MUSIC

GENERAL EDITOR
SEAN EGAN

MUSIC

CASSELL
ILLUSTRATED

A CASSELL BOOK

An Hachette Livre UK Company

First published in the UK 2007 by
Cassell Illustrated, a division of
Octopus Publishing Group Ltd.
2-4 Heron Quays,
London E14 4JP

Text, design and layout © 2007 Octopus Publishing Group Ltd.

A CIP catalogue record for this book is available from the
British Library.
ISBN-13: 978-1-84403592-2 (UK Edition)
ISBN-10: 1-84403-592-1 (UK Edition)

Distributed in the United States and Canada by
Sterling Publishing Co., Inc
387 Park Avenue South, New York, NY 10016-8810

ISBN-13: 978-1-84403606-6 (U.S. Edition)
ISBN-10: 1-84403-606-5 (U.S. Edition)

10 9 8 7 6 5 4 3 2 1

Commissioning Editor: Laura Price
Project Editor: Joanne Wilson
Editor: Ruth Patrick
Assistant Editor: Eoghan O'Brien
Designer: John Round

Printed in China

CONTENTS

CONTRIBUTORS

Hugh Barker is a writer, publisher, and ex-musician, currently living in North London. His book *Faking It: The Quest for Authenticity in Popular Music*, (co-written with Yuval Taylor) is published by Faber & Faber and W.W. Norton.

Angus Batey has written extensively on music since the early 1990s. He is a regular contributor to *Hip Hop Connection*, *Mojo*, *The Guardian*, and *The Times*, for whom he also writes about cricket. He can be contacted on angus@hiphop.com.

Johnny Black, author of acclaimed books including *Eyewitness Hendrix* and *Reveal: The Story of R.E.M.*, has contributed for over twenty years to *Mojo*, *Blender*, *Music Week*, and *Q*. He also maintains a vast popular music database, the Rocksource Archive.

Melissa Blease is a freelance writer specializing in music, food, and book reviews and features, mouthy opinion pieces, erotic fiction, and plays. Her work is regularly published in *Venue* and *Folio* magazines but her ambition is to become a bestselling novelist.

Ken Bloom has written three definitive works on popular song: *American Song*, *Tin Pan Alley*, and *Hollywood Song* plus the bestselling *Broadway Musicals: The 101 Greatest Musicals of All Time*. He is

president of independent record company Harbinger Records.

Fred Dellar has spent the past forty years contributing to such publications as *NME*, *Vox*, *Q*, *Smash Hits*, *Hi-Fi News*, *Empire*, *The Stage*, and *Mojo*. He has also penned or co-written books on country music, rock movies, and jazz.

Robert Dimery is a freelance writer and editor. In addition to working for *Vogue*, *World of Interiors,* and *Time Out*, he served as general editor for *1001 Albums You Must Hear Before You Die*.

Bruce Eder has written for *Village Voice* and *Newsday*, and produced vintage rock, soundtrack, and classical CD reissues for Sony Music and Polygram. He is also a writer-producer-narrator of commentary tracks for classic films on DVD for *The Criterion Collection*.

Sean Egan has written for, among other outlets *Goldmine*, *RollingStone.com*, *Uncut*, and *Vox*. He has written several books, including works on The Animals, Jimi Hendrix, The Rolling Stones, and the critically acclaimed rock 'n' roll novel *Sick Of Being Me*.

Sara Farr has written for more than thirty newspapers and magazines, including *Music Inc.*, *Dayton (Ohio) Daily News*,

Impact Weekly, *Groupeez*, *Cincinnati CityBeat*, and the *Los Angeles Newspaper Group* family of publications. She lives in Los Angeles.

Gillian G. Gaar's books include *She's A Rebel: The History of Women in Rock & Roll*, *Nirvana: In Utero*, and *Green Day: Rebels With A Cause*. She has written for many publications and worked on Nirvana's box-set *With The Lights Out*.

Gary Pig Gold launched Canada's first musical fanzine *The Pig Paper*, produced records for the USSR's Melodiya label, contributed to the *Music Hound Essential Album Guides*, almost ran off to Australia with Jan and Dean, and surfs today out of www.GaryPigGold.com

Chris Goodman was Music Editor at the *Sunday Express* for five years where he wrote weekly music reviews, news, and interviews. He has contributed to *Mojo*, *The Word*, *Classic Rock*, and other publications.

Ralph Heibutzki is the author of *Unfinished Business: The Life & Times Of Danny Gatton*, and has written for the *All Music Guide*, *Goldmine*, and *Guitar Player*, among others. For details on his music and projects, see www.chairmanralph.com.

Thomas S. Hischak is the author of sixteen books on theater, film, and popular music, including *The Tin Pan Alley Song Encyclopedia*, *The Oxford Companion to American Theatre*, and the award-winning *The American Musical Theatre Song Encyclopedia*.

In 1984 **Steve Jelbert** reviewed his own band for the *NME*. He has since written for *The Times*, *Independent*, *Independent on Sunday*, *Mojo*, and many now-defunct publications. He lives in East London, surrounded by empty wine bottles, toys, and crates of records and books.

Rob Jovanovic has written for all the major music magazines over the past decade and penned books on sport and music, covering such diverse subjects as Beck, Kate Bush, Nirvana, Big Star, R.E.M., and George Michael.

Ignacio Julià is the publisher of *Ruta 66*, a Spanish magazine devoted to rock history and contemporary alternative scenes. He has written a dozen books, including worldwide distributed Velvet Underground and Sonic Youth biographies.

Miles Keylock writes on music and culture in South Africa. He has written features for the *Mail & Guardian* and *GQ South Africa* magazine, where he is currently the contributing music editor. His reviews can also be read in *1001 Albums You Must Hear Before You Die*.

Spencer Leigh has been broadcasting *On The Beat* on BBC Radio Merseyside for 25 years. He has contributed to various magazines and newspapers and penned several books. Details of his books with sample chapters can be found at *www.spencerleigh.co.uk*.

David McNamee co-founded and edited *Plan B* magazine. He acted as reviews editor on *Careless Talk Costs Lives*. His work has also appeared in *The Guardian*, *Dazed & Confused*, *Metro*, *Kerrang!*, *Metal Hammer*, *Loose Lips Sink Ships*, and more.

Alex Macpherson has written for *The Guardian*, *Plan B*, *Careless Talk Costs Lives*, *thelondonpaper*, *Stylus*, *Undercover*, *New Statesman*, and *Resident Advisor*.

As a columnist for regional daily newspapers in his native Wessex, **Kevin Maidment** spent several years thwarting the ambitions of local musicians. He has subsequently written for the *BBC*, *Music 365*, *Books On Line*, *NME*, *amazon.com*, and *The Morning Star*.

Gavin Michie has written authoritatively on rock, folk, electronic, and popular music for *Rock CD*, *Rock'n'Reel*, *The Listener*, *CD Review*, *More Music*, *The Beat*, and *New York Rocker* along with many other publications and websites worldwide.

Andre Millard is Professor of History and Director of American Studies at the University of Alabama. He has written on Thomas Edison and the early entertainment industry, music technology, the history of recorded sound and the electric guitar.

Joe Muggs has written regularly for *The Daily Telegraph*, *Mixmag*, *Word*, *The Face*, and *BBC World Service*. He has a long involvement as a promoter, performer and musician with the underground post-rave scene.

Alongside numerous encyclopedia contributions and magazine articles, **Alex Ogg**'s writing includes the books *The Hip Hop Years* (accompanying the TV series), *No More Heroes*, *Top Ten*, and works on rap lyrics, and biographies of Def Jam Records, Radiohead, and others.

Pierre Perrone spent his formative years in Marseilles watching *The Avengers* and listening to *The Who*. A UK resident for the last 27 years, he is a regular contributor to *The Independent*, the *Bergens Tidende* in Norway, and *Rock & Folk* in France.

Michael Portantiere is an editor and writer for *TheaterMania.com*, having previously held editorial positions at *InTheater* and *Back Stage*. He edited and contributed reviews to *The TheaterMania*

Opposite The Beatles

Guide to Musical Theater Recordings and has written for *Playbill* and *Stagebill*.

Mike Princeton is a NYC-based script consultant who has anonymously doctored several developing and out-of-town "musicals in trouble." Under several "house" and "pen" names he has written both erotic romance and men's action novels.

A British ex-pat living in Decatur, Georgia, **Leila Regan-Porter**'s thirst for music knowledge has her delving into Atlanta's music history for *Performing Songwriter*, interviewing acts new and old for *Paste*, and discovering local music for the *Atlanta Journal-Constitution*.

William Ruhlmann writes for the *All Music Guide*.

A journalist who makes her home in Warren, Ohio, **Tierney Smith** has been a contributor to *Relix*, *Discoveries Goldmine*, and Cleveland's *Scene*. She also contributed to the book *100 Albums That Changed Music*.

Former editor of *Mojo* magazine and author of *The Fame Game*, **Mat Snow** writes and broadcasts about music and more. He was immortalized by his former flatmate Nick Cave in the song "Scum," every word of which is true.

David Spencer is a composer, lyricist, and librettist whose works include *The Fabulist* and versions of *Phantom of the Opera* and *Les Misérables*. He is author of *The Musical Theatre Writer's Survival Guide* and *Passing Fancy*, an Alien Nation novel.

Giancarlo Susanna has contributed to *Rockerilla*, *Audio Review*, and *L'Unita*. He is the author of books on Neil Young, Jeff Buckley, Coldplay. and R.E.M.

Jeff Tamarkin has edited *Goldmine*, *Relix*, *CMJ*, and *Global Rhythm*, and currently writes for *Mojo*, *Harp*, *All Music Guide*, *Jazz Times*, *Boston Phoenix* and others. He is the author of *Got a Revolution! The Turbulent Flight of Jefferson Airplane*.

Dave Thompson is the author of over one hundred rock biographies and encyclopedias, and a regular contributor to a multitude of magazines and publications. He lives in Delaware with cats.

John Tobler has written for *Melody Maker*, *NME*, *ZigZag*, *Folk Roots*, and *Country Music People*. He is the author of books on The Beach Boys, The Carpenters, The Doors, and Buddy Holly and has written many liner notes.

Richie Unterberger is the author of several rock history books, including *The Unreleased Beatles: Music and Film*, *Unknown Legends of Rock 'N' Roll*, and a two-volume history of 1960s folk-rock, *Turn! Turn! Turn!/Eight Miles High*.

David Wells has written extensively for *Record Collector* magazine, including sole authorship of their stand-alone publication *100 Greatest UK Psychedelic Records*. He has also compiled and written sleevenotes for several hundred CD reissues.

INTRODUCTION

Histories of popular music are usually somewhat partial affairs. Generally, publishers of pop books seem to think that popular music started with Elvis Presley's shoot to stardom in 1956 and fill their tomes exclusively with artists and records that emerged thereafter. This approach has the effect of ignoring more than half a century of popular music. It also makes the illogical assumption that people who love rock and other forms of post-'56 music have no interest in other genres like big bands, musicals and crooning, whereas most will appreciate that rarely does such rigid demarcation exist in human taste.

In this book, we have striven to correct this imbalance. Here we look at a century of music for the masses, starting at the dawn of the twentieth century with artists whose wares were still distributed on cylinder as well as disc (the latter yet to establish its dominance) and finishing in the early years of the twenty-first century with people whose art is increasingly delivered to the public via downloads, a method that would have been the stuff of the science fiction of the then still-living Jules Verne to purchasers of the music of those artists featured in the early pages. In between, we take in every genre of music that has been popular with the public in that timeframe, including barbershop quartets, operetta, music hall/vaudeville, musicals of both stage and screen, novelty songs, folk, jazz, blues, big band, country, rock, reggae, rap, techno, and more.

We have also dispensed with the absurd attitude that the only valid popular music is that which originates from the UK or America or is English-language. Herein you will find artists from all across the planet. Whether they be from Norway or Nigeria, Jamaica or Germany, if their popularity merits it, they are in. With similar inclusiveness, we have not concerned ourselves with notions of street credibility when selecting entries. Though we have certainly not indulged in hagiography – our multi-national team of more than forty seasoned and expert writers has too much integrity for that – we have seriously and honestly attempted to analyse and explain the reasons for the success of every artist featured, whether or not they be "cool."

In addition to profiling artists and their works, we, unusually, address the significant events on the musical timeline – the moments that provided the framework for the music industry to exist and/or flourish, whether it be the formation of songwriters' unions, the publication of the first charts, or the technological inventions that gradually improved the sound quality and distribution methods of music.

While it would be unwise for any publisher to claim complete comprehensiveness, we consequently feel that within these pages you will find represented every key person (whether it be via a mini-biography or detailing of a major song, significant concert or important album) and occurrence within the "popular" sphere of the first full century of recorded music.

Sean Egan

Acknowledgements
The editor wishes to extend his grateful thanks to the following people for providing help with research: Johnny Black, Doug Hinman, Ray Jackson, Steve Boone, Russell Hayward.

Key Event **Introduction of Gramophone recordings**

The gramophone and its discs were the work of the inventor Emile Berliner who first demonstrated them in 1888. The sound waves were cut laterally in the groove (from side to side), which distinguished it from the hill and dale (up and down) of the records – as they were already called – invented by Thomas Edison and Alexander Graham Bell. Edison's phonograph and Bell's graphophone (developed with Charles Tainter) used the cylinder format, a thumb-sized vehicle with a soft wax coating housed in a protective tube. Of the two formats the "talking machine" industry was divided between, the cylinder format seemed if anything the superior one because it enabled the consumer to record, not just listen.

Eldridge Johnson was a mechanic who joined with Berliner to improve the performance of the gramophone's spring motor and went on to develop all parts of the machine and its 7-inch diameter solid wax disc. Johnson made the machines that Berliner's American Gramophone company marketed, and eventually merged his patents with Berliner in 1901 to form the Victor Talking Machine Company. Berliner had also sold the rights to his gramophone in Europe and beginning in 1897 companies were set up in England, Germany, and France who built their own record pressing plants. The revolving disc format was now established and in a position to challenge the cylinder record as the basis of commercial recording of music.
Andre Millard

Date 1900

Country USA

Why It's Key Paved the way for the eventual domination of the revolving disc as the primary medium for sound recording.

Opposite "His Master's Voice" became the Gramophone company logo

Key Song **"Absence Makes The Heart Grow Fonder"**

Though "Absence Makes The Heart Grow Fonder" first appeared as the title of an anonymous English poem in 1602, it took two hundred years for the sweet, elegant phrase to catch on. Thomas Haynes Bayley's song "Isle Of Beauty" contained the line, "Absence makes the heart grow fonder, Isle of beauty, Fare thee well!" The song was published in 1850, long after Bayley's death in 1839.

In the first year of the twentieth century, popular songwriter Arthur Gillespie used the phrase as the title of a song with the accompanying music by Herbert Dillea. The number premiered in the musical *The Floor Walkers*, which opened at New York's Grand Opera House on January 29, 1900. The song was typical of the overwrought, emotional ballads popular at the time. Similarly sentimental hit songs from just the same year included "A Bird In A Gilded Cage," "Goodbye, Dolly Gray," and "Tell Me Pretty Maiden."

A later song from 1930 by Sam M. Lewis and Joe Young used the familiarity of both the phrase and the Gillespie/Dillea song to put a spin on it with "Absence Makes The Heart Grow Fonder (For Somebody Else)," a charming warning to a lover that "when the cat's away, the mice will play."
Ken Bloom

Published Date 1900

Nationality USA

Composers Arthur Gillespie, Herbert Dillea

Why It's Key From line in a poem to line in a song to song title to parody – and all in only 328 years.

His Master's Voice

Key Song "Just Because She Made Dem Goo-Goo Eyes" Dan W. Quinn

The publication of "Just Because She Made Dem Goo-Goo Eyes" in 1900 introduced an expression that would quickly become part of the American vernacular. With the twentieth century came an abundance of slang in popular music and this number by John Queen and Hughie Cannon (music and lyrics), about a gal who can flirt outrageously with her eyes, popularized the phrase "Goo-goo eyes," a nonsense expression yet one that suggested all kinds of provocative things. The song was first given recognition when Querita Vincent sang it on the vaudeville stage, then it was popularized by a recording by Dan W. Quinn – somewhat fitting, as the first chart entry of that prolific artist had been the equally colloquial "Daddy Wouldn't Buy Me A Bow-Wow." Arthur Collins also had a successful record of the ditty. By World War I the song had become rather obscure but the expression "Goo-goo eyes" remained in usage. It was eclipsed somewhat in 1938 when the song "Jeepers Creepers" popularized the term "peepers" for eyes, though the former bit of slang still holds on.

In the 1940s "Just Because She Made Dem Goo-Goo Eyes" was revived as a popular nonsense song, the sort of novelty number that proliferated at the time. It received several new recordings but by the late-1950s the song was again forgotten and only the old "Goo-goo eyes" expression remained.

Thomas Hischak

Published Date 1900

Nationality USA

Composers John Queen, Hughie Cannon

Why It's Key Showed how popular song can bequeath a phrase while itself being discarded.

16

Key Song
"When You Were Sweet Sixteen"

Songwriter James Thornton was born in Liverpool, England but his Liverpudlian family became Bostonians when he was around eight. "When You Were Sweet Sixteen" came into existence because the by now grown-up Thornton was asked by his wife if he still loved her. Came the reply, "I love you as I did when you were sweet sixteen."

Published in 1898, the song was released by both George J. Gaskin and Jere Mahoney in 1900. The next year Henry Macdonough and J.W. Myers had successful recordings but it was Al Jolson's version that established the song as a standard. The song was given a second life when sung by Bing Crosby in the boxer biopic, *The Great John L* (1945). When Crosby's movie opened, Perry Como covered the song and sold over a million copies. Como's hit inspired Jolson to rerecord his version on Decca Records. Vocal groups took a liking to the melody with covers by the Mills Brothers and the Ink Spots amongst others.

It was presumably because Thornton in no way predicted all this success that upon writing the song he unfortunately gave two separate publishers supposedly exclusive deals. This all ended up with Stern and Marks Publishing suing Witmark Music Publishing, who had to pay U.S. $5000 to the former when they demonstrated that they had paid an advance to Thornton of $15 for it.

As recently as 1981, The Fureys with Davey Arthur had a UK Top 20 with the song.

Ken Bloom

Release Date 1900

Nationality USA

Composer James Thornton

Why It's Key True love inspires a ballad but deception mars its success.

Key Person
Len Spencer

Len Spencer just might have been the first nationally known recording star.

He entered the business just at its beginnings and realized early on that he could have successes with songs written by others. As was typical of the times, Spencer, a white man, recorded several "coon songs" and other songs associated with the American South but he sang in practically any style, save opera. Among his greatest hits were "Ta-Ra-Ra-Boom Der E" in 1892, "Little Alabama Coon," and "Dat New Bully" in 1895, "A Hot Time In The Old Town," and "Oh, Mister Johnson, Turn Me Loose," both in 1897, and "Hello! Ma Baby" in 1899.

His biggest hit was "The Arkansaw Traveler," his version of which entered the U.S. chart on November 3, 1900. (This date, like all U.S. chart entry dates and positions in this book prior to 1955, is an estimate on the part of chart experts Joel Whitburn and Steve Sullivan – practically a comedy sketch with music, the novelty number ended up selling around a million copies.

Spencer made famous many of the songs he recorded, a surprising number of which are sung to this day. He also contributed mightily to the early success of the Columbia and Victor labels.

Born in 1867, Spencer's death in 1914 ended one of the most successful recording careers of any era.
Ken Bloom

Role Recording Artist

Date November 3, 1900

Nationality USA

Why It's Key Pop idoldom starts here.

Key Song
"Coon! Coon! Coon!"

The "coon song," or, as it was originally called, "coon shout," is a mostly forgotten American musical genre. Written by black people as well as whites, coon songs used Southern clichés as their lyrical motifs, and early syncopation in much of their music. The lyrics weren't usually racist – and often portrayed black people as admirable underdogs – but their patronizing attitudes and of course the word "coon" consigned them to oblivion as America entered a more enlightened era.

The first coon song was "New Coon In Town," written by Paul Allen in 1883. Ernest Hogan, the author and performer of "All Coons Look Alike to Me," (1896), was black himself and later concluded that the song was demeaning but its success led to a spate of imitations. Some of them, like "Mammy's Li'l Coal Black Rose," and "Mammy's Little Pumpkin Colored Coon," were beautiful, heartfelt ballads. Some coon songs were out and out racist rants but some reflected the thoughts and outlooks of African-Americans at the time (though even these musings are today regarded as politically incorrect).

"Coon! Coon! Coon!," published in 1901, could conceivably, at a stretch, be considered to be in the latter category. Introduced by Lew Docksteader, a white man who performed in blackface, its verse sees the narrator declaring that he would like a different shade, concluding, "I'd rather be a white man instead of bein' a coon." "A Change Is Gonna Come" it's clearly not.
Ken Bloom

Published Date 1901

Nationality USA

Composers Leo Friedman, Gene Jefferson

Why It's Key A song that epitomized a popular genre that is now jaw-dropping.

Key Event **Musicians Union tries to prohibit ragtime**

Ragtime music and the American Federation of Musicians (AFM) were created at the same time – the first published rag appeared a year after the formation of this musicians' union in 1896.

The AFM worked to protect the interests of people who made a living from live music. In 1901, the AFM publicly denounced ragtime music and declared that their members should not play it. Their ban might have been based on their opposition to an army of amateur piano players banging out the ragtime hits or "ragging" existing music. Alternatively, it could have been the consequence of their discrimination against African Americans and their music. There were also questions about the propriety of the many dances associated with ragtime, such as the "cakewalk."

The ban occurred when the syncopated marching beat that constitutes ragtime was becoming vastly popular. Scott Joplin's "Maple Leaf Rag" of 1899 had brought international attention to this form of "Negro" music and it was followed by a mass of imitators, both vocal and instrumental. The ban was spectacularly unsuccessful. By 1911 the ragtime craze was dominating American popular music and dance and some music was even being marketed as "ragtime" when it was not.

One wonders whether some of the musicians who defied the edict were indulging in the same youthful rebelliousness that kids would later display in the face of elders who scorned the equally black, equally exciting rock 'n' roll.

Andre Millard

Date 1901

Country USA

Why It's Key Possibly the first example of an attempt to ban popular music that backfired.

Opposite **The cakewalk**

Key Song **"He Laid Away A Suit Of Gray To Wear The Union Blue"**

In 1901, the publication of "He Laid Away A Suit Of Gray To Wear The Union Blue" and its subsequent popularity signaled the ability of popular music to create success by riding a tangential wave. The Spanish-American War at the turn of the century influenced popular song and suddenly patriotic ballads and marches became more popular than they had been for decades. Not all of the songs were about the war with Spain; the era conjured up memories of the Civil War, which it is now astonishing to think had taken place just forty years earlier, and a number of new songs were written about that conflict.

A favorite theme of these ballads was the southerner who was torn between his loyalty to the South and his belief in the Union. Such was the subject of this song, by Edward M. Wickes (lyric) and Ben Jansen (music). In it, a southerner realizes he must hide away the gray uniform of the Confederate Army and join Lincoln's men in order to preserve the Union.

Vaudeville entertainers Lillian Mack, J. Aldrich Libbey, and Lydia Barry each sang the heart-tugging ballad very dramatically on stage and thereby encouraged patriotic unity. Sheet music sales were substantial but after the war ended the song faded away. When World War I came around in the next decade, patriotic songs would change to more enticing approaches and references to the Civil War were deemed ineffective.

Thomas Hischak

Published Date 1901

Nationality USA

Composers Ben Jansen, Edward M. Wickes

Why It's Key The song that illustrated how one war's songs could become another's.

Key Song
"We Shall Overcome"

Placing "We Shall Overcome" in 1901, is necessarily arbitrary. The origins of the song, like many that evolved from a folk tradition, are murky, and the points along the timeline where it was the subject of incremental modifications and development ultimately leading to its present-day form are many and various.

The song developed from the gospel traditions of both blacks and whites in the late 1800s. The more recent development of the song began in 1946 when Lucille Simmons, on strike against the American Tobacco Company, sang a version of the song, titled "We'll Overcome" on a picket line. Folk activist Pete Seeger learned it and it may have been he who changed the lyric to "We shall overcome." He made additions to the lyric and in a continuation of the "passing on" folk tradition, it was taken up as an anthem of the burgeoning civil rights movement. Folk singer Joan Baez helped bring the song to a wider audience through her participation in marches and, most importantly, at the 1969 Woodstock festival.

Quintessentially Sixties, "We Shall Overcome" served a function that only music could: a spoken catalogue of grievances from strikers or demonstrators was hardly practical but the song – a non-belligerent but emphatic expression of suffering and determination – acted as a superb form of shorthand, especially in combination with the placards and banners also common in such situations.

Ken Bloom

Date 1902

Nationality USA

Composers Pete Seeger, Zilphia Johnson Horton, Guy Carawan, Frank Hamilton

Why It's Key The anthem of the disenfranchised and downtrodden that illustrates the immense power of popular song.

Key Event
Mass production of records begins

After several inventors had perfected talking machines based on spring motors in the 1890s, the great obstacle to the commercial development of recorded sound was the time and expense of duplicating master recordings. Performers were asked to make hundreds of identical recordings. Thomas Edison began experiments to find a way to duplicate his phonograph cylinders at the end of the 1880s and soon afterwards Eldridge Johnson – like Edison, based in New Jersey, which probably led to a diffusion of ideas between the two – worked on machines to mass produce gramophone discs.

Both inventors started with a master recording made out of wax. Then they coated layer after layer of metal (often gold) on the surface of the master to make a metal matrix of the grooves in the record. In the case of the gramophone, this matrix could simply be used to stamp out identical copies of the master. Edison's phonograph cylinder presented a much trickier process in which hot wax was injected into the cylindrical master and then left to cool and fall away.

By 1902 both began to build facilities to mass produce their new recordings. Edison's "High Speed Hard Wax" cylinders appeared in 1903. The impact was immediate as prices fell from U.S. $1 or $2 per recording to 75 and 50 cents. Within a few years one could buy a record for as little as 25 cents.

Andre Millard

Date January 1902

Country USA

Why It's Key Cylinder prices tumbled and turned records from an expensive luxury into a household commodity.

Opposite **Edison's phonograph**

THE Edison PHONOGRAPH

EDISON ·TRIUMPH· PHONOGRAPH

UNCLE SAM TAKES OFF HIS HAT.

THE TRIUMPH $50.00

NONE GENUINE WITHOUT THIS

TRADE *Thomas A. Edison* MARK

NATIONAL PHONOGRAPH COMPANY
ORANGE, N. J.
83 CHAMBERS STREET, NEW YORK.

Key Event
Caruso makes his first recordings

A handful of recordings made by an up-and-coming young opera singer became a landmark in the recorded sound industry. Enrico Caruso was far from being an international star when he agreed to make some recordings for the Gramophone Company of Great Britain in 1902. At this time, sound recordings were so imperfect (and unflattering to the performer) that none of the big names in classical music had made records and the talking machine reproduced only popular songs, short vaudeville turns, and often coarse humorous skits. But Caruso's powerful and often emotional tenor was perfectly suited to the limitations of acoustic reproduction and Fred Gaisberg, the recording engineer, made the most of the primitive recording equipment.

Music lovers of "discernment" on both sides of the Atlantic were rapturous in their reception of these recordings, praising the clarity of Caruso's voice as it emerged from the horns of their players. The Victor company used the success of these recordings to create a series of high-priced records of "good music" on its Red Seal label.

Caruso made his own fortune out of the records, obtaining a contract to perform at the Metropolitan Opera House in New York and bringing his music to millions of people. In 1907 his rendition of "I Pagliacci-Vesti la Giubba" became one of the first records to sell a million copies.
Andre Millard

Date April 11, 1902

Country Italy

Why It's Key Told the middle and upper classes that the talking machine business had something for them too.

Key Person
Arthur Collins

In his time, Arthur Collins (1864–1933) was the most popular recording artist in America. In his late teens and twenties, he toured with in repertory theatre and later joined the De Wolf Hopper troupe, specializing in early musical comedies. He had a long stage career but it was in recordings that he made his mark. In 1898, Collins was asked by the Edison Company to audition and made his first wax cylinder recordings on May 18. One contemporaneous critic said of his vocal abilities, "There probably has never been a sweeter, more naturally musical baritone voice than his." Two years later, Byron G. Harlan joined the Edison company and the two men became a singing team, the most popular in America. Collins continued on his own and, beginning in 1906, also sang as a member of the Peerless Quartet.

On July 12, 1902, his first huge hit "Bill Bailey, Won't You Please Come Home" hit the charts. In 1905, came his blockbuster record "The Preacher And The Bear." Collins also recorded Irving Berlin's "Alexander's Ragtime Band" and helped popularize Berlin.

Many of Collins' recordings were performed in black dialect. Although these "coon songs" were often excellent, they are politically unacceptable today and this helps explain why his fame was fleeting. Collins also recorded songs by Bert Williams and Alex Rogers and those of many other black songwriters that were not so objectionable. Collins retired in 1926.
Ken Bloom

Role Recording Artist

Date July 12, 1902

Nationality USA

Why It's Key Once hugely important, an artist now forgotten because of the dubious nature of some of his output.

Key Performances *Florodora* stage musical

By the time *Floradora* closed on Broadway on January 25, 1902, it had racked up two important milestones. Not only did its 552 performances make it the second-longest running musical up to that point but it was also the first musical to have originated in the UK to become a wow with Americans.

It concerns a perfume maker on the Phillipine island of Florodora who has stolen the business from the family of a young woman, who herself falls in love with a disguised nobleman. But it wasn't the fanciful plot that earned *Florodora* – which opened in London in 1899 – its fame; rather, it was the fact that the show's publicist, Anna Marble, ingeniously elevated the chorus girls into stars. The "*Florodora* girls" became a phenomenon, if one with a perpetually revolving line-up. Over 70 girls made up the sextet at one time or another during the show's two-year run: they kept being pursued by and subsequently marrying wealthy admirers.

However, the show's music should not be overlooked. Marble decided to push the show's highlight song, the chirruping double sextet "Tell Me, Pretty Maiden," and it became one of the first popular hits from a Broadway show. Other hits from the musical include "The Silver Star Of Love" and "The Fellow Who Might." Though Leslie Stuart (music), Edward Boyd-Jones and Paul Rubens (lyrics) contributed the original score, additional songs were interpolated as the show's run continued.

Florodora was revived as quickly as 1902 and again in 1905 and 1920.

Andre Millard

Closing Night
January 25, 1902

Country UK

Director Lewis Hopper

Cast Sydney Deane, R. E. Graham, Fannie Johnston

Composers Leslie Stuart, Edward Boyd-Jones, Paul Rubens

Why It's Key The first British hit to successfully transfer to Broadway.

Key Song "Land Of Hope And Glory"

In 1898, Edward Elgar – composer of works like *The Enigma Variations* (1899) and *The Dream Of Gerontius* (1900) – wrote to a friend, "I hope someday to do a great work – a sort of national thing, that my fellow Englishmen might take to themselves and love."

He fulfilled his ambition, but not in the way he'd envisaged. Starting in 1901, Elgar wrote five marches in the series *Pomp And Circumstance*. He was so pleased with the first ("March No. 1 In D Major") that he thought of turning it into a symphony. When Henry Wood conducted the first performance of the march, "the people simply rose and yelled," he later recollected. The new king, Edward VII, heard the march and told Elgar that if it had some stirring words, it would go round the world. Elgar was uneasy about that but by the following year, poet Arthur Benson had provided those words. The song became "Land Of Hope And Glory" and was played at Edward's coronation on August 9, 1902.

With its proud asking of the land in question, "How shall we extol thee/Who are born of thee?," some of the public considered they had another national anthem. Others of more leftist bent questioned the imperialist tenor of its talk of "Wider still and wider/Shall thy bounds be set." However, the song remains an irreplaceable feature of the annual British classical event the Last Night of The Proms.

Spencer Leigh

Published Date 1902 (music), 1904 (lyric)

Nationality UK

Composers Edward Elgar, Arthur Benson

Why It's Key Stirring patriotic song created almost by accident.

THE ENTERTAINER

Music by SCOTT JOPLIN
Words by JOHN BRIMHALL

CHARLES HANSEN
EDUCATIONAL MUSIC & BOOKS

Key Song
"The Entertainer"

"The Entertainer" proved popular music's potential for generation-spanning endurance by enjoying wide popularity at two different points of time separated by seventy years. Joplin wrote the rag composition in 1902 and, because of the great success of his previous "Maple Leaf Rag," it was immediately published and garnered considerable sheet music sales. The song follows classic ragtime structure but it is unique in its tone: the rag is quieter, more leisurely, and usually played slower than most rags. It also has the distinction of being rather melancholy when the tempo is played haltingly. Less difficult to play than many rags, the number was a favorite at parlor pianos.

Over the years other Joplin pieces remained more well known than "The Entertainer," though there were excellent recordings by Mutt Carey's New Yorkers in 1947 and by Ken Colyer's Jazzmen in 1955. The song later took on an entirely new lease of life however, when Joplin pieces were used for the soundtrack for the retrospectively set popular film *The Sting* (1974), starring Paul Newman and Robert Redford. Marvin Hamlisch's distinctive arrangement of "The Entertainer" became the theme song for the movie. Hamlisch's piano recording was released on single and boosted to a U.S. No. 3 by people whose parents often hadn't been alive when the song first appeared. There followed a general revival of Joplin's work in America. Even his unproduced opera *Treemonisha* was finally staged in 1975. As a result of the film, "The Entertainer" replaced "Maple Leaf Rag" as the most well-known Joplin composition.
Thomas Hischak

Published Date 1902

Nationality USA

Composer Scott Joplin

Why It's Key The ragtime number revived after a whole lifetime.

Opposite "The Entertainer"

Key Event **The moniker "Tin Pan Alley" is coined**

Although the music business in America had flourished since 1885, it was not given a name until 1903 when newspaper columnist Monroe Rosenfeld is credited with coining the phrase "Tin Pan Alley." A stretch of 28th Street between Fifth Avenue and Broadway in New York was comprised of old brownstone apartments that had become dominated by music publishers' offices. In this labyrinth of little rooms, tunesmiths, and pluggers banged away on cheap upright pianos trying to sell songs to publishers as well as influential singers and producers. In warm weather when all the windows were open, the noise coming from the many pianos must have been both annoying and exhilarating.

When Monroe did a series of articles on the music business for the *New York Herald* in 1903, he wrote that the racket sounded like a lot of people banging on tin pans and he dubbed the location Tin Pan Alley. Monroe probably did not come up with the phrase himself; many believe songwriter Harry Von Tilzer had created the expression. But it was Monroe who popularized the term and it would stick for over half a century. By 1919 most music publishers relocated uptown to the Brill Building and surrounding buildings on Broadway and 49th Street so Tin Pan Alley as a place only existed for sixteen years, but the expression continues to linger in the language to refer to the music business.
Thomas Hischak

Date 1903

Country USA

Why It's Key A piece of descriptive shorthand that has survived a century.

Key Event
The barbershop quartet boom

Barbershop singing is so-called because its origins – just before the turn of the twentieth century – lie in African-American barbershops, centers of socializing as well as tonsorial parlors.

The era was known for a worldwide interest in choral singing, and a cappella music reached its zenith in African American church choirs, which utilized songs and harmonies that originated with field hands around the Civil War era. Like jazz, barbershop harmonies crossed into the white mainstream and "Sweet Adeline" by Richard H. Gerard and Harry Armstrong became the most notable of barbershop tunes. It was introduced and recorded by vaudeville and burlesque performers The Empire City Quartet in 1903, though it wasn't until The Quaker City Four's 1904 recording of the song that it became a hit. The Hayden Quartet and The Peerless Quartet also recorded it.

Despite its penchant for simple tunes and easy-to-understand lyrics, barbershop singing is quite sophisticated musically, relying on seventh chords which resolve around circles of fifths. Tonalities and frequencies are constantly changing in order to keep the tonal center constant.

Though its status is far from the massive popularity the likes of The American Quartet, The Hayden Quartet, and The Peerless Quartet, enjoyed up to the 1920s, barbershop singing continues to this day. Though the sexes had always been restricted to their own groups, in recent years mixed-gender barbershop groups have become common.

Ken Bloom

Date 1903

Country USA

Why It's Key The vocal format so sweet and sophisticated that audiences didn't miss musical instruments.

Key Performance *Babes In Toyland*
stage musical

The British started a trend with their pantomimes, children's entertainments that owed more to music hall than musical theater. Soon these shows were expanded into adult entertainment. The most famous of these fantasy musical comedies was the stage version of *The Wizard Of Oz* (1902).

That show's great success led its producer, Fred R. Hamlin and director Julian Mitchell to seek to replicate it. They commissioned the greatest theater composer of his day, Victor Herbert, to provide the music and Glen MacDonough to supply the libretto and lyrics for a show based on the Mother Goose fairytales, *Babes In Toyland*. The show instantly became a classic of the American musical theater. Among its greatest songs, still played today, are "The March Of The Toys" and "Toyland," each firm Christmas time playlist staples. Other delights are the sweetly simple (but not cloying) "I Can't Do The Sum" and "Go To Sleep, Slumber Deep."

The lush and lavish visual spectacle represented by *Babes In Toyland*, was a big contributory factor to its success. James Gibbons Harker, writing in *The Sun*, was so dazzled by the settings and effects that he gave what must be one of the most gushing write-ups ever, one which concluded, "What more could the spirit of mortals desire?" The operetta has been filmed several times, probably most memorably – if not faithfully – in 1934, with Laurel and Hardy starring.

Ken Bloom

Opening Night October 13, 1903

Nationality USA

Director Julian Mitchell

Cast William Morris, Mabel Barrison, George Denham

Composer Victor Herbert, Glen MacDonough

Why It's Key The musical for the big kid in all of us.

Key Song
"Hiawatha"

"Hiawatha" began as a 1901 march by Charles Daniels that was popularized by John Philip Sousa. In 1903, words were added to the rhythmic melody by James O'Dea. A flurry of recordings followed. The April 11, 1903 Columbia Orchestra version was the first to enter the charts but there were two other hit versions that year, the most successful by Harry MacDonough, which made U.S. No. 1.

Henry Wadsworth Longfellow's 1855 epic poem *Song Of Hiawatha* about the life of a chief of the Iroquois tribe might seem like an unlikely source of material for the popular music industry at the turn of the century, but it was already awash in sentimental material about the pre-Civil War South and the unreconstructed West. Though Longfellow's tale boasted very little historical truth, the country's imagined past (still within living memory for some) included romantic treatments of the Native American experience and this song perfectly fitted this interpretation. MacDonough's success encouraged other songwriters to produce works about Native Americans, including "Red Wing" and "Navajo" and rhythmic drum beats as a shorthand for the music or appearance of "Red Indians," as they were then called, became a cliché.

Those who might observe that the song now has a somewhat corny tang might be interested to learn that as early as October 1903, Arthur Collins and Byron Harlan made the U.S. chart with "Parody On 'Hiawatha'."

Andre G. Millard

Published Date 1903

Country USA

Composers Charles Daniels, James O'Dea

Why It's Key Popular song propagates inaccurate view of the Wild West – even though some purchasers had been alive to see the truth.

Key Song
"When We Were Two Little Boys"

"When We Were Two Little Boys" was published in 1903 and was another song that illustrated America's revived interest in numbers about battle and sons away at war and loved ones separated in the time of the Spanish-American War. "When We Were Two Little Boys" by Edward Madden (lyric) and Theodore F. Morse (music) was perhaps the most potent example of the genre. The ballad tells of the friendship between two men of the same town, from their childhood days when they played together, through their schooling and courting days, up until they served together in the war. It is there that one friend saves the life of the other and their longtime bond is solidified. The song was introduced on tour by F. W. Hollis of West's Minstrels and they sang it dressed in rough rider's uniforms. The same year the number was published, Billy Murray made a very successful recording of it. Murray was primarily a comic singer but his wistful rendition of the ballad was very popular. Sheet music sales were considerable but, like many wartime songs, the public quickly lost interest once peace returned and the ballad was little-known a decade later.

That, you might think, was that. But in 1969 Rolf Harris scored a UK No. 1 with the song, albeit retitled "Two Little Boys." That swinging England could embrace the number proved that evocative songwriting touches emotions whatever the context.

Thomas Hischak

Published Date 1903

Nationality USA

Composer Theodore F. Morse (music), Edward Madden (lyric)

Why It's Key The battle tale popular in both war and peace.

Key Performance *In Dahomey*
stage musical

At the turn of the twentieth century in New York, it was not unusual to have African American performers in musicals, though not usually on their own terms. Successful black vaudevillian team George Walker and Egbert Austin Williams put together *In Dahomey* after Walker came up with the idea of using the African elements of their background in a new show. The show was a farce about a scheme to enable unhappy American Negroes to "return" to Africa. Though neither knew much of the African culture (West Indies-born Williams was raised in California and Walker was from Kansas), the idea was fresh and new.

Though the musical only found moderate success on Broadway (53 performances), *In Dahomey* toured Britain, playing at the Shaftesbury Theatre to rave reviews and huge audience fervor. The Prince of Wales, Edward VII, even had the play performed at Buckingham Palace for his birthday. Will Marion Cook's infectious music paired with Paul Lawrence Dunbar and Alex Rogers' high-spirited lyrics made hits out of songs "I May Be Crazy But I Ain't No Fool" and "Miss Hannah From Savannah."

The show provided African Americans with theater ambitions, if not an opened door, then a cracked one. A sign of the slowly changing climate came when Williams went on to star in *Ziegfeld Follies* (1910). He was met with a boycott by the white performers but they yielded when Florenz Ziegfeld threatened to fire them all.

Leila Regan-Porter

Date February 18, 1903

Nationality USA

Director George Walker

Cast George Walker, Egbert Austin Williams, Lottie Williams

Composers Will Marion Cook, Paul Lawrence Dunbar, Alex Rogers

Why It's Key The first full-length Broadway musical written or played by African Americans.

Key Event
First double-sided discs

The first double-sided discs were experimental ones produced in limited numbers in Europe as early as 1904 but the first serious attempt to commercially introduce the innovation was a series of discs introduced by the Columbia company in 1908 in Britain and the United States. At this time, the record companies organized their products in series, which grouped recordings under technical advantages or types of music. They hoped to build customer loyalty around the technological or aesthetic returns of a specific series of recordings rather than market records on their individual merits. The rivalry between cylinder and disc at this point was a serious impediment to the growth of the record industry. Once a customer had bought into a system, it was impossible to play the products of the competing format. The double-sided disc was a strategy to end this rivalry and center the industry around the disc format. The response of the companies producing cylinders was a cylinder which doubled the playback time – but only up to four minutes! The problem with the double disc was that it encouraged customers to wait until a new standard emerged. Very few disc manufacturers had the nerve to follow Columbia into the new format, and it took at least a decade before the industry fully accepted double-sided discs as standard. When it did so, of course, the format reigned supreme for many, many years.

Andre Millard

Date 1904

Country USA

Why It's Key The death knell for the cylinder – eventually

Opposite Double-sided disc

A.M.CASSANDRE 32

Pathé

L'ENREGISTREMENT ELECTRIQUE LE PLUS PERFECTIONNE

Key Song "Meet Me In St. Louis, Louis"
Billy Murray

This topical song that celebrated the 1904 Louisiana Purchase Exposition held in St. Louis reflected the enthusiasm and confidence of a nation on the rise. The World's Fair was a source of great national pride and over 20 million Americans visited the vast fair grounds in St. Louis, marveling at such innovations as air conditioning and wireless telegraphy (radio).

In this composition of Kerry Mills (melody) and Andrew B Sterling (lyric), the titular Louis returns home to find that his wife Flossie has abandoned their boring life for the wonders of the World's Fair, and encourages him to join her in that city. "Don't tell me that the lights are shining anyplace else but there," she says in her note, promising that if he comes she will be his "tootsie-wootsie."

First published in 1904, the first performer to successfully record this song was Billy Murray, whose strong voice and unusually clear intonation made it easy to distinguish the words of the song on the scratchy phonograph cylinder. Murray was followed by legions of other singers who recorded this song into the 1920s. The excitement and pride generated by the World's Fair produced several other songs, as well as a play that was turned into a film, *Meet Me In St. Louis*. The latter, starring Judy Garland, was itself a landmark musical insofar as its songs genuinely advanced the plot. Quite a development from a brief song.

Andre Millard

Published Date 1904

Nationality USA

Composer Kerry Mills, Andrew B. Sterling

Why It's Key Displayed the ability of popular song to exploit current events and feelings.

Key Performance "The Yankee Doodle Boy" *Little Johnny Jones* stage musical

Vaudeville songwriter-singer-dancer George M. Cohan finally broke into the legitimate theater on November 7, 1904 with his musical comedy *Little Johnny Jones*. The show changed the sound of the Broadway musical and *Little Johnny Jones*'s signature tune, "The Yankee Doodle Boy," became the new model for the Broadway hit song. Cohan wrote the book, music, and lyrics, and also co-produced, directed, and starred in *Little Johnny Jones*. He played the American jockey Johnny in London to ride in the Derby, boasting about his native pride in the catchy song. The cocky number can be looked at as a modern, ragged variation of the pre-Colonial days ditty "Yankee Doodle (Went To Town)." The song immediately caught on and it became a kind of theme song for Cohan's long career. Like the rest of the Cohan score, "Yankee Doodle Dandy," as it is more commonly known today, is brash, colloquial, and part of a musical rebellion against operetta and other European-sounding theater songs. Critics thought Cohan's numbers too slangy and unpoetical, but the public loved the new conversational approach to songwriting and his songs crossed over to become favorites in vaudeville, sheet music, piano rolls, and early recordings. James Cagney sang "The Yankee Doodle Boy" in the Cohan movie biography *Yankee Doodle Dandy* (1942) and Joel Gray sang it in the Broadway musical *George M!* (1968).

Thomas Hischak

Opening Night November 7, 1904

Country USA

Director George M. Cohan

Cast George M. Cohan

Composer George M. Cohan

Why It's Key Where pop met nationalism.

Key Song "Alexander, Don't You Love Your Baby No More?"

Just as the word "baby" was used in songs to indicate a young black woman ("Baby, Won't You Please Come Home," "I Can't Give You Anything But Love, Baby"), so the name "Alexander" was used in early twentieth century compositions as shorthand for a black male.

The usage started with the vaudeville and musical comedy team of James McIntyre and Thomas K. Heath. While Al Jolson portrayed a black man named "Gus" in many blackface appearances at the Winter Garden Theater, in blackface McIntyre was always named "Alexander." In vaudeville and the musicals *The Ham Tree* and *Hello, Alexander*, McIntyre and Heath used the name "Alexander" as a running gag in their blackface comedy routines.

One day in 1904, composer Harry von Tilzer overheard a black woman in the Winter Garden's lobby remark, "Don't you love your baby no more?" He added the name "Alexander" to the comment and had his lyricist, Andrew Sterling, write a "coon song" with that title. The name became so associated with black characters that Irving Berlin used the name in his 1910 song, "Alexander And His Clarinet." Berlin used that song's lyric as the basis for "Alexander's Ragtime Band," written a year later.

Interestingly, while "baby" is now universally used in popular song to refer to a lover – white or black, male or female – and its etymology is unknown to the performers who employ it, "Alexander" has fallen out of lyrical use.

Ken Bloom

Published Date 1904

Nationality USA

Composers Harry von Tilzer, Andrew Sterling

Why It's Key Birth of the name Alexander in popular song to denote a black male.

Key Event "The Preacher And The Bear" is recognized as the first million-seller

Although it is eminently arguable that this comedy number by Arthur Collins was the first million-seller – nobody really knows how many records or how much sheet music was sold at that time – it has gone down in history as such.

Not that the song is the type to celebrate for reasons other than being a significant indicator of how the recorded sound industry had mushroomed in a few short years. It marked the high water mark of minstrelsy in the United States, in which white performers imitated and mocked African American dialect and stereotypes. Indeed because Collins' specialty was "coon songs," he was billed as a "coon singer," even though he used other dialects in his comic songs, imitating Irish immigrants and country "rubes."

Collins' songs were issued by practically every American record company during his two-decade career and "The Preacher And The Bear" was recorded many times on several different labels, as was the custom with hit songs at this time. The introduction of four-minute cylinders allowed a fuller version of the song to be issued in 1908. The song tells the story of a man of the cloth who is confronted by a grizzly on a hunting trip and involves a humorous dialogue between the trapped preacher (actually referred to as a coon in the lyric) and the animal: "If I should give you just one big juicy bite would you go away?" the preacher wails.

Andre Millard

Date June 1905

Country USA

Why It's Key Sales milestone in the still-young recording industry.

Key Event
Variety is published

The trade journal of the U.S. entertainment industry was founded in 1905 in New York. It was to be a vehicle for vaudeville artists to fight for better payments for bookings and for composers to publicize their songs.

Though it may now have the aura of establishment, it endured some tumultuous times in its early days. Sime Silverman, its publisher, offended Edward Albee of the mighty Keith-Albee vaudeville circuit and endured a boycott of the new publication, leading Silverman to publish articles about the injustices of low payments to performers and songwriters. However, contemporary printed window on the growing business of entertainment *The Talking Machine World* is the periodical that has disappeared from memory, not *Variety*.

Variety played an important part in the debate about payments to songwriters, gratuities paid to plug songs, and the formation of organizations like ASCAP.

The development of the new mass media meant that *Variety*'s interests started to go well beyond the live, vaudeville, and circus business areas it had originally covered and articles on "Pictures" and "Radio" appeared prominently in it. Significantly it opened an office in Los Angeles. The magazine kept a close eye on sales and published weekly statistics, although suspicions of rigged numbers led it to occasionally drop its weekly popularity charts. Nevertheless *Variety* remained the main arbiter of the success of a song and a highly influential reporter on the news and gossip of popular entertainment.
Andre Millard

Date December 16, 1905

Country USA

Why It's Key *Variety*'s growth in circulation and influence reflected the public's increasing fascination with the "score card" of the entertainment industry.

Key Song "Give My Regards To Broadway" Billy Murray

Broadway is today the center of American theater, musical and non-musical, the place where a show has to make it in order to be perceived as genuinely successful. Its standing was the same a hundred years ago. The theater-studded New York strip got its unofficial anthem when "Give My Regards To Broadway" was first heard in the stage musical *Little Johnny Jones* (1904). Billy Murray, who had already had a U.S. No. 1 with the show's "Yankee Doodle Boy," entered the U.S. chart with his version on June 17 1905 on his way to the top once more.

Composer George M. Cohan had worked so many years in vaudeville, dreaming of crossing over to the legit stage, that he had a huge reverence for Broadway. His works are filled with song and show titles that salute Broadway as the pinnacle of all-American entertainment. None were more potent than this one. In *Little Johnny Jones*, the American jockey Johnny is wrongly accused of throwing the Derby in England and

must remain to face charges. He sings the song to his friends as they depart by ship to return to New York without him. Once he finds he is cleared of the charges, Johnny explodes into a jubilant song and dance reprise of the number.

"Give My Regards To Broadway" remains one of the most recognized of all-American songs, so much so that Paul McCartney could play on its familiarity in the title of his movie *Give My Regards To Broad Street* (1984).
Thomas Hischak

Chart Entry Date June 17, 1905

Nationality USA

Composer George M. Cohan

Why It's Key The song that showed the Great White Way was already famous enough to get a theme tune.

Opposite George M. Cohan

Key Event **Music first transmitted over Radio** Reginald Fessenden

Although Guglielmo Marconi is considered to be the father of radio technology, he was actually only one of numerous inventors in the United States and all over Europe who were experimenting with generating and receiving electromagnetic waves in the 1890s. The name first given to the technology reveals the intent of all these inventors: wireless telegraphy. Radio was seen as an improved method of sending information.

Two of the leading North American experimenters saw radio in a broader light. Lee de Forest and Canadian Reginald Fessenden were scientists who had experience in the business world and both recognized that radio might have commercial applications in entertainment. Fessenden was a graduate of Thomas Edison's famous research laboratory in West Orange, New Jersey and after he left he devoted his experiments to wireless telegraphy. He set up a laboratory in Brant Rock, Massachusetts and on December 24, 1906, achieved the first broadcast of

music. It was a modest affair, involving him playing "O Holy Night" on the violin as well as reading from the Bible and it could only be heard by ships at sea. However, the event opened up a new world, "an invisible empire of the air," (as de Forest envisaged it) that would transform entertainment in the twentieth century. Four years later De Forest transmitted music from the Metropolitan Opera to over 20 listening stations in New York. Although these two events were experimental and not commercially exploited, the first steps in entertainment broadcasting had been taken.
Andre Millard

Date December 24, 1906

Country USA

Why It's Key A new concept: music that comes to you, not vice versa.

Opposite **Reginald Fessenden**

Key Performance *The Red Mill* stage musical

Victor Herbert, then the most famous American composer, saw the comedy team of Dave Montgomery and Fred Stone as the Tin Man and Scarecrow in the stage musical *The Wizard Of Oz*. The brilliance of their performance led Herbert to commission lyricist and librettist Henry Blossom to invent a new show in which the team could star.

The result, *The Red Mill*, transcended its purpose as a showcase for the two comics. The plot revolved around a pair of traveling vaudeville performers who, whilst making their way through Holland, allow their soft hearts to get them embroiled in romantic intrigue. Opening on September 24, 1906, it was an exceptional hit in its time but when the show was revived in 1945, it played twice as long as the original. Even now, though the libretto, fashioned around the particular talents of Montgomery and Stone, by necessity has dated, the score is still one of the masterpieces of the American musical theater. Its "Every Day Is Ladies Day

With Me" and "The Streets Of New York," have become standards. *The Red Mill* is still occasionally revived, and though its libretto is usually updated, it never fails to amuse and entertain, capitalizing on its beautiful melodies.

An interesting historical footnote to the original production is that it prompted the producer to put an electric windmill image at the front of the theater, thus creating the first of the moving neon signs for which the Broadway district is now famous.
Ken Bloom

Opening Night September 24, 1906

Country USA

Director Fred G. Latham

Cast Dave Montgomery, Fred Stone, Augusta Greenleaf

Composers Victor Herbert, Henry Blossom plus (one song), Harry Williams, Egbert Van Alstyne

Why It's Key The Broadway show cast before it was written.

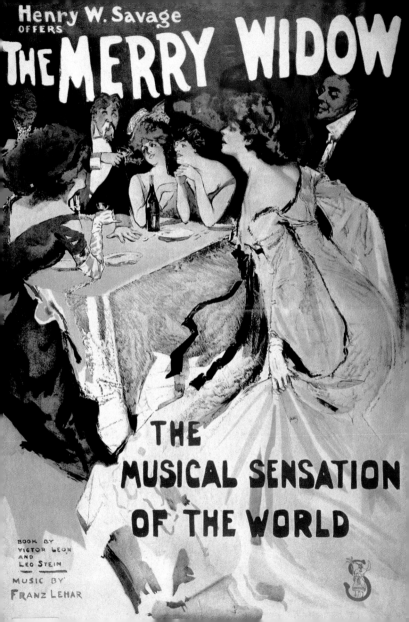

Key Song "**We've Been Chums For Fifty Years**" R. J. Jose

While love songs in the 1890s tended to eschew slang and conversational lyrics, the turn of the century brought a looser, less reverent approach to declaring love. Some of this came about because of ragtime and a less predictable musical line, but even old-fashioned ballads started to drop "thee" and other archaic words. "We've Been Chums For Fifty Years," published in 1906, illustrates the new tone. Thurland Chattaway wrote the ballad that is sung by a spouse on a fiftieth wedding anniversary and the language is gentle and casual. The lyric emphasizes the friendship that has grown over the years rather than the romantic or passionate declarations found in most love songs. Chattaway's music is flowing and low-key, matching the lyric in its depiction of the twilight years. The song was written for R. J. Jose to sing on tour and he recorded it too, also in 1906.

The sentiments of "We've Been Chums For Fifty Years" were not completely original; the same idea was popularized in song during the previous century with such beloved standards as "When You And I Were Young, Maggie" (1866) and "Silver Threads Among The Gold" (1873). But it was Chattaway's ballad that introduced an informality that would allow a spouse to lovingly call a mate a "chum."

Thomas Hischak

Published Date 1906

Nationality USA

Composer Thurland Chattaway

Why It's Key Revealed a new kind of informal love song on Tin Pan Alley.

Key Performance *The Merry Widow* stage musical

The Merry Widow was the high point of imported European operetta – and one of the most successful in that genre of opera-lite, which included spoken dialogue as well as music. After enormous success in its native Vienna in 1905, an English adaptation of the original vision of composer Franz Lehár and librettists Viktor Léon and Leo Stein was provided by Britons Basil Hood and Adrian Ross. Following more success in London, the show landed in New York on October 21, 1907 and, as Leonard Bernstein put it, "swept the Broadway public off its feet."

Based on the Henri Meilhac work *L'Attaché d'Ambassade* (1861), the operetta followed the fortunes of a bereaved but rich woman from the poor country of Pontivedro (a fictional Montenegro) attempting to find a new husband. The narrative piled in all the marvelous qualities the genre was known for – quarreling lovers, dancing, amusing circumstance, champagne, European frivolity – and inspired a new style of American musical.

With its plot and a setting of "Gay Paree", the music and action were inevitably vivacious, naughty and fun. The Parisian backdrop allowed for can-can dancing at the famous Maxim's during the song "You'll Find Me At Maxim's" and the background of the titular widow meant the music could switch to a joyful folk dance, as in the song "Vilja."

The Merry Widow caused a surprisingly modern merchandising sensation, hats, cigars, cocktails, shoes, perfumes all being sold off its back.

Leila Regan-Porter

Opening Night October 21, 1907

Nationality Austria/UK

Director Viktor Léon

Cast Mizzi Gunther, Louis Treumann

Composers Franz Lehár, Viktor Léon, Leo Stein

Why It's Key Advanced the evolution of the American musical with its comedic styles and lighthearted dancing.

Opposite *The Merry Widow*

Key Event **Ada Jones and Billy Murray arguably invent popular music**

The recording career of vaudeville and early musical comedy star Ada Jones didn't receive great notice until she teamed up with Billy Murray. Their first No. 1 was "Let's Take An Old-Fashioned Walk," which entered the U.S. charts on November 9, 1907.

What made their recordings such a success – and so revolutionary – was the team's style of singing. Rather than the operatic approach favored by such recording greats as Caruso or the pure voiced, round-toned style of sopranos and baritones singing sentimental ballads, Jones and Murray sounded like ordinary people singing (albeit to a somewhat higher level than the average Joe manages in the bathtub). In fact, many of their duets were practically conversed rather than sung in a traditional way. In addition, the fun they clearly had performing together was contagious to listeners. On many of their joint recordings, they adopted characters for their performances, utilizing different accents and regional pronunciations of words. Among their other duets are "Wouldn't You Like To Have Me For A Sweetheart," "Cuddle Up A Little Closer, Lovey Mine," "Shine On Harvest Moon," and "Be My Little Baby Bumble Bee." Theirs was a new type of popular music, wholly American in its flavor and rhythms.

The singing style of the team (who each had successful solo careers) influenced many later singers, including Bing Crosby who adopted and extended their relaxed naturalism, sense of fun, and all-American everyman personae.

Ken Bloom

Date November 9, 1907

Country USA

Why It's Key A duetting pair whose style codifies the most successful form of music the world has seen.

38

Key Song
"I Do Like To Be Beside The Seaside"

In the late nineteenth century, British coastal towns like Blackpool and Brighton became magnets for holidaymakers as a consequence of the growth of the railway network and the introduction of bank holidays.

John Glover-Kind (1881–1918) celebrated this phenomenon with "I Do Like To Be Beside The Seaside." It is his most famous song, and no wonder. This masterpiece had one verse that concluded with a near-genius onomatopoeic flourish – "Where the brass bands play tiddly-on-pom-pom" – and another choc-full of delicious wordplay and alliteration: "There are lots of girls, besides/That I'd like to be beside/Beside the seaside, beside the sea." Never one to miss an opportunity, Glover-Kind's sheet music had words for both Blackpool and Brighton. The song was so popular that Glover-Kind wrote a follow-up (or perhaps rebuttal), "I Don't Like To Be Beside The Seaside."

However, there is a dark underbelly to this delightful, humorous ditty. In a day and age when the British proletariat endured grinding, soul-destroying poverty despite their country being the richest on earth, The Tariff Commission of 1907 condemned their indolence, complaining of the working man, "He is more interested in the next football match and the nearest public house than he is in his work." Faced with attitudes such as that, it is little wonder that they so enthusiastically temporarily fled their urban squalor to snatch the small taste of paradise the seaside constituted.

Spencer Leigh

Published Date 1907

Nationality UK

Composer John A. Glover-Kind

Why It's Key Showed that an ostensibly popular song could mask real-life bleakness.

Key Song
"On The Road To Mandalay"

Rudyard Kipling's famous poem, "Mandalay" was first published in 1892 in the collection, *Barrack Room Ballads*. In 1907, Oley Speaks – famous for "The Shooting Of Dan McGrew" – adapted Kipling's verse into a song.

As well as a literary sensibility, the song also boasted a cockney sensibility rare to American ears, for Kipling's poem was written in the vernacular of a working-class London soldier who has served in the Far East. He is pining for a banjo playing Burmese girl named Supi-Yaw-Lat and knows that she misses him too. The time constraints of the music industry at the time being a couple of minutes, Speaks had to distil the poem to its essence and chose to chop out all but the first and last of the six quite long verses. Though it loses something in this process, the resultant "On The Road To Mandalay" still packs far more exotic backdrops, atmospheric phrases, and cultural richness into its running time than just about anything else then around.

The glum subject matter is given a suitably slow, almost doomy melody with a dramatic piano part. The melody has a natural feel, not like an arrangement in which inviolable words long since settled are being shoehorned. This "setting" is an impressive achievement.

Of all people, Frank Sinatra recorded a cover of this quintessentially English imperialist lament in 1958.
Ken Bloom

Published Date 1907

Nationality UK/USA

Composers Oley Speaks, Rudyard Kipling

Why It's Key The song that brought a rare literary sensibility to the popular music field in the first decade of the twentieth century.

Key Person
Byron G. Harlan

The first big hit of Byron G. Harlan (1861–1936), an early minstrel performer and singer, was 1899's "Please, Mr. Conductor, Don't Put Me Off the Train," a typical tearjerker of the period. In 1903, Harlan recorded "Please Mother, Buy Me A Baby" and "The Vacant Chair," two more narrative songs meant to pull at the heartstrings. There were exceptions including the bliss-soaked "Wait Till The Sun Shines, Nellie" and war anthem "Tramp! Tramp! Tramp!" The tenor's version of Gus Edwards' "School Days" entered the U.S. charts on May 11, 1907 and the success of that recording helped make it a standard for almost 100 years.

In his recordings, Harlan would often assume a character when singing a song. An early review enthused, "He is at home whether his personation be that of a typical Yankee, a wench, or an end man in a minstrel show. His success… is due in a large measure to the way in which his own delightful personality reveals itself through his records."

Harlan was later paired with Arthur Collins, another early recording star. The two were billed as the "Half-Ton Duo" due to their respective girths. It seemed almost inevitable that they would turn to comic songs like "Down Where The Wurzburger Flows," "The Right Church, But The Wrong Pew," "Oh How She Could Yacki Hacki Wicki Wacki Woo," and "Alexander's Ragtime Band," the success of all of which was yet another sign of this one-time balladeer's great versatility.
Ken Bloom

Role Recording Artist

Date 1907

Nationality USA

Why It's Key A recording pioneer who was as much impersonator as singer.

Key Song "Maple Leaf Rag"
Scott Joplin

Scott Joplin's first and most influential piano rag, "Maple Leaf Rag," was written in 1899 when Joplin had settled in Sedalia, Missouri, and performed with his band at the Maple Leaf Social Club. The composition was daring for its time, building the music on four distinct themes in which the bass rhythm of the left hand is contrasted by the syncopated (or off-the-beat) treble rhythm of the right hand. This form would become the structure for classic piano ragtime. When Joplin introduced the song at the social club, it immediately gained attention. When it was published soon after, the rag went on to be the first of its genre to sell over one million copies of sheet music. A recording by the U.S. Marine Band in 1907 put the song on the recording charts for the first time on March 16, 1907 and it became the most famous of all the ragtime compositions of the era. Also in 1907, Vess Ossman, dubbed the "King of the Banjo," recorded it and the rag was thereby found just as effective with other instrumentation besides the piano. Best-selling recordings of the song over the years include those by the New Orleans Feetwarmers (1932), Tommy Dorsey (1936), Art Hodes (1944), and Eddie London (1950).

Interest in Joplin and his rags was rekindled after the release of the film *The Sting* (1974) and "Maple Leaf Rag" saw many new recordings.
Thomas Hischak

Published Date 1907

Nationality USA

Composer Scott Joplin

Why It's Key The model from which the ragtime genre blossomed.

Key Event The "Take Me Out To The Ball Game" foul-up

A version of baseball anthem "Take Me Out To The Ball Game" that has long been attributed to Billy Murray and Hadyn Quartet, made the U.S. charts on October 24, 1908 and was a No. 1. Its immense popularity – officially, the biggest of Murray's many, many hits – makes it all the more strange that nobody seems to have noticed that it was not Murray singing the lead on the record but in fact Harry MacDonough.

Perhaps this is because the credit error was a retroactive one. The record's original label did not cite Murray as appearing. It seems to be the case that only when the recording was erroneously attributed to Murray and the Haydn Quartet – with whom he sometimes sat in as lead vocalist – in a 1911 catalog did the incorrect billing begin. In a day and age before television or film had created the cult of the celebrity, it was much easier for something like this to go unnoticed. As to why the artists themselves don't seem to have taken the trouble to point it out, it's difficult to speculate, but with them issuing a dozen or more titles per year under various identities, it would hardly have been a priority. The error remained uncorrected until the experts at oldies label Archeophone Records spotted the mistake in 2002.

Ironically, neither of the song's writers Jack Norworth and Albert Von Tilzer had ever actually been to a baseball game but Murray was a big baseball fan.
Ken Bloom

Date October 24, 1908

Country USA

Why It's Key A century-long credit error.

Opposite "Take Me Out To The Ball Game"

Key Song "Mother Hasn't Spoken To Father Since" Billy Murray

For most people in 1908, divorce was not a subject of fun, "Mother Hasn't Spoken To Father Since" by William Jerome (lyrics) and Jean Schwartz (music), first published in that year, is a slightly daring example of a lighthearted song about such domestic trouble.

It also illustrates how pop has changed. While no pop song today would be written about one's parents, before the Roaring Twenties it was not uncommon to find songs about family; parents were particularly favorite subjects, whether the tone was comic or tragic. In this novelty number's seven verses, a series of squabbles between two parents are chronicled as they lead up to a divorce. The song never gets sentimental over the break up and by the last verse the lyric sarcastically lists famous love song titles about domestic bliss. Vestra Victoria introduced the ditty in vaudeville and recorded it, as did singing comic Billy Murray and the team of Arthur Collins and Byron G. Harlan. Because of its satiric tone, the song was not a major sheet music seller; this was not the kind of song to be sung by the family around the piano. But it was enjoyed in vaudeville and on records for a while. By the time America entered World War One, such anti-domestic ditties would be frowned upon in an era when the family was often anxiously awaiting a son's return home from the war.

Thomas Hischak

Published Date 1908

Nationality USA

Composers Jean Schwartz (music), William Jerome (lyric)

Why It's Key Illustrated popular song's capacity for the sly in a satire on a then very serious matter.

Key Song "Cuddle Up A Little Closer, Lovey Mine" Ada Jones and Billy Murray

"Cuddle Up A Little Closer, Lovey Mine" was written by composer Karl Hoschna and lyricist Otto Harbach for the musical The Three Twins, which opened on June 15, 1908. It was Harbach's first hit song, although as "Hauerbach" – he changed his name to something less Germanic when America entered World War I.

In 1908, Harbach was at the start of a notable career as the most prolific librettist/lyricist in the American musical theater but the lyric for "Cuddle Up A Little Closer, Lovey Mine" shows little of the reasons for his future success. The verse tells of a boyfriend and girlfriend on the beach. When the temperature drops and the girl thinks it's time to depart, the boy isn't ready. He whispers to her the chorus of the song, starting with the song's title. The boy declares that he loves to feel the girl's cheeks, which are rosy. Harbach then proceeds to blithely rhyme "rosy" with "comfy cozy" before ending in a flourish of banality: "'Cos I love from head to toesy, lovey mine." He then repeats the chorus without offering an additional verse.

When it was recorded in late 1908 by Ada Jones and Billy Murray however, the song was a U.S. No. 1. Partly, it was the sweet tune that carried the day. Mostly it was the delightful, twinkle-eyed, bursting-with-personality performances of the two singers, who actually turn the wince-making contortions of the lyric into something that's actually endearing.

Ken Bloom

Release Date 1908

Nationality USA

Composers Karl Hoschna, Otto Harbach

Why It's Key Proves that it's sometimes all in the delivery.

ple
Quartet

ery popular when acoustic
oming an important element
t. The record companies liked
ween tenors, baritone and
rdings vocal peaks and some
encies of the tenor voice
estricted range of acoustic
artet began as the in house
ording operation and was
e Quartet. Its two tenors were
acDonough, its baritone was
s was William Hooley. They
tet to be able to record for
me was a tribute to the
was later amended to

s appeared as early as 1898,
Old Kentucky," entered the
oneer recording company

Berliner, formed by the inventor of the disc record.
The material the Hayden Quartet sang was extremely
sentimental, often nostalgic, and unashamedly
commercial, such as "Put On Your Old Gray Bonnet,"
which entered the U.S. chart on December 11, 1909
and was their biggest hit. Other Hayden Quartet hits
included "Take Me Out To The Ball Game" and "By The
Light Of The Silv'ry Moon," songs still familiar today.

The group disbanded in 1914.

Andre Millard

son
MacDonough

o, Harry MacDonough (his
ohn MacDonald but his first
name as MacDonough and
hyphenate of the nascent
mong the most popular
twentieth century and
ng director and director of

his career before 1900,
an Electric Company's coin-
nes. In 1898 he cut his first
e, Sweet Dream, Good-Bye."
of Edison's most popular
ders by 1905. An additional 250
all popular ballads. His biggest
st Moon," which entered the
909. The tenor also sang with
ding the Schubert Trio and the
dovn/Hayden Quartet

As long as he performed, his records remained
popular. But once he ceased singing in 1912 to devote
his time to executive duties with the Victor company,
the number of MacDonough recordings available
dropped precipitously. In 1917, there were 77 titles
on the market and only four by 1927.

In 1923, MacDonough moved from sales manager
to Manager of Artists and Repertoire at the Victor
Talking Machine Company. He moved to Columbia in
1925 as director of their studios, a role he held until
his death in 1931.

Ken Bloom

Key Song **"I Wonder Who's Kissing Her Now"** Joe E. Howard

"I Wonder Who's Kissing Her Now" was one of Tin Pan Alley's most popular songs, selling over three million copies of sheet music after its 1909 publication and remaining a favorite for many decades. Joe E. Howard got the idea for the song when he heard a Chicago college student say the title phrase to a friend. Howard composed the flowing melody and Will H. Hough and Frank R. Adams penned the lyric, the wistful – but by pop's then-affected standards, matter-of-fact – reflection of a rejected beau about what lies his former honey is telling, who is buying her wine and whose lips are kissing hers. Henry Woodruff introduced the ballad in a Chicago production of the musical *The Prince Of Tonight* (1909) but it was Howard himself who popularized it on stage. In 1947 Harold Orlob, Howard's musical arranger, came forward and claimed authorship of the music; he sued Howard and won. Orlob received no money but his name was added to subsequent sheet music.

Henry Burr made one of the first recordings of the song and in 1947 Perry Como revived interest in it with a popular recording with Ted Weems' Orchestra. In addition to many other recordings, the ballad was sung in several movies, including *The Time, The Place And The Girl* (1929) and the Howard bio-film *I Wonder Who's Kissing Her Now* (1947).

Thomas Hischak

Published Date 1909

Nationality USA

Composers Joe E. Howard, Will H. Hough, Frank R. Adams

Why It's Key One of the first torch songs to use a direct, down-to-earth lyric rather than a melodramatic one.

Key Event **The dawn of the album** Nutcracker Suite

In the early years of the twentieth century a major problem facing the talking machine industry was the inability to compress more than four minutes of music on a record. This prevented the recording of symphonic music and kept the record companies out of classical music, an extremely affluent and prestigious market. While inventors desperately looked for means to increase recording times, the record companies made do by issuing multiple disc sets that contained abridged versions of symphonies.

The HMV company in London released Verdi's *Ernani* in 1903 in a set of 40 single-sided discs, a cumbersome and expensive product. The German Odeon company came up with the marketing tool of collecting the discs in a leather-bound album, much like the albums used to store photographs. When they released Tchaikovsky's *Nutcracker Suite* on four double-sided discs in 1909, they opened the way for the recording and marketing of whole symphonies. The record companies also used the album concept to market collections of classical music, such as Victor's Music Arts Library of 1924. Although long playing technology – and packaging – was transformed in the '30s and '40s, the name "album" stuck and when microgrooved long-playing discs were introduced in 1948, they too were called albums.

The term remains in use even in the CD and download age, although its actually more appropriate twin "long player" has largely fallen into disuse.

Andre Millard

Date April 1909

Country Germany

Why It's Key Recorded music can finally be listened to more than couple of minutes at a time.

Opposite *Nutcracker Suite*

Key Performance *The Arcadians*
stage musical

The Arcadians took romantic elements from operetta, the satire of Gilbert and Sullivan and humor from the music halls to make one of the earliest musical comedies in the modern style, with songs related to the plot.

Howard Talbot and Lionel Monckton, hugely successful songwriters of the time, and lyricist Arthur Wimperis supplied a charming score and Mark Ambient and Alexander M. Thompson a sly libretto. *The Arcadians* proved to be an immense success. From April 28, 1909, the show ran a total of 809 performances at the Shaftesbury Theatre, a remarkable record in a time when 200 performance runs were considered smash hits.

An American production followed, as did mountings in Vienna, Bombay, Paris, and Melbourne, making the musical the first great international success. Audiences throughout the world thrilled to the story of a stranded aviator landing in the mythical paradise Arcadia, where he is taught about truth, honor, and other noble ideals. A changed man (dipped in the Well of Truth as he was), he returns to London with some Arcadians where he attempts to sway the local population into becoming better people. Despite songs like "The Girl With The Brogue," "Arcady Is Always Young," and "All Down Piccadilly," the Londoners are immune to higher thoughts and the Arcadians return to their retreat, leaving the wider world behind.

Perhaps they and the rest of the world should have taken the message of Arcadia: the horrors of the Great War were just around the corner.
Ken Bloom

Opening Night April 28, 1909

Country UK

Director Unknown

Cast Phyllis Dare, Harry Helchman, Alfred Lester

Composers Lionel Monckton, Howard Talbot, Arthur Wimperis

Why It's Key Possibly the first globally successful musical.

Opposite **The Arcadians**

Key Person
Billy Murray

He is forgotten today but the name of Billy Murray (1877–1954) was known to everyone with an interest in recorded music in the first two decades of the twentieth century. When "By The Light Of The Silvery Moon" entered the U.S. charts on April 16, 1910 on its way to No. 1, he was only about halfway through his peak years. He racked up a mind-boggling 169 Top 30 hits – and that's not counting the commercial successes he had with various vocal groups and duets with the likes of Ada Jones, which themselves total over 100.

Perhaps it is only right then that whereas most recording pioneers came from vaudeville or musical theater, Billy Murray seemed to spring fully formed from the Edison cylinder: he was the first star whose reputation existed solely through recordings. Philadelphia-born and Denver raised, he was a tenor whose trademark was loud and fast delivery. Many of the songs he chose were inspired by the exciting developments of the time. 1904's "Meet Me In St. Louis, Louis" commemorated the St. Louis Exposition, "Come Take A Trip In My Air-Ship" was the first song to commemorate the Wright Brothers' flight and "In My Merry Oldsmobile" was a song written in honor of the first transcontinental auto race.

Ironic then that technology overtook Murray. When the acoustic horn was replaced by the microphone, his loud style began to look histrionically old-fashioned as the crooner age began.
Ken Bloom

Role Recording Artist

Date 1910

Nationality USA

Why It's Key The superstar of the recording industry up to 1920.

Key Person
Bela Bartok

Where his musical countrymen seemed content to recycle their own stylistic hallmarks, the Hungarian pianist Bela Bartok (1881–1945) made his reputation by striking out in unlikely directions. Best known for his piano works, Bartok blended folk and modernist melodies. Consequently, he is considered a founder of ethnomusicology, or the study of folk music. He also deserves credit for doing his own bit in breaking down barriers between "elitist" classical and "common" folk.

The most celebrated example of this is *Romanian Folk Dances*, six short piano pieces based on old Magyar folk melodies that Bartok and his colleague, Zoltan Kodaly, collected starting in 1910 (and which were commercially released in 1915). However, where Kodaly's pieces continued quoting these melodies, Bartok used them as inspiration for his own writing.

When the Nazis took power in Germany, Bartok stopped giving concerts there, but his views inevitably ran afoul of right-wingers in his own country. In 1942, Bartok reluctantly fled to the United States – where his profile was lower and his eclectic style attracted less attention. However, Bartok's lot improved with the commissioning of *Concerto For Orchestra*, which eased his financial difficulties, and became his most popular work. A renaissance seemed due – notably, his *Sonata For Solo Violin* was commissioned by Yehudi Menuhin – only to be scuppered by Bartok's September 1945 death by leukemia.

He remains a towering figure, a fact symbolized by the 1988 reburial of his remains in a newly non-Communist Hungary, with a full state funeral.
Ralph Heibutzki

Role Composer

Date 1910

Nationality Hungary

Why It's Key A founder of ethnomusicology.

Key Song "Some of These Days"
Sophie Tucker

African-American songwriter Shelton Brooks (1886–1975) was born in Canada. His family moved from Ontario to Detroit in 1901 and he made his living performing in vaudeville and early musical comedy as well as songwriting. In time, his songs – which included "At The Darktown Strutters' Ball," "Swing That Thing," "There'll Come A Time," and "Walkin' The Dog" – were wildly successful but when he wrote "Some Of These Days" he was an unknown.

For this reason, when in 1910, he tried approaching the successful singer Sophie Tucker with it, she wouldn't see him. Tucker's maid, Mollie Elkins, convinced her to give the guy a break, chiding her, "That's no way for you to be going on, giving a nice boy like that the run-around." As Tucker recalled, "The minute I heard "Some of These Days," I could have kicked myself for almost losing it… It had everything… I've turned it inside out, singing it every way imaginable, as a dramatic song, as a novelty number, as a sentimental ballad, and always audiences have loved it…" Tucker recorded the song on February 24, 1911 on an Edison cylinder and it was a hit the following summer.

Tucker predicted that "the song will be remembered and sung for years and years to come, like some of Stephen Foster's." Tucker was right; she and countless others have recorded it, recognizing "Some Of These Days" as one of the greatest torch songs in Tin Pan Alley history.
Ken Bloom

Published Date 1910

Nationality USA

Composer Shelton Brooks

Why It's Key A scolding maid ensures exposure for a classic.

Key Event
Sheet music sales peak

While the sale of cylinders, player piano rolls, and early records were all used to help gauge the popularity of a song, in 1910 the sales of sheet music remained the preferred, most accurate, and most profitable measure of what was a hit. That year the sale of sheet music in America reached a peak of a massive two billion copies, at a time when the U.S. population was only 93,402,000. It was a symptom of a time when many households boasted both a piano and members able to play it and of a day and age before radio or television where people had to make their own entertainment.

In addition to the hundreds of popular songs already printed and on sale, 1910 saw the introduction of such mammoth hits as "Let Me Call You Sweetheart," "Ah, Sweet Mystery Of Life," "Some Of These Days," "Mother Machree," "Down By The Old Mill Stream," "I'm Falling In Love With Someone," "Put Your Arms Around Me, Honey," "Come Josephine In My Flying Machine,"

"The Stein Song," "Italian Street Song," and "Play That Barbershop Chord."

After 1910 the music business would gradually change. The days of the parlor piano being the center of music in the home were waning and by the Roaring Twenties sheet music would no longer be the mighty business it had been. Sheet music sales would eventually be superseded by records, radio play, and other technological wonders.

Thomas Hischak

Date 1910

Country USA

Why It's Key A peak but the beginning of the end for a way of measuring musical popularity.

Key People
The American Quartet

Barbershop quartets had been popular in the nineteenth century but the introduction of the frenetic ragtime at the turn of the century made such a cappella, intricate, mannered harmonizing seem old fashioned. That changed with the coming of records, particularly the entry in the U.S. charts of The American Quartet's recording of "Casey Jones" on June 18, 1910.

The group was formed in 1910 by tenor Billy Murray who, though a recording star at Victor Records, wanted to be featured in a quartet. He hired tenor John Bieling, baritone Steve Porter, and bass William F. Hooley. "Casey Jones" was their first hit. Over the next fourteen years The American Quartet would have 65 Top Ten hits, including such Number One songs as "Come Josephine In My Flying Machine," "Oh, You Beautiful Doll," "Moonlight Bay," "Everybody Two-Step," "Call Me Up Some Rainy Afternoon," "Rebecca Of Sunnybrook Farm," "Chinatown, My Chinatown," "Oh Johnny, Oh!" and "Over There." The membership of the

group changed during its fourteen-year existence. Birling left in 1914 and was replaced by John Young, and when Hooley died in 1918 he was replaced by Donald Chalmers. When The American Quartet was revamped in 1920, only Murray remained and his new partners were Albert Campbell, John Meyer, and Frank Croxton. The group disbanded in 1925 but their records remained popular for decades, keeping four-part singing alive long after the barbershop heyday had passed.

Thomas Hischak

Role Recording Artists

Date 1911

Nationality USA

Why It's Key Revived the nation's interest in four-part harmony songs.

Key People
The Peerless Quartet

The Peerless Quartet were the most recorded of the vocal quartets who dominated American popular song at the turn of the twentieth century and whose harmonized singing covered every sort of song from hymns and classical music to minstrel routines.

Formed in the late nineteenth century as a vehicle for recordings of the Columbia Phonograph Company, The Columbia Male Quartet were renamed in 1906 as The Peerless Quartet and continued (with different personnel) until they were disbanded in 1928. The key figures in their foundation were their two tenors Henry Burr and Albert Campbell, both of whom were performers and entrepreneurs. In 1906 Frank Stanley replaced Tom Daniels as the bass anchor of the group and Stanley managed the quartet until his death in 1910 when Burr took over as leader.

"Let Me Call You Sweetheart," which entered the U.S. chart on November 4, 1911, was their second No. 1. A syrupy love song with a placid tempo that places few demands on the vocalist, it was typical of the vaudeville sing-along of the era, is still sung at karaoke sessions and is revived every Valentine's Day. As recently as Christmas 2006, a version by Laurel and Hardy was being used in a UK mobile phone television campaign. The height of The Peerless Quartet's popularity was in and around World War I, when they had a string of hits, including the protest number "I Didn't Raise My Boy To Be A Soldier."

Andre Millard

Role Recording Artists

Date 1911

Nationality USA

Why It's Key One of America's most influential vocal groups.

Key Person
Irving Berlin

Irving Berlin was born in Russia on May 11, 1888 and died in New York city on September 22, 1989. During his long lifetime, he wrote the music and lyrics for more than 3,000 songs, even though he never learned to read music beyond a very basic level and could only play the piano in one key. "Alexander's Ragtime Band" – published on March 28th, 1911 was a huge hit in an era when a song's success was rated largely on sheet music sales. The infectious, up-tempo ditty made the "Hit Parade" by selling more than one million copies in sheet music form. Though the song is not a pure example of ragtime, it helped popularize the idiom. In addition to Berlin's stand-alone popular songs, he composed the scores for 21 Broadway shows and 17 films. "God Bless America," "White Christmas," "Easter Parade," "Blue Skies," "There's No Business Like Show Business," "Puttin' On The Ritz," "Cheek To Cheek," and "Always" are among the many songs he wrote that became standards. "Alexander's Ragtime Band" inspired a 1938 movie of the same title, starring Alice Faye, Tyrone Power, Don Ameche, and Ethel Merman. The song is also featured prominently in the amazingly hokey flick *There's No Business Like Show Business* (1954), in which it's performed by Merman, Dan Dailey, Donald O'Connor, Mitzi Gaynor – and Johnnie Ray!

Michael Portantiere

Role Composer

Date 1911

Nationality USA

Why It's Key Proved that limited technical skills did not prevent somebody being possibly the defining songwriting talent of his era.

Opposite **Irving Berlin**

Key Song
"Any Old Iron"

Harry Champion was one of Britain's best-loved music hall stars. He was born William Crump in 1866 in the Shoreditch area of London and the songs he picked (and sometimes wrote) reflected Cockney working class life. Despite the squalid conditions in which many of the proletariat lived and worked, his songs were upbeat and cheerful and ideal for parties, none more so than "Any Old Iron." Written by the team of Charles Collins, Fred Terry, and E. A. Sheppard, it was first recorded on October 17, 1911.

The narrator has been left a watch and chain by his Uncle Bill. He thinks it looks smart, but everywhere he goes he is taunted by the cry of people, unimpressed by the legacy, of "Any old iron?," the refrain of dealers who toured neighborhoods who were prepared to give cash to those able to furnish them scrap metal. As usual with Champion, he performed the song almost ridiculously fast. A close inspection of the blurred lyric however reveals it to be stupendously good, packed with local color ("He dashed up in a canter with a carriage and a pair") and clever rhymes ("I began to wonder, when their dials began to crack/If by mistake I'd got my Sunday trousers front to back".)

Peter Sellers made the UK Top 20 in 1957 with a skiffle version of "Any Old Iron."

Spencer Leigh

Published Date 1911

Nationality UK

Composers Charles Collins, Fred Terry, E. A. Sheppard

Why It's Key Brilliant proletarian vignette by a master of the art.

Key Song
"The March Of The Women"

In Great Britain, a campaign to gain women the right to vote began in 1872. It became increasingly militant after 1905, with "suffragettes" – the more militant advocates of women's suffrage – engaging in protests that often involved public vandalism.

One of the leading suffragettes was Emmeline Pankhurst, who founded the Women's Social and Political Union. In 1910 composer Ethel Smyth saw Pankhurst speak, and, falling in love with her, promptly joined the WSPU and devoted the next two years of her life to the suffragette cause. She also wrote songs for the movement, including "Laggard Dawn, 1910, A Medley" and "The March Of The Women," both of which were premiered at a rally at London's Albert Hall on March 23, 1911.

"The March Of The Women" quickly became a popular number performed at suffragette rallies and demonstrations. The words, by Cecily Hamilton, didn't address the issue of suffrage directly, but rather addressed the need to stand strong during the struggle ("Wide blows our banner and hope is waking"). One of its most famous impromptu performances came in 1912, when Smyth was sent to Holloway Prison following a suffragette protest: as the prisoners exercised in the yard, Smyth leaned out of her window and led the group through the "March," conducting with her toothbrush.

In 1918, women over the age of 30 finally received the right to vote in Britain, extended to all women over 21 in 1928.

Gillian G. Gaar

Published Date 1911

Nationality UK

Composers Cecily Hamilton (lyrics), Ethel Smith (music)

Why It's Key The first popular song of the twentieth century feminist movement.

Opposite Suffragette march, London, 1911

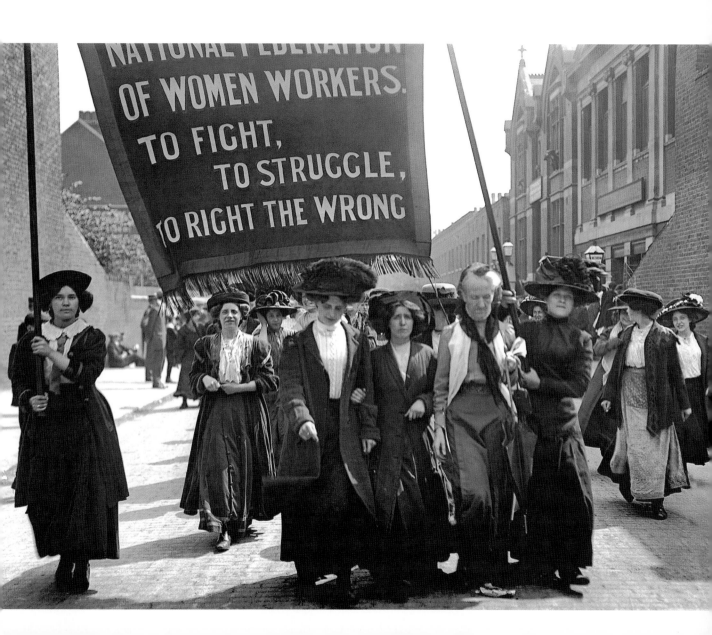

Key Song
"It's A Long Way To Tipperary"

In January 1912, Jack Judge, a music hall singer of Irish descent from Oldbury, Worcestershire, was appearing at the Grand Theatre, Stalybridge. He bet some friends five shillings (U.S. 50c) that he could compose a new song and perform it the following night. Whilst walking to his lodgings, he heard someone asking for directions and getting the response, "It's a long way." Judge added the name of the Irish town, Tipperary, and the next morning he completed the song in a local pub. He asked Horace Vernon, the conductor at the theater, to arrange it and, as promised, performed it that night.

Even though five shillings was a day's wages back then, the song proved far more lucrative than winning the bet meant – and not only for Judge. When times were bad, Judge worked in a fish market and to honor one of his creditors, Harry Williams, he added his name as a composer to the song. "It's A Long Way To Tipperary" became a highlight of Judge's act. He sometimes performed it with performing seals keeping time with their flippers. It became a favorite when it was taken up (without seals) by the music hall star Florrie Forde. The song was adopted by the Connaughts, an Irish regiment in the British Army, who warmed to its combination of a marching beat with a sentimental story of a lover yearning to be back home, and they took it to the trenches during World War I.

Spencer Leigh

Composed January 1912

Nationality UK

Composers Jack Judge, Horace Vernon

Why It's Key The evergreen written on a bet.

Key Song "The Elevator Man Going Up, Going Up, Going Up, Going Up!"

Though the dopey romantic rhyme of moon and June has come to be a shorthand for Tin Pan Alley, American popular song was never just about love songs. Romance may have been the main subject but early popular music lyrics also covered events, notables and fads, helped wartime propaganda, spurred support for political candidates, and celebrated new technology.

The latter category then, as now, gave an extra frisson to a song, making it seem to gleam with the same freshness as the inventions it discussed. When "The Elevator Man Going Up, Going Up, Going Up, Going Up!" was published on July 5, 1912, the widespread use of safe elevators that allowed buildings to rise past six stories was still a relatively new phenomenon. The epicenter of elevator use was of course skyscraper-studded New York, whose resident Irving Berlin came up with a typically witty ditty about them. Berlin exploited the fact that elevators then usually came with an attendant and the issue of chance meetings in enclosed spaces to create a tale of burgeoning romance and marriage (ceremony in the elevator), albeit one with an unexpected twist when the titular protagonist is subsequently caught in compromising circumstances in the elevator with another woman.

Cutting-edge though the whole scenario may have been at the time, the song's inhabitation of times past is demonstrated by a passing reference to a "funny coon" and the fact that the protagonist is "Andy Gray, young and gay."

Ken Bloom

Published Date July 5, 1912

Country USA

Composer Irving Berlin

Why It's Key Demonstrated the way new and developing technology was incorporated into popular song.

Opposite **Elevator man**

Key Song
"My Melancholy Baby"

"My Melancholy Baby" was a mainstay of vaudevillians who made audiences weep with the sweetness of its lyric. Though lines about clouds having silver linings, waiting until the sun shines through, and smiling through tears sound clichéd to modern ears, the lyric has a line that still sparkles: "Fears are foolish fancy."

The song, originally titled "Melancholy," had a lyric by composer Ernie Burnett's wife, Maybelle E. Watson and was published in Denver in 1911. The publisher hired George A. Norton to rewrite the lyric and reprinted the song in 1912 with Burnett and Norton receiving credit. In 1940, Maybelle Watson (divorced from Ernie by that time) sued. The court agreed with Watson and she was awarded copyright as well as damages on back royalties owed to her.

But that is not the whole story. In 1965, songwriter Ben Light died. His son, Alan, claimed that Light and Norton wrote the song while Light was working at a Denver nightclub and that Burnett stole the song and copyrighted it under his own name. According to Light's obituary in *The New York Times*, "Mr. Light was urged by his friends to claim authorship and in the early '40s he went on the radio with an orchestra, was announced as the author, and told of the circumstances under which he had written it." Light gathered affidavits attesting to his authorship of the music but Norton had died and Light could never prove his case.

Published Date 1912

Nationality USA

Composers Ernie Burnett, George A. Norton, Maybelle E. Watson

Why It's Key Such a sweet song, such a tortured history.

Key Song
"When Irish Eyes Are Smiling"

Depictions of Irish characters and Irish culture formed a large and important part of popular entertainment on both sides of the Atlantic in the early twentieth century. The term "music hall Irish" refers to commonly held stereotypes that were fostered by songwriters and comedians and eagerly consumed by mass urban audiences.

Chauncey Olcott, the co-author of "When Irish Eyes Are Smiling," had a very successful career as singer, actor, and composer within this genre but he was an American born of Irish immigrants in New York state. As an international star of music halls and the Broadway stage he helped form the imagined world of Irish characters that ignored the poverty, violence, and hopelessness of life in a depressed British colony.

"When Irish Eyes Are Smiling" – first published in 1912 and taken into the U.S. charts by Olcott on June 21, 1913 after featuring in Broadway musical *Isle O' Dreams* – offers the typical view of a happy, optimistic Irishman with a charmed life. The song includes key words that were associated with Irish dialect: "Sure, 'tis like the morn in spring." Although this kind of sentimental ballad was enjoyed all over the world, it had special resonance in the United States with its large Irish diaspora yearning for a homeland they now saw through rose-tinted glasses. It was American audiences who made such songs popular and tenors like Chauncey Olcott and John McCormack (a real Irishman) superstars.

Andre Millard

Published Date 1912

Nationality USA

Composers James Graff, Chauncey Olcott

Why It's Key A significant element in disseminating stereotypes of Irish culture in popular entertainment.

Key Event
The first record charts

With the early-twentieth-century discovery that recorded popular music could be a viable business, record companies and publishers alike wanted a way to quantify successes.

In the late nineteenth century, magazines *Edison Phonograph Monthly* and *The Phonoscope* listed good-selling recordings but they were unranked. In July 1913, *Billboard* inaugurated the chart era when it started ranking sheet music sales by polling five and dime chains like Woolworth's and McCrory's as well as a selection of department stores with sheet music departments and larger independent stores. Though then hardly scientifically accurate, these charts effected an important cultural shift, perfect as they were for trumpeting success both in trade papers and in the stores themselves, creating a snowball effect as people began to base their purchasing decisions partly on what was demonstrably popular.

September 1914 saw *Talking Machine World* publish lists of top selling records. In 1934, *Billboard* and *Variety*, by then the leading music industry publications, began publishing Top 10 charts. On January 4, 1936, *Billboard* printed its first Hit Parade and four years later the first Music Popularity Chart was published.

For a long while the chart of *Cash Box* magazine was competition to that of *Billboard* but with the demise of *Cash Box* in 1996, *Billboard*'s "Hot 100," as it has been called since August 1958, has reigned supreme in America. Airplay and sales now determine positions, not sheet music, now consigned to history, with human pollsters replaced by computer collation.
Ken Bloom

Date July 1913

Country USA

Why It's Key The idea of the Hit Parade is born.

Key Person
James Reese Europe

On December 29, 1913, the Victor Talking Machine Company financed some recordings by James Reese Europe. When the first of them was released the following year – "Castle House Rag" – it became the first commercially available phonographic recording made by an African American.

Europe, the conductor and arranger of the record, was born in Mobile, Alabama, in 1881, and played piano as a boy. In 1904 he went to New York and soon became one of the most respected of conductors, arranging the music for all-black musical revues. By 1910 he had formed his own orchestra and opened the Cleft Club, an organization dedicated to getting jobs and payments for black musicians. Also in 1910, he conducted the Broadway musical *Watch Your Step*.

At the outbreak of World War I, Europe joined the army and became director of the famous 369th Light Infantry Band, which toured the nation in 1919 and made several records as well. That same year Europe

was stabbed to death in an argument with one of his musicians.

Although he worked in the waning days of ragtime and before jazz had established itself, Europe was the model and inspiration for up-and-coming artists such as Eubie Blake, Noble Sissle, King Oliver, and Louis Armstrong. He was also the foot in the door that allowed every African-American musician there has been since the right to get their talent heard.
Thomas Hischak

Role Recording Artist

Date 1913

Nationality USA

Why It's Key Inspired a generation of black songwriters and musicians.

Key Event **Premiere of *The Rite Of Spring***
Igor Stravinsky

It had seemed a very civilized proposition: the staging of a ballet about primitive pagan cultures with choreography by the premier ballet star of his era, presented by an acclaimed company to an audience comprising the cream of Paris's cultural elite. But the premiere of *The Rite Of Spring* ended in outrage, scandal, and physical violence.

Igor Stravinsky, a young, driven composer, wrote the piece for Ballet Russes producer Serge Diaghilev. Stravinksy's rhythmically complex, aggressively discordant score stretched a large orchestra to its limit and Vaslav Nijinsky's interpretation of the music did the same to the dancers. He created steps that were deliberately ungainly and frequently painful. Rehearsals were bedeviled by rows between composer, choreographer, and impresario; the dancers threatened mutiny.

The audience was as split as the company at the show's premiere on May 29, 1913. Sensibilities attuned to far less confrontational material were affronted. Boos and heckling turned into arguments, then actual fighting, in the Theatre des Champs-Elysees stalls. Nijinsky had to stand on a chair in the wings, bellowing the rhythm to dancers who could barely hear the music.

The planned run of six performances went ahead without further event, with Diaghilev quietly delighted to have provoked such a sensation. Stravinsky's astoundingly prescient music, anticipating rock's visceral dynamics, would go on to influence everyone from Jim Steinman to Sonic Youth but would never have acquired the patina of legend without the conflagrations of its opening night.

Angus Batey

Date May 29, 1913

Country France

Why It's Key Arguably the first ever rock music is appropriately greeted with the first rock riot.

Opposite *The Rite Of Spring*

Key Performance ***Adele***
stage musical

In the rich history of Broadway, its most mysterious show is musical *Adele*, which opened on August 28, 1913. Its music was credited to Jean Briquet and Adolf Philipp and its libretto and lyrics to Philipp and Edward Paulton.

The program claimed that the show was based on an unnamed French show by Briquet and Jean Herve. But no record exists of a show by that team. Briquet's previous show was *Alma, Where Do You Live?* in 1910, and credited as from the German of Adolf Philipp. Ditto *The Midnight Girl* in 1914 and two shows in 1915, *The Girl Who Smiles* and *Two Is Company*. The problem arises when one tries to research any of these individuals. According to some sources Herve was one of Philipp's pseudonyms. He apparently acted in and wrote a few silent films and built the Bandbox Theater in New York. Paul Herve was, apparently, also a pseudonym as his name is unknown apart from the shows that Philipp claimed to have adapted from his works. Edward Paulton, at least, was a real person who contributed to 16 Broadway productions.

It seems that Philipp and Paulton conspired to create a false source as the basis for their shows, inventing the names Herve and Briquet. Perhaps they were attempting to create an air of intrigue and mystery? They may have succeeded: their shows were successful in their time (this one transferred to London), although they are forgotten today with none of any of the songs achieving any fame.

Ken Bloom

Opening Night August 28, 1913

Country USA

Director Unknown

Cast Georgia Caine, Hal Forde, Grace Walton

Composers Adolf Philipp, Edward Paulton

Why It's Key Broadway's greatest mystery.

Key Song "Trail Of The Lonesome Pine"
Henry Burr and Albert Campbell

The romantic ballad "Trail Of The Lonesome Pine" was written by Harry Carroll and Ballard MacDonald. It described the picturesque Blue Ridge mountains of Virginia where the singer's sweetheart lives in a rustic log cabin. Henry Burr and Albert Campbell took it into the U.S. charts on June 21, 1913 and it made No. 1. From that point the song languished and might have been forgotten but for its fortuitous inclusion in a popular film comedy a generation later.

Following the introduction of talking pictures, the major studios diversified into record production and then bought interests in music publishers to integrate their music operations. The movies turned out to be an excellent way of marketing both their contracted singers and the songs they owned. The comedians Laurel and Hardy were no vocalists but their version of this song, which they performed as a duet in their 1937 western *Way Out West*, demonstrated that exposure in films could reinvigorate a song and connect it to a new market, even if the song might have been for some cheapened in the process. The performance of its lyric by the pair was comedic not merely because they were comedians but because its worshipful attitude was by now the product of bygone and slightly laughable sensibilities. Subsequently, a British release of Laurel and Hardy's version of the song in 1975 saw it make UK No. 2.

Andre Millard

Release Date 1913

Nationality USA

Composers Harry Carroll, Ballard MacDonald

Why It's Key Illustrated the way that a song could achieve a new – if contrasting – lease of life when resurrected in a different medium.

Key Song
"Danny Boy"

The apparent source of the tune to "Danny Boy" is a nameless piece of supposedly ancient Irish music given the title "Londonderry Air" after the hometown of a woman who said she heard a fiddler play it, although some have even posited that the – financially naïve – lady wrote it herself.

In 1912, Margaret Weatherley heard gold prospectors in Colorado sing said tune. She sent a copy of the music to her brother-in-law, songwriter Fred Weatherly. He had already written a song titled "Danny Boy" and adapted his lyric to the miners' tune, which was published in 1913 and first recorded in 1915. With imagery like, "The pipes are calling from glen to glen" it has proven to be hugely successful as an unofficial Irish anthem, though more popular in the Americas than in Ireland itself, though it is used as the anthem of Northern Ireland in the Commonwealth Games.

Interpreters have differed on who is the character singing the song. Most agree it is a love song from a woman to a man but it is vague enough in its lyric to be interpreted as from a parent to a man who has gone off to war. Weatherly himself intended the lyric to be from a mother to a son but in 1918 he wrote an amended lyric to allow for men to sing the song.

This flexibility seems somehow only fitting. Weatherly was an Englishman who may never have visited Ireland.

Ken Bloom

Published Date 1913

Nationality UK

Composers Traditional, Fred Weatherley

Why It's Key A song that is all things to all men.

Key Event
The founding of ASCAP

Although copyright laws passed at the turn of the century protected composers, lyricists and music publishers from the illegal reprinting of their sheet music, American artists and their publishers received no payment when orchestras performed their work in restaurants, ballrooms, and other public places. This was completely at odds with the situation in Europe, something that led to the formation of the American Society of Composers, Authors, and Publishers (ASCAP).

Composer Raymond Hubbell, lawyer Nathan Burke, and publisher George Maxwell approached the famous composer Victor Herbert about the idea and the powerful artist used his influence and popularity to get the project rolling. On February 13, 1914, 22 publishers and 170 songwriters met at Manhattan's Hotel Claridge and drafted the charter for ASCAP. The new organization announced that fees would have to be paid to the organization any time the works of one of their artists were performed. Orchestras ignored the ruling until a test case in 1915. ASCAP sued Shanley's Restaurant for playing selections of Herbert's operetta Sweethearts and the case went all the way to the Supreme Court before ASCAP won.

With the growing popularity of radio and invention of other forms by which music could be disseminated, these "performance royalties" became even more important, particularly as they were a more reliable source of income than the "mechanical royalties" paid by record companies to their artists, which were susceptible to creative accounting.
Thomas Hischak

Date February 13, 1914

Country USA

Why It's Key Songwriters were now able to gain full remuneration for their skill and craft.

Key Song
"Colonel Bogey March"

In 1914, Lieutenant Frederick Joseph Ricketts, the bandmaster of the British second battalion, Argyll and Sutherland Highlanders was intrigued by a soldier who whistled a couple of notes in place of the traditional "Fore!" as he played golf. He used the notes at the start of each line of a new march he'd written, which he called "Colonel Bogey," "bogey" being a golfing term.

Ricketts published this and many other marches under the pseudonym of Kenneth Alford, as forces personnel were not officially meant to have outside interests. The jolly tune quickly became a favorite with military bands everywhere. Ricketts himself became a director of music for the Royal Marines and was appointed major. Though he died in 1944, he had lived long enough to hear his march acquire a ribald, unofficial lyric during the second great war of his lifetime: "Hitler has only got one ball/The other is in the Albert Hall/Himmler has somewhat similar/But poor old Goebbels has no balls at all."

The composer Malcolm Arnold incorporated the march into his music for the 1957 film, *The Bridge On The River Kwai*, starring Alec Guinness. It led to a U.S. hit single for Mitch Miller and his Orchestra. Another of Ricketts' marches, "The Voices Of The Guns," appears in the film, *Lawrence Of Arabia*. "Colonel Bogey" crops up in comedy situations today and the lyric need only to be alluded to for a laugh.
Spencer Leigh

Published Date 1914

Nationality UK

Composer Kenneth Alford

Why It's Key Popular marching tune that became even better known in its unofficial version.

W. C. Handy's
SAINT LOUIS BLUES

City of St. Louis
1872

HANDY BROTHERS MUSIC CO., Inc.
PUBLISHERS
"Genuine American Music"
1650 BROADWAY, NEW YORK, N. Y.

Key Song
"St. Louis Blues"

In 1914 songwriter W. C. Handy (1873–1958), co-writer of "The Memphis Blues" (1912) was looking around for a suitable subject for another blues song. He remembered a woman he had seen on Memphis' notorious Beale Street who had unsuccessfully tried to take the edge off her grief by heavy drinking. She muttered as she stumbled along, "My man's got a heart like a rock cast in the sea," giving Handy a very memorable key line for the resultant "St. Louis Blues." The St. Louis reference was to a woman from that city who had enticed the narrator's lover away. "St. Louis Blues" was partially based on a section of Handy's instrumental "Jogo Blues," written the year before.

The song was first recorded in 1916 by Prince's Band and the first vocal recording was by Marion Hutton in 1920. When the Original Dixieland Jass Band issued a version in 1921, the song became a smash hit.

Much of the song followed the classic 12-bar blues structure of verses starting with two identical lines. However, it wasn't pure blues because it adopted a tango rhythm in other parts. Nonetheless, much of the American public had never heard any variant of the blues before and "St. Louis Blues" couldn't have been more successful in introducing them to it; in the half century after its composition, it was the most recorded American song.

Ken Bloom

Published Date 1914

Nationality USA

Composer W. C. Handy

Why It's Key The song that spectacularly brought the blues to the masses.

Opposite "St. Louis Blues"

Key Event
Birth Of A Nation score

Silent movies were never silent because there was always a piano to add a background to the action on the screen. The Edison company began to circulate suggestions for musical accompaniment to its films at the turn of the twentieth century as film exhibition moved from small shop front operations to theaters specially designed to show movies. Exhibitors soon grasped the importance of music in establishing mood and continuity for film narratives. In those days, this importance was underlined by the fact that many of their immigrant audience could not read the inter-titles but even today, with speech long since added to films, it is virtually unthinkable for one not to have a score.

D.W. Griffith's 1914 epic *Birth Of A Nation* had a special score that was painstakingly cued to match the action on the screen and which spurned the single pianist or small groups common in larger theaters for full symphonic orchestra. Much of the music was taken from the classics. Griffith also used folk songs and popular song to key into the audiences' associations with well-known music.

The music for *Birth Of A Nation* took the movies from mere entertainment to lifelike spectacle that moved film audiences like never before. The movies may have been the new rage but the realization had soon been made that good old music was by no means redundant even here.

Andre Millard

Date 1914

Country USA

Why It's Key First orchestral score written specifically for a motion picture.

Key Person
Jerome Kern

Jerome Kern was born in New York in 1885 and quit school as a teenager to study music. By 1903 his songs were heard in London and on Broadway. His "They Didn't Believe Me" in 1914 is considered the first modern ballad and it laid the foundation for theater songs for the decades that followed. The Princess Musicals in the 1910s were a series of small-scale, contemporary musicals that eschewed the more melodramatic operetta format and with Kern's score for inaugural Princess *Musical Very Good Eddie* – which opened on December 23, 1915 – the sound on Broadway became more jazz-influenced. After several hit musicals, such as *Leave It To Jane, Sally,* and *Sunny,* Kern wrote the music for the landmark *Show Boat* (1927), the first American musical play and a score that combined blues, folk, operetta, and jazz.

Later, he wrote for both Broadway and Hollywood, providing many song standards in collaboration with lyricists such as Oscar Hammerstein, Ira Gershwin, and Dorothy Fields in such works as *Music In The Air* (1932), *Roberta* (1933), *Swing Time* (1936), and *Cover Girl* (1944). Amongst his classic songs are "Ol' Man River," "Smoke Gets In Your Eyes," and "The Way You Look Tonight."

He died suddenly in 1945. Kern's endless variety with melody and his continual experimentation with musical forms make him one of the most innovative pioneers in American popular song.

Thomas Hischak

Role Songwriter

Date 1915

Nationality USA

Why It's Key Music writer who pioneered the ballad and introduced jazz and other idioms to Broadway and Hollywood musical scores.

Key Song "Pack Up Your Troubles In Your Old Kit Bag And Smile, Smile, Smile!"

"Pack Up Your Troubles In Your Old Kit Bag And Smile, Smile, Smile!" was a popular music hall song, written by the vocalist George Powell and his pianist brother Felix, and published by Chappell and Co.. They introduced it during their residency at the Bridge Pavilion in Ilkley, Yorkshire, UK. It tells of Private Perks, who keeps smiling despite the many adversities of war. All this hardy soul asks is a Lucifer (match) to light his fag (cigarette). The song was first recorded by Murray Johnson in 1916 and it became a favorite with British soldiers in World War I.

Despite the horrors of the Great War, there's no reason to believe that the soldiers who heartily joined in the recitation of this song in the trenches were doing so ironically. Some of the most popular songs from that war accepted the soldiers' pitiful conditions unquestioningly. However, "Pack Up Your Troubles…" is the product of an era now quite clearly gone forever. The unthinking obedience and almost village idiot like cheeriness of Private Perks was something that the powers that be, come the '60s, could never count on again.

The flavor of that decade was summed up by Bob Dylan's intense commentary on armed conflict "Masters Of War" and Buffy St Marie's scathing "Universal Soldier." Following their lead, the best-known songs from the Vietnam conflict are questioning, rather than jingoistic.

Spencer Leigh

Published Date 1915

Nationality UK

Composer George Powell, Felix Powell

Why It's Key Loved at the time but a servile soldier's singalong that would now be unthinkable.

Key Song
"Jelly Roll Blues"

"Jelly Roll Blues" was the work of Ferdinand Morton, a pianist and composer who had a reputation – mostly justified but partly built by himself – as an originator of jazz.

Born in New Orleans around 1890 as something like Ferdinand Joseph La Menthe (the facts of his life cannot be distinguished from the myths he created), Morton got his musical education in Storyville, the legendary red light district of New Orleans. Like many Creoles, Morton was an accomplished musician who absorbed many European musical influences but "Jelly Roll Blues" has the swinging tempo and rhythmic attack that gave jazz its distinctly African-American flavor.

This song, which was possibly written as far back as 1910 but first recorded in September 1915, was an important stage in the evolution of jazz from its ragtime and march step roots. An instrumental, it relied on the rhythmic base of the left hand while the right hand provided the melody. This song, like many in the early canon of jazz, was reproduced and reinterpreted many times, and appeared in many different forms, some with vocals added. Ironically, when Jelly Roll Morton (as he had been dubbed after his creation) and His Red Hot Peppers had a hit with it in 1927 after recording it on the Victor label, it was rechristened "Original Jelly Roll Blues." The song by them had become so well-known that it was referred to in another famous early jazz song, "Darktown Strutters' Ball."

Andre Millard

Release Date 1915

Nationality USA

Composer Ferdinand Lamothe [sic]

Why It's Key A vital element in the emergence of jazz.

1910–1919

65

Key Song
"If You Were The Only Girl In The World"

The Clifford Gray (lyric) and Nat D. Ayer (music) ballad "If You Were The Only Girl In The World" was introduced by George Robey and Violet Loraine in the London revue *The Bing Boys Are Here*, which opened on April 19 1916. It was soon a favorite in British music halls but it was over a decade before America discovered it. Sung as a duet, the lyric posited a modern-day garden of Eden: "If you were the only girl in the world/And I were the only boy/Nothing else would matter in the world today/We could go on loving in the same old way."

When Rudy Vallee sang the number with the Connecticut Yankees in the movie *The Vagabond Lover* (1929), American audiences finally embraced it and Vallee's recording was a bestseller. As if to make up for that belated Atlantic crossing, another American artist made it a hit again after an even longer period, Perry Como taking it into the Hit Parade in 1946. The ballad was performed by Doris Day and Gordon MacRae in the period movie *By The Light Of The Silvery Moon* (1952) and by Ann Blyth (dubbed by Gogie Grant) in *The Helen Morgan Story* (1957). The hyperbolic song remained popular for so many years because of its innocent, nostalgic quality that appealed to listeners born long after the World War I era in which it was written.

Thomas Hischak

Release Date 1916

Nationality UK

Composers Nat D. Ayer, Clifford Gray

Why It's Key Showed that a song could still become a U.S. hit even if it initially failed to bridge the Atlantic.

Key Performance
Chu Chin Chow stage musical

London's audiences during World War I wanted escape. Magical tales of faraway places were the ideal method to distract a tired and tormented mind. On August 31, 1916, the perfect remedy came in the form of a musical based on the story of Ali Baba and the 40 Thieves.

After seeing the Arabian Nights-inspired play *Kismet*, writer Oscar Asche called on composer Frederic Norton to help create his own escape to the East, although the interpolated title character – an Arab in disguise – hailed ostensibly from the Orient. For the economically tight days of English wartime, *Chu Chin Chow* was a mammoth production. Costing £5,300 (a huge amount at the time) with a cast of 64 adults and eight children, the lavish extravaganza paid off better than could have ever been imagined. Not even the intervention by the Lord Chamberlain over the scanty clothing of the cast's slave girls could stop the success.

Running for five years – more than twice as long as any previous musical – and an unprecedented 2,235 performances (a record that wouldn't be beaten for almost 40 years), *Chu Chin Chow* gave weary soldiers and battered civilians a welcome diversion from the horrors of war. Sumptuous sets and beautifully dressed exotic characters took audiences to another world, yet the sounds of songs like "Any Time's Kissing Time" and "The Cobbler's Song" were comfortingly British and would stay in the minds of the nation for decades to come as singers added them to their repertoires.

Leila Regan-Porter

Opening Night
August 31, 1916

Nationality UK

Director Oscar Asche

Cast Oscar Asche, Frank Cochrane, Courtice Pounds

Composers Frederic Norton

Why It's Key A magic carpet ride out of war-depressed London.

Opposite *Chu Chin Chow*

Key Song "What Do You Want To Make Those Eyes At Me For?"

Howard Johnson, Joseph McCarthy, and James V. Monaco's "What Do You Want To Make Those Eyes At Me For (When They Don't Mean What They Say?)" was in a series of 'optic' songs that premiered in the first decades of the new century like "I Just Can't Make My Eyes Behave" and "Tell Me What's The Matter, Loveable Eyes".

The titular eyes, belonging to an attractive lady, put ideas in the singer's head. They make him glad, sad and "They make me want a lot of things that I never had." However, he laments that the flirtatious eyes are deceiving. Those ideas have the suitor so revved up, he tells the girl she is playing with dynamite.

The song proved a success for Ada Jones and Billy Murray in 1917. Henry Lewis also recorded the tune in 1917. It is ironic that Hollywood, when it wanted to evoke an earlier, simpler era, often trotted out "What Do You Want to Make Those Eyes at Me For?", for the song has surprisingly endured, with a variety of singers

and bands. Amazingly, the song hit No. 1 on the UK chart in 1959 – 43 years after its publication – with a recording by Emile Ford and the Checkmates. Even more amazingly, it was produced by Joe Meek, although this was not one of the studio genius' more "way out" recordings. Ray Peterson covered it in 1960 and The Librettos made a version in 1965.

Ken Bloom

First Published 1916

Nationality USA

Composers Howard Johnson, Joseph McCarthy, James V. Monaco

Why It's Key The eyes have it – for several different generations.

- THREE NILE BEAUTIES -

Key Song **"O Sole Mio"**
Enrico Caruso

Written in 1897 by the composer Eduardo Di Capua and the poet Giovanni Capurro for the Naples Piedigrotta Festival, "O Sole Mio" has become not only a synonym for the town but for all of Italy, a country loved around the world for its natural beauties, the sea, and especially the sun: the title means "my sun."

The great tenor Enrico Caruso's world renown comes from his prescient decision to make records. Although Caruso had picked up the then fabulous sum of £100 (U.S. $200) in April 1902 for recording ten opera arias, it was a four year gap, by which time he was famous in the wider world, before he chose to tackle "O Sole Mio," a song then only well-known within Naples, partly because its dialect was Neapolitan. He recorded it on February 5, 1916 in a studio in New Jersey, United States, with an orchestra conducted by Walter B. Rogers. The released version was his first and only take. "O Sole Mio" immediately became a sensational hit in America, where anything Italian sounded exotic and therefore the parochial nature of the language didn't matter. The other reason of course was Caruso's magnificent voice. A legal judgment in 2004 meant that transcriber Alfredo Mazzucchi's name was appended to the writing credits.

Inevitably, the song has had English translations and to many is now better known as "It's Now Or Never" as soaringly sung by Elvis Presley in 1960.
Giancarlo Susanna

Release Date 1916

Nationality Italy

Composers Eduardo Di Capua, Giovanni Capurro, Alfredo Mazzucchi

Why It's Key Local song that became almost Italy's unofficial national anthem.

Key Performance *The Bing Boys Are Here*
stage musical

During World War I, one of the solaces of Londoners was *The Bing Boys Are Here*, which jolly caper-packed musical premiered in the West End on April 19, 1916.

The show, which described itself as "A Picture of London Life, in a Prologue and Six Panels," was based on a French show, *Le Fils Touffe*. Though the show was essentially a revue it did have a plot that linked the episodes together. The Bing Boys – Oliver and (the curiously named) Lucifer – yearn to leave Binghamton to see the world, meaning London. The Bings' cook, Emma, loves Lucifer and she decides to try her luck in London too, resulting in her marrying the Duke of Dullwater and being dubbed Miss Fuschia of Valparaiso. She becomes a performer on the stage under the pseudonym Mary McGay. Hilarity ensued as well as several jolly songs and dances.

Despite the escape it offered from World War I, the show ironically gave its name to a famous cartoon of soldiers dubbed the "Byng Boys" after Sir Julian Byng, the commander of the Canadian Corps.

Though the show was such a success that it spawned two sequels, the mists of time have closed over it. With one exception: the modern general public who have, generally speaking, never heard of it still know the hit song of the show, "If You Were The Only Girl In The World."
Ken Bloom

Opening Night April 19, 1916

Country France/UK

Director Gus Sohlke

Cast George Robey, Alfred Lester, Violet Lorraine

Composer Nat D. Ayer, Clifford Gray

Why It's Key Wartime escapist fare – but it still gave a name to battle imagery.

Key Song **"Livery Stable Blues"**
Original Dixieland Jass Band

In the era before mass media like radio, new styles in music would remain regional or even limited to one urban area. This was the case with jazz, which was restricted to certain parts of New Orleans until the Original Dixieland Jass Band (ODJB) released this record in 1917.

Jazz was the name given to up-tempo African-American music based on blues forms and march cadences that evolved into dance music, much of which was improvised. The runaway success of "Livery Stable Blues" brought jazz to millions of listeners in the United States and Europe. It opened the floodgates for white bands like ODJB to exploit the jazz craze of the '20s while African American musicians were enabled to play to much larger, integrated audiences.

The title of Original Dixieland Jass Band was a misnomer, for this was a group of white musicians from New Orleans who imitated the music they heard played by black performers. Segregation in the South and discrimination in the North kept the original jazz players out of recording studios and the prestigious venues. ODJB played in Chicago and then New York before signing to the major Victor label. "Livery Stable Blues" is more like an uptempo rag with many comic effects than the hot jazz that is associated with the music of the Jazz age. Yet there was so much press attention given to this song that it really brought home to Americans that here was a new and exciting musical form.

Andre Millard

Release Date 1917

Nationality USA

Composer Ray Lopez, Alcide Nunez, Marvin Lee

Why It's Key First jazz song ever recorded.

Key Event **The exclusive patents of Victor, Columbia, and Edison expire**

As with all nineteenth century businessmen, the inventors who set up the talking machine industry hoped that a strong patent position would enable them to maintain monopolistic control.

The basic process of acoustic recording could not be protected with patents but the key processes of duplicating records were the key to keeping interlopers out of a growing business. When many of these patents expired around the time of World War I, the doors were opened and the Big Three record companies were faced with strenuous competition from much smaller start-up businesses. The figures tell the story: in 1914 there were 18 establishments in the American talking machine industry and their output was valued at U.S. $27 million. By 1919 these numbers had grown to 166 establishments with an output of U.S. $158 million.

The effect of this event could be seen at the bottom end of the product line where very cheap machines and records flooded the market. At the same time demand for recorded sound increased dramatically because of the war: Music was a vital factor in maintaining morale at home and on the front. There was a boom in patriotic songs and sentimental ballads as millions of people were caught up in the emotions of war. Falling prices meant that there was a machine and a record priced for every pocket.

Andre Millard

Date 1917

Country USA

Why It's Key A factor in the massive expansion of the record industry.

Key Performance *Oh, Boy!*
stage musical

The new team of Jerome Kern (music), P. G. Wodehouse, and Guy Bolton (lyrics and book) created a new form of American theater with the Princess Theatre shows. The third Princess Theatre musical, *Oh, Boy!*, which opened on February 20, 1917, was the third-longest running musical of its decade.

Like other Princess musicals, the show was simple and unpretentious, with one setting for the first act and another for the second, and *Oh, Boy!* eschewed the exotic, foreign locales of operettas, placing its action in modern, American settings. Musicalized comedies of manners, featuring marital mix-ups, the Princess shows were also notable for being another step forward in the true integration of song and story. Despite this, there was room for special material jammed into the plot. The characters were sometimes mere caricatures but all were essentially good people. The tone and style of the show was unwavering, rejecting too much energetic farce and overworked emotion.

The libretto was remarkably pun free and the turns of its plot points were natural and unforced. Charm was uppermost in the creator's minds, so they designed a relaxing evening in which the audience could feel slightly superior to the silly undertakings on stage and enjoy the melodic, lyrically witty but undemanding songs. The hit song of the show proved to be one of Kern's most beautiful and enduring works, "Till the Clouds Roll By."

Ken Bloom

Opening Night
February 20 1917

Country USA

Director Edward Royce

Cast Hal Forde, Anna Wheaton, Tom Powers

Composers Jerome Kern, P. G. Wodehouse, Guy Bolton

Why It's Key Represented the transition point between the haphazardly written musicals of the past and the newer, more deliberate musical comedies.

1910-1919

Key Song
"For Me And My Gal"

A romantic ballad about wedded bliss, "For Me And My Gal," published in 1917, has a rather gushing lyric by Ray Goetz and Edgar Leslie about bells ringing and birds singing as two turtle doves go off to their wedding. However, its George W. Meyer-written music is positively adventurous. It stays within an octave in a traditional thirty-two measure structure yet goes off in surprising directions at times, revealing a pattern that would later be used in jazz.

The number was popularized in vaudeville by such beloved performers as Van and Schenck, Sophie Tucker, Al Jolson, Eddie Cantor, Belle Baker, and George Jessel. Over three million copies of sheet music were sold by the '20s. No parlor piano at that time was complete without a copy of the song. Interest in the song was revived when Judy Garland and Gene Kelly sang the ballad in the movie *For Me And My Gal* (1942). Among the many artists to record the number are Bing Crosby, Cliff Edwards, Arthur Godfrey, Bob Grant, Dick Shannon

and His Society Sextet, Les Elgart, The Chordettes, Perry Como, The Cliff Adams Singers, Freddy Cannon, Tiny Tim, and Harry Nilsson. Jolson, who had sung the ballad throughout his career, dubbed the song for Larry Parks in the film *Jolson Sings Again* (1949).

Thomas Hischak

Published 1917

Nationality USA

Composers George W. Meyer, Ray Goetz, Edgar Leslie

Why It's Key The musical arrangement foreshadowed the jazz age.

Opposite *For Me And My Gal*

Key Song
"Good-Bye-ee!"

Novelty songwriters, Bob Weston and Bert Lee wrote "Good-bye-ee!" during World War I. It told of how Brother Bertie psyched himself up for battle by pretending he was going on holiday. He memorably tells his sweetheart that though their parting is hard, "I'll be tickled to death to go!" The song with its marching chorus became a favorite with the troops in 1917, but by 1965, it was a relic.

Following the success of the celebrated revue, *Beyond The Fringe*, two of its stars Peter Cook and Dudley Moore formed a comedy double act. Moore was an outstanding jazz pianist but Cook was tone deaf. Needing something to close each episode of their BBC television series, *Not Only… But Also*, it was suggested – for reasons fatuous or comedic – that "Good-bye-ee!" would be appropriate. Moore tried it out but sitting at the piano and not knowing all the words improvised some passages with some "fa-ta-ta-ta"s. The director Joe McGrath considered that this was fine as it was, and Peter added a sentimental spiel about farewells. A hit single – credited to Peter Cook – followed. There was another UK hit version of the song in 1975 by the act 14-18.

Weston had died in 1936 but his songs enjoyed something of a revival in the Swinging Sixties: "Paddy McGinty's Goat" became associated with Val Doonican; Joe Brown and Herman's Hermits sang "I'm Henry VIII I Am" and "What A Mouth" was recorded by Tommy Steele.

Spencer Leigh

Date 1917

Nationality UK

Composers Bob Weston, Bert Lee

Why It's Key World War I anthem that got an unexpected rebirth.

Key Event
The age of vaudeville

Coming out of the French revue, American minstrel and English music hall "variety" traditions, American vaudeville began in the 1890s. Within 20 years, vaudeville circuits criss-crossed the United States. In an age before radios, movies, and television, it was the main source of entertainment, especially for the poor, and its peak year was 1918.

Because vaudeville employed thousands of specialty acts, singers, dancers, and actors, it required a huge amount of material. Competition was fierce among singers, who wanted to introduce the newest songs, and song pluggers, who were anxious to place their songs with the hottest acts. The greatest of the acts were offered the best material and stars would find their portraits on the sheet music covers preceded by the byline, "introduced by." Stars might also commission hot writers to write songs and whole acts especially for them. Publishers also distributed cheaply printed music sheets to orchestra leaders, record producers, entertainers, and bookers. "Gifts" and outright payments sometimes induced performers to take their songs on the road.

The onset of the Depression and the emergence of first, the parlor piano and records, then sound films helped kill vaudeville. Thousands of musicians were thrown out of work and vaudeville theaters were converted to movie usage or torn down. All that survive are ghostly memories of the famous theater names – The Palaces, Orpheums, and Strands – and the great vaudeville presenters – Proctor, Pantages, Keith-Albee, and Orpheum – who owned them.

Ken Bloom

Date 1918

Country USA

Why It's Key How music was heard before home entertainment systems.

Opposite **Vaudeville production**
A Modern Cinderella

A NOTABLE PRODUCTION OF THE LAST WORD IN MUSICAL COMEDY

A MODERN CINDERELLA

BOOK & LYRICS BY CASPAR NATHAN ——— MUSIC BY HAMPTON DURAND

Ackermann-Quigley
Litho. Co.
KANSAS CITY

Key Person
Henry Burr

Henry Burr was the unrivaled master of the quiet song delivery style. Considered the "dean of ballad singers" in the early decades of the twentieth century, he had a unique way with a nostalgic song, quite different from the "coon-shouters" and Broadway belters of the time, and his early recordings were among the first bestsellers in the genre. Born in Canada in 1882 as Harry McClaskey, he took his stage name from a vocal teacher called Kate Stella Burr. Burr had not spent much time in vaudeville before he turned to the new recording technology and cut several cylinders in the early 1900s. He had hits with with "I Wonder Who's Kissing Her Now" and "Meet Me Tonight In Dreamland," both in 1909. With his vaudeville partner Albert Campbell, Burr popularized "I'm Forever Blowing Bubbles" and "The Trail Of The Lonesome Pine" in variety. His recording of "Just A Baby's Prayer At Twilight" by Sam Lewis, Joe Young (lyric), and M. K. Jerome (music) – which hit the U.S. charts on April 18, 1918, went on to sell over a million records, one of the first to do so. In addition to his solo material, he recorded with The Peerless Quartet, even acting as their manager from 1912.

Burr was involved in pioneering radio experiments. When he sang down telephone wires to California from New York, it was called the first "transcontinental broadcast." Burr died in 1941.

Thomas Hischak

Role Recording Artist

Date April 18, 1918

Nationality Canada

Why It's Key Popularized a new style of ballad delivery.

Key Song
"I'm Always Chasing Rainbows"

Lyricist Joe McCarthy and composer Harry Carroll wrote "I'm Always Chasing Rainbows" for the Broadway show *Oh Look!* which opened on March 7, 1918. With a melody based on Chopin's "Fantasie Impromptu In C Minor," a slow, plodding tempo and a lyric that was dark and pessimistic, it was an unexpected hit. The tenor Charles Harrison immediately recorded the song and it sold a million copies and reached the top of the Hit Parade in 1918. It was soon covered by Harry Fox, Sam Ash, and Charles Princes, making it one of the most popular songs in the dark fall of 1918. At this time World War I had dragged on for four years and the hopelessness expressed in the songwords certainly struck a chord in a weary public: "But my life is a race, a wild goose chase and all my dreams have been denied."

The song was revived by the young Judy Garland in the middle of World War II. Her version appeared in the film *Ziegfeld Girl* in 1941 and although it did not become a big hit it brought renewed attention to the song. Several artists recorded it after the war including Helen Forrest, Dick Haymes, and Harry James but it was Perry Como who made the song his own and who kept it alive in his very popular television shows that defined the easy listening market in the '50s and '60s.

Andre Millard

Release Date January 1918

Nationality USA

Composers Joe McCarthy, Harry Carroll

Why It's Key A wartime lament that become a staple of easy listening.

Key Song
"Swanee"

Lyricist Irving Caesar had an idea: writing a one-step in 2/4 time like the current hit "Hindustan." The new song would be an all-American version. As was popular at the time, Caesar and his musical foil, a 21-year-old unknown named George Gershwin, set the song in the American South. They began writing it on an uptown bus on the way to Gershwin's apartment building. By the time they arrived, the song was mapped out lyrically. 15 minutes after that, the music was also done. The lyric dripped with references to Southern staples like strumming banjos and contained a somewhat contrived, if delightful, rhyme: "Among the folks in D-I-X-I-E - ven now my Mammy's waiting for me."

The song was interpolated into a revue, *Demi-Tasse*, which opened on October 24, 1919 but was a flop, completely ignored by the audience. One evening at a party for Al Jolson, Gershwin sat at the piano and played "Swanee." Jolson was immediately entranced. He not only interpolated the number into the touring version of *Sinbad* but recorded it in January 1920. The great success of Jolson's recording led to gigantic sheet music sales, with Gershwin's royalties in the first year amounting to over $10,000.

Gershwin abandoned his ideas of becoming a concert pianist and could concentrate on writing complete score, not simply interpolations. The world will never know how long, without Jolson's ear for a good tune, Gershwin might have waited to become famous.
Ken Bloom

Date 1919

Nationality USA

Composers Irving Caesar, George Gershwin

Why It's Key An initial damp squib ultimately creates the phenomenon of George Gershwin.

Key Song "Take Your Girlie To The Movies (If You Can't Make Love At Home)"

It sounds amazingly risqué for the period but "Take Your Girlie To The Movies (If You Can't Make Love At Home)" had a more innocent meaning when Billy Murray took it into the U.S. charts on September 27, 1919. Then, "making love" meant merely kissing and necking.

In an era when unmarried women still lived with their parents, alternative locations to the parlor sofa and porch swing for such activity were necessary. When the parks were closed, the balcony of a movie theater proved the ideal place for what was also then called "spooning," as lyricists Edgar Leslie and Bert Kalmar detailed in this song, to a melody devised by Pete Wendling.

With movies then a young medium, the song was highly topical. The popular culture relevance was ratcheted up by the fact that the lyric is written as a reply to suggestions sought on places to kiss by a reader of the advice column of the then well-known journalist Beatrice Fairfax. The song also references celluloid legend Douglas Fairbanks and movie and stage star Billie Burke. (When Dean Martin later sang the song he replaced Billie Burke's name with that of the better-known Tyrone Power.) Miss Fairfax makes another point that the balcony is "far away from cranky dad and mother's eagle eye." In a few years women would interpret such sentiments in a different way and leave home to make their way in the big city.
Ken Bloom

Published Date 1919

Nationality USA

Composers Edgar Leslie, Bert Kalmar, Pete Wendling

Why It's Key A song absolutely of its time – in differing ways.

Key Song
"A Pretty Girl Is Like A Melody"

Producer Florenz Ziegfeld commissioned various songwriters for each edition of his lavish *Ziegfeld Follies* revues but the 1919 edition – which opened on June 16, 1919 – was almost completely scored by Irving Berlin, who came up with the finest set of songs yet heard in the series. The most famous number, "A Pretty Girl Is Like A Melody," is a graceful ballad that even today conjures up visions of beautiful women in luxurious costumes descending a staircase. In the original production, John Steele sang the paean to beauty and the parading girls were dressed as classical music selections. During the number the orchestra played fragments from Dvorak's "Humoresque," Mendelssohn's "Spring Song," Schubert's "Serenade," and other classical pieces.

"A Pretty Girl Is Like A Melody" was very different from Berlin's songs hitherto, which had alternately been comedic numbers and conventional ballads. It managed to straddle both songwords that were in the vernacular and melodic gracefulness. Gradually, this became Berlin's favorite type of composition and where he led, the musical world followed: by the '20s, just about everyone of note was writing in this way.

Steele and Ben Selvin's Novelty Orchestra were among the first to record the number which became a particular favorite at fashion shows and beauty pageants. Interest in the song was revived in the '30s when it was used as the centerpiece of the film *The Great Ziegfeld* (1936).

Thomas Hischak

Published Date 1919

Nationality USA

Composer Irving Berlin

Why It's Key Pioneered the slow, elegant song.

Key Song
"I'm Forever Blowing Bubbles"

The Broadway musical, *The Passing Show Of 1918*, was just that. It is forgotten today except for one song, the waltz "I'm Forever Blowing Bubbles." The song – first published the following year – was a popular hit and recorded by many artists including Ben Selvin's Novelty Orchestra and the Original Dixieland Jass Band from New Orleans. However, the song's continuing fame came about unexpectedly.

The Victorian artist, John Everett Millais, painted a syrupy picture of a curly-haired boy, Bubbles, which from 1886, in one of the first such advertising deals, was used to sell Pear's Soap. A player for London soccer club West Ham United had attended school with a boy named Billy Murray, who resembled the boy in the painting. By a convoluted route, by the '20s the crowds at the club's Upton Park stadium were singing "I'm Forever Blowing Bubbles" on match days. It was one of the first football anthems and many other popular hits have been commandeered in this way, notably "You'll Never Walk Alone" (Liverpool Football Club, UK). However, though many of those appropriations are witty or rousing, few can match the melodic pathos of "Hammers" fans in full cry stating that their bubbles fly so high as to nearly reach the sky, "Then like my dreams, they fade and die."

The tune has made the UK charts for the West Ham Squad (1975) and punk band and West Ham fans the Cockney Rejects (1980).

Spencer Leigh

Published Date 1919

Nationality UK

Composers John Kellette, Jaan Kenbrovin

Why It's Key A song given immortality by soccer fans' adoption.

Key Person
Mamie Smith

Mamie Smith (1883–1946), actress, dancer, singer, and pianist, enjoyed an early career in black vaudeville. Music entrepreneur Perry Bradford cast Smith in his 1918 all-black musical, *Made In Harlem*.

When white chanteuse Sophie Tucker took ill and had to drop out of a recording session on Valentine's Day 1920, Bradford talked Fred Hager of Okeh Records into letting Smith record two sides of Bradford's blues compositions, "That Thing Called Love" and "You Can't Keep A Good Man Down." Smith's record, on which she was accompanied by a white band, was a success.

She was asked back to Okeh that same year and recorded Bradford's "Crazy Blues" and "It's Right Here for You, If You Don't Get It, 'Tain't No Fault Of Mine." These recordings, the first vocal blues recordings by a black performer, were immense successes, selling over a million copies in one year. That same year, Smith became the first black singer to record with a black jazz band (The Jazz Hounds). Smith's recordings sold to black audiences, a market that record companies had not hitherto considered.

Billed as "The Queen of the Blues," Smith recorded with Okeh and Victor and toured throughout the United States and Europe. She also appeared in the 1929 film *Jail House Blues*. Smith retired in 1931, returning to performing in 1939 in the film *Paradise In Harlem*. She followed with five more musical films, finally retiring for good in 1943.

Ken Bloom

Role Recording artist

Date 1920

Nationality USA

Why It's Key The woman who proved there was a black record-buying market.

Key Person
Ben Selvin

Although the violinist Ben Selvin (1898–1980) is not as well-known as other giants of the big band era such as Ellington or Dorsey, he recorded more 78rpm sides than any other artist of his times, as many as 20,000 different songs in some estimates. His career began in 1919 when, as Selvin's Novelty Orchestra, he had a hit with "I'm Forever Blowing Bubbles". The next year he recorded "Dardanella" which, after hitting the U.S. charts on January 24, 1920, became the first record estimated to have sold 5 million copies.

Throughout the 1920s and most of the 1930s he produced several hit songs every year, and in some years he managed to place ten or more records in the Top 20. Although he was officially a Columbia recording artist from 1924 onwards, he recorded under different names and on many different labels. His output covered hit songs from Broadway shows, romantic ballads, instrumentals, comic songs and even holdovers from the minstrel shows.

Ben Selvin And His Orchestra enjoyed their last hit record in 1934 but Selvin proved to be a highly influential figure in the record industry for several more decades as he acted as an A&R man for the Columbia and Victor companies. In the 1950s he was supervising the recordings of such important artists as Frank Sinatra and Doris Day.

André Millard

Role Recording artist

Date 1920

Nationality USA

Why It's Key The most prolific band leader of the 1920s and 1930s.

Key Song
"The Cuckoo Waltz"

In the first decades of the twentieth century, the waltz and two-step dominated the ballroom floor and popular song. Waltz music is defined by its elegant 1-2-3 count and triple meter. It is this very elegance, perhaps, that made it seem old hat as the Roaring Twenties got underway. Jonasson and Stranks' "The Cuckoo Waltz," published in 1920, was one of the last popular waltzes before the onslaught of the fox-trot and other syncopated dances more suitable to the frantic era of the flappers and the speakeasies.

Stranks' lyric is certainly not the reason for its success. The opening line, "Cuckoo! Cuckoo! Let's waltz to the melody," is about as sophisticated as it gets. Rather, as in many waltzes, it's the music that matters and "The Cuckoo Waltz" with its repetitions on the word "Cuckoo," provides a nice structure and rhythm for the song as well as being unique and fun. Ken Griffin charted with "The Cuckoo Waltz" in the summer of 1948, which was late for such an old-fashioned song to hit the charts without its music and rhythm altered.

By 1920, the fox-trot was all the rage. The Victor Records bulletin of March 1923 reported, "The fox-trot today is the greatest social dance of the entire world. It has gone far beyond the waltz, the polka, the tango." Still, as it dates from the eighteenth century, the waltz can be said to have had a good run.

Ken Bloom

Published Date 1920

Nationality USA

Composers J. E. Jonasson, Alan Stranks

Why It's Key Not a bad way for the waltz to effectively bow out.

Key Song "I'll Be With You In Apple Blossom Time" Nora Bayes

Though published in 1920, "I'll Be With You In Apple Blossom Time" was a traditional waltz, a rhythm that firmly rooted it in the turn-of-the-century. Nora Bayes, the famed vaudeville and Broadway performer and sometime songwriter herself, introduced and recorded the song. A nostalgic paean from one inamorata to another, the song promises that the loving pair will get together in apple blossom time and finally tie the knot.

The nostalgic feel of the composition is what sold it, certainly not the lyric itself which rhymes "tree" and "me," "May" and "say," "and has such "false" rhymes as "time" and "mine" and "vain" and "again." Not lyricist Neville Fleeson's greatest moment.

Yet time and circumstance has a way of making the banal poignant. In 1941, the song was revived by The Andrews Sisters. Sung in the Abbott and Costello film *Buck Privates*, the sisters swung the song in 3/4 time, thus modernizing the tune. The lyric was retained wholesale, though, and possessed new meaning to thousands of couples separated by war praying to be reunited in an "apple blossom time" that might never come.

The modernized version proved even more popular than the original, with the Andrews Sisters reprising their performance in the 1944 film *Follow the Boys*. Their jazzy interpretation has persisted through the years, with recordings by Bill Haley And His Comets, Jo Stafford, Tab Hunter, Wayne Newton, and others.

Ken Bloom

Published Date 1920

Nationality USA

Composers Neville Fleeson, Albert von Tilzer

Why It's Key The corny song made profound by the heartache of war.

Key Song "I Belong To Glasgow"
Will Fyffe

Will Fyffe, who was born in Durham in 1885, toured the music halls, performing soliloquies from Shakespeare and comic monologues about engineers, bridegrooms and expectant fathers. One night he was harangued by a drunk at Glasgow railway station who, when asked by Fyffe if he belonged to Glasgow, responded, "The way I feel tonight, Glasgow belongs ta mae." This prompted Fyffe to write "I Belong To Glasgow," a number which related the drunken escapades of a gang of men and which advised the listener of all the benefits of a drop or two, culminating in the fact that when one got home, "You don't give a hang for the wife!"

Fyffe offered the song to a star name: Harry Lauder. Lauder liked it but felt that he could not sing anything which advocated heavy drinking. Fyffe performed the song himself and it became very popular – although not necessarily in Glasgow. One critic of the would-be city anthem caustically pointed out that the only time he had ever heard "I Belong To Glasgow" sung in the named city was by professional performers. This may have been less to do with aesthetic considerations than a sensitivity to the reputation for Glaswegian drunkenness the song was helping to cement.

What lack of attraction the song may have for the city's inhabitants is more than compensated for by its global popularity: it has been rendered by such bizarre honorary Glaswegians as Danny Kaye and Eartha Kitt.
Spencer Leigh

Published Date 1920

Nationality UK

Composer Will Fyffe

Why It's Key The city anthem that the city didn't want.

Key Song "Ma! He's Makin' Eyes At Me"
Eddie Cantor

Songwriters Con Conrad (music) and Sidney Clare (lyric) were very familiar with comic vocalist Eddie Cantor's talent for singing exclamatory numbers and the way he could hold a note as he rolled his eyes to suggest something exciting or even lewd. They wrote "Ma! He's Makin' Eyes At Me" for Cantor, giving him the punctuated word "Ma!" to grab the listener's attention then proceeded with a lyric that loudly announced that a beau is looking closely, then acting nice, then proposing marriage and finally kissing. The popularity of such a slangy, unsentimental love song at the beginning of the Roaring Twenties led the way for a new kind of songwriting on Tin Pan Alley, for what made the song unique is that the lyric is ambiguous about whether the female narrator is boasting or complaining to her mother about this attention.

Cantor liked the song right off and interpolated it into his Broadway show The Midnight Rounders (1921), then recorded it. By the end of the year, the ditty was on the charts and years later there would also be very popular discs by Pearl Bailey in the '40s and by ten-year-old Scottish singer Lena Zavaroni in 1974. Other notable recordings were made by Tennessee Ernie Ford, Oscar Peterson, and Leslie Uggams. The song was heard in the films Ma! He's Makin' Eyes At Me (1940), Singin' In The Corn (1946) and The Eddie Cantor Story (1953), where Cantor dubbed it for Keefe Braselle.
Thomas Hischak

Release Date 1921

Nationality USA

Composers Con Conrad, Sidney Clare

Why It's Key A cleverly sustained exercise in ambivalence.

Key Song "The Sheik of Araby"
The Club Royal Orchestra

A piece originally called "My Rose Of Araby" took on another dimension entirely when the music publisher Harry Warren mentioned that the novel *The Sheik* had been a bestseller and it might be an idea to devise a song around the same theme. Only days after the song had been completed, an announcement was made that a movie was to be made of the novel.

The Club Royal Orchestra entered the U.S. charts with the song (then known as just "The Sheik") on March 25, 1921. The phenomenal success of the motion picture in 1921 naturally played an important part in the song's popularity. Its star Rudolph Valentino took the United States by storm in his performance as the sheik and the cultural fallout of his depiction of a sensuous ethnic other included the rise of new dances such as the tango. The song's lyric played on the distinctly foreign pattern of seduction, the narrator promising the woman addressed that when she was asleep at night, "Into your tent I'll creep."

Yet it was a surprisingly short time before both Valentino's sensuousness came to seem comically effeminate and the song a guffaw-inducer. Spike Jones played the song – now generally called 'The Sheik of Araby' – for laughs on his 1943 recording. Versions of the song performed in public gatherings added new lyrics at the end of each line ("With no pants on!") that turned it into a burlesque.

Andre Millard

Release Date 1921

Nationality USA

Composers Henry B. Smith, Francis Wheeler, Ted Snyder.

Why It's Key The romantic ballad that was transformed by changing attitudes into a comic song.

Opposite *The Sheik*

Key Song
"Way Down Yonder In New Orleans"

The publication of the Dixieland jazz classic "Way Down Yonder In New Orleans" in 1922 gave the Louisiana city its most memorable theme song with more recordings than any of the many other New Orleans numbers over the years.

J. Turner Layton composed the pulsating music that used repeated notes so effectively that it can be described as a stomp. His fellow African-American Henry Creamer wrote the vibrant lyric about the yearning to return to the southern city and his use of "Stop!" in the lyric punctuates the musical line and gives the number a bounce beloved by jazz musicians. Contrastingly, the city is dreamily described as a place wherein "Creole babies with flashin' eyes softly whisper with tender sighs."

The song was written for the all-Negro revue *Strut Miss Lizzy* (1922) but it was cut before opening, so Layton and Creamer introduced the number themselves in the Broadway revue *Spice* (1922).

It was Blossom Seeley who popularized the song in vaudeville, on records and in her nightclub act for years. Interest in the number was revived in 1960 with Freddie Cannon's best-selling rock 'n' roll version.

Among the hundreds of other recordings were notable ones by Louis Armstrong, Lester Young, Bix Beiderbecke, Buddy Clark, Fred Astaire, Pete Fountain, Dean Martin, and Jan and Dean. The song was also heard in such films as *The Story Of Vernon And Irene Castle* (1939) and *Is Everybody Happy?* (1943).

Thomas Hischak

Published Date 1922

Nationality USA

Composers Henry Creamer, J. Turner Layton

Why It's Key A bizarre but splendid mixture of the frenetic and the fairytale.

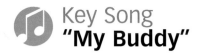

Key Song
"My Buddy"

Walter Donaldson and his new collaborator, Gus Kahn had a great success with their first co-written song, "My Buddy." With its melancholy lyric, the song resonated with the many people who had lost friends and family in the world wars. In fact, Donaldson wrote the music to mark the death of his fiancée.

Though the gender-neutral title phrase might suggest a song about friendship, there is little ambiguity in the line, "Miss your voice, the touch of your hand." It's slightly surprising therefore that it has indeed come to mean more than romance. The song was popular in all eras but its premiere in 1922 – not too long after World War I – and the aftermath of World War II were the periods of its greatest success. The perceived fallen comrades subtext was only enhanced by the song's use by cinema musicians during screenings of the 1927 silent war movie *Wings*.

Jazz musicians were particular fans of the tune and Chet Baker, Lionel Hampton, Benny Carter, Sonny Stitt, and Stan Getz all performed notable instrumental versions. Sweet bands were naturals to take up the song and ensembles led by Jackie Gleason, Jerry Gray, and Glenn Miller had hit recordings of the song. Frank Sinatra had a success with "My Buddy" as did his daughter Nancy. Though the sentiments might seem too lachrymose for today's taste, such recent performers as Doctor John, Barry White, and Jerry Jeff Walker have covered the title.
Ken Bloom

Published Date 1922

Nationality USA

Composers Walter Donaldson, Gus Kahn

Why It's Key A bereaved man's grief assumes an unintended resonance.

Opposite **Hank Williams**

Key Song
"Lovesick Blues"

"Lovesick Blues" was a Tin Pan Alley song written by Cliff Friend and Irving Mills. Emmett Miller's version (1925, subsequently re-recorded in 1929) was typically vaudevillian. Miller was a country singer who incorporated a great deal of African-American influences into his music and performances. He began his career in the black-face tradition of minstrelsy. Like Jimmie Rodgers, Miller grew up in the Deep South and had considerable exposure to black culture. As a member of touring vaudeville companies, Miller played all over the country. He had the ability to break into falsetto in the middle of the song, much like Rodgers' "blue yodeling," and this distinctive effect brought him to the attention of other performers and the record companies in the early '20s, especially the Okeh label which had a considerable catalogue of African American "race" recordings.

Other performers, notably Rex Griffin (1939), turned "Lovesick Blues" into a country song with a strong bluesy feel. By yodeling at the end of every line – "I got a feeling called the blues" – Griffin keeps the song's symmetry while bending and stretching the lyric much like a blues guitarist would add *vibrato* to a blue note. Many other country singers would use this for emotional effect, especially Hank Williams in his successful 1949 recording. The jaunty tempo and easily remembered lyric made this song a standard in country music for much of the twentieth century.
Andre Millard

Published Date 1922

Nationality USA

Composers Cliff Friend, Irving Mills

Why It's Key One of the most important white blues in country music.

Key Song
"Carolina In The Morning"

Songwriter Walter Donaldson's first big hit was "How Ya Gonna Keep 'Em Down On The Farm After They've Seen Paree," with lyrics by Sam M. Lewis and Joe Young. They also had a hit with "My Mammy," which Al Jolson popularized. Jolson became a booster of Donaldson and interpolated several of his songs into his Broadway shows including "Carolina In The Morning," written with lyricist Gus Kahn and published in 1922.

"Carolina In The Morning" was another in a long string of pseudo-Southern songs, including "Swanee" and "Waiting For The Robert E. Lee," usually written by New York Jews who had never been farther south than 14th Street. Even so, Kahn's lyric made a good case for its chorus proposition that "Nothing could be finer than to be in Carolina in the morning," rhapsodizing over morning glories twining around the door, pearly dew, and kissing buttercups.

The song found its way into the Broadway revue *The Passing Show* (1922). After Jolson's recording, it became a huge hit and was recorded by a diverse group of singers including Bing Crosby, Jimmy Durante, Danny Kaye, and, in 1957, a rock version by Bill Haley And His Comets.

Because the song doesn't specify whether North or South Carolina is the state in question, some wags have suggested that the song's Carolina in which nothing could be finer than to be in of a morning is, in fact, a woman.

Ken Bloom

Published Date 1922

Nationality USA

Composers Walter Donaldson, Gus Kahn

Why It's Key Tribute to the South – from the distance of the East Coast.

Key Song "Down Hearted Blues"
Bessie Smith

Mamie Smith's historic recording of "Crazy Blues" alerted the record companies to the large urban market for African-American "race" music, but her subsequent recordings never moved beyond the black audience. This was the achievement of Bessie Smith, the "Queen of the Blues" who made it palatable to the white audience and brought a commercial form of blues to millions of listeners. While other blues artists recorded for small companies and had to enter the studio by the freight elevator, Bessie Smith was the star performer for the giant Columbia label and the massive sales of her records kept this company solvent throughout the '20s.

The story of this recording – made on February 16, 1923 – is clouded by myth. Smith had considerable experience in recording studios. Although none of her earliest recordings have surfaced, she was far from being a raw and inexperienced blues singer but rather a professional vaudeville entertainer who was often billed as a "comedienne." "Down Hearted Blues," a desolate but defiant song of a wronged lover written by Lovie Austin and Alberta Hunter, showcases the power and intensity of her voice but it is a controlled performance which does not challenge the conventions of popular music of the time. The sales of this record were astounding: 800,000 units sold in six months, proving that African-American music could cross over.

Andre Millard

Release Date 1923

Nationality USA

Composers Lovie Austin, Alberta Hunter

Why It's Key The recording that launched the career of Bessie Smith and helped bring "race" music to a larger audience.

Key People
Bert Kalmar and Harry Ruby

Bert Kalmar (1884–1947) and Harry Ruby (1895–1974) were both born in New York and worked in vaudeville. Ruby was a pianist who started writing music in 1917 and had moderate success with songs like "Daddy Long Legs" but when he met Bert Kalmar in 1920, he found his perfect lyrical foil. Amongst the first of their memorable hits was "Who's Sorry Now," although unusually they wrote its lyric and a third party, Ted Snyder, provided the melody. Isham Jones took it into the U.S. charts on August 11, 1923. Another of the duo's famous '20s hit was "I Wanna Be Loved By You." They also did plenty of work on Broadway.

They might have stayed in New York for the entirety of their careers, as did many other successful songwriters, but in 1930 they moved to Hollywood, where demand for songwriters was suddenly high following the introduction of synchronized sound in 1926 and the rise of the musical and the insertion of featured songs in dramas and comedies. Kalmar and Ruby not only wrote songs for movies, they also collaborated on the scripts, notably for the Marx Brothers' classic *Duck Soup* (1933). Significantly when Hollywood chose to produce a film about the trials and tribulations of songwriting teams, they based it on Kalmar and Ruby. The 1950 melodrama starred Fred Astaire and was called *Three Little Words* after their 1930 hit song.

Andre Millard

Role Songwriters

Date August 11, 1923

Nationality USA

Why It's Key The writing team who epitomized the migration of many songwriters from New York's boards to Hollywood celluloid.

Key Performance *Earl Carroll Vanities*
stage musical

There were three great revue series that graced Broadway in the early years of the twentieth century: the *Ziegfeld Follies*, *George White's Scandals*, and the *Earl Carroll Vanities*. Each of the three had its own trademark, the special stamp of their titular producers. Florenz Ziegfeld relied on star-filled extravaganzas featuring top talents performing material by some of America's greatest composers. George White produced jazzy, fast moving revues with flappers and sheiks and a hint of bawdiness. Earl Carroll, on the other hand, employed few great stars and relied on mostly second-rate material but surpassed his competitors with vulgarity, burlesque-inspired humor and ample nudity.

A famous sign hung over Carroll's stage door: "Through These Portals Pass the Most Beautiful Girls in the World." It was a direct challenge to Ziegfeld whose aim was "Glorifying the American Girl." There were 11 editions of the Vanities, starting on July 5, 1923, and two Earl Carroll Sketchbooks. Among the stars that appeared in the series were Patsy Kelly, W. C. Fields, Milton Berle, Ray Dooley, Jack Benny, Helen Broderick, Lillian Roth, and Jimmy Savo.

Commissioning substantial scores was not Carroll's strong point. He wrote many of them himself and others were written by Morris Hamilton and Grace Henry. However, at least one enduring song came from the Vanities: "I Got a Right to Sing the Blues" by Harold Arlen and Ted Koehler.

Ken Bloom

Opening Night July 5, 1923

Country USA

Director William Collier

Cast Joe Cook, Margaret Davies, Gertrude Lemmon

Composer Earl Carroll plus (one song) Roy Turk, William Daly, Russell J. Robinson

Why It's Key The annual revue that proved that the consideration of musical quality can sometimes be negated by the allure of flesh.

Key Event
The Charleston dance craze

Most dance crazes begin with a song and no number created a more popular dance phenomenon than the introduction of James P. Johnson and Cecil Mack's "Charleston" in 1923. The music is made up of short, propulsive bursts of music that accommodated the halting dance step. The song and the dance were introduced in the all-black revue *Runnin' Wild* where Elizabeth Welch performed the frenetic, knee-knocking, high-stepping number but the dance dates from well before that, with the residents of an island near Charleston, Carolina reputedly having been doing it as far back as the turn of the century.

The dance and its accompanying music is now inextricably associated with the Roaring Twenties. It would be danced at speakeasies as an act of defiance to those who supported prohibition and thought the Charleston decadent. The female dancers came to be called flappers because of the way some of the dance movements required them to resemble birds.

Both the song and new step quickly caught. For the next five years the Charleston dominated dance halls across America and in Europe. Other dance numbers using the same halting tempo were written and a whole repertoire of "Charleston"-like songs flooded the market. When an unknown Joan Crawford danced the Charleston in the movie *Our Dancing Daughters* (1928), she became a star.

Thomas Hischak

Date 1923

Country USA

Why It's Key The first dance to define a generation.

Opposite The Charleston

Key Song "Yes, We Have No Bananas"
Eddie Cantor

Songwriters Frank Silver and Irving Cohn got the idea for "Yes, We Have No Bananas" from a Greek fruit peddler who used the expression to a patron. The contradictory notion was expanded into a nonsense lyric and a bright and vigorous melody was added. The music is filled with sly references to such famous compositions as the "Hallelujah Chorus," "My Bonnie," and "I Dreamed That I Dwelt In Marble Halls." Silver's group The Music Masters introduced the silly ditty in restaurants and clubs, where Eddie Cantor heard it. He subsequently interpolated it into his Broadway revue *Make It Snappy*. Cantor and the song stopped the show each night. He recorded it soon after and made a U.S No. 1. Irving Berlin collaborated with Silvers and Cohn on a parody version that spoofed opera and it was sung by Al Jolson in the film *Mammy* (1930). It was also sung "straight" in several other movies.

To this day, British schoolchildren who have never heard any of the many recordings of the song know its chorus. This is the legacy of the fact that the song's title was used by shopkeepers during World War II as a way to admit to its clientele that it did not have the stock they wanted while still retaining the "Blitz spirit." Silver and Cohn intended to amuse but little could they have known that their ditty would help Britons through their darkest days.

Thomas Hischak

Release Date 1923

Nationality USA

Composer Frank Silver, Irving Cohn

Why It's Key Showed that popular song intended to amuse could unintentionally have far more profound benefits.

Key Song "Nobody Knows You When You're Down And Out"

"Nobody Knows You When You're Down And Out" was written by vaudeville performer Jimmie Cox and published in 1923. It has remained a favorite of blues singers ever since Bessie Smith made her bestselling record in 1929. Smith's very solemn version became her signature song and in many ways it could even have been written specifically for this woman with a hardship-strewn life.

Yet though Smith apparently learned the song from the composer when she appeared on a bill with him in vaudeville, when Cox performed it he played it for laughs. After all, he was known as the "Black Charlie Chaplin." This was in the tradition of many black performers in the early years of the twentieth century who refused to play black stereotypes, and instead created characters for themselves who, while suffering the blues, were also humorous. The best-known of these is Bert Williams who played a down-on-his-heels character who sang "Nobody..."

and other sad songs but rendered it in a style you might call tragi-comedy.

Cox's song has a narrator who was once a millionaire who took all his friends out for a good time and bought them bootleg alcohol. Of course, once his fortunes changed, his friends disappeared for the reason of human nature that the song title starkly lays out. The lyric concludes that when you are finally back up on your feet again, "Ev'rybody wants to be your long lost friend."

Ken Bloom

Published Date 1923

Nationality USA

Composer Jimmie Cox

Why It's Key A classic blues lament that actually started out in far less serious mode.

Opposite Radio days

1920-1929

Key Event
Radio Christmas

The first radio sets were made available to the public by 1920. These were weak, battery-powered machines with earphones rather than speakers. The radio set was conceived as a "music box" by the Radio Corporation of America (RCA) which saw it as a replacement to the various "talking machines" that stood in so many American and West European households. By 1921 there were over half a million radio sets in the United States and 200 broadcasting stations but the talking machine industry dismissed radio as a threat, thinking (wrongly) that not allowing their contracted performers or their records to be used on the radio would eliminate all sources of programming. Where radio didn't just ignore the edict, they used local musicians or non-musical programming.

By 1923 it appeared that the first "radio boom" had died down because sales of receivers were flat and the programming of radio stations remained limited and of

very poor sound quality. But the "Radio Christmas" of 1924 was a disaster for the talking machine business as consumers bought radios rather than gramophones or phonographs. Sales plummeted at least 50 per cent and some companies suffered even more. Improved machines with much louder sound, lower prices, and improved, more structured, and thoughtful programming (plus live musicians) took radio from a hobby of technical enthusiasts to a mass-market commodity that everyone had to have.

Andre Millard

Date December 1924

Country USA

Why It's Key Radio became the dominant force in the music business.

Key Performance *Rhapsody In Blue*
jazz concerto

Paul Whiteman, the most successful bandleader of his day, was not satisfied with million-selling records, sold-out nightclub appearances, international tours, and appearances in Broadway musicals. He longed to give the orchestral popular music he called "symphonic jazz" the respectability of classical music. In that pursuit, he announced a performance at New York's Aeolian Hall on February 12, 1924 that he billed as "An Experiment in Modern Music," and for which he commissioned new concert pieces by such composers as Victor Herbert and George Gershwin, who were better known for their work in the musical theater.

Whiteman was well acquainted with Gershwin, having scored hits with his songs "Do It Again!" and "(I'll Build A) Stairway To Paradise." The composer was typically busy writing show music (among his four musicals to open on Broadway or in the West End during 1924 was the memorable *Lady, Be Good!*, which appeared on December 1), but that didn't keep him from dashing off a masterpiece for Whiteman at the last minute. In fact, he accompanied Whiteman's orchestra on-stage for his *Rhapsody In Blue*, playing piano improvisations where written music was absent.

The work became one of Gershwin's most celebrated compositions and the highlight of Whiteman's career. The two collaborated for a two-sided record version that became a hit. That was only the first of many recordings of *Rhapsody In Blue*, which cemented Gershwin's claim to being among the most important American composers.

William Ruhlmann

Date February 12, 1924

Venue Aeolian Hall, New York, USA

Nationality USA

Why It's Key Marked Gershwin's successful crossover from writing show music to contemporary classical music.

90

Key Person
Irving Caesar

The lyricist Irving Caesar lived over a hundred years (1895–1996) and wrote more than a thousand songs. His career began with the rise of the American popular song at the time of World War I and ended when freelance songwriters, especially lyricists, were largely irrelevant in popular music.

He spent his whole life in New York City, the center of professional songwriting and the home of Tin Pan Alley. His first major hit came in 1919 when he collaborated with George Gershwin on "Swanee." He worked with Vincent Youmans on two songs that energized the Broadway musical *No No Nanette*, and brought him lifelong acclaim: "I Want to Be Happy" and "Tea for Two." Both were first recorded in 1924, have become American standards, and have been reinterpreted numerous times.

Irving Caesar continued to write for Broadway shows and Hollywood musicals during the '30s and '40s. A founder of the Songwriters Guild of America, he was dismayed at the changes in the structure of the music business in the '50s that gradually sidelined the composer and lyricist working together to produce popular songs. Not only did performers more and more write the songs they played, but the newer forms of music were clearly not to his taste. Caesar complained that nobody wanted to hear good songs anymore and that a "musical juvenile delinquency" had taken over American popular music.

Andre Millard

Role Songwriter

Date 1924

Nationality USA

Why It's Key Personified the rise and fall of Tin Pan Alley.

Key Song
"It Had To Be You"

In 1924 Gus Kahn was already established as a lyricist with a string of songs introduced by Al Jolson in his shows at the Winter Garden Theater. Isham Jones was established only as a popular bandleader.

The new team of Gus Kahn and Isham Jones wrote three of the most successful songs of 1924, all of which have become standards, a remarkable record. Even more remarkable considering "I'll See You in My Dreams," "The One I Love Belongs To Somebody Else," and "It Had to Be You" were Jones' only successful compositions. More remarkable still: he banged out their melodies in an hour on a baby grand piano his wife had just given him for his birthday.

All three songs boast surprisingly sophisticated music in a period known for catchy melodies, with upbeat tempi suitable for fox-trotting around the dance floor. The songs are often assumed to have been written in the '40s, as they had a kind of Forties feeling and slang-free lyrics, and enjoyed a renewed popularity in that decade. Additionally, Kahn's lyric to "It Had to Be You" had a sophistication that popular music, for all its charm, rarely displayed in the Roaring Twenties. No moon-eyed devotional, it admits the ambiguities and contradictions of love, summed up in the line, "With all your faults, I love you still".

Naturally, it has been covered many times since its publication in 1924, including by Doris Day and Frank Sinatra.

Ken Bloom

Published Date 1924

Nationality USA

Composers Isham Jones, Gus Kahn

Why It's Key Product of an amazingly successful partnership – for one year, anyway.

1920-1929

91

Key Song
"California, Here I Come"

Of all the songs written about the Western state, none has remained as popular over time as 1924's "California, Here I Come," even the official state song "I Love You, California." B. G. DeSylva wrote the declarative lyric to "California, Here I Come" about leaving the cold and snow and returning "Right back where I started from" and Joseph W. Meyer composed the forceful music that has the drive of a speeding train. The number is most associated with Al Jolson. For a while, it was used as a sort of theme tune for any character in a Warner Brothers cartoon who was making a hasty, enforced exit.

Although his name appeared on the sheet music as co-lyricist, it is questionable if Jolson actually helped write the song. But he did popularize it on stage and on records and soon just a musical phrase from the song – let alone the words – conjured up for listeners the image of rushing to the West Coast. Those words of the title phrase though entered and remained in the language. Even two or three generations removed, an announcement by an individual that they are on their way to the Golden State is often couched in exactly those words. Even if it is not, the announcement very frequently brings forth a jolly rendition of the title phrase from the person addressed – who is also frequently rewarded with groans.

Thomas Hischak

Published Date 1924

Nationality USA

Composers Joseph W. Meyer, B. G. DeSylva

Why It's Key Demonstrated that a musical statement related to a place will have only one consequence.

Key Song "Does Your Chewing Gum Lose Its Flavor On The Bedpost Over Night?"

Chewing gum was frowned upon by the older generation because it was considered bad etiquette and unhealthy, so the Spearmint company was thrilled when the novelty number "Does The Spearment [sic] Lose Its Flavor On The Bedpost Over Night" became a hit.

Ernest Breuer wrote the hoedown-like music and Billy Rose and Marty Bloom penned the comic lyric that asked if you "swallow it in spite" when your mother doesn't allow chewing gum. Harry Richman introduced the song in concert but it was a record by Ernest Hare and Billy Jones that hit the U.S. charts on July 12, 1924. The song was so popular that other gum manufacturers complained about all the free advertising Spearmint was getting every time it was played on the radio so the title was altered to the one that has lasted up to today. Other '20s songs plugged particular products but none had the lasting popularity of the chewing gum number.

Interest in the song was revived in 1959 with a successful disc by British skiffle singer Lonnie Donegan who had a UK No. 3 with it and – two years later – a U.S. Top 5. Donegan's success in Britain would have been impossible without that decision way back when to change from the brand name to the generic: BBC rules on advertising were then so strict that no airplay would have been allowed.

Thomas Hischak

Release Date 1924

Nationality USA

Composer Ernest Breuer, Billy Rose, Marty Bloom

Why It's Key Madison Avenue and Tin Pan Alley cross paths with a ditty that inadvertently invents product placement in songs.

Opposite **Lonnie Donegan**

Key Event
First Electrical Recording

When Bessie Smith came into Columbia's New York recording studios in 1925 she found out that she no longer had to shout into a large acoustic horn. She now stood in front of a microphone and the new Western Electric system did the rest, amplifying the signal of her voice electronically and using electro-magnetic cutters to inscribe the sound wave onto the master record. The frequency range of records was now increased by more than two octaves. This, the most important technological innovation in sound recording in the twentieth century, took mechanical reproduction into a new realm of reality.

Ironically the Big Three record companies – Edison, Victor and Columbia – were not interested in the new system that Western Electric laboratories demonstrated to them in 1924, but falling sales and the growing threat of radio made them change their minds. Once they adopted the system they found it bolstered their oligarchic business strategies, making the big

companies more powerful and weeding out the mass of smaller competitors. Control of new technologies like electric recording reinforced the move towards large, integrated companies that dealt in both industrial and artistic arenas, ensuring that popular entertainment would remain the preserve of the major business players.

Much the same process occurred in the movie industry when electrical recording was employed to make talking pictures. The large studios' initial reluctance evaporated when they saw Warner Brothers' huge success with the *The Jazz Singer*. The electrical age had arrived and there was no going back.

Andre Millard

Date 1925

Country USA

Why It's Key The invention that transformed the aural quality of records.

Key People
Gus Kahn and Walter Donaldson

Walter Donaldson (1893–1947) had already great success with lyricists Sam M. Lewis and Joe Young when he met Gus Kahn (1886–1941), who had his first standard, "Memories" published in 1915. Both songwriters had contributed to the career of Al Jolson.

Jolson introduced their first hit together as a team, "Carolina In The Morning" in 1922, the same year as their next hit, "My Buddy." As the '20s continued, the team wrote many successes including, "Beside A Babbling Brook" in 1923 and "Ukulele Lady" in 1925. That was also the year of two Donaldson and Kahn songs with the word "baby" in their titles, "I Wonder Where My Baby Is Tonight" and "Yes Sir! That's My Baby." The latter, with which Gene Austin entered the U.S. chart on August 1, 1925, is perhaps the song which best shows the way their talents complemented the other's, Donaldson's instantly memorable jolly melody the perfect accompaniment to Kahn's brilliantly colloquial, repetition-friendly songwords.

In 1928, Donaldson and Kahn wrote a highly successful musical comedy, *Whoopee* that was laden with smashes, including, "I'm Bringing a Red, Red Rose," "Love Me Or Leave Me," "Makin' Whoopee," and "My Baby Just Cares for Me." They were asked to adapt *Whoopee* for the motion pictures. They wrote another Samuel Goldwyn-produced musical, *Kid Millions*, in 1934 which featured "When My Ship Comes In."

The pair's hit-strewn partnership came to an end when Kahn passed away in 1941.
Ken Bloom

Role Songwriters

Date 1925

Nationality USA

Why It's Key The team who wrote some of the biggest hits of the '20s and '30s.

94

Key Song "If You Knew Susie"
Eddie Cantor

The "new woman" of the jazz age cut her hair short, smoked, drank, and went out dancing without a chaperone. Known as "flappers," they became the subject matter of popular songs that characterized the hedonism of the Roaring Twenties.

One such number is "If You Knew Susie," which highlighted the fact that though women inhabited roles as mothers and daughters, they were also sexual beings. That Susie is clearly the kind of girl who would be happy to be "known" in the way the narrator implies would have been amazing and appalling to many, not least because the song is patently not about a couple who have recited wedding vows. Susie is described as wearing tight dresses and as possessing quite a "chassis." Even more outrageously, the narrator concedes that all those listening may "know" her too. Although African-American songs often showed sexually aggressive women, this type of depiction was rare on Tin Pan Alley.

The song is forever linked to the singer and comedian Eddie Cantor, whose Columbia recording entered the U.S. chart on July 18, 1925 on its way to the top but it was popular on both sides of the Atlantic and sung in music halls, pubs, and private homes. Its frenetic tempo ideally suited the popular music of the jazz age and the emphasis on the "Oh" in the chorus gave music hall orchestras the opportunity to introduce comedic emphasis.
Andre Millard

Release Date 1925

Nationality USA

Composers Buddy De Sylva, Joe Meyer

Why It's Key The song that represented the changing role of women in the '20s.

Opposite Margaret Kerry plays Eddie Cantor's daughter in the 1948 film, *If You Knew Susie*

Key Song **"Sweet Georgia Brown"**
Ben Bernie and his Orchestra

Ben Bernie, Ken Casey (lyric) and Maceo Pinkard (melody) collaborated on "Sweet Georgia Brown," a scintillating number about a new gal in town who comes from Georgia, upsetting all the women because all the men are dazzled by her. The sly lyric notes that the only men Georgia can't get are those "she ain't met yet." The bright and bouncy music is deceptively tricky, using chord lines with all sorts of changes and is actually difficult to sing correctly. This early jazz classic foreshadowed the swing sound to come along a decade later and was one of the first songs to lend itself to improvisation, making it a favorite of jazz musicians.

Ben Bernie and his Orchestra introduced the song on a record that entered the U.S. chart on June 27, 1925, and it caught on immediately. Though it has been the subject of dozens of recordings over the years, the number should have been destined for the same forgotten status as any other composition of a bygone era, no matter how high quality. Popular music however, is always throwing curves in the way it manages to preserve itself. Today the tune is familiar to anybody who has ever watched the basketball performers The Harlem Globetrotters on television and in exhibitions: their inimitable ball twirling and trickery is always accompanied by their signature tune, a whistled rendition of "Sweet Georgia Brown."

Thomas Hischak

Release Date 1925

Nationality USA

Composers Ben Bernie, Ken Casey, Maceo Pinkard

Why It's Key Proves how unpredictable the reason for the extension of a song's shelf life can be.

Key Person
Paul Whiteman

Purists dismiss Paul Whiteman (1990–1967) because they find his adopted nickname "The King of Jazz" absurd. Paul Whiteman and his Orchestra may never have been a real jazz band but Whiteman brought popular music into the jazz age in a form acceptable to the masses. He understood how popular music needed to change and abetted those changes through the hiring of up-and-coming talents (e.g. Bing Crosby) and providing a showcase for new kinds of music (he commissioned *Rhapsody In Blue*). His importance lies in his codification of the big band.

When "Valencia" entered the U.S. chart on June 26, 1926 on its way to the top, he had already been achieving chart activity for six years. There would be nearly twenty further years of hits, including, immediately afterwards, another No. 1 in the shape of "The Birth Of The Blues." With such popularity, Whiteman set the standard for future bands and also set the format for performance. His was the first band to feature a female vocalist (Mildred Bailey). Later he hired Bailey's brother, Al Rinker, along with Harry Barris and Bing Crosby, and introduced the idea of a vocal trio. With Ferde Grofe, Don Redman, and Bill Challis on payroll, Whiteman was the first to use written arrangements. Grofe and Whiteman introduced the full reed and brass sections to the big band, another first. Booking the band into vaudeville and going on a European tour constituted two more.

Ken Bloom

Role Recording Artist

Date 1926

Nationality USA

Why It's Key The man who set the rules for the big band.

Opposite Paul Whiteman

Key Performance *Oh, Kay!*
stage musical

Wodehouse got the call from overextended American librettist Guy Bolton that help was needed with the new musical Bolton was writing with George and Ira Gershwin, Wodehouse was apprehensive, even though he and Bolton, with composer Jerome Kern, had pretty much invented American musical comedy in writing their Princess musicals. Wodehouse was not merely a librettist but one of the era's most sought-after lyricists. With Ira as George's permanent partner, was Wodehouse only to be Bolton's book doctor?

As it turns out, Bolton had an agenda. He'd become enamored of British performer Gertrude Lawrence after seeing her in London vaudeville and wanted to bring her to American audiences. He was convinced, though, that she had to be established not in a revue but a book musical designed for her. He therefore convinced his producers to bring in Wodehouse, the most renowned of British wits,

famous for his Jeeves and Wooster comedy of manners fiction, to provide Lawrence with pithy lines for her English rhythms.

Oh, Kay! a comedy involving bootlegging, bathing beauties, and the eponymous heroine, looking to find a man she met on an ocean cruise, turned out to be a success on all fronts, indeed making Lawrence a U.S. star and giving Wodehouse some of his happiest memories.

Among the standard songs to emerge from the score were "Do Do Do" and "Someone To Watch Over Me."

David Spencer

Opening Night
November 8, 1926

Country USA

Director John Harwood

Cast Gertrude Lawrence, Victor Moore, Oscar Shaw

Composer George Gershwin, Ira Gershwin

Why It's Key The musical that made British celebrity Gertrude Lawrence an American star.

Key Song
"Are You Lonesome Tonight?"

The plaintive ballad "Are You Lonesome Tonight?" was written by the Tin Pan Alley songwriting team of composer Lou Handman and lyricist Roy Turk. An unabashed tearjerker, the sentimental song is sung in the voice of a scorned lover who wonders if a former romantic partner now regrets their breakup. It reaches its emotional climax in a spoken-word passage leading to a final, pleading chorus.

Published in 1926, "Are You Lonesome Tonight?" was introduced on radio and records by Vaughan DeLeath in 1927 but her version may have been outsold by the competing one by Henry Burr, for whom it was one of his last hits. Al Jolson featured it onstage. Other notable initial recordings include those by Little Jack Little, Jacques Renard and His Orchestra with vocals by Franklyn Baur and Blue Barron and His Orchestra (narration handled by disc jockey John McCormick). Jaye P. Morgan took it back into the charts in 1959.

It was the version by Elvis Presley that was the most unexpected. Recorded in 1960 at the suggestion of his manager Tom Parker, it proved that beneath Presley's animalistic stage moves and rock 'n' roll hits, there was a genuinely superb singer. His beautiful, sustain-packed version was a Transatlantic chart-topper. The song achieved yet another hit recording in 1973 as a U.S. Top 20 vehicle for Donny Osmond, making it one of the most popular songs of the twentieth century.

William Ruhlmann

Published Date 1926

Nationality USA

Composers Lou Handman, Roy Turk

Why It's Key A song that remained relevant down the decades to artists across the musical spectrum.

Key Song "Baby Face"
Benny Davis

"Heaven save us/From Benny Davis," once remarked Howard Dietz. Dietz was mocking the propensity of his fellow lyricist Davis to write fast and in the process render false rhymes – just like "save us" and "Davis." "Baby Face" contains just such a lyrical "crime" in its matching of "jumpin'" and "something" – yet the rhyme hints at the very casualness and colloquialism that made Davis' songs such fun. Certainly, this song was so loved by the public that it was a hit for four different artists in 1926 alone.

"You got the prettiest little baby face" is essentially the sum total of the idea conveyed in a number written in the style of the English music hall tradition. Yet a simplistic lyric is on closer examination also quite canny. The use of words like "jumpin'," "somethin'," and "ev'ry" gives it a nice slangy quality, while the fact that it is mostly a torrent of one-syllable words grants it a momentum that makes it fun to listen to and even more fun to sing.

The first recording was made by Jan Garber's orchestra, with Benny Davis himself as vocalist. A U.S. No. 1, it hit the charts on September 25, 1926. Many, many covers followed. The song was used for ironic effect as background music in the Barbara Stanwyck vehicle *Baby Face* (1933) in a pre-Code romp wherein she sleeps her way to the top.
Ken Bloom

Published Date 1926

Country USA

Composers Benny Davis, Harry Akst

Why It's Key The song symptomatic of a lyricist who broke all the rules but still came up trumps.

Key Person
Gene Austin

"The Voice of the Southland," honey-voiced tenor Gene Austin (1900–1972) was one of the top singers of the '20s and '30s.

After returning from World War I as a bugler and schooling in dentistry and law, Austin decided to try his luck as a singer. He formed his own band and appeared in vaudeville and on radio before turning to recording. Austin was also an accomplished songwriter, collaborating with vaudeville partner Roy Bergere on hits "How Come You Do Me Like You Do" and "When My Sugar Walks Down the Street." His groundbreaking mellow, relaxed, and intimate singing style paved the way to later crooners like Bing Crosby, Nick Lucas, and Russ Columbo.

He made his first records on the Vocalion label beginning in 1924. Austin moved to Victor, with whom he sold almost 90,000,000 records. Among his hit recordings were "Bye, Bye, Blackbird," "My Melancholy Baby," "The Lonesome Road," "Girl Of My Dreams,"
"Ramona" (renowned for its unique pipe organ instrumentation), and "Carolina Moon."

His biggest hit was his recording of Walter Donaldson and George Whiting's "My Blue Heaven," which sold over twelve million copies after entering the U.S. charts on December 3, 1927, becoming the largest-selling record of all time, a record held until Bing Crosby's "White Christmas."

He appeared in eight films, including three with his friend Mae West, *Belle of the Nineties* (1934), *Klondike Annie* (1936), and *My Little Chickadee* (1940). Austin's last chart appearance was in 1957 with "Too Late."
Ken Bloom

Role Recording Artist

Date 1927

Nationality USA

Why It's Key The inventor of crooning.

Key Performance *Show Boat*
stage musical

Though many scholars point to Rodgers and Hammerstein's *Oklahoma!* of 1944 as the first "mature," integrated book musical, it is in fact 1927's *Show Boat* (originally produced by Flo Ziegfeld!) that really heralded the future. (Not coincidentally, Oscar Hammerstein II was librettist-lyricist here too, his composer the redoubtable Jerome Kern.) It's just that its authors' contemporaries weren't ready to build on its innovations.

Perhaps, though, it's understandable why *Show Boat*, which opened on December 27, 1927 and was based on Edna Ferber's 1926 novel, didn't instantly spearhead a trend of sophistication, despite famous songs like "Bill" (lyrics by P. G. Wodehouse), "Can't Help Lovin' Dat Man," "Make Believe," and the immortal "Ol' Man River." Its ambitious structure may have camouflaged the road map for emulation: rather than featuring one central, contained story, it's a multi-generational, multi-plot family epic (starting in the 1880s) spanning four decades of a show business family with roots in Mississippi's show boat circuit. Yet, more than merely a "potboiler," *Show Boat* also examines racism, dramatizing miscegenation in a society intolerant enough to outlaw it.

While clearly meant as a condemnation of bigotry, the show is still a product of its era, and has thus sparked controversy since. Significantly no two mainstream productions have been alike; throughout its revival history the book has been revised and reshaped, and the score's content altered (drawing upon a wealth of alternate, archived drafts) to match the sensibility of the day.
David Spencer

Opening Night
December 27, 1927

Country USA

Director Zeke Colvan, Oscar Hammerstein II

Cast Helen Morgan, Jules Bledsoe, Howard Marsh

Composer Oscar Hammerstein II, Jerome Kern, plus one song each from P. G. Wodehouse, Josepf E. Howard, and Charles K. Harris

Why It's Key The first American musical to properly intertwine plot and song.

Opposite Jerome Kern

Key Event
Country music's big bang

Late in July of 1927, Ralph Peer, the recording director of the Victor Talking Machine Company, came to Bristol, Tennessee to record some of the local talent. The "Bristol Sessions" are known as country's big bang, its consequence the breaking out of this hitherto backwoods genre into the U.S. mainstream. Among those recorded at Bristol were the Alcoa Quartet, the Teneva Ramblers, Henry Whitter, and Uncle Eck Dunford, and – greatest of all among the solo acts – Jimmie Rodgers, around whom an industry formed.

For many, it was the July 31 sessions that proved the most important. On that day, the Carter Family – singer A. P. Carter, his wife Sara (autoharp), and sister-in-law Maybelle Carter (a talented guitarist) – arrived from Maces Springs, Virginia. The trio, who had never recorded before, received U.S. $50 for the six sides they cut that day and went on to become legends. There had been country hits before them like John Carson's "Little Old Log Cabin In The Lane" and Pop Stoneman's "The Sinking Of The Titanic" but with releases like "Wabash Cannonball," "Will the Circle Be Unbroken," "Wildwood Flower," "Keep on The Sunny Side," and many others the Carters brought the music out of the fields and into urban living rooms, popularized both the guitar as a lead instrument and the flat-picking style and preserved possibly hundreds of Appalachian songs for posterity.

The Carter Family recorded for decades and were the first group inducted into country's hall of fame.
Bruce Eder

Date July 31, 1927

Country USA

Why it's key Effectively marked the birth of country music.

Key Performance *The Jazz Singer* the movie

Contrary to modern misconception, when *The Jazz Singer* was released on October 6, 1927, it was not the first movie with music and sound effects (that was *Don Juan*, 1926) nor the first all-talking feature length film (an honor that belongs to *Lights Of New York*, 1928). A production that still had the "intertitles" of silent films, it was more accurately the first significant feature-length motion picture with synchronized dialogue. Significant because the six songs that Al Jolson sang in the film and its two minutes of mainly ad libbed dialogue created a sensation.

Apart from D. W Griffiths' *Dream Street* (1921), the first song – "My Gal Sal," performed by Robert Gordon – was the first time the enraptured audience had both seen and heard a human being sing on celluloid. Jolson's first song, "Dirty Hands, Dirty Face," and his further warbling only incited them more. People who knew of Jolson but had never witnessed him on stage were captivated by his charisma and power. The iconic image of the film will forever be the closing scene where a blackfaced Jolson sings "My Mammy" on bended knee.

All of cinema was now changed permanently, of course, but *The Jazz Singer* was particularly important for music in the medium: the phenomenon of the movie musical was now unleashed, as was the tie-in smash: the following year "Sonny Boy" (by Jolson) became the first record to be a hit as a direct consequence of appearing in a movie.

Ken Bloom

Movie Release Date October 6, 1927

Country USA

Director Alan Crosland

Cast Al Jolson, May McAvoy, Warner Oland

Composer Louis Silvers

Why It's Key A new medium for music to be purveyed through.

Key Event
First Juke Boxes

The earliest cylinder phonographs came equipped with numerous ear tubes to bring their songs to groups of paying listeners. However, it was not until the loud playback made possible by electrical recording and the development of automatic record changers in the early '20s that provided the means to store and manipulate stacks of disc records that "coin slot" talking machines became an important force.

The first machine to incorporate these innovations was introduced by the Automatic Music Instrument Company in 1927. Soon other manufacturers like Seeburg, Wurlitzer, and Rockola joined them. After the repeal of prohibition, Americans found themselves in bars where a juke box provided the music instead of live performers. They were also installed in restaurants, bus stations, stores, and hotels. They were ubiquitous in the South, where "jooking" (black slang for dancing) to records in small drinking establishments ("juke joints") was common. Not only did juke boxes now play a vital part in the exposure and marketing of popular songs, but by 1939 juke boxes accounted for 13 million disc sales a year. The introduction of the small 45 rpm disc provided the ideal format for juke boxes and the '40s and '50s marked the high point of this technology.

Today, juke boxes are moving over to "streamed" music but despite the huge increase of music choices the internet enables, the elaborate, (then) modernistic designs of Wurlitzers and Rockolas playing black vinyl will probably always have the greater sensual and emotional appeal.

Andre Millard

Date 1927

Country USA

Why It's Key Provided a major outlet for popular music.

Key People
George and Ira Gershwin

Ira Gershwin (1896–1983) had just started piano lessons when his younger brother George (1898–1937) demonstrated such amazing musical abilities that Ira turned to lyric writing while George pursued composing. By 1919 George had a bestseller with "Swanee" while Ira quietly wrote lyrics for others, using the pen name of Arthur Francis so as not to capitalize on his brother's fame. The two men wrote their first Broadway score together with *Lady, Be Good!* (1922) and from that point on they worked almost exclusively with each other.

Funny Face, which opened on November 22, 1927, was their fifth show together and their biggest hit to date. For the next ten years the Gershwins would continue as one of the most innovative and successful of American songwriting teams. Writing for Broadway and Hollywood, they penned such varied standards as "I Got Rhythm," "'S Wonderful," "Embraceable You," "Summertime," "Someone To Watch Over Me," "Strike Up The Band," "Love Walked In," "It Ain't Necessarily So," and "Let's Call The Whole Thing Off." They also collaborated on the landmark musical satire *Of Thee I Sing* (1931) and the American folk opera *Porgy And Bess* (1935) before George's untimely death in 1937.

A measure of the public affection in which their output was held is illustrated by the reaction of novelist John O' Hara to the latter tragic news: "I don't have to believe it if I don't want to."

Thomas Hischak

Role Composers

Date November 22, 1927

Nationality USA

Why It's Key The brothers whose talents were perfectly complementary.

Key Song **"The Song Is Ended (But The Melody Lingers On)"**

Just as Irving Berlin wrote the unofficial theme songs for Christmas, Easter, showbusiness, and America, this number can be viewed as the theme for all popular music.

The Berlin standard, published in 1927, has a haunting melody that is almost ghostlike in its echoing qualities. Its lyric describes a lover and the ballad that was "their song" and states that while both are gone, neither can be forgotten: "We sang a love song that ended too soon." Ruth Etting's version entered the U.S. charts in February 1928 and the number was soon shorthand to explain the lasting power a song can have on the populace. Among standout recordings was that of Nat "King" Cole but the disc that brought the song back into favor was Nellie Lutcher's 1948 record. Singers and bands sometimes liked to place "The Song Is Ended" at the end of a concert or nightclub set, letting the number reverberate in the audience's memory just as the lyric suggests. The song was used in the movie *Blue Skies* (1946) but ironically only as background.

While the song itself may not have lingered for anyone except aficionados of Tin Pan Alley-era classics, its title phrase has. When 1992 Democratic presidential candidate Paul Tsongas pulled out of the race, an admiring British newspaper cartoonist drew a picture of a man walking past a newspaper hoarding bearing the headline "Tsongas over" and remarking "But the melody lingers."

Thomas Hischak

Published Date 1927

Nationality USA

Composer Irving Berlin

Why It's Key The epitome of the onomatopoeic in popular song.

Key Event **A fire nearly cuts short Django Reinhardt's budding career**

Though only 18, Django Reinhardt was already an accomplished acoustic guitarist with his first recordings behind him when an accident on the above date changed both his life and the course of jazz. Gifted on the instrument since childhood, the Belgian-born, French-speaking musician was living with his wife in a caravan when a candle engulfed their home in flames. Reinhardt's left hand was scorched and two fingers were rendered useless. With his right leg also injured, Reinhardt was bedridden for 18 months. However, he spent the time wisely, utilizing his guitar as necessary physical and psychological therapy by honing his playing skills.

As his reputation spread, Reinhardt learned to compensate for the handicap and developed a unique swinging style that brought him wide recognition. He is considered by many historians to be the first important (and to this day, most renowned) European jazz musician, as well as one of the most influential guitarists within any genre. In 1934, Reinhardt joined an all-string band called Le Quintette du Hot Club de France, which also included the violinist Stéphane Grappelli. The group enjoyed great popularity but disbanded with the onset of World War II. Reinhardt and Grappelli reunited intermittently but Reinhardt's spiraling fame soon took him to America, where he performed with such jazz giants as Duke Ellington and Coleman Hawkins. He also experimented with electric guitar.

Django Reinhardt was only 43 years old when he died in France in 1953, but his stamp on music remains incalculable.

Jeff Tamarkin

Date November 2, 1928

Country France

Why It's Key Far from hindering the Gypsy guitarist, it arguably contributed to his singular technique.

Opposite Django Reinhardt with Le Quintette du Hot Club de France

Key Person
Jimmy McHugh

The first published song by Jimmy McHugh (1895–1969) was "Emaline" (1921), with lyrics by George A. Little. McHugh had his first hit with "When My Sugar Walks Down The Street' (1925), written with Gene Austen and Irving Mills.

In 1926, McHugh teamed with lyricist Dorothy Fields. Their first success was Lew Leslie's *Blackbirds of 1928*, which opened on May 9, 1928. As well as standards like "I Must Have That Man," and "Diga Diga Do," it featured "I Can't Give You Anything But Love." Fats Waller and Andy Razaf claimed they wrote the latter song and sold it to McHugh. Waller recorded the song and Razaf was heard to say that it was the song of which he was most proud. Leslie produced *The International Revue* (1930) and the team supplied the show with "On The Sunny Side Of The Street." Some have accused McHugh of buying that from Waller and Razaf. We'll never know the truth of these claims but they shouldn't be allowed to overshadow the great work of McHugh that was indisputably his own, including subsequent hit collaborations with Fields "I'm in the Mood for Love" and "I Feel a Song Comin' On" (from movie *Every Night At Eight*, 1935), and hits co-written with Harold Adamson like "Comin' In On A Wing And A Prayer," "I Couldn't Sleep A Wink Last Night," and "It's a Most Unusual Day."

Ken Bloom

Role Composer

Date May 9, 1928

Country USA

Why it's key A gifted composer whose career is overshadowed by allegations about passing off the songs of others as his.

Key Song
"I Wanna Be Loved By You"

Only the '20s could have produced such a bizarre standard as this farcical ditty by Harry Ruby, Herbert Stothard (music), and Bert Kalmar (lyric), introduced in the Broadway musical *Good Boy*, which opened on September 5, 1928. The squeaky-voiced Helen Kane sang it with Dan Healy. Her "Boop-boop-a-doop" at the end of each refrain was both juvenile and sexy. Kane's recording was an instant success, became her signature song for the rest of her long career and labeled her the "Boop-a-Doop Girl." Mae Questral would later imitate Kane when she voiced the pointedly named character Betty Boop in a series of popular cartoons.

There were recordings by other artists, such as Lee Wiley, Ray Anthony, Barney Kessel, and Annette Hanshaw. The song was sung on screen by Carleton Carpenter and Debbie Reynolds (dubbed by Kane) in *Three Little Words* (1950), Jane Russell, Rudy Vallee, and Jeanne Crain (dubbed by Anita Ellis) in *Gentlemen Marry Brunettes* (1955), Ann-Margaret in *The Swinger* (1966), and, more recently, British actress Jane Horrocks in *Little Voice* (1998). These interpretations ranged from sly to naïve to lusty, illustrating the ambiguous quality of the song.

The most enduringly famous rendition of the song is surely that of Marilyn Monroe in the film *Some Like It Hot* (1959). Her live version – climaxing with her eyebrows meeting her fringe as she enunciates the diddlee-dee-diddle-dee finale – is the definition of endearing.

Thomas Hischak

Release Date 1928

Nationality USA

Composer Harry Ruby, Herbert Stothard, Bert Kalmar

Why It's Key The number that epitomized the craze for baby-talk numbers in the Roaring Twenties.

Opposite **Marilyn Monroe** in *Some Like it Hot*

106

Key Performance *The Threepenny Opera*
stage musical

For all the reputed lethality of Mack The Knife, the anti-hero of *The Threepenny Opera* doesn't really do anything throughout the show except pursue the easily corruptible ingénue Polly Peachum and express smug pride in his past crimes having been expunged from the official police record. Hardly the heroic proletarian symbol he is posited as.

Why then the fascination the frequently revived *Threepenny* – which debuted in Berlin on August 31, 1928 – continues to have? First, Bertolt Brecht's libretto, filled with spiky and bizarre characters, is a perennially relevant and cohesive socialist critique of the capitalist world and breaches the "fourth wall" to directly confront the ethics of its audience, a self-styled "alienation technique" which is the attractive cornerstone of his imprimatur. Second, the score is easily Kurt Weill's most memorable, and likewise defines the insistently rhythmic and angular style with which he is associated, its heavy American jazz influence put through a distinctly Germanic filter of outrage that almost makes attitude the active main character.

Finally, one can't underestimate the power of an idiosyncratic hit tune. Of all things, "The Ballad Of Mack The Knife" (lyric from the hit 1954 off-Broadway translation by Marc Blitzstein – to date the only hit production of the show in New York), which introduces our caddish hero as a shadowy presence and a stone killer, was transformed by the American singer Bobby Darin, into a hip, chart-busting swing standard.

David Spencer

Opening Night August 31, 1928

Country Germany

Director Erich Engel

Cast Harold Paulsen, Roma Bahn, Lotte Lenya

Composer Bertolt Brecht, Kurt Weill

Why It's Key The only early foreign language musical to ever enter the American repertoire.

Key People **Buddy DeSylva, Lew Brown, and Ray Henderson**

The songwriting team of lyricist Buddy DeSylva (1895–1950), lyricist Lew Brown (1893–1958), and composer Ray Henderson (1896–1970) only worked together for five years but the trio's songs dominated Broadway from 1925 to 1930 and in many cases are still performed today.

They had all worked in Tin Pan Alley before they came together and were well versed in sentimental and nostalgic ballads. They worked on Broadway's *George White's Scandals* of the '20s, their "Birth Of The Blues" emanating from the 1926 production. As their collaboration grew stronger they produced songs that were more sophisticated, insouciant, and clever. "You're The Cream In My Coffee" from the Broadway musical *Hold Everything* which opened on October 10, 1928, is a prime example of their craft.

Brown/Henderson's "Life Is Just A Bowl of Cherries" (1931) has a touch of self-deprecating humor that marked the music of the jazz age. It also has a title that is part of the common language, as does the trio's "The Best Things In Life Are Free."

Although this songwriting team went their separate ways in the '30s, all three made their mark in the heyday of the Hollywood musical when the best songs were written for the movies. Unlike the other masters of Tin Pan Alley, DeSylva, Brown, and Henderson moved with the times and adapted to the new types of popular entertainment. DeSylva was one of the founders of Capitol Records in 1942.

Andre Millard

Role Songwriters

Date 1928

Nationality USA

Why It's Key Their three-pronged attack was temporary but its legacy eternal.

1920-1929

Key Performance
Broadway Melody the movie

Talking movies were the final step for stage performers to shine on the big screen. Now, at last, the vaudeville stars who sang in theaters could sing to audiences all over the world, not just on Broadway. *The Jazz Singer* had already made its mark as the first significant talking picture but when it came to the lavish productions from New York stages, *Broadway Melody*, released on February 1, 1929, was the first to make the transfer to celluloid.

Loosely based on the lives and careers of vaudevillians The Duncan Sisters, the story of young hopefuls trying to make it big and having their fair share of romantic troubles along the way may seem tried and hokey by today's standards but in the days of the first talkies the intertwining songs, plot and dance numbers were groundbreaking.

From the opening number, with lead actor Charles King singing the praises of "The Great White Way," to the huge "Wedding Of The Painted Doll," complete with a line of lavishly dressed girls kicking in unison, it marked the beginning of MGM's vast musical-making machine. It also marked the first all-talking feature for the studio, and was the first talkie to win an Oscar for Best Picture. The songs – written by Arthur Freed and Nacio Herb Brown – commenced Freed's reign over MGM's studios with his hit-churning "Freed Unit" (featuring films with Judy Garland, Frank Sinatra, and Fred Astaire).

Leila Regan-Porter

Movie Release Date February 1, 1929

Country USA

Director Harry Beaumont

Cast Charles King, Bessie Love, Anita Page

Composer Arthur Freed, Nacio Herb Brown

Why It's Key The first all-talking movie musical.

Key Person
Leo Reisman

The '20s saw the emergence of the big bands. These dance bands grew out of the nineteenth-century traditions of Sousa, Creatore, and other brass-heavy martial music. In the '20s with the development of the fox-trot rhythm, their popularity really took off.

Black bands led by Duke Ellington, Cab Calloway, and Count Basie became musically influential. The great white bands of the '20s (for bands weren't integrated yet) were the ensembles of Paul Whiteman, Coon-Sanders Nighthawks, George Olsen, and Leo Reisman. Reisman (1897–1961), a violin player and vocalist, formed his ensemble in 1919. His first No. 1 was "The Wedding of the Painted Doll," which entered the U.S. chart on May 25, 1929. It was Reisman who, in 1931, recorded one of the first 33 ⅓ sets. It contained songs from the Dietz and Schwartz revue *The Band Wagon* and featured stars Fred and Adele Astaire.

The bandleader who bridged the styles of the races was admired by Broadway composers. Jerome Kern dubbed Leo Reisman and his Orchestra band, "The string quartet of dance bands." Cole Porter was also a fan, Reisman's 1932 recording of "Night and Day" being one of the bandleader's greatest successes. Reisman ultimately had over 80 hits, including "Paradise" (1932), "Stormy Weather" (1933), and "The Continental" (1934). His final hit was 1941's "Bewitched," no less than 20 years after his chart debut.
Ken Bloom

Role Recording Artist

Date 1929

Nationality USA

Why It's Key The bandleader who trod a middle road between the jazzy black bands and the sweet white bands to some illustrious acclaim.

Key Person
Andy Razaf

The introduction of the song classic "Ain't Misbehavin" in 1929 was a triumph for one of the finest of all jazz lyricists, the African-American Andy Razaf, who collaborated with some of the most renowned composers of the '20s and '30s.

He was born Andreamennentania Paul Razafinkeriefo in Washington, D.C. in 1895, the nephew of Queen Ranavalona III of Madagascar, and by birth a Grand Duke. He was educated in public schools but studied music privately and began his career writing for nightclubs revues in New York and Chicago in the 1910s. By the Roaring Twenties, Razaf was collaborating with such outstanding black composers as Thomas "Fats" Waller, Eubie Blake, Joe Garland, and James P. Johnson, and scoring the celebrated Broadway shows like *Keep Shufflin'*, *Hot Chocolates*, and *Blackbirds Of 1930*. In addition to "Ain't Misbehavin" (music by Waller), Razaf's other Tin Pan Alley hits include "Honeysuckle Rose," "Stompin' At The Savoy," and "In The Mood."

Despite his noble lineage, Razaf was a master of using black slang and idioms in his lyrics, giving his white listeners an insight into the African-American world that they would not otherwise have. While his songwords' satirical and flippant tone was usually unthreatening, when the gangster Dutch Schultz demanded he write a song from the perspective of a girl unhappy about the lot of a black female, Razaf responded with the disquieting, pained "(What Did I Do To Be So) Black And Blue."
Thomas Hischak

Role Lyricist

Date 1929

Nationality USA

Why It's Key Brought a black sensibility to popular song.

Key Song
"Star Dust"

Among the most performed and recorded songs of the twentieth century, "Star Dust" (sometimes rendered "Stardust") was written as an instrumental composition by Hoagy Carmichael at a class reunion at Indiana University in 1927. Carmichael recorded it for the first time that year at a dance tempo. He also played on the first popular recording, by Irving Mills and His Hotsy Totsy Band. Mills was Carmichael's publisher and it was he who was responsible in 1929 for a quite remarkable reinvention and rejuvenation of the composition by commissioning staff writer Mitchell Parish to provide a lyric (Carmichael had in fact previously devised one but abandoned it).

Parish's words may be a little over the top for some but the public loved the richness of lines such as the one wherein a nightingale tells a fairy tale "of paradise where roses grew." The version that really attracted attention was the one by Isham Jones that slowed the tempo down to ballad speed; it became a U.S. No. 1 hit in April 1931. Bing Crosby's version of this new incarnation with words became a hit in the late summer of 1931. Louis Armstrong, Wayne King, Lee Sims, and Benny Goodman also recorded it but a full list of who covered it would literally run over several pages, for that decision to add words proved amazingly lucrative. "Star Dust" has been ranked as the third-most recorded song published between 1890 and 1954.
William Ruhlmann

Published Date 1927 (melody) 1929 (lyric)

Nationality USA

Composers Hoagy Carmichael, Mitchell Parish

Why It's Key An uptempo instrumental jazz tune gets a new life as a pop ballad.

Opposite **Hoagy Carmichael**

Key Song
"Happy Days Are Here Again"

Some songs take forever to write and some seem to emerge from the writers' pens fully formed. "Happy Days Are Here Again" is one of the latter. In the last week of production of the musical *Chasing Rainbows* (1930), the producer called lyricist Jack Yellen and asked him to write a song for a scene where a group of World War I soldiers receive news of the Armistice. Yellen called upon his old collaborator Milton Ager and the composer came over the next afternoon. Ager asked if Yellen had a title in mind and Yellen spontaneously suggested, "Happy Days Are Here Again." Ager plunked out the first notes that came to mind and Yellen wrote what he later described as "corny lyrics" ("The skies above are clear again"). The only argument the two had was when Ager opined the song's lyric should start with the title and Yellen disagreed with him.

The song was later adopted for the 1932 presidential campaign of Democrat Franklin D. Roosevelt during the height of the Depression. Since then, the Democrats have adopted the song as their own. Journalist Steven Neal's book about the 1932 Democratic convention and how FDR became president was called *Happy Days Are Here Again*.

The song was recorded by Leo Reisman in November 1929 and subsequently almost 100 albums have featured it. One of the most notable versions is that of Barbra Streisand who, in 1963, slowed down the tempo with intriguing results.
Ken Bloom

Published Date November 1929

Nationality USA

Composers Milton Ager, Jack Yellen

Why It's Key The apolitical song that came to be associated with a political party.

Key Person
Dorothy Fields

"On The Sunny Side Of The Street," which Ted Lewis took into the U.S. chart on April 5, 1930, is one of the best-remembered songs of lyricist-librettist Dorothy Fields. These days it is a cliché to talk of a woman making her way in a man's world but Fields (1905–1974) genuinely did that.

Dorothy Fields was born to a famous theatrical family. She began writing lyrics as a student and by 1928 her songs were heard in nightclubs and Broadway revues. For *The International Revue* (1930), Fields collaborated with composer Jimmy McHugh and wrote "On The Sunny Side Of The Street," one of the earliest and best of the flock of cheery '30s anti-Depression songs.

Fields' particular talent was for lyrics that were both sophisticated and down-to-earth, giving a refreshing slant to clichés and everyday expressions. Witness, from the breathless "If My Friends Could See Me Now," "What a set-up, holy cow!" She even sometimes invented phrases, such as "I don't pop my cork for every guy I see" in the raunchy "Big Spender." She was the first woman to win an Oscar for Best Song with her Jerome Kern collaboration "The Way You Look Tonight." Fields was also an adept librettist, coauthoring such Broadway musicals as *Up In Central Park* (1945) and *Annie Get Your Gun* (1946). She was still writing lyrics for Broadway shows in the '60s and '70s, such as *Sweet Charity* (1966) and *Seesaw* (1973).
Thomas Hischak

Role Lyricist

Date 1930

Nationality USA

Why It's Key A rare distaff songwriting presence in Broadway and in Hollywood.

Key Performance *The Blue Angel*
the movie

German director Josef von Sternberg wanted his movie *Der Blaue Engel* to be an international hit and tried unsuccessfully to get Gloria Swanson and other widely known actresses to be in it. Instead he chose unknown German Marlene Dietrich, a student from the local acting academy, and filmed the movie both in German and English. Dietrich played a nightclub singer named Lola who seduces, marries, then destroys Rath, a stodgy school teacher (Emil Jennings).

Friedrich Hollander wrote a handful of original songs for Lola to sing at the club, most memorably the world weary "Ich Bin Von Kopf Bis Fuss Auf Liebe Eingstellt" ("Falling In Love Again"). Dietrich delivered the number in her low, slurring voice, leaning lazily on a chair, looking bored and tired but effortlessly sexy too. The film – released in the United States on April 1, 1930 – was a sensation on two continents, partly because it was such a powerful early talkie. Dietrich was whisked off to Hollywood. Dietrich's recording of "Falling In Love Again" (given an English lyric by Sammy Lerner) became a bestseller. She sang it throughout her long career as her signature song, her German tones only adding to its sensuality.

That decision to settle for a local girl for the movie certainly proved fortunate: any English language rendition of "Falling In Love Again" now sounds somehow wrong if not performed with an accent that indicates English is the singer's second language.
Thomas Hischak

Movie Release Date April 1, 1930

Country Germany

Original Title *Der Blaue Engel*

Director Josef Von Sternberg

Cast Marlene Dietrich, Emil Jannings, Kurt Gerron

Composer Friedrich Hollander, Sammy Lerner

Why It's Key Generated a famous song whose foreign inflections only added to its appeal.

Opposite **Marlene Dietrich** in *The Blue Angel*

Key Song
"Georgia On My Mind"

The composition of "Georgia On My Mind" in 1930 introduced one of the few Tin Pan Alley songs of the era that crossed over to be sung by blues, folk, jazz, and pop singers.

Someone suggested to Hoagy Carmichael that he write a song about the state of Georgia. However when he and lyricist Stuart Gorrell collaborated on the number, they fashioned it with Carmichael's sister Georgia in mind. Yet the lyric is ambiguous enough that the number can be a lament about the loss of a sweetheart named Georgia or a homesick ballad about the Southern state. Whether intended or not, both homesick ex-residents of the state were now guaranteed to buy it as well as beaus of girls called Georgia as an unimaginative present.

"Georgia On My Mind" is a very conversational number and performers sometimes talk-sing the heartfelt lyric. A 1931 recording by Frankie Trumbauer popularized the song and there were other early recordings of note by Mildred Bailey and Louis Armstrong, among others. Interest in the slow and lazy ballad was revived by Ray Charles in 1960 with a version that made U.S. No. 1. It is generally considered the definitive rendition of the number. As recently as 1990, Michael Bolton took a version into the U.S. top 40.

The issue of what the song is about was sort of settled in 1979: in that year, it was adopted by Georgia as official state song.

Thomas Hischak

Release Date 1930

Nationality USA

Composers Hoagy Carmichael, Stuart Gorrell

Why It's Key Illustrates the doubled commercial viability engendered by ambiguity.

Key Song "Our Don Bradman"
Art Leonard

Though an enigma to much of the globe, the sport of cricket exercises an almost religious power on its devotees and in Australia, a land particularly obsessed by the game, no cricketing name is more sainted than that of the late Sir Donald Bradman. "The Don" is routinely regarded as the finest batsman who ever lived. His batting average in international Test matches of 99.94 still stands.

1930 was the year Bradman's star turned supernova, with a then world-record Test score of 334. Intuiting the seismic impact of what was going on and distilling the moment into song, in that year writer Jack O'Hagan, through the mouthpiece of recording artist Art Leonard, combined the traditions of the music hall and the methodologies of folk music to hymn this fast-rising superstar.

After positing the question of who all of Australia is raving about and then suggesting there are those who might conclude it is airwoman Amy Johnson or cartoon character Mickey Mouse, O'Hagan reveals, "No, it's just a country lad who's bringing down the house." Such quasi-lyrical fatuousness hints at the fact that their creation is not exactly a milestone in artistic achievement, something underlined by the recording's tinny orchestra and careful enunciation. But Leonard's ditty was one that showed that pop music could do for stars of sport what folk did for medieval knights, and turn contemporary heroes into immortal legends.

Angus Batey

Release Date 1930

Nationality Australian

Composer Jack O'Hagan

Why It's Key An early crossover between those twin great pleasures of the ordinary man – popular song and sport.

Opposite **Don Bradman**

Key Person
Bing Crosby

By the time "Out of Nowhere" entered the U.S. charts on the April 25, 1931 – on its way to becoming his first No.1 – Bing Crosby was already a popular entertainer Stateside. But 1931 saw the young artist take the first steps on what would become an unprecedentedly successful solo singing career.

Crosby had turned professional in the '20s, prior to which the dominant popular vocal style had emerged from vaudeville. Stars of this earlier era, such as Al Jolson, needed to really work to project their voices to the back of the theaters in which they performed. But the start of Crosby's career coincided with the pioneering use of microphones, both in public performance and (in more sophisticated form) in the recording studio. This development enabled singers to create an intimate performance on recordings; Crosby's mellow baritone was ideally suited to the new technology, while his familiarity with the work of contemporary jazz styles helped him to evolve a distinctive, seemingly casual approach to phrasing. This unfussy but sophisticated style soon came to epitomize a new vocal genre – "crooning."

The same year that "Out of Nowhere" hit the top, Crosby launched himself as a solo vocalist, backed by the Carl Fenton Orchestra, on a CBS radio show. Crooning – which permitted a far more personal connection between performer and listener – was ideally suited to radio, and Crosby was a smash. The laid-back legend was up and running.
Robert Dimery

Date 1931

Nationality USA

Why It's Key Epitomized a new type of singing on record.

Opposite Bing Crosby

116

Key Song "Minnie The Moocher"
Cab Calloway

Songs that provided opportunity for a reply or echoing effect from the audience or listener were popularized with this scat singing classic in which even the recordings had members of the band singing out the repeats.

The number has always been associated with Cab Calloway, who wrote it with Irving Mills and Clarence Gaskill. Calloway introduced it with his band in the Cotton Club in Harlem, recorded it as his first disc, and reprised it on radio, in films, on television, and in concerts for over 50 years. The song is a narrative piece, telling the story of "hoochie coocher" Minnie who is loved by Smokey who takes her to parties in Chinatown and showers her with gifts. But big-hearted Minnie ends up going crazy, is put in a mental asylum, and dies. The morose story is contrasted by the red-hot music and the repeated phrase "Hi-de-hi-de-hi-de-hi," which audiences couldn't help but gleefully chant back. The latter and other scat sounds lend a primitive, tribal flavor to the song. Calloway's 1931 disc entered the U.S. charts on March 21, 1931 and he became known as the "Hi-De-Ho Man." The number is often listed as "The Hi-De-Ho Song."

Although it was always thought of as Calloway's exclusive domain, "Minnie The Moocher" was recorded by Adelaide Hall, the Mills Blue Rhythm Band, Duke Ellington, and even Danny Kaye.

Larry Marshall played a young Calloway singing the song in the film *The Cotton Club* (1984).
Thomas Hischak

Release Date March 1931

Nationality USA

Composer Cab Calloway, Irving Mills, Clarence Gaskill

Why It's Key The classic "call-and-response" number.

Key People
Flanagan and Allen

Though primarily comedians, Bud Flanagan and Chesney Allen were also hitmakers, their music steeped in working class London life. Yet despite their apparent parochialism, they crossed boundaries. During World War II, an American DJ played their record "Underneath The Arches" six times over and it became an international success.

Bud Flanagan cowrote "Underneath The Arches" in 1926 as a comment on friendship and poverty. Flanagan sang the song with Allen, as was his trademark style, doing little more than speaking his lines. It became one of their best-known songs, along with "Run Rabbit Run" and "Shine On Harvest Moon."

In November 1931 the impresario Val Parnell had the concept of putting Flanagan and Allen together with fellow popular British music hall entertainers "Monsewer" Eddie Gray, Jimmy Nervo, Teddy Knox, Charlie Naughton, and Jimmy Gold, billing them as the Crazy Gang for a London Palladium revue. The show was a tremendous success and although they still worked separately, the Gang appeared together for over 20 years.

Flanagan later sang the theme song for BBC television's long-running wartime comedy *Dad's Army*, a song that sounds like it was written as a tribute to the morale raising style that Flanagan and Allen used in the wartime number "We're Going To Hang Out The Washing On The Siegfried Line."

Chip Hawkes of the Tremeloes liked Chesney Allen's Christian name so much that he gave it to his son, himself later a No. 1 hitmaker.
Spencer Leigh

Role Recording Artists

Date 1931

Nationality UK

Why It's Key Asserted the validity of their own culture as American songs grew ever more pervasive.

118

Key Person
Howard Dietz

Howard Dietz (1896–1983) was the primary lyricist for 15 musicals that played on Broadway between 1924 and 1963. He wrote sketches and librettos for those shows, and he sometimes directed them, too. He also wrote and produced films and translated operas.

Yet Dietz actually had a full-time day job running the publicity and advertising department of movie company Metro-Goldwyn-Mayer. In that capacity, he came up with Leo the Lion as the growling corporate logo, as well as the motto "Ars Gratia Artis" (roughly Latin for "Art for Art's Sake").

Although he collaborated with composers including George Gershwin and Jerome Kern, Dietz was best known for the musical revues he wrote with Arthur Schwartz, particularly *The Little Show* (1929), *Three's A Crowd* (1930), *The Band Wagon* (1931), *Flying Colors* (1932), *At Home Abroad* (1935), and *Inside U.S.A.* (1948). These shows threw off such song hits as "Moanin' Low," "I Guess I'll Have To Change My Plan," "Something To Remember You By," and "Dancing In The Dark." *The Band Wagon*, which ran for 260 performances (a healthy number in the early '30s) after its opening on June 3, 1931, marked the final appearance of the team of Fred and Adele Astaire before she retired and he went solo. Twenty-two years later, Fred Astaire starred in a successful film adaptation of *The Band Wagon* for which Dietz and Schwartz wrote another song standard, "That's Entertainment."
William Ruhlmann

Role Songwriter

Date 1931

Nationality USA

Why It's Key Fine lyricist whose songwriting was almost moonlighting.

Key Performance *Cavalcade*
stage musical

Noel Coward, the urbane chronicler of the upper crust, was Britain's preeminent hyphenate: playwright-songwriter-performer. As a songwriter, he was regarded by many as the British Cole Porter.

Coward's plays were smart, sophisticated comedies of manners, although with few exceptions his musical revues and humorous musical shows did not cross to America. One of his greatest successes was the pageant *Cavalcade*, which opened on October 13, 1931. The show was a patriotic tableau incorporating traditional music hall songs as well as a new song by Coward, "Twentieth Century Blues." The latter title gives a idea of the plot, which traced the lives of two families, one well-off, the other poor, from the turn of the twentieth century to the (then) present, with the events of the day viewed from the perspective of the protagonists, including World Wars I, the death of Queen Victoria, and the sinking of the Titanic.

A film version (1933) won an Oscar for Best Picture and that version is the one by which *Cavalcade* is destined to be remembered, for the show's scale and sweep has prohibited full-scale revivals. However, its impact at the time cannot be denied. It premiered shortly before the British general election and it is said its patriotic tone helped the Conservative Party win several seats. Cavalcade also lost Coward some friends who were dismayed that this previously iconoclastic-seeming, anti-war figure should depict the workers as happily servile.
Ken Bloom

Opening Night
October 13, 1931

Country UK

Director Noel Coward

Cast John Mills, Binnie Barnes, Arthur Macrae

Composer Noel Coward

Why It's Key The musical that helped decide a general election.

1930-1939

Key Song
"Goodnight Sweetheart"

Ray Noble, Jimmy Campbell, and Reg Connelly collaborated on this flowing standard that offers comfort to a dear one, asking her not to cry as they part and promising that "sleep will banish sorrow." There is a lullaby quality to the number, yet it has a continuous, even insistent, pattern that defines the fox trot song. It was introduced in the UK where Henry Hall's BBC Orchestra played it on the radio in 1931. Rudy Vallee introduced the song to American audiences the same year with a best-selling record, and it was quickly interpolated into the Broadway revue *Earl Carroll's Vanities Of 1931*, where it was sung by Milton Watson and Woods Miller.

Of the many subsequent recordings, the most successful were those by Al Bowlly and by Guy Lombardo and the Royal Canadians. Amongst movies to feature the song were *Stardust On The Sage* (1942, sung by Gene Autry), and *Stage Door Canteen* (1943, a rendition by Kenny Baker). For obvious reasons, the song was often chosen as the final number of the evening in dance halls, nightclubs, and concerts.

The song's title was used for a popular BBC television comedy series that ran from 1993 to 1999 that depicted a time traveling man who lives parallel lives in World War II and the then present day. Naturally the song was the program's theme tune.
Thomas Hischak

Date 1931

Nationality UK

Composers Ray Noble, Jimmy Campbell, Reg Connelly

Why It's Key The public's attachment to this gentle farewell song helped turn the fox trot into the preferred tempo for romantic songs in the '30s.

Key Person
Maurice Chevalier

The release of the film musical *Love Me Tonight* on August 13, 1932 secured the reputation of French performer Maurice Chevalier. Chevalier was the quintessential Parisian singer, exuding a carefree, romantic, and bemused attitude in all that he did, epitomized by the straw boater he wore however formal the rest of his dress.

He was born in the French capital in 1888 to a poor family and struggled with various jobs before finding fame as a comic singer at the Folies-Bergère in 1909. By 1929 he was over in Hollywood appearing in movie musicals such as *Innocents Of Paris* (1929). He was apparently fully aware of the power of his Gallic charm: he instructed the film's composers Whiting and Robin to bear in mind his French accent and it was this that made them alight on the name "Louise," which became one of his signature songs, just as his accent became a trademark in his performing style.

Love Me Tonight introduced another signature song, "Isn't It Romantic?" If "Thank 'Eaven For Leetle Girls" (as it were) from *Gigi* (1958) skirted self-parody, it was knowingly and the song was adored enough for Americans to forgive him over erroneous reports of Second World War "collaboration."

Although both his singing voice and acting talents were limited, Chevalier had a stage persona that was bigger than life. A last hurrah before his death in 1972 was the accolade of singing the title tune to the 1970 Disney movie *The Aristocats*.

Thomas Hischak

Role Recording Artist

Date August 13, 1932

Nationality France

Why It's Key Injected Gallic charm into world pop.

Key Person
Ted Lewis

One of America's best-loved performers, Ted Lewis (1890–1971) brought audiences to their feet when he asked, "Is everybody happy?" The self-proclaimed "Medicine Man for Your Blues" specialized in novelty syncopated tunes.

Though Lewis played the clarinet on his first recording in 1917 with Earl Fuller's Jazz Band, the instrument was really just as much a prop as his battered top hat. The admittedly schmaltzy Lewis might not have been a great instrumentalist but he knew enough to hire the top clarinetists, including Benny Goodman, Jimmy Dorsey, and Don Murray. His jazz credentials were also supported by trumpeter Muggsy Spanier, pianist Fats Waller, and trombonist George Brunis. Lewis's signature tune was "Me And My Shadow" and he also popularized "When My Baby Smiles at Me" (which he cowrote) and "I'm a Musical, Magical Man."

Lewis and the band appeared on hundreds of radio and television shows. Though tastes in music changed, like many of his era, Ted Lewis remained popular through the decades. His "In A Shanty In Old Shanty Town," which entered the U.S. chart on June 4, 1932, was a 10-week chart topper fully 12 years after his first No. 1. He and his band were appearing in Las Vegas into the '60s. There were three movies with or about Lewis spanning 1929 to 1943. All were titled *Is Everybody Happy?*

Ken Bloom

Role Recording Artist

Date 1932

Nationality USA

Why It's Key Bandleader who was no virtuoso but knew his musical onions.

Key Song
"Brother Can You Spare A Dime?"

Lyricist E. Y. Harburg knew about poverty, having grown up on the Lower East Side of Manhattan. As he said, "I know what it is for a neighbor to come and ask for a piece of bread." The great Depression precipitated by the stock market crash of 1929 made life for the poor even more hard. One day during its grip, when Harburg and his first songwriting collaborator Jay Gorney were walking through New York's Central Park, they were accosted by one of the heartbreaking sights that were then commonplace: a beggar asked them, "Buddy, can you spare a dime?".

Substituting the word "brother" for "buddy," Harburg span off a classic lyric in whose chorus the narrator counterpointed each line detailing his past hard work ("Once I built a railroad, now it's done"), with the title phrase. Harburg's references to khaki suits and being told of building a dream with peace and glory ahead made clear his disgust for the way that those who had fought for their country in World War I were now being discarded by it. Jay Gorney teased out the lyric's aching sadness with a slow, mordant melody.

The song debuted in Broadway revue *Americana*, which opened on October 5, 1932. Both Rudy Vallee and Bing Crosby had number one hits with the song. Coming out just before the presidential election of Franklin Delano Roosevelt, the song became a rallying cry for a change in the American political landscape.
Ken Bloom

Release Date
October 5, 1932

Nationality USA

Composers Jay Gorney, E. Y. Harburg

Why It's Key Practically the official anthem of the Depression.

Key Song
"The Teddy Bears' Picnic"

As discussed elsewhere in this book, there are many examples in pop music history of instrumental compositions that had lyrics added later. Few such processes were quite as inspired as that attending the evolution of "The Teddy Bears' Picnic."

The jaunty tune was written by Broadway and Tin Pan Alley composer John W. Bratton (1867–1947), who was inspired by the name for a toy bear cub first used in 1902 by the cartoonist C. K. Berryman in reference to President Theodore ('Teddy') Roosevelt's love of hunting. Published by Witmark in 1907, it achieved immediate popularity.

Yet however pleasant and whistle-able the melody was, there was nothing about it to particularly make one think of teddy bears or picnics. When in 1932 British songwriter James B. Kennedy (1902–1984) devised a lyric, he achieved the quite amazing feat of doing so in a manner that was so free of contrivance that it sounded like the new words were always meant to be. His clever tricks like the line-ending rhyming of "there was" and "because" was swept along delightfully by the original tune and he deftly side-stepped trying to shoe-horn in the title where it wouldn't go by making the refrain not the title phrase but "Today's the day the teddy bears have their picnic."

An updated "The Teddy Bears' Picnic" was recorded by Henry Hall, transforming the 25-year-old song into a four-million seller and an evergreen.
William Ruhlmann

Published 1907 (music), 1932 (lyric)

Nationality USA/UK

Composers John W. Bratton, James B. Kennedy

Why It's Key The song whose added lyric sounded like it had been separated from the melody at birth.

My Best wishes
To Doc Turner!
From
Louis Armstrong
3/20/33

JOHNNY COLLINS
PRESENTS
THE INTERNATIONAL
STAR
LOUIS ARMSTRONG

Key Person
Louis Armstrong

Louis Armstrong revolutionized jazz with a talent for improvisation on the trumpet that had never been heard before he arrived in Chicago from his native New Orleans in August 1922 at the age of 21. Engaged to play with a band led by his mentor, King Oliver, Armstrong made his first recordings under his own name three years later, leading bands called the Hot Five or Hot Seven. These tracks are among the most revered in jazz history.

Armstrong was not just a great instrumentalist, however. Although his singing voice was not technically great, in performance it was a marvel of expressiveness. Deep and gravelly, his vocals matched his trumpet playing in its sly departures from the melody, as well as employing phrasing that toyed with and gently mocked the lyrics of the songs he sang. They were also of a piece with his ingratiating, comic persona, which helped make him a star far beyond the field of jazz. In a career that extended until his death

at 69 in 1971, he became a mainstream entertainer featured in films and on television, with a string of popular recordings.

Jazz purists were not pleased with Armstrong's more entertaining qualities, and were not impressed with performances like his rendition of the pop standard "All Of Me," but that didn't keep it from becoming his first U.S. No. 1 on February 20, 1932.
William Ruhlmann

Role Recording Artist

Date 1932

Nationality USA

Why It's Key One of the great pop vocalists of the twentieth century and quite possibly the most important jazz musician of all time.

Opposite **Louis Armstrong**

Key Event
Death of Jimmie Rodgers

The tuberculosis that claimed Jimmie Rodgers' life on May 26, 1933, was the result of his years spent working on the railroads. But those railroads were the subjects of his songs and those songs thereby helped break country music out of a ghetto in which traditionally only the daily concerns of mountain folk were addressed.

Rodgers – born 1897 and raised in Meridian, Mississippi – melded folk songs with the blues, also adding the unique selling point of yodeling. Dubbed "The singing brakeman" because of his discussion and mythologizing of the railroads, his recording career started in 1927 when he auditioned for Ralph Peer at Victor Records. His prolific songwriting ability produced a string of timeless hits like "T For Texas, T For Tennessee," "Waiting For A Train" (later covered by Boz Scaggs with Duane Allman, who, like Bob Dylan, was an admirer of Rodgers), and "In The Jailhouse Now" (covered by Webb Pierce and Johnny Cash,

among others). Many of his songs used the title of "Blue Yodel," plus a number – for example, "Mule Skinner Blues" was known as "Blue Yodel #8" – and it is widely felt that had he enjoyed better health, he could easily have continued reaching the U.S. pop charts, where he enjoyed eight hits during his lifetime, including 1928's million-selling "Blue Yodel" (aka "T For Texas").

Rodgers retrospectively became known as "The Father Of Country Music" and he inspired many later country stars, including Hank Snow, Ernest Tubb, and Gene Autry.
John Tobler

Date May 26, 1933

Country USA

Why It's Key A death inextricably bound up with the artist's innovations.

Key Person
Al Dubin

Al Dubin (born 1891) was born in Zurich, Switzerland, and emigrated to America at the age of two. After serving in World War I, he started working for music publishers in New York but found greater success in Hollywood where he began scoring early movie musicals with composer Joe Burke.

Dubin's most productive collaborator was Harry Warren and together they wrote songs for the Gold Diggers and other Depression-era musicals. His most celebrated Depression-era song was "We're In The Money," introduced by Ginger Rodgers in *Gold Diggers Of 1933*, released on May 27 1933. The almost ridiculously catchy and perky number, which sarcastically boasted of spending power in an era where few had any ("We never see a headline about breadlines today"), immediately appealed to the public and is still widely known.

His lyrics could be romantic, slangy, optimistic, torchy, or silly, as seen in such standards as "I Only Have Eyes For You," "Forty-Second Street," "You're Getting To Be A Habit With Me," "Tip Toe Through The Tulips," "Painting The Clouds With Sunshine," "With Plenty Of Money And You," "Shuffle Off To Buffalo," and "Lullaby Of Broadway," the latter an Academy Award winner in 1935.

Ironically for someone who was able to ride the Depression by dint of his talent, Dubin succumbed to the vices to which many resort to escape their financial misfortunes: after a lifetime of alcoholism, over-eating, and drug abuse, he died an untimely death in 1945.
Thomas Hischak

Role Lyricist

Date 1933

Nationality USA

Why It's Key Lyricist who became the unofficial voice for '30s escapist popular music.

Opposite *Gold Diggers Of 1933*

124

Key Person
Otto Harbach

Lyricist-librettist Otto Harbach (1873–1963) was one of the first songwriters to strive for precise, careful lyrics that were integrated into Broadway shows. Though little known today, he authored fifty musicals and the success of his still renowned ballad "Smoke Gets In Your Eyes" has outlived him.

He was born Otto Hauerbach in Salt Lake City and began a college teaching career before going to New York in 1901 to work on a doctorate at Columbia but his money ran out so, in his mid-thirties, he turned to writing scripts and lyrics for Broadway. By 1910 he had a major hit with *Madame Sherry* (music by Karl Hoschna), which introduced "Every Little Movement (Has A Meaning Of Its Own)." Because of anti-German sentiments during World War I, he changed his name to Harbach and went on to score popular musicals with Vincent Youmans, Jerome Kern, Rudolf Friml, and Sigmund Romberg. To his young pupil Oscar Hammerstein, he preached the importance of carefully thought-out lyrics and logical librettos in which the songs were interwoven into the plot. Yet while Hammerstein would become massively celebrated, Harbach rarely enjoyed his levels of success. Though his musical with Kern, *Roberta*, which debuted on November 18, 1933, was not well-received, the song it introduced, "Smoke Gets In Your Eyes," was an immediate hit on the radio and it was filmed with Astaire and Rogers in 1935. The song illustrates Harbach at his best: poetic, haunting, and sophisticated.
Thomas Hischak

Role Lyricist

Date 1933

Nationality USA

Why It's Key The man who began writing songs because he was broke.

Key Person
Ray Noble

Multi-talented Ray Noble (1903–1978) was a famous bandleader, noted composer, actor, and arranger. In his native UK, he began his career as the leader of the New Mayfair Dance Orchestra, the house band for HMV Records. The band's recording debut came in 1929. Noble's collaborations with singer Al Bowlly helped define the British sound to American audiences and Noble soon found himself leading separate bands in the UK and the United States.

His first U.S. No. 1 was "Love Is The Sweetest Thing," which entered the chart on July 15, 1933. It was written by Noble, as was another great hit of his, "Cherokee." His great standard "The Very Thought of You" is probably the best-known of his compositions. Previous to the success of that song, it was probably "Goodnight, Sweetheart." Other notable recordings include "The Touch of Your Lips" and "I Hadn't Anyone Til You."

Noble showed up in a number of English and American films. He appeared with his orchestra in The Big Broadcast of 1936, The Pride of the Yankees (1942), and Lake Placid Serenade (1944). He also played a part in the Gershwin brothers film musical, Damsel In Distress (1937). Noble acted on radio too; he was a regular on The Burns and Allen Show, where he also led his band. Noble was the regular bandleader on the Edgar Bergen and Charlie McCarthy radio show.
Ken Bloom

Role Recording Artist

Date 1933

Nationality USA

Why It's Key One of the only British bandleaders to achieve fame on the American side of the Atlantic.

Key Performance
42nd Street the movie

Based loosely on the grittier novel by former hoofer Bradford Ropes, black and white movie *42nd Street* told exactly the kind of rags-to-riches story America desired during the Depression Era. And if it didn't define the archetypes – ailing producer (Warner Baxter), rookie chorine (Ruby Keeler), incapacitated headliner (Bebe Daniels), goldigger chorine (Ginger Rogers), and sleazy sugar daddy (Guy Kibbee) – it at least immortalized them.

Though the narrative segments were originally assigned to Mervyn LeRoy, illness led to his being replaced by Lloyd (*Footlight Parade*) Bacon. Technically less proficient than LeRoy, Bacon nonetheless had a then-rare instinct for cinematic pace and built compellingly to the final reel's full burnished musical numbers (only hinted at earlier in the movie). These were iconically directed and choreographed by Busby Berkeley in a manner that was lavish and gaudy, innocent and erotic, his use of the camera as inventive as the colossal geometry of his dance patterns.

Songwriters Al Dubin (lyrics) and Harry Warren (music) – who appear in a cameo as, what else, beleaguered songwriters – contributed numbers that still remain recognizable standards: "Shuffle Off To Buffalo," the peppy "Young And Healthy," the addictive "You're Getting To Be A Habit With Me," and the title song – a racy, roaring inducement in minor.

In 1980, *42nd Street* was refashioned as a Broadway stage musical (the script reconceived for the interpolation of additional Warren-Dubin songs) that ran for 3,486 performances.
David Spencer

Movie Premier Date February 2, 1933

Country USA

Director Lloyd Bacon

Cast Warner Baxter, Ruby Keeler, Ginger Rogers, Guy Kibbee

Composer Al Dubin, Harry Warren

Why It's Key The backstage musical that defined backstage musicals.

Key Song **"Stormy Weather"**
Harold Arlen

When one thinks of "Stormy Weather," composer Harold Arlen and lyricist Ted Koehler's classic bluesy lament, one also thinks of Lena Horne. But Arlen and Koehler wrote "Stormy Weather" with a completely different performer in mind. It was devised for Cab Calloway to perform in *The Cotton Club Revue* of Spring 1933. So tailor made was it for him that it begins with his trademark "Hi-de-ho" phrase, here using the words "Don't know why." The song continues with an unusual 36-bar blues melody in which the singer relates romantic disappointment to overall depression ("Gloom and mis'ry everywhere") as well as unstable climactic conditions. But Calloway dropped out of the revue, and Arlen himself introduced the song in a recording that entered the U.S. charts on March 25, 1933 and hit No. 1. Guy Lombardo recorded a cover version, and the song went into *The Cotton Club Revue* sung by Ethel Waters, who also had a U.S. No. 1 with it and claimed it for a while as her signature

song. Versions by Duke Ellington and Ted Lewis also charted in 1933.

Lena Horne made a claim to "Stormy Weather" by recording it in 1941. That claim was consolidated by her starring role in the 1943 movie *Stormy Weather*, in which she sang it as the Katherine Dunham troupe danced. Thereafter, Horne sang the song continually, including in her triumphant 1981 Broadway revue *Lena Horne: A Lady And Her Music*.

William Ruhlmann

First Released 1933

Nationality USA

Composers Harold Arlen, Ted Koehler

Why It's Key The number written for Cab Calloway that ended up as a Lena Horne signature song.

1930-1939

Key Person
Cole Porter

Cole Porter (1891–1964), the urbane, worldly composer/lyricist, hailed from Peru, Indiana. He was the epitome of soignée wit in the '30s. His songs were usually of a markedly higher level of sophistication than the plots of the shows in which they appeared.

Porter came from a well-to-do family but was disinclined to work in the coal and timber industries like his grandfather. By the age of ten, having learnt both violin and piano, he was writing operettas. Though he was pushed into law early on, he had already written 300 songs before he enrolled at Harvard Law School so it was perhaps inevitable that he would transfer into Arts and Sciences.

Porter could write both sinuous ballads ("Night and Day," "Begin The Beguine," "Love For Sale") and delightful "list" songs full of up-to-date references and sometimes incredibly shocking double entendres: "Let's Do It," "You're the Top," and the title tune of *Anything*

Goes, which opened on November 21, 1934, and featured another of his classics, "I Get A Kick Out Of You." During this run of hits, Porter suffered a fall from a horse that crushed both his legs. A virtual cripple, he endured constant pain and over 30 operations, finally undergoing an amputation in 1957.

Around the World (1946) was a failure but after a two-year absence from Broadway he returned with his greatest work, *Kiss Me, Kate*.

Ken Bloom

Role Songwriter

Date 1934

Nationality USA

Why It's Key The man who transported the victims of the Depression with the glamour, fantasy, and filth of his songs.

Key Person
Duke Ellington

When Duke Ellington's recording of the Coslow-Johnston song "Cocktails for Two" entered the charts on May 5 1934, it was a surprise, for the renowned African American artist was mostly known for his own compositions. Perhaps it shouldn't have been a surprise, for Ellington was also intelligent enough to know the limits of the composer: he devised songs that enabled his band members to contribute distinctive solos.

In the late '20s, Duke Ellington was a composer, band leader and pianist whose variety and innovations were distinctive. He was born Edward Kennedy in Washington, D.C. in 1899 and began his music career playing piano with local groups. He formed his own band in 1923 and was soon playing in New York City clubs, most importantly the Cotton Club in Harlem beginning in 1927. It was there he developed the "jungle sound" of jazz, using muted instruments and growl techniques to create a sleek but passionate concoction. Ellington's band was soon on the radio, on Broadway playing Gershwin music in *Show Girl* (1929), and on screen performing in *Check And Double Check* (1930). That same year his own celebrated composition, "Mood Indigo" was introduced, followed by "It Don't Mean a Thing If It Ain't Got That Swing," "Sophisticated Lady," "Take the A Train," and other smooth jazz classics.

Ellington, whose band remained popular into the '60s, died in 1974. His music was celebrated in the Broadway revue *Sophisticated Ladies* (1981).

Thomas Hischak

Role Recording Artist

Date 1934

Nationality USA

Why It's Key Pioneer in developing a more refined kind of jazz.

Opposite Duke Ellington and his band

Key People
Rodgers and Hart

Composer Richard Rodgers (1902–1979) first teamed up with lyricist Lorenz Hart (1895–1943) in 1920. The pair became famous when their song "Manhattan" was introduced in the Broadway revue *The Garrick Gaieties* (1925). They had a string of stage hits in the '20s and '30s, as well as a handful of films. The team were known for their fresh, lively songs that could be slangy or romantic in tone, or both. Of the hundreds of tunes that Rodgers and Hart wrote for Broadway and Hollywood, their single greatest hit was "Blue Moon," a sentimental, operetta-like ballad very atypical of their work. It was introduced in the movie *Manhattan Melodrama*, which was released in 1934.

Among their other great songs are "Mountain Greenery," "Ten Cents A Dance," "Dancing On The Ceiling," "The Most Beautiful Girl In The World," "My Funny Valentine," "The Lady Is A Tramp," and "Bewitched, Bothered And Bewildered."

Their working relationship was a strained one. Hart was short of stature, self conscious of his looks, and an unhappy homosexual who often turned to alcohol and drugs. By the early '40s, Hart was so unreliable that Rodgers started looking for a new partner. Hart died of alcoholism in 1943, the same year that Rodgers first teamed up with Oscar Hammerstein. Ironically, the quality of Hart's writing did not diminish as his life unraveled. The last lyric he wrote, "To Keep My Love Alive," is as fresh and masterful as any in his catalog.

Thomas Hischak

Role Composer (Rodgers) and Lyricist (Hart)

Date 1934

Nationality USA

Why It's Key The team who made beautiful music together professionally but were discordant privately.

Key Song
"Deep Purple"

Mitchell Parish was key to turning an instrumental piece into a popular song hit on more than one occasion. Having made "Star Dust" immortal by adding words to its existing tune, he did the same thing again a decade later with this enduring standard.

Composer Peter DeRose wrote "Deep Purple" as a lilting instrumental piece in 1934 and it was introduced by Paul Whiteman's Orchestra with modest success. In 1939 Parish added a torchy lyric about watching the sky turn purple and the stars come out, all of it reminding one of a lost love who appears in "deep purple dreams." The new version was popularized by Larry Clinton's Orchestra and each decade for the next 40 years would see a revival of interest in the romantic song. Success was achieved with it in the '40s (Bing Crosby), the '50s (Billy Ward and his Dominoes), the '60s (Nino Tempo and April Stevens), and the '70s (Donny and Marie Osmond). Of the many others who recorded the number, Doris Roberts used it as the theme song on her radio show and billed herself as the "Deep Purple Girl." The song was also a favorite of baseball legend Babe Ruth, who had DeRose come and sing it to him on his birthday during the last ten years of Ruth's life.

More recently, though it was hardly a part of their repertoire, a group of heavy metal merchants named themselves after the song.

Thomas Hischak

Date 1934

Nationality USA

Composer Peter DeRose, Mitchell Parish

Why It's Key Lyricist works his enhancement magic again.

130

Key Song
"On The Good Ship Lollipop"

Richard A. Whiting began his composing career in the 1910s and '20s writing mainly with Raymond B. Egan. He went to Hollywood in 1929 and teamed up with Leo Robin at Paramount Pictures. In 1933, he moved to Fox where he was most often partnered with staff lyricist, Sidney Clare. At Fox the duo wrote for the leading star at the time, Shirley Temple, the little girl whose pictures literally saved Fox from bankruptcy during the Depression.

The two were assigned the Temple vehicle, *Bright Eyes*. In the film, the child's birthday party is held on an airplane. While cavorting on the plane, Shirley was meant to sing a song. Struggling to find a number for Temple, inspiration struck Whiting one day when his daughter came into his room with a big, sticky lollipop. She managed to get her father, his piano, and his music sticky. Remonstrating with her, Whiting suddenly stopped in mid-sentence and rushed to the phone to inform Clare, "I've got the title!"

The resulting song saw Miss Temple insisting that she would grow up to be a pilot and would have an aircraft named Lollipop. Clare's actually somewhat surreal lyric sees her imagining cruising in a world where everything is made of candy. Whiting's jaunty melody contains regular little flourishes for lines like, "On the sunny beach of Peppermint Bay." Both the film – released on December 28, 1934 – and the song were huge hits, with "… Lollipop" becoming Temple's signature song.

Ken Bloom

Release Date December 28, 1934

Nationality USA

Composers A. Whiting, Sidney Clare

Why It's Key A standard inspired by a naughty, sticky child.

Opposite Shirley Temple

Key Event *Your Hit Parade* is the first broadcast chart program

Popular music was disseminated through live performances, radio broadcasts, films, and record and sheet music sales in the first third of the twentieth century. But it was not until the advent of *Your Hit Parade* on April 20, 1935, that songs were assigned a weekly rank for their national popularity. The radio show, initially broadcast by the NBC network and always sponsored by Lucky Strike cigarettes, spent an hour, starting on Saturday night at 8 P.M., counting down the most successful songs, which were performed by a cast of singers and an orchestra at first conducted by Lennie Hayton.

And how were those rankings determined? The publicity agency that handled the show kept the specifics a secret but said that the criteria included requests sent in to radio stations, sheet music sales, and jukebox statistics. Record sales were also a factor but they were so low in 1935 that they couldn't have been a major one. Significantly, *Your Hit Parade*

measured the popularity of songs, not of specific recordings of those songs. At a time when the record industry opposed the playing of records over the air, fearing it would cut into sales, the radio show did not promote individual renditions. Nevertheless, when "Soon" turned out to be the No. 1 song the first week, most people associated it with Bing Crosby's recording.

Your Hit Parade was superseded by other charts but it continued to broadcast on radio, and then television until 1959.

William Ruhlmann

Date April 20, 1935

Country USA

Why It's Key Began the obsession with ranking songs by popularity.

Key Performance *Porgy And Bess* stage musical

Originally, George Gershwin thought of basing an opera on the Yiddish classic *The Dybbuk* (1914) but when the rights proved unavailable, he turned to the notion of a story from "Negro" life, to explore the realms of jazz, spirituals, and folksong that had been as strong an influence as his own Jewishness. After reading DeBose Heyward's novel *Porgy*, and subsequent play, loosely modeled on real events in the author's native South Carolina, Gershwin had his source material.

He took some time to get started – Heyward, who needed money, had to consider a "blackface" version that would have been written for Al Jolson – but the collaboration between Gershwin and Heyward (as librettist-lyricist) with lyrics also by George's brother Ira, eventually went full force into new territory, blending popular song forms with operatic protocols, performed by an all-black cast. Notable numbers were "I Got Plenty O' Nuttin," the gossamer "Summertime,"

and the skeptic's anthem "It Ain't Necessarily So." The work opened to predictable controversy: populist critics loved the songs but disdained the recitative and classicism; legit critics felt the reverse. And many blacks denounced it as Uncle Tom territory, resenting its dialect.

The original run was 124 performances (disappointing but well over the miniscule opera house average for a new work) but that was enough to establish a presence in the literature, which has led to thousands more performances worldwide, and complete artistic/social vindication.

David Spencer

Opening Night
October 11, 1935

Country USA

Director Robert Mamoulian

Cast Todd Duncan, Ann Wiggins Brown, John W. Bubbles

Composer George Gershwin, Ira Gershwin, Dubose Heyward

Why It's Key Synthesized popular music with opera techniques to become the quintessential American crossover work.

Opposite *Porgy And Bess*

Key Event
The birth of the DJ

In the first decades of radio's history, most programs were live or transcribed news and entertainment programs. Things started to change slightly when in 1927, Christopher Stone hosted phonograph concerts of classical music on the BBC. He called himself a "presenter." In the United States, nameless announcers gave specifics of the records they played without personality or explanation. In the early '30s, Al Jarvis created the *Make Believe Ballroom* program on KFWB in Los Angeles. Jarvis's program spotlighted one band, giving the illusion of a real ballroom performance.

In 1935, on New York's WNEW, one Martin Block decided to play records between news broadcasts on the Lindbergh kidnapping, an unusual combination. He then took the idea and title of Jarvis's program and began his own *Make Believe Ballroom* on February 3, 1935. Via chatting, Block's personality shone through and newspaperman Walter Winchell dubbed him a "disc jockey," the first usage of the term. Bock's

pioneering helped lead to a truce between previously warring radio stations and record companies, as the latter realized that their wares were being given free advertizing. Block's show was nationally syndicated in 1940. It was so popular, a 1948 musical short featured Block discussing the show and in 1949 Columbia Pictures made a musical film called *Make Believe Ballroom*.

Block left the program in 1954 for *The Martin Block Show* on the ABC Radio Network. *Make Believe Ballroom*, with different hosts, has continued to this day.
Ken Bloom

Date February 3, 1935

Country USA

Why It's Key A revolution in the way of presenting music on the airwaves.

Opposite The birth of the DJ

Key Song **"Begin The Beguine"** from *Jubilee*

In some senses, Cole Porter's "Begin The Beguine" is a novelty number, referencing a then popular rumba-esque dance that gave the author opportunity to paint an exotic backdrop. Yet the song was also extremely innovative. Before "Begin The Beguine," 32 measures was considered the standard length for a popular song and to go much beyond that was risking success. Yet this much-loved ballad runs 108 measures, still the longest pre-rock popular song ever written.

Porter once said he got the tribal-like musical accompaniment for this number from a war dance he heard in the Indonesian islands during a world cruise with writer Moss Hart. Later he said he got it from Martinique natives performing in a Parisian dance hall. One thing is certain: it was first sung by June Knight in the Broadway musical *Jubilee*, which opened on October 12, 1935, and then danced by her and Charles Walters. In addition to its length, "Begin The Beguine" is unique in other ways. The ballad has no verse and

drives ahead without benefit of distinct stanzas or a clear-cut release that relieves the surging melody. It is also one of the most difficult Porter songs to sing, a situation that kept it from gaining widespread popularity at first. It was not until Artie Shaw's swing version in 1938 that the song achieved the fame it deserved. Eddy Heywood's version (1944) sold over a million copies.
Thomas Hischak

First Released October 1935

Nationality USA

Composer Cole Porter

Why It's Key Showed that popular song could hold the attention – if it was good enough.

Key Song
"It Ain't Necessarily So"

Though the first production of George Gershwin's *Porgy And Bess* was not a success, several of the songs became standards. The most famous one is "It Ain't Necessarily So," which Leo Reisman first took into the U.S. charts on December 14, 1935 and whose atheist/skeptic slant has made it so enduringly popular that it has been covered by modern day artists like Bronski Beat, Cher, the Moody Blues, and Sting.

The number is sung by the no-account gambler Sportin' Life, who mischievously questions the stories in the Bible to a church group on a picnic. The title of the song was the dummy one thought up by Ira. Once he had the rhymes "li'ble"/"Bible" and "Goliath"/"dieth", Ira knew the song was not only possible but would be a success. The musical theme of the piece is in a sort of limerick form, ideally suited to the lyric's meter. John Bubbles, the brilliant hoofer and singer, portrayed Sportin' Life and helped make the song a success.

The song has become a favorite of singers including Sammy Davis, Jr. in the 1959 film version of *Porgy And Bess* and Cab Calloway, who appeared opposite Leontyne Price and William Warfield in a tour sponsored by the State Department. When the show went to Russia (which had previously co-opted the songs, royalty free) it transpired that the Russians had mis-translated "Li'l David was small but oh my… " as "Li'l David was impotent but oh my… "

Ken Bloom

Release Date 1935

Nationality USA

Composers George Gershwin, Ira Gershwin

Why It's Key A '30s song of continuing relevance to the rock generation.

Key Person
Benny Goodman

When Benny Goodman's recording of "Goody, Goody" made U.S. No. 1 on February 29, 1936 he was given the title "King of Swing". Arguably the finest clarinet player of the twentieth century, Benny Goodman was an innovative band leader and composer, as well as a renowned musician, and one of the giants of the Big Band era.

He was born in Chicago in 1909 and was playing clarinet professionally at the age of 12. Five years later he recorded his first record and was playing in the top ballrooms in New York City and Los Angeles. Goodman formed his own band in 1934. When swing – a form of jazz with infectious riffs alternating with virtuoso solos – was introduced soon after, he immediately became one of its leaders. In addition to his clear tone and inventive solo playing, Goodman was recognized as a superior conductor-arranger with an eye for talent. He used African-American musicians in his concerts when most orchestras were segregated. Many famous bands'

leaders, such as Harry James, Gene Krupa, and Lionel Hampton, started as players in Goodman's band and he popularized such singers as Helen Ward, Mildred Bailey, Helen Forrest, and Peggy Lee. Goodman's jazz concert at Carnegie Hall in 1938 was a highlight in a career that also included world tours, appearances in films, and composing such swing standards as "Swingtime In The Rockies" and "Stoppin' At The Savoy." The orchestra disbanded in 1944. Goodman died in 1986.

Thomas Hischak

Role Recording Artist

Date February 29, 1936

Nationality USA

Why It's Key The head of the vanguard of swing.

Opposite **Benny Goodman**

Key Person
Eddy Duchin

Pianist, composer, and bandleader Eddy Duchin (1910–1951) was born in Cambridge, Massachusetts, and studied to be a pharmacist before turning to music when he got a job as pianist for Leo Reisman's Orchestra in 1929. The next year Reisman had a major hit record of "Body And Soul" with Duchin at the piano. Duchin formed his own band in 1931 and developed a style in which a solo piano would start a song, followed by the band entering in parts before moving into a full orchestra sound. Soon Eddy Duchin and his Orchestra had hit recordings of "Ain't She Sweet," "It Had To Be You," "Easy Come, Easy Go," "Let's Fall In Love," "Moon Over Miami," and "Brazil." His trademark sound was perhaps best heard in his hit recording of "I'll Sing You A Thousand Love Songs," which entered the U.S. charts on November 28, 1936. This number by Harry Warren and Al Dubin was introduced in the film *Cain And Mabel* (1936) but it was Duchin's U.S. No. 1 chart record that popularized it.

Duchin has been dismissed by some as a Liberace prototype but he was far more musically-oriented than the latter. He was also even involved in a bit of a scandal when his recording of "Old Man Mose" (1938) seemed to feature the words "Fuck it" from vocalist Patricia Norman (if true, the first f-word on any record) and was banned in Britain as a consequence.

Thomas Hischak

Role Recording Artist

Date 1936

Nationality USA

Why It's Key The performer who blended a big band with a solo piano.

Opposite Eddy Duchin (left)

Key Person
Johnny Burke

The facility of Johnny Burke (1908–1964) with songwords made him one of the most in-demand lyricists in Hollywood during the 30's and '40s.

His first hit, with Joe Young and Harold Spina, was 1933's "Annie Doesn't Live Here Anymore." At Twentieth Century Fox, Burke was paired with composer James Van Heusen. The first of their many standards for Bing Crosby was "It's Always You." Among their hits were "Moonlight Becomes You," "It Could Happen To You," and "Swinging On A Star." Though their Broadway shows were flops, with the exception of Dubin and Warren, no team wrote as many great songs for Hollywood as Burke and Van Heusen. Burke put words to Erroll Garner's "Misty" in 1954, and it was a major success. It would be his last hit song.

Burke's most famous song today is probably "Pennies From Heaven," written in collaboration with his first Hollywood musical foil Arthur Johnston. The most successful of four hit versions of it in 1936 was

Bing Crosby's, which made the U.S. charts on November 28 that year. However, it gained immortality as a consequence of it being the title of Dennis Potter's acclaimed BBC television series and subsequent film starring Steve Martin more than 40 years later. The way it was used therein made it permanently a sort of shorthand for the style of the golden age of American song for those who weren't alive to see it when it was happening.

Ken Bloom

Role Lyricist

Date 1936

Nationality USA

Why It's Key A successful songwriter in his day but additionally one whose work was given life everlasting decades later.

Key Performance *On Your Toes*
stage musical

It was originally intended to have been a movie musical starring Fred Astaire. Composer Richard Rodgers and lyricist Lorenz Hart had cobbled together a story about a bespectacled hoofer-turned-music teacher who gets mixed up with the Russian Ballet and some good old American gangsters, with some romantic entanglements thrown in: our hero's girl-next-door honey is jealous of his contact with a predatory prima ballerina. Astaire didn't take it on as the story wouldn't gave him the opportunity to appear in his "native" white-tie-and-tails element.

The lankier, more comic, less suave Ray Bolger was retained instead and the proposed movie became a Broadway show. George Abbott was engaged as librettist to streamline and clarify a convoluted plot. By the time the musical emerged on April 11, 1936, it built to a show within the show; the Russian company's controversial debut of an American jazz ballet. The ballet itself tells a noir story culminating in a fatal gunshot. And while it's being performed on opening night, our hero (who has of course assumed the lead) realizes there are actual gangsters offstage waiting to deliver him an actual fatal shot at the crescendo…

The now-legendary choreography was by George Balanchine. Introduced along with the city-smart music of the ballet were the peppy title song and the delicately cuddle-close standard "There's a Small Hotel."

David Spencer

Opening Night April 11, 1936

Country USA

Director C. Worthington Miner

Cast Ray Bolger, Doris Carson, Monty Wooly

Composer Richard Rodgers, Lorenz Hart

Why It's Key The musical whose show within a show introduced a classical ballet.

Key Song
"I've Got You Under My Skin"

Cole Porter was inspired to write "I've Got You Under My Skin" by a French song, "Mon Homme," which opened with the line, "I've got him so much in my skin." Like some of Porter's other great songs, it had an unusual structure, consisting of 56 measures rather than the usual 32, with each of the seven eight-measure phrases slightly different; its beguine-like rhythm was also unconventional. But that did not keep it from serving as a dance for the team of Georges and Jalna as it was sung by Virginia Bruce in the film *Born to Dance*, released in November 1936.

Even before the movie came out, Hal Kemp And His Orchestra, with Skinnay Ennis on vocals, entered the U.S. charts with the song in November 1936. They were overtaken by Ray Noble And His Orchestra, with Al Bowlly singing, who scored an even bigger hit with it. After its initial success, "I've Got You Under My Skin" became a perennial hit, sung in other films and recorded by many artists including Ella Fitzgerald, Frank Sinatra, and Perry Como. It also returned to the pop singles charts periodically in sometimes wildly different versions, including a 1959 novelty rendition by Stan Freeburg and a 1966 pop/rock treatment by The 4 Seasons that returned it to the U.S. Top 10 after 30 years. In 1993, Sinatra and U2's Bono sang it on Sinatra's *Duets* album.

William Ruhlmann

Release Date 1936

Country USA

Composer Cole Porter

Why It's Key The song that got under the skin of so many that it spanned the generations.

Key Song
"Let's Face The Music And Dance"

The Fred Astaire and Ginger Rogers vehicle *Follow The Fleet*, released on February 20, 1936, featured a score from Irving Berlin that was one of the finest of his Hollywood efforts.

One featured number, "Let's Face The Music And Dance," was one of Berlin's most unconventional songs. The song has no verse and is a remarkable 66 bars long. Each of the four sections of the song contains a different number of bars and even the harmonies are unusual. Because Astaire and Rogers and the orchestrators were so adept, audiences never noticed the song's lack of symmetry.

The song for many is inextricably entwined with the dance that accompanied it in the film, choreographed by Astaire and Hermes Pan. Astaire and Rogers appear as Art Deco sculptures come to life, posing exaggeratedly. The song begins slowly and builds to a frenetic climax, ending with the two dancers frozen in place once more. Famously, in the single, almost three minute take used for the film, Rogers' beaded sleeve whacks her partner in the face.

However, the fame of the song is due to more than just its appearance in the movie. The lyric has a sense of dread about an unknown future (first line: "There may be trouble ahead"), urging a live-for-today attitude. With the world seemingly inevitably headed toward war, Americans were already feeling a sense of uncertainty perfectly expressed in Berlin's lyric.
Ken Bloom

Published Date 1936

Nationality USA

Writer Irving Berlin

Why It's Key The song that expressed the national desire for oblivion in the face of doom.

1930-1939

141

Key People
Rainger and Robin

Rainger and Robin were never household names but the composing team wrote dozens of familiar songs for the movies.

Composer Ralph Rainger (born 1901) was born in New York and was a practicing lawyer before turning to music professionally. He was in Hollywood writing film scores by 1930. Lyricist Leo Robin (1895–1984) was born in Pittsburgh and worked as a newspaperman and an actor before writing songs for Broadway shows in the '20s. When the Depression crippled Broadway, Robin went west and teamed up with Rainger for the first time in 1932. Over the next ten years the team scored 34 movie musicals that included such noteworthy songs as "Love In Bloom," "June In January," "Blue Hawaii," "With Every Breath I Take," and "Please." When they were asked to write a song for Bob Hope and Shirley Ross to sing in *The Big Broadcast Of 1938* (1937), the pair came up with the bittersweet "Thanks For The Memory," whose music and lyric have an aching subtext that is highly unusual for a non-theater song of the era. It won the Oscar for Best Song. Hope used the number throughout his very long career as his theme song.

Rainger's and Robin's partnership was tragically ended by Rainger's death in an airplane crash in 1942, although Robin collaborated with other musical foils for another 13 years.
Thomas Hischak

Role Composer (Rainger) and Lyricist (Robin)

Date 1937

Nationality USA

Why It's Key Their names left no abiding memory with the public – ironically considering the title of their song that did.

The jitterbug dance craze

When 21,000 jitterbuggers pranced frantically to the music of Benny Goodman And His Orchestra on March 3, 1937, the first night of the band's residency at New York's Paramount Theater, Goodman was declared the King Of Swing. In retrospect, that evening's wider significance was that it marked white America's open embracing of a dance craze that had started among the black clientele of Harlem's legendary Savoy Ballroom.

The jitterbug was a wild, abandoned, and improbably athletic dance, originally named the Lindy Hop, in tribute to aviation pioneer Charles Lindberg's Transatlantic crossing. The dance's crazed movements, however, prompted onlookers to compare it to the uncontrollable shaking of alcoholics, known in black slang as "the jitters." The new name took hold after bandleader Cab Calloway recorded a track called "Jitterbug" in 1934. By June 1939, with recording stars like Goodman and Ella Fitzgerald having boosted the dance's appeal, The World's Biggest Jitterbug Contest was held at the Los Angeles Coliseum. On a 12,000 square foot dance floor, over 1,000 contestants cut the rug from 7 A.M. until 6 P.M. Before the year was out, another song called "Jitterbug" became the first number written for *The Wizard Of Oz*. Though it was deleted from the final cut, the very fact that the producers thought of shoehorning the trendy reference into this fantasy film testifies to the universal appeal of the dance.

Johnny Black

Date March 3, 1937

Country USA

Why It's Key The dance craze that united white and black music lovers on an unprecedented scale.

Opposite The jitterbug

1930-1939

143

Key Performance *Snow White And The Seven Dwarfs* the movie

Originally, *Snow White And The Seven Dwarfs* was nicknamed "Disney's Folly." Walt Disney had to remortgage his house to finance the U.S. $1.4 million budget for his adaptation of the Brothers Grimm fairytale. Believing that feature length cartoons could make more profit than his usual animated shorts, Disney decided to broaden his studio's horizons while pushing the boundaries of film cartoons. *Snow White…* was the first full-length English language animated film, not to mention the first film ever to have a spin-off album to help boost sales.

Though the lush beauty of the film's visuals is indisputable, the songs of Frank Churchill and Leigh Harline certainly merited a life separate from the movie. (Paul J. Smith was responsible for the incidental music.) "Some Day My Prince Will Come," "Heigh-Ho," and "Whistle While You Work" became staples in every child's songbook, with, in addition, the latter famously customized by Allied troops during World War II to make scurrilous remarks about Hitler and his cronies. Because at the time releasing an accompanying album for a film was unheard of, the studio didn't have its own music publishing company. Instead the studio relied on the Bourne Co., who, uniquely for Disney's now large catalog, control the film's songs to this day.

Released on December 21, 1937, "Disney's Folly" quickly became the highest-grossing motion picture there had yet been, paving the way for the Disney company's stronghold on the American songbook and cinema.

Leila Regan-Porter

Movie Release Date December 21, 1937

Country USA

Directors William Cottrell, Wilfred Jackson, Larry Morey, Perce Pearce, Ben Sharpsteen

Cast Adriana Caselotti, Lucille La Verne, Roy Atwell

Composers Frank Churchill, Leigh Harline

Why It's Key The first film to have an accompanying soundtrack album.

Key Performance *Me And My Girl* stage musical

Bill Snibson had been the hero of a musical called *Twenty To One* in 1935. He became so popular, as personified by star Lupino Lane, that Lane commissioned that first show's librettist, L. Arthur Rose, to create a new misadventure for Snibson, in collaboration with lyricist Douglas Furber and composer Noel Gay.

Me And My Girl – which went on a short tour of Britain before opening at London's Victoria Palace on December 16, 1937 – was a sort of *My Fair Lady* with the genders reversed, the impoverished cockney Snibson inheriting an Earldom but only on the provision that he becomes more refined. Snibson loyally refuses to ditch Sally – his titular girl – to make this easier. The score contained some wonderful numbers, including the title song, and "The Lambeth Walk," which gave birth to a dance and become the work's title when it was filmed. Other songs for which the musical is known were actually inserted into later productions:

"The Sun Has Got His Hat On" and "Leaning On A Lamp Post."

The show was a huge morale booster during World War II. Performing twice nightly, it racked up an astonishing run of 1,646 performances and even generated Lane-Snibson dolls.

For decades the show was thought too British to make a mark in the United States, but a 1985 West End revival proved so popular that it, its star (Robert Lindsay) and director (Mike Ockrent) were successfully imported to Broadway a year later.

David Spencer

Opening Night
December 16, 1937

Country UK

Director Lupino Lane

Cast Lupino Lane, George Graves, Teddie St. Dennis

Composer Douglas Furber, Noel Gay

Why It's Key The "Lambeth Walk" musical epitomizes British musical comedy.

Opposite *Me And My Girl*

144

Key Song **"Let's Call the Whole Thing Off"** from *Shall We Dance*

"Let's Call The Whole Thing Off" is frequently assumed to be a song that examines the different way words are pronounced by American and English people. This is in fact erroneous, for its impetus was the lesser highlighted variations in dialect within America's shores.

The song was written by George and Ira Gershwin for the Fred Astaire and Ginger Rogers vehicle *Shall We Dance*, released on May 13, 1937. While working on it one day, Ira was speaking to his brother-in-law, English Strunsky. The latter was telling Ira that the local New Jersey farms didn't understand when Strunsky said "to-mah-to" and not the more common American pronunciation "tomay-to." Ira responded that Strunsky's sister, Lenore, insisted to Ira that the proper pronunciation for "either" was "eye-ther" while Ira said "ee-ther."

Ira ran with the theme and devised a lyric in which a narrator begins by telling his partner that he is tired

of a romance that has gone flat and that their inability to get along is illustrated by the fact that they even pronounce words differently. In the middle of this, the narrator has a change of heart, realizing he doesn't want to lose his girl and so instead pledges to "wear 'perjammas' and give up 'pyajarmahs'," i.e. change to suit his girl's tastes and preserve the relationship.

Pretentious or not, Strunsky's pronunciation led to one of the greatest songs in the popular repertoire.

Ken Bloom

Published May 13,1937

Nationality USA

Composers George Gershwin, Ira Gershwin

Why It's Key The song that is actually about one – not two – countries divided by a common language.

Key Event
Death of Robert Johnson

Sometime in August, 1938, Robert Johnson played a juke joint in Three Forks, Mississippi. It was a busy Saturday night, with a lot of dancing and other activity, in the course of which Johnson was handed a jug of moonshine. Unbeknown to the musician and ladies' man, the moonshine had been spiked with poison – possibly lye – probably by a jealous husband. He got sick that night and was taken to a boarding house, where he lay ill for days. He beat the poison but developed pneumonia and died on August 16, 1938.

Johnson was buried in an unmarked grave, a typical end for an itinerant bluesman, but the only thing "typical" about this man. For the last eight years, the rural blues world had been dazzled by the range of Johnson's mellifluous playing, impassioned singing, and haunted lyrics (a disproportionate number of which seemed to concern being chased by demons). He already had a certain myth attached to him – that his rapid progression on the guitar was as a result of selling his soul to the devil – but now Johnson's name was suddenly engulfed by the even greater myth that early death (aged 27) generates. His tiny catalog and negligible sales were instantaneously rendered irrelevant as he inspired a legion of disciples drawn to him by his legendary aura, including many rock artists more than one generation removed from him who became superstars, The Rolling Stones and Eric Clapton included.
Bruce Eder

Date August 16, 1938

Country USA

Why It's Key The death that piled myth upon myth.

1930–1939

Key Person
Tommy Dorsey

Although he was an accomplished trombonist, Tommy Dorsey's most conspicuous talent was as the head of a consistently popular big band in the '30s and '40s. In the age of swing, Dorsey was – commercially – king, doing arguably the most of any band leader to shape the manner and course of that then-dominant musical style, even if he was never as personally popular as Benny Goodman or Glenn Miller.

Dorsey's organizational abilities were not diminished by his notoriously short temper, even though that got him into trouble occasionally. He was closely associated with his saxophone-playing older brother Jimmy, and the two initially co-led a band, The Dorsey Brothers Orchestra, starting in 1934. A year later, however, Tommy Dorsey stormed off the bandstand after an argument, and soon he was in charge of his own band.

Tommy Dorsey and His Orchestra was a hit right away, with its leader's savvy mixture of hot and sweet playing, as exemplified by "Music, Maestro, Please," his sixth number-one hit, which entered the U.S. chart on June 18, 1938. Even before he happened across young vocalist Frank Sinatra, Dorsey was at the top of the band business. Sinatra stayed with him less than three years, but that was longer than many of the musicians who worked for the restless bandleader. In later years, the fad for swing subsided, but Dorsey kept on, and he could make a strong claim to having given crucial assistance to the career of Elvis Presley by giving him his first television exposure on his show.
William Ruhlmann

Role Recording Artist

Date 1938

Nationality USA

Why It's Key The stormy sultan of swing.

Key Song "You Must Have Been A Beautiful Baby" Dick Powell

Dick Powell introduced "You Must Have Been A Beautiful Baby" in the film *Hard to Get*, released in November 1938. Although the song was newly written by the successful Hollywood songwriters Harry Warren (music) and Johnny Mercer (lyric), the simple melody had the feel of a tune from decades earlier. Mercer wrote the lyric after being given the melody.

The title phrase came from his wife Ginger, who said it on a visit back to his home town with him when she espied a picture of Mercer as a baby on a rug. The revelation from Mercer's proud mother that he had in fact won a blue ribbon in a baby contest was incorporated into the lyric, albeit one that was made the standard romantic one: the narrator imagined the female subject aging from infancy to her attractive prime, telling her she must have been a beautiful baby, "'cause, baby, look at you now!" The words, employing such unusual rhymes as "appreciate" / "super-great", were colloquial and slangy, which somehow perfectly suited a melody that was almost breathlessly fast and full of turnarounds.

Tommy Dorsey and His Orchestra, with Edythe Wright on vocals, had the first hit with it and Bing Crosby the most successful. By the '60s, one might think the song seemed old fashioned and even a bit campy, but that didn't keep Bobby Darin or the Dave Clark Five from taking it back into the U.S. Top 40 in that decade.

William Ruhlmann

Release Date
November 1938

Nationality USA

Composers Harry Warren, Johnny Mercer

Why It's Key Lyricist's own infant beauty inspires romantic song.

Key Person
Noel Gay

The British public who vaguely know the name "Noel Gay" through talent agency Noel Gay Artists would be surprised to discover that the man after whom the organisation is named wrote or co-wrote many songs familiar to them.

Richard Armitage, who was born in Wakefield, Yorkshire, UK, in 1898, was a child prodigy, proficiently playing the cathedral organ. He studied at the Royal College of Music and Cambridge University, whilst also working as a choir director and organist. A successful career in liturgical music beckoned but he became intrigued by musical comedy and had success with the revue *Clowns In Clover*. He became Noel Gay to avoid embarrassing the church authorities with his creative extra-curricular activities.

In 1930 he co-wrote "The King's Horses" and during the decade, others of his songs included "The Fleet's In Port Again," the chipper "The Sun Has Got Its Hat On," the anti-hunting "Run Rabbit Run," "I Took My Harp To A Party" (Gracie Fields), and George Formby's signature song "Leaning On A Lamp Post." His score for the show, *Me And My Girl*, bequeathed a song so famous that in October 1938 the *London Times* ran an editorial celebrating "The Lambeth Walk," poetically stating, "While dictators rage and statesmen talk, all Europe dances – to The Lambeth Walk."

After World War II Gay struggled with deafness and died in 1954. His son, Richard, turned his business into Noel Gay Artists, one of the UK's biggest entertainment agencies.

Spencer Leigh

Role Songwriter

Date 1938

Nationality UK

Why It's Key A real and talented person behind a famous name.

Key Person
Harry Warren

With Louis Armstrong's entry into the U.S. chart on February 4, 1939 with "Jeepers Creepers," the relatively unknown composer Harry Warren had one of the biggest hits of his long career. Although he never became a household name like his contemporaries Cole Porter or Irving Berlin, Warren was the quintessential Hollywood composer. He scored nearly 60 movie musicals over a period of 30 years, adapting to the changing styles in popular music.

He was born Salvatore Guaragna in Brooklyn in 1893. Warren taught himself to play the piano and eventually nine other instruments as well. He worked as a song plugger on Tin Pan Alley where he had a surprise hit with his first composition, "Rose Of The Rio Grande" in 1920. Warren went to California in 1931 and, teaming with lyricist Al Dubin, scored many Warner Brothers' Depression musicals, including *42nd Street* (1933), *Footlight Parade* (1933), *Dames* (1934) and four Gold Diggers movies. He remained in Hollywood into the '60s, working with such lyricists as Johnny Mercer, Ira Gershwin, and Mack Gordon. Amongst his immortal compositions are "The More I See You," "I Only Have Eyes For You," and "September In The Rain." Although he rarely wrote directly for Tin Pan Alley, Warren saw several of his movie songs score on the charts. He retired in the '60s but interest in his songs was revived with the Broadway version of *42nd Street* (1980). He died the following year.

Thomas Hischak

Role Composer

Date 1939

Nationality USA

Why It's Key Demonstrated to composers how to move with the times.

Key Song "Strange Fruit"
Billie Holiday

Penned by Jewish schoolteacher Abel Meeropol under the pen name Lewis Allan, the song "Strange Fruit" was inspired by the 1930 Indiana lynching of two black men, Thomas Shipp and Abram Smith. Meeropol saw photographs of the lynching and wrote a poem expressing his horror. The poem explained that Southern trees bore strange fruit: "The bulging eyes and the twisted mouth." Later he set the poem to downbeat music and, following a Madison Square Garden performance of the song by black vocalist Laura Duncan, it came to the attention of black jazz diva Billie Holiday.

Though Holiday felt strongly about the song, her record label, Columbia, refused to let her record it due to the song's controversial content and she was forced to take it to the minor Commodore label. It made a U.S. No. 16 after entering the U.S. charts on July 22, 1939, but was hardly Holiday's biggest hit of the period (she'd notched a U.S. No. 1 with "Carelessly" in 1937). In time, though, it became the song with which the singer was most readily associated. Certainly she felt passionate about its content, Holiday's accompanist, Bobby Tucker, claiming that Billie frequently broke down after performing Meeropol's chilling creation.

Soon the anthem of the anti-lynching movement, "Strange Fruit" was recorded by bluesman Josh White in 1944 and it was his Decca/Brunswick version that first introduced the song to the UK. It has since been recorded by Nina Simone, Sting, Tori Amos, Robert Wyatt, and many others.

Fred Dellar

Date July 22, 1939

Nationality USA

Composer Lewis Allan

Why It's Key Prototypical protest hit

Opposite Billie Holiday

Key Person
Ivor Novello

Contemporary British songwriters who receive Ivor Novello Awards are generally ignorant of it but the man after whom the awards are named was a multi-talented superstar.

Ivor Novello was born into a musical family in Cardiff, Wales, in 1893. He wrote the music for uplifting World War I song "Keep The Home Fires Burning" (1914) and served in the army. From 1919, he appeared in films, including as a Jack the Ripper suspect in Alfred Hitchcock's *The Lodger* (1926). The broodingly handsome Novello became a Hollywood film star and heartthrob, idolized by female fans who mistook his bachelorhood for availability. In reality, he was a tormented homosexual who had an affair with the poet Siegfried Sassoon.

As a playwright, he had major success with the musical, *Glamorous Night* (1935), about a man, played by Novello, who invents television and is paid by radio executives to disappear. Novello usually wrote songs with lyricist Christopher Hassell as in *The Dancing Years*, which opened on March 23 1939 and became the most successful London musical of the war years. His victory musical *Perchance To Dream* (1945), which saw Novello write both lyrics and melodies, features perhaps his most famous song, the reunion number "We'll Gather Lilacs."

Novello died in 1951. His sentimental music has not endured as much as his name: the "Ivors" are so-called because of Novello's sterling work for British composers in founding the British Academy Of Songwriters, Composers And Authors, which grants them.
Spencer Leigh

Role Songwriter

Date 1939

Nationality UK

Why It's Key The man who gave his name to one of the ultimate songwriters' accolades.

Key Performance *The Wizard Of Oz*
the movie

Amazingly, there were at least half a dozen *Wizard Of Oz*-related movies before 1939. All of them have, of course, been completely forgotten, eclipsed by the dazzling majesty of the version starring Judy Garland released on August 25, 1939.

Those coming to L. Frank Baum's novel *The Wonderful Wizard Of Oz* (1900) after experiencing the movie might find it quite dull but there was no cinematic competition around in those days and readers were so entranced that it generated thirteen sequels. It also led to a 1902 stage musical version, although the score for that was not the one used here. Instead the songwriting team of Harold Arlen (melodies) and "Yip" Harburg (lyrics) was hired to come up with an entirely new set of numbers. The result was a memorable score that was peppered with songs instantly destined to be as iconic as lead character Dorothy's magic ruby slippers: "Ding Dong The Witch Is Dead," "You're Off To See The Wizard," "If I Only Had A Brain," and, most iconic of all, "Over The Rainbow," the yearning lament of Kansas-shackled Dorothy with its lovely bobbing bridge.

The movie failed to turn a profit in its first ten years of release. However, subsequent rereleases and its ultimate status as a staple of both American and British Christmas television schedules gradually helped seal its immortality. The Academy Award people got it right however: It won Oscars for best original song ("Over The Rainbow") and best score.
Sean Egan

Movie Release Date August 25, 1939

Country USA

Director Victor Fleming

Cast Judy Garland, Frank Morgan, Ray Bolger

Composer Harold Arlen, "Yip" Harburg

Why It's Key Now immortal musical that was initially a flop.

Opposite *The Wizard Of Oz*

Key Person
Hoagy Carmichael

Hoagy Carmichael (1899–1981) hailed from Bloomington, Indiana. Carmichael was urged to try his hand at composition by musician Bix Beiderbecke and his first piece, "Riverboat Shuffle," was to be Carmichael's first composition, first recording, and first published piece of music.

Beiderbecke joined Paul Whiteman's aggregation but didn't forget Hoagy. In November of 1927, Whiteman recorded his "Washboard Blues" with Carmichael handling the piano chores and singing Fred B. Callahan's lyric. That same year Carmichael's most successful composition, "Star Dust," was released. Now the hits came fast and furious, "Rockin' Chair," recorded with Louis Armstrong, "Georgia On My Mind," with a lyric by Stuart Gorell, and "Lazy River." On October 1, 1938, Larry Clinton's version of "Heart And Soul" made the U.S. chart, the most successful of three versions of this number written by Carmichael with Frank Loesser to chart that year.

In the early '30s, Carmichael moved further toward mainstream Tin Pan Alley writing and away from his jazz roots. In 1936, he left New York for Hollywood. He appeared in the films *To Have And Have Not*, where he sang "How Little We Know," and "The Best Years Of Our Lives," among others and recorded for Decca. His voice had a county twang and a wry quality. In an age when composers' visages were not that well-known, author Ian Fleming was able to assume a knowledge of Carmichael's face amongst the public when describing his hero James Bond as resembling him in his work.
Ken Bloom

Date 1939

Nationality USA

Role Songwriter

Why It's Key Probably the most recognizable songwriter in America.

Key Song
"Three Little Fishes"

Saxie Dowell wrote the ostensibly silly and contagious number about a mother fish and her children who swim over a dam, the lyric using such nonsense phrases as "Dit dit ditty." The song was introduced on a successful record by Hal Kemp and his Orchestra with Dowell doing the vocals with The Smoothies, which entered the U.S. chart on April 22, 1939. Even more popular was a disc by Kay Kyser (vocal by Ish Kabibble) that sold a million copies.

The number remained a familiar favorite throughout the '40s and beyond. Among the others to record "Three Little Fishes" were Paul Whiteman (vocals by The Modernaires), Spike Jones, The Hoosier Hot Shots, Glenn Miller, Ambrose and his Orchestra, Guy Lombardo, Red Norvo, Bebe Daniels, Maurice Denham, and Shelley Duvall. The most unlikely figures brought the song back to the charts again in 1967: rock band Mitch Ryder and the Detroit Wheels combined the number with "Too Many Fish In The Sea" to make

U.S. No. 24. Despite its grammatically incorrect title, the song was a nursery and school favorite for several years, and still is to some extent, perhaps because the song contains a moral: after ignoring their mother's instructions not to swim too far, the trio of fish are confronted by a shark and realize the benefits of their "Itty bitty pool," to which they go scurrying back.
Thomas Hischak

Release Date 1939

Nationality USA

Composer Saxie Dowell

Why It's Key An empty novelty song – or is it?

Key Performance *Pal Joey*
stage musical

John O'Hara's fast-talking Chicago cad, Joey Evans, began life as the star of *New Yorker* short stories in the form of letters, signed "Pal Joey". Fittingly, it was a letter from O'Hara to Richard Rodgers (composer) and Lorenz Hart (lyricist), asking if they'd be interested in a Joey musical, that started the ball rolling. O'Hara himself fashioned the seamy, steamy libretto.

Broadway history claims the show, starring Gene Kelly, was not a success upon its December 25 1940 opening. The public, we're told, simply wasn't ready for a complex anti-hero to be a musical's main character. Possibly, but that doesn't explain why revivals since a fairly successful 1952 remounting failed even more conspicuously, long after audiences had become more sophisticated.

The more likely reason is subtler. The show was conceived before book musicals began to adopt what we now consider true integration of script and score, which involves not only elements of structure but style and tone. Pal Joey never found quite the right balance because the tools for that balance were yet to be refined. Joey wasn't just a musical main character ahead of his time, he was an idea ahead of available technique. And in revival, the disparity shows.

Still, there's no denying the insinuating power of the score whose standards include the smooth charm of "I Could Write a Book", the helpless infatuation of "Bewitched, Bothered and Bewildered" and the brazen striptease suggestiveness of "Zip".

David Spencer

Opening Night December 25, 1940

Country USA

Director George Abbott

Cast Gene Kelly, Vivienne Segal, June Havoc

Composers Richard Rodgers, Lorenz Hart

Why It's Key The first genuinely dark mainstream musical with musical theatre's first genuine anti-hero.

153

Key Event
The Formation of BMI

By 1939, ASCAP licensed about 90 per cent of the music played, recorded, and broadcast in America. With such power, the organization was able to make demands that radio stations considered extreme. In retaliation, the radio networks created Broadcast Music, Incorporated (BMI) on April 1, 1940 as an alternative for songwriters.

Despite the smack of conflict of interest, this organization endeared itself to many composers by opening its doors to writers of country and western, rhythm and blues, and other genres generally ignored by ASCAP. ASCAP called a strike in January 1941 in an attempt to raise the percentage of advertising revenue they received from radio stations by 50 per cent. Radio stations scrambled for tunes to fill the airtime. In addition to doing new arrangements of songs by pre-copyright composers such as Stephen Foster, the networks promoted new songwriters joining BMI.

Even after the strike was settled in 1943, BMI's catalog of songs continued expanding in quality and number. Also, for the first time country music, African-American sounds, and other little known genres started to get national broadcasts. The audiences for such music grew – some even suggest rock 'n' roll would not have taken off in the way it did had the old Tin Pan Alley songs not been deprived of exposure for so long – and American music became more diverse. Today BMI represents over 300,000 songwriters and has 6.5 million songs in its catalog.

Thomas Hischak

Date April 1, 1940

Nationality USA

Why It's Key A new music organization that provided a more populist selection of songs.

Key Album *Dust Bowl Ballads*
Woody Guthrie

Woody Guthrie sang folk music in the vernacular of society's victims, giving his tales of hardship, wandering, and perseverance an authentic resonance.

Commenting upon events and social conditions of the day was a centuries-old tradition in folk music when Guthrie, a native Oklahoman, recorded *Dust Bowl Ballads* in one day on April 26, 1940. The worst of the Depression might have been over, but its aftershocks continued to haunt the American working class and poor, especially those who had been displaced from their farms by the Dust Bowl storms of the '30s. Topical references had made their way into folk, and even some pop, recordings since the record industry had taken off in the early part of the twentieth century. With this material, however, Guthrie was offering a voice to the dispossessed in an especially concentrated, articulate, even anthemic way.

Released in two volumes by RCA Victor in July 1940, the initial commercial and social impact of *Dust Bowl Ballads* was modest. However, it was immediately recognized as a key document by the burgeoning urban folk music community, remaining one as the folk revival picked up steam in the '50s and early '60s. Bob Dylan was so mesmerized by *Dust Bowl Ballads* that he adapted Guthrie's style as his own at the outset of his career. Guthrie's topical bite and social consciousness is heard to the present day in the work of singer-songwriters such as Bruce Springsteen and Billy Bragg.

Richie Unterberger

Release Date July 1940

Nationality USA

Tracklisting The Great Dust Storm (Dust Storm Disaster), I Ain't Got No Home, Talking Dust Bowl Blues, Vigilante Man, Dust Can't Kill Me, Dust Pneumonia Blues, Pretty Boy Floyd, Blowin' Down The Road (I Ain't Going To Be Treated This Way), Tom Joad – Part 1, Tom Joad – Part 2, Dust Bowl Refugee, Do Re Mi, Dust Bowl Blues, Dusty Old Dust (So Long It's Been Good To Know Yuh)

Why It's Key Invented modern protest music.

Opposite Woody Guthrie

Key Song **"When You Wish Upon A Star"**
from *Pinocchio*

Disney animated movies have featured many songs down the decades but none that have had the exposure of "When You Wish Upon A Star."

It made its first appearance in the film *Pinocchio*, released on February 7, 1940. The Jiminy Cricket, character, voiced by Cliff Edwards, sat on the shoulder of the wooden puppet turned real boy of the title and acted as his conscience. It was he who sang this dreamy lullaby-like number, about wishes coming true if you firmly believe in yourself ("Anything your heart desires will come to you") written by Ned Washington (lyric) and Leigh Harline (music).

The number won the Oscar for Best Song and it would live on to represent the Walt Disney Company. The ballad was immediately embraced by moviegoers and was a favorite with big bands in the '40s, such as Harry James (vocal by Dick Haimes) and Glenn Miller. Interest in the ballad was revived when Disney used it as the theme song for its weekly television show starting in the '50s. Even as the nature of that show changed, and later when Disney had its own television network, the song remained and just the sound of its seven opening notes came to represent everything Disney, from movies to cruise ships. By the '90s, pop singers such as Ringo Starr, Johnny Mathis, Billy Joel, and Linda Ronstadt had recorded their versions of the perennially popular ballad.

Thomas Hischak

Movie Release Date February 7, 1940

Nationality USA

Composer Ned Washington, Leigh Harline

Why It's Key The pop ballad that became the theme song for a corporate empire.

Key Person
Burton Lane

When Burton Lane had his first stage success with *Hold On To Your Hats*, which premiered on September 11, 1940, he was finally established on Broadway as a composer of reputation. Younger and less known than his colleagues Cole Porter, Irving Berlin, Arthur Schwartz, and Dorothy Fields, Lane was still responsible for immortal compositions.

He was born Burton Levy in New York in 1912 and by the time he was 18 his songs were being interpolated into Broadway revues. By 1933 he was in Hollywood scoring musicals with lyricists Harold Adamson and Frank Loesser. He collaborated with lyricist E. Y. Harburg on *Hold On to Your Hats*, a popular Al Jolson vehicle on Broadway. Lane and Harburg worked together again on their most memorable stage musical, *Finian's Rainbow* (1947), which introduced "How Are Things In Glocca Morra?," "If This Isn't Love," and "Old Devil Moon." With lyricist Alan Jay Lerner, Lane scored the movie *Royal Wedding* (1951) and the

Broadway musical *On A Clear Day You Can See Forever* (1965). The golden age of the Hollywood music was waning when Burton was at his peak so many of the outstanding songs he wrote are buried in second-rate films. Burton died in 1996. He had a particular talent for writing romantic, atmospheric music with a lively, insistent beat, such as in "Everything I Have Is Yours," "The World in My Arms," and "How About You?."

Thomas Hischak

Role Composer

Date 1940

Nationality USA

Why It's Key A top-ranked composer writer for Broadway and Hollywood who never became as famous as his songs.

Key Song **"Boogie Woogie Bugle Boy"**
The Andrews Sisters

Don Raye and Hughie Prince penned "Boogie Woogie Bugle Boy," which is similar in spirit to their hit, "Beat Me Daddy, Eight to the Bar." The joyous song is about a Chicago-based trumpeter who gets drafted and becomes depressed that he cannot practice anymore. A compassionate captain responds by drafting a band with whom he can play, the upshot of which is "Now the company jumps when he plays reveille."

The unmistakable three-pronged attack of The Andrews Sisters' version of "Boogie Woogie Bugle Boy" entered the U.S. chart on March 1, 1941. However, when the United States entered World War II at the end of the year, the song took on a new focus as men had to cope with the reality of facing up to life in the army. Yet Bette Midler was able to take it into the U.S. Top 10 in 1973, its purchasers presumably a new generation. Another generation later the female group En Vogue covered the song in 1990. In 2000 the Puppini Sisters also recorded it. 2007 saw a sort of reemergence with

the appearance of "Candyman" by Christine Aguilera. The tribute Aguilera was paying "Boogie Woogie Bugle Boy" via this composition was made explicit by a video in which the artist appeared as a three-woman uniform-wearing vocal group. However, The Andrews Sisters would never have contemplated a line like this song's declaration that the object of Aguilera's fascination made her "panties drop."

Ken Bloom

Release Date 1941

Nationality USA

Composers Don Raye, Hughie Prince

Why It's Key A song that had resonance in wartime but which has shown surprising durability.

Opposite The Andrews Sisters

Key Person
Glenn Miller

Trombonist-composer-bandleader Glenn Miller was born in 1904 in Clarinda, Iowa, and attended the University of Colorado for a time before quitting to play with bands led by, amongst others, Benny Goodman, the Dorsey Brothers, and Ray Noble. He formed his own band in 1938 and soon developed his distinct trademark of letting a high-register clarinet play over the saxophone section. The thrilling and romantic arrangement helped propel Glenn Miller And His Orchestra to the top.

Miller was famous for promoting many fine vocalists, such as Ray Eberle and Marion Hutton. Yet his signature songs include instrumentals "In the Mood" and "Tuxedo Junction." He and the band appeared in a handful of movies, most memorably *Sun Valley Serenade* (1941) in which "Chattanooga Choo-Choo" was introduced. Harry Warren (music) and Mack David (lyric) wrote this swinging number and it was played by Miller and the band while Tex Beneke, Paula Kelly, and the Modernaires sang it. Miller's version of "Chattanooga Choo-Choo," recorded on May 7, 1941, ultimately became the first record to go gold; that is, to sell 1,000,000 copies.

From 1939, Miller dominated American music. The more improvisation-oriented jazzers might not like his formal approach much but the public lapped up records like "Stairway to the Stars," "Careless," "That Old Black Magic," and "Pennsylvania 6-5000."

A wartime troops entertainer, Miller died in 1944 when the plane he was traveling in to Paris went down in the English Channel.

Thomas Hischak

Role Recording Artist

Date 1941

Nationality USA

Why It's Key The man whose band was the most popular of the swing era.

Key Event **The invention of the solid-bodied electric guitar**

The quest to increase the volume of the guitar began in the big band era of the '30s when it was hardly heard and relegated to the rhythm section. Adding a pickup to the hollow-bodied acoustic guitar provided enough volume for jazz guitarists to be heard but increases in volume caused unwanted and unmusical resonance.

Les Paul was principally a virtuoso guitarist but he was also a talented inventor (he developed the system of multi-track recording still in use today). While experimenting with electrical pickups in 1941, Paul attached one to a 4 x 4-inch piece of solid pine to which he had glued a fretboard. He actually played this device during performances but the audience was so confused by the look of it that Paul attached two halves of an Epiphone guitar to each side of the "Log."

Les Paul's log did not go into production but it helped dispel anxieties about using a solid body for an electric guitar. On his urging the Gibson company developed a solid bodied electric guitar which had unprecedented levels of volume and sustain. By 1952 these guitars were introduced along with Leo Fender's version of the same idea. Although the term rock 'n' roll was not yet coined, the availability of these cheap and easily mastered instruments played a major role in its growth. Ironically the famous Les Paul model that keeps his name alive was largely the work of Gibson's own design team.

Andre Millard

Date 1941

Country USA

Why It's Key Provided the dominant sound of rock 'n' roll.

Key Song "When I See An Elephant Fly" from *Dumbo*

In the Disney movie musical *Dumbo*, released on October 23, 1941, after the titular big-eared elephant and his mouse friend Timothy accidentally imbibe alcohol, they awake to find themselves mysteriously perched in the branches of a tree. A group of crows are perturbed to find their natural habitat invaded. A discussion ensues as to how Dumbo came to be up there. The loyal Timothy insists it must be because Dumbo flew. The crows – a sassy bunch – ridicule this. Cue a delightful pun-laden jazzy concoction by Ned Washington (words) and Oliver Wallace (music) in which the crows variously contend that while they have seen a house fly, a dragon fly, a peanut stand, a baseball bat, etc. "I be done seen about everything when I see an elephant fly!"

The black vernacular contained in that chorus line gives an indication of the problem some have had with the number. Critic Richard Schickel opined that the sequence was "distasteful," complaining that the crows were "Negro caricatures." Fellow critic Leonard Maltin has responded that the crows were "black characters, not black stereotypes," and said of their jive-talk, "if offence is to be taken in hearing blacks call each other 'brother,' then the viewer is merely being sensitive to accuracy."

Apart from leader Jim Crow, the crows' voices were rendered by the Hall Johnson Choir, a groundbreaking black spiritual vocal group, hardly a casting that implied sinister motives on the part of the Disney staff.
Sean Egan

Movie Release Date October 23, 1941

Nationality USA

Composer Ned Washington, Oliver Wallace

Why It's Key Rarely has a song been so unfairly maligned.

Key Song "The White Cliffs Of Dover" Vera Lynn

The uplifting "The White Cliffs Of Dover" was amongst the most celebrated songs of World War II and, as rendered by forces sweetheart Vera Lynn, did much to raise the morale of British troops.

However, the composition was by a pair of Brill Building writers who were American through and through, Nat Burton and Walter Kent. Burton, the lyricist, had never been to the UK but he knew how picturesque the titular white cliffs were and how they could be the first sight of Britain for someone returning home. He had no idea whether there were bluebirds over the white cliffs of Dover (there aren't) but their inclusion in the lyric tapped into the same sentimentality as the "pretty little bluebirds" flying in "Over The Rainbow." Similar sentimentality attends the passages where it is declared that the future holds "peace ever after." While easy to mock from today's vantage point of continued conflict, it cannot be underestimated how such rhetoric would have aggravated the tear ducts for soldiers enduring the aching misery of separation from loved ones and the terror of the possibility of death at any moment.

The original recording was by the U.S. bandleader Kay Kyser with a vocal from Harry Babbitt, and there were several other American versions, including Glenn Miller's, before Vera Lynn made it her own in 1941. The song was revived by the Righteous Brothers (1966) and Robson and Jerome (1995).
Spencer Leigh

Release Date 1941

Country USA

Composers Writers Nat Burton, Walter Kent

Why It's Key A British patriotic anthem written by Americans.

Key Event
Musicians go on strike

As the jukebox became increasingly popular in small venues, the small combos and individual musicians they often replaced began to perceive records as the greatest threat to their continued employment.

Additionally, more time was afforded record shows by radio companies. They were cheaper to run and less problematic than airing big bands, usually from outside locations. Eventually the American Federation Of Musicians decided that things were getting out of hand. Musicians were paid a meager, one-off fee for recording dates. They observed the huge sales achieved by many recordings which they had helped fashion and demanded that they should be paid a royalty in addition to session rates. When the record companies refused to accept this, union leader James Petrillo called a strike on August 1, 1942, declaring that no musicians would make records until an agreement had been reached.

The strike lasted two years, during which only singers made recordings, stars such as Bing Crosby being forced to record with the aid of choirs and vocal groups. As a result, the popularity of dance and swing bands waned and vocalists, still producing hit records to promote their talent, gained the ascendancy. (Luckily for Nat "King" Cole, he had recorded chart-topper "Nature Boy" just prior to the strike date with an orchestra). Ultimately, though, the musicians obtained justice: after a year Decca capitulated and in November 1944 RCA and Columbia also signed an agreement on AFM's terms. The principle of "performance royalties" became accepted.

Fred Dellar

Date August 1, 1942

Country USA

Why It's Key Musicians achieve greater recognition – and renumeration.

Key Person
Kay Kyser

Born James King Kern Kyser in Rocky Mountain, North Carolina, Kay Kyser (1906–1985) formed his first band as a student at the University of North Carolina and by the '20s was conducting professionally. Kyser usually used vocalists at the top of a song then let the band take over, putting the two together for the final refrain. By 1936 he had his own radio show and two years later introduced his popular radio program Lucky Strike Kollege of Musical Knowledge, a combination quiz show and music show. Kay Kyser And His Orchestra were featured in '40s movies and such was Kyser's fame that he once appeared in cartoon form in a Batman comic. In February 1941, Kyser became the first artist to perform at a military camp, predating Bob Hope's ventures in this area.

Kyser had a zany, larger than life stage personality. His playful approach to the big band sound was best heard in his interpretation of light novelty numbers such as "(I've Got Spurs That) Jingle, Jangle, Jungle," which entered the U.S. chart on July 4, 1942. A clip-clopping cowboy ditty written by Joseph J. Lilley (music) and Frank Loesser (lyric), it sold a million.

The Kollege show moved over to television in 1949. When it was cancelled after two seasons, Kyser – who had sometimes talked of retiring before – decided to make his premature exit from showbusiness to pursue religious and philanthropic interests. He never went back.

Thomas Hischak

Role Recording Artist

Date 1942

Nationality USA

Why It's Key Hugely popular bandleader who turned his back on music.

Opposite Kay Kyser

Key Event **Frank Sinatra breaks free from his onerous contract with Tommy Dorsey**

In the days of the big band, nobody apparently thought twice about the fact that the names of the bandleaders were what attracted the consumer to concerts, radio shows, and records. Things however began to assume a logic with Frank Sinatra.

Sinatra's incredible personal and vocal charisma ensured that he was given unusual prominence on recordings by the Tommy Dorsey Orchestra instead of being treated as merely one of the sonic attractions. Sinatra himself began to be aware of his pulling power, if not that the age of the singer/vocalist/frontman was coming. In 1941, he told Dorsey he was going solo. Dorsey, barely speaking to him as he began serving out his year's notice, told him he was going to hold him to his contract, signed in ignorance and haste. It dictated that after they parted company in September 1942, Sinatra had to give Dorsey a third of all his future earnings plus a further 10 per cent to Dorsey's agent.

Eventually, Dorsey released Sinatra from his contract. How he was persuaded to do so has long been a matter of ferocious conjecture. Italian-American Sinatra associated with Mafia figures throughout his life and a rumor circulated that Dorsey signed Sinatra away for one dollar with someone's gun in his mouth. The evidence for this is conflicting. Even if not true, however, the irony is that Sinatra – who loved what he considered the glamor of the Mob – probably enjoyed people thinking it was.

Sean Egan

Date September 1942

Country USA

Why It's Key An essential part of Sinatra mythology.

Opposite **Frank Sinatra**

Key Song
"That Old Black Magic"

"That Old Black Magic" was written by Harold Arlen and Johnny Mercer for the 1942 film *Star-Spangled Rhythm*, where it was performed with a languorous dance by Vera Zorina.

Mercer later revealed that he took inspiration from a Cole Porter song. Porter's number "You Do Something To Me" had a phrase in it that went: "Do do that voo-doo that you do so well." "That thing about voodoo must have stuck with me, because I paraphrased it in 'Old Black Magic,'" said Mercer. Arlen, ever the gentleman, gave the lion's share of the credit to Mercer's lyric, which tells of a man who is bewitched by his lover's charms and knows it, talking of "Icy fingers up and down my spine," with the final line of the song clarifying that the old black magic in question is called love. "The words sustain your interest, make sense, contain memorable phrases, and tell a story," Arlen said. "Without the lyric, the song would be just another song." He was too modest: the sensual

excellence of their joint creation weaves a spell of its own on the listener.

The song is among the most covered popular standards. Notable recordings include those by Frank Sinatra, Margaret Whiting, Sammy Davis, Jr., and Glenn Miller And His Orchestra, whose 1943 version peaked at No. 1 on the *Billboard* chart.

Ken Bloom

Release Date 1942

Country USA

Composers Harold Arlen, Johnny Mercer

Why It's key The song that showed cannibalizing the past can lead to wonderful new works.

Key Performance *Holiday Inn* the movie

From its charity premier on August 4 1942 at the Paramount New York, *Holiday Inn* proved a hit both with both audiences (it became the biggest-grossing musical movie up to that point) and critics ("The best musical drama of the year," enthused *The New York Post*). Key to that success is the song at the heart of the film.

The film teamed Bing Crosby, Fred Astaire, and Marjorie Reynolds as a love triangle whose *denouement* is played out in the titular Inn, to which Crosby's character had prematurely retired from the song-and-dance act he had pursued with Astaire's character. Set-piece numbers abound, as one would expect in a movie that teamed the best singer and the best dancer of the era but the song the movie is now chiefly famous for is a one-man-and-his-piano scenario: Crosby sings "White Christmas" with only Reynolds in attendance.

The wistful warmth of the sentiment of Irving Berlin's celebration of Yuletide and Crosby's mellifluous delivery proved enduringly captivating. Uniquely, it returned to the charts during each of the following 20 years. "White Christmas" went on to become the best-selling single ever, with sales of around 50 million to date.

Berlin had known he'd hit on something special straightaway: after writing "White Christmas" in early 1940, he told his musical secretary: "Grab your pen and take down this song. I just wrote the best song I've ever written – hell, I just wrote the best song that anybody's ever written!"

Robert Dimery

Movie Release Date August 4, 1942

Nationality USA

Director Mark Sandrich

Cast Bing Crosby, Fred Astaire, Marjorie Reynolds

Music Irving Berlin

Why It's Key The largely forgotten movie that gave us a song we will never forget.

Key People
Rodgers and Hammerstein

Few foresaw on March 31, 1943 when the curtain went up on *Oklahoma!* that a new era in Broadway musicals was born. Composer Richard Rodgers (1902–1979) and librettist-lyricist Oscar Hammerstein (1895–1960) had each enjoyed successful careers on Broadway, but when they collaborated professionally for the first time on *Oklahoma!* they not only launched the most renowned partnership in the history of Broadway musicals but also changed the direction of the American musical. It was the first fully integrated musical in which songs, dance, and story were logically and artistically interwoven, instead of slapped together in a semi-contrived way, and all subsequent musicals were influenced by it.

Hammerstein came from a famous theatrical family and began writing lyrics and librettos for Broadway in the '20s. Working with such composers as Jerome Kern and Sigmund Romberg, he found fame for such shows as *Rose-Marie* (1924), *The Desert Song* (1926), and *Show Boat* (1927). Rodgers teamed up with lyricist Lorenz Hart in the '20s and the team presented a series of hit musical comedies into the '40s. When that partnership ended, it seemed impossible that Rodgers would be able to forge another pairing of such chemistry but *Oklahoma!* was just the start of an even more successful team-up that would continue to break new ground in such imperishable works as *Carousel*, *Allegro*, *South Pacific*, *The King And I*, and *The Sound of Music*, as well as providing a long list of beloved song standards.

Thomas Hischak

Date 1943

Roles Composer (Rodgers) and Lyricist (Hammerstein)

Nationality USA

Why It's Key Changed the face of the musical.

Opposite Richard Rodgers and Oscar Hanmmerstein

Key Person
Fats Waller

The untimely death on December 15, 1943, of jazz pianist, composer, and performer Thomas "Fats" Waller at the age of 39 as he rode the Santa Fe Chief train cut short a remarkable career of a unique talent.

Waller was born in 1904 in Waverly, New York, the son of a Baptist Reverend. The young Waller learned to play the organ at his father's Harlem church then in the '20s made a living playing piano in Washington, D.C. movie houses before finding success in vaudeville and later major theaters in Chicago and New York. His freewheeling way of singing as he played and interjected ad libs soon caught on and his recordings of his own songs and those by others became popular.

Waller had started composing music in the '20s and, working with such lyricists as Andy Razaf, he wrote many jazz favorites, such as "Ain't Misbehavin," "Honeysuckle Rose," "Joint Is Jumpin," "I've Got A Feeling I'm Falling," and "Keeping Out of Mischief Now." He scored two "Negro" revues on Broadway, *Keep Shufflin'* (1928) and *Hot Chocolates* (1929), and performed his songs in Hollywood movies. His "stride" piano playing could be breathtaking, although some admirers feel that his almost cartoonishly playful stage persona obscured his abilities.

A heavy drinker and eater, Waller lived carelessly and, as tragic as it was, few were surprised at his death. Interest in Waller's works was revived with the long-running Broadway revue *Ain't Misbehavin'* (1978).
Thomas Hischak

Role Recording Artist

Date December 15, 1943

Nationality USA

Why It's Key A man whose clowning belied his magnificent talent.

Key Album *Oklahoma!*
original cast recording

Oklahoma! is generally regarded as the very first original Broadway cast album. There were some precursors, and many records of individual songs from shows in pop-style arrangements had been released prior to 1943, but this is the first recording of the bulk of a musical's score as performed by the Broadway cast, led by the original conductor and featuring the orchestrations heard in the theater. It's interesting to note that, although the show opened at the St. James Theater on March 31, 1943, the cast album wasn't recorded until October 20 and 25 of that year and wasn't released until December 2, 1943. The bundle of several 78-rpm discs – a literal "album," as was then the standard format – included such songs as "Oh, What A Beautiful Mornin," "The Surrey With The Fringe On Top," "Kansas City," "I Cain't Say No," "People Will Say We're In Love," and the title number. Howard da Silva, who played Judy Fry, is heard only in the duet "Pore Jud Is Daid" (with Drake); his solo, "Lonely Room" was not recorded for this collection. A supplementary volume, including three songs from the show that had been omitted from the first one, was recorded on May 24, 1944 and released in January 1945 – but "Lonely Room" is sung by Drake, not da Silva. The *Oklahoma!* cast album established a recording genre that was immensely popular through the pre-rock era and, to a lesser degree, beyond.
Michael Portantiere

Release Date December 2, 1943 (Volume I); January 3, 1945 (Volume II)

Nationality USA

Track Listing Overture, Oh, What A Beautiful Mornin', The Surrey With The Fringe On Top, Kansas City, I Cain't Say No, Many A New Day, It's A Scandal! It's A Outrage!, People Will Say We're In Love, Pore Jud Is Daid, Lonely Room, Out Of My Dreams, The Farmer And The Cowman, All Er Nuthin', Oklahoma!, Finale

Why It's Key The album that spawned an industry.

Opposite *Oklahoma!*

Key Event
Muddy Waters moves to Chicago

Back home in Louisiana, he was just another Delta bluesman but when in 1943 McKinley Morganfield – already better known as Muddy Waters – headed north to try to become a professional musician, he changed the course of popular music for good.

It would be five years before the move to the Windy City yielded a record release for Waters but he proved to be the lightning rod that sparked life into one of the most powerful musical monsters of the twentieth century. A crucial fact is that during those five years, Waters took possession of his first electric guitar.

His first hit was the classic "I Can't Be Satisfied" (ironically a reworking of "I Be's Troubled," which blues historian Alan Lomax had recorded Waters performing before the move north) and the success of the 78 rpm single set a template that his label, Chess, would use for the next three decades. Waters' adoption and popularization of an electric, group format changed the

blues from a rustic, backwoods, man-on-a-stool genre into something more modern-sounding and galvanizing. He became the lynchpin of a roster that included Howlin' Wolf, Bo Diddley, and Chuck Berry. The Chicago electric blues sound would form a cornerstone of the rock 'n' roll of the '50s, the R&B and beat boom of the '60s (The Rolling Stones took their name from one of Waters' songs), and heavy metal in the '70s.
Angus Batey

Date 1943

Country USA

Why It's Key A relocation leads to one of the most influential American musical styles of all time.

Opposite Muddy Waters

Key Event
Charles Trenet writes "La Mer"

World War II was not good for Charles Trenet. Though the exuberant music hall star nicknamed "The Singing Fool" was known in happier times for his white felt hat, angelic blond curls, sparkling blue eyes, light baritone voice, and poetic turn of phrase, he was no more immune to the rest of the French population to the horrors of Nazi occupation. During that conflict he had the misfortune to be reported dead and suspected of being both Jewish and a collaborator.

Yet during this same period while on a train journey along the coast with his friends Roland Gerbaud and Léo Chauliac, his piano accompanist, he managed to cowrite the most tranquil of songs. The romantic ballad "La Mer" – which reportedly took Trenet and Chauliac only 20 minutes to complete – celebrated the shimmering beauty of the Mediterranean before the developers moved in. Trenet originally found the chanson "too solemn" but when he recorded it at the end of the war, he

caught the mood of the French nation and it became his best-known song.

Trenet (1913–2001) also appealed to Francophiles the world over and followed in the footsteps of Maurice Chevalier, who had been the first person to sing "Y'a d'la Joie," another Trenet composition, in 1937. Recorded hundreds of times in dozens of languages, "La Mer" was adapted into English by Jack Lawrence and became "Beyond The Sea," Bobby Darin's biggest hit of 1960.
Pierre Perrone

Date 1943

Country France

Why It's Key Proof that not even the Nazis could suppress the artistic impulse.

Key Person
Kate Smith

Possessed of a big, rich, booming voice and a physique to match, Kate Smith (1907–1986) was one of the most popular singers of the first half of the twentieth century. Smith knew exactly how to control the power of her voice and made sure never to rely on her sound alone, this and her perfect diction making her an excellent interpreter of lyrics. She concentrated on songs that had mass appeal, speaking to the regular guy on the street or on the farm.

She made her first splash in the shows *Honeymoon Lane*, *Hit the Deck*, and *Flying High*. In 1926, she began recording. Nineteen of her recordings sold over a million copies. In 1931 she got her own radio show and her theme song became "When The Moon Comes Over The Mountain," to whose lyric she contributed. Simultaneously she had a daytime talk and news show, making her the most successful woman in radio. On August 14, 1943, she got her second theme song when she sang Irving Berlin's "God Bless

America" in the film *This Is The Army*, released on that date. A hit for her three times over, it was adopted by hockey team the Philadelphia Flyers, who still occasionally run a video of her performing the song before games. Smith was voted one of the three most popular women in America alongside Helen Hayes and Eleanor Roosevelt. In 1950, she made the medium of television yet another of her conquests.

Ken Bloom

Role Recording Artist

Date 1943

Nationality USA

Why It's Key Known – even to non-initiates – as the "God Bless America" woman.

Key Song
"Bésame Mucho"

During World War II, the entertainment business embraced Latin American stories, themes, performers, and songs. This Mexican number was taken to its heart, and became one of the most popular love songs of the era.

Consuelo Velazquez wrote the passionate Spanish lyric and the rhythmic, pulsating music before she was even 16 and it was so successful in Mexico that Sunny Skylar was commissioned to write an English lyric about a fervent declaration of love; he retained the Spanish title which roughly translates as "Kiss Me Deeply." The song was released by Jimmy Dorsey and his Orchestra (vocals by Kitty Kallen and Bob Eberle) in late 1943 and went to No. 1 on the U.S. charts the following year, another successful version by Abe Lyman and his Orchestra soon following. When Andy Russell made a test record of the song with George Siravo's Orchestra, it was deemed worthy of release and went on to sell a million copies.

"Bésame Mucho" remained a favorite long after the war years. Russell recorded it again in 1957, as did such diverse talents as Josephine Baker, Xavier Cugat, The Flamingos, Nat King Cole, Mantovanni's Orchestra, Sammy Davis, Jr., Steve Lawrence with Eydie Gorme, Charo, Charlie Byrd, the Ray Conniff Singers, Dave Brubeck, Diana Krall, and Richard Clayderman. Most lucratively of all, it featured on The Beatles *Anthology 1* album (1995) – even though it was one of the songs with which the Fab Four failed to impress Decca Records in 1962.

Thomas Hischak

Release Date 1943

Nationality Mexico/USA

Composer Consuelo Velazquez

Why It's Key The Latin sound – long before Ricky Martin.

Key Performance *Cover Girl*
the movie

So she didn't sing her own songs. Rita Hayworth may have had her vocals in *Cover Girl* courtesy of Martha Meers, but the face and the moves were all her own. Swept along by Gene Kelly's choreography genius, Hayworth's legs staked their claim as the best movers in Hollywood.

The film also made Gene Kelly a star – for both acting and choreography – worth his weight in tap shoes. The producers gave Kelly complete control over the creative side of the film, giving him the chance to try out new tricks, such as dancing with himself in "Alter Ego," a technological and artistic marvel for a film in 1944.

Not only did *Cover Girl* propel these stars to Hollywood's A-list, but it also paved a new road for American musicals. Gone were the days of random, lavish stage numbers plopped in whenever a vaudeville star or hit-making pop song cropped up, although admittedly when the story's leads are dancers

struggling to make it to the top, it makes "melding" a lot easier. A string of Gershwin and Kern songs – including the lovely "Long Ago And Far Away" – and comedic slapstick from star Phil Silvers complemented Hayworth's dramatic chops and Kelly's smart moves. The film was nominated for five Oscars and won for Best Music and Scoring of a Musical Picture.
Leila Regan-Porter

Date 1944

Nationality USA

Director Charles Vidor

Cast Rita Hayworth, Gene Kelly, Phil Silvers

Composers Jerome Kern, Ira Gershwin

Why It's Key Now songs in musicals were a part of the plot and dance numbers mirrored the action, instead of distracting from it.

1940-1949

171

Key Song **"Ac-cent-tchu-ate the Positive"**
from *Here Come The Waves*

Composer Harold Arlen and lyricist Johnny Mercer wrote the score for the wartime navy musical *Here Come The Waves*, released on December 18, 1944. Among the hit songs from the score was "Ac-cent-tchu-ate The Positive," sung by Bing Crosby in the film.

Mercer and Arlen were riding home from the studio after a conference about devising a song for the sailors in the movie. Arlen began singing a melody for the proposed song. The minute he did so, something jumped into Mercer's mind "as if it dialed a phone number." In 1939, Mercer had been working with Benny Goodman and had fallen into conversation with a publicity man who told him he had been to see a sermon by one Father Divine. Mercer was amused to hear that the subject of his sermon was, "Accentuate the positive and eliminate the negative." "It sounds so Southern and so funny that I wrote it down on a piece of paper," Mercer recalled. He admitted, "It doesn't

really fit. The accent is all different. I just think there's some kind of fate connected with it."

The public didn't seem to share Mercer's apparent feeling that the phrase had been inappropriately shoehorned into the melody. Mercer's own recording of the song was a hit, as was that of Crosby and the Andrews Sisters. Many years later, the song was used to close the 1986 Mary Martin- and Carol Channing-led play *Legends!*
Ken Bloom

Movie Release Date December 18, 1944

Country USA

Writers Harold Arlen, Johnny Mercer

Why It's Key A sermon plants a seed – which sprouts five years later.

Key Performance *Meet Me In St. Louis*
the movie

There's not much dramatic conflict in *Meet Me In St. Louis*, a family saga about nice people trying to be nice to other nice people. A measure of the crises involved is the part late in the tale where the teenage heroine's beau sadly announces he can't take her to the big dance because his tuxedo is stuck in a closed tailor's shop and he doesn't know how to contact the proprietor. But its release on November 28, 1944, was two years before the end of World War II, and the musical movie's look at simpler times in small-town life provided exactly the escapism America wanted.

Based on popular stories by Sally (Junior Miss) Benson, that eventually became the basis of a hardcover collection (deliberately named for the film, by then in production, to capitalize on its release), the film starred a young Judy Garland. The Hugh Martin/Ralph Blaine songs she introduced herein were "The Trolley Song" (which became a signature of her career) and the now universally known "Have Yourself A Merry Little Christmas." Other, lesser standards to emerge were that title song and "Under The Bamboo Tree."

Meet Me In St. Louis was also an early film of director Vincente Minelli, containing some of his signatures too, including the famously eerie Halloween sequence and some authentic and rare for the time night-time outdoor filming. It was during the shoot that Minelli met his future wife Garland, mother of their future daughter, Liza with a "z."

David Spencer

Movie Release Date November 28, 1944

Nationality USA

Director Vincente Minelli

Cast Judy Garland, Margaret O'Brien, Mary Astor

Composer Hugh Martin, Ralph Blaine

Why It's Key Feel-good movie that cheered wartime America – and fostered a showbiz marriage.

Opposite *Meet Me In St. Louis*

Key Song **"Swinging On A Star"**
Bing Crosby

When composer James Van Heusen and lyricist Johnny Burke wrote songs for the Bing Crosby film *Going My Way*, released on May 3, 1944, the title ballad was highlighted in the movie, sung three times with the hope of an Oscar nod. Ironically, it was the novelty ditty "Swinging On A Star" that captured moviegoers' attention, won the Academy Award for Best Song, and passed into history.

The number is an amusing piece with a catchy, swinging melody and a clever lyric that uses different animals to illustrate some of the seven deadly sins and to merrily teach a lesson. It was sung in the movie by Crosby and the Robert Mitchell Boys choir on the stage of the Metropolitan Opera House as part of an audition for a music publisher. Burke got the idea for the lyric after hearing Crosby scold one of his sons for "acting like a mule." He wrote the wry lyric in which an animal name jarringly ends each refrain without rhyming. Crosby's recording of the song with the Williams Brothers sold over a million records, as did a disc by the John Scott Trotter Orchestra. The number was reprised in films *Duffy's Tavern* (1945, a parody version by Crosby and others) and *The Joker Is Wild* (1957, Frank Sinatra, using a revised lyric by Harry Harris). The song even crossed over and was a hit record for folk singer Burl Ives.

Thomas Hischak

Release Date February 1944

Nationality USA

Composers James Van Heusen, Johnny Burke

Why It's Key Showed that it isn't always the obvious song that becomes a standard.

Key Person
Perry Como

When his recording of "Till The End Of Time" hit the U.S. charts on August 18, 1945, former band singer Como (1912–2001) came into his own as one of the best-selling vocalists of the post-war years.

Born Pierino Roland Como in Canonsburg, Pennsylvania, he began a career as a barber at the age of fifteen – but sang in barbershop quartets. By the '30s he started singing professionally and first received some recognition as the vocalist for the Ted Weems Orchestra in 1936. He went off on his own in the early '40s and recorded five singles before striking the jackpot with "Till The End Of Time," a fervent love ballad that Buddy Kaye and Ted Mossman adapted from Chopin's "Polonaise in A Flat Minor." Como's warm, smooth crooning style garnered him eleven singles that were million-sellers during the '50s. "Hot Diggity," "Round And Round," and "Catch A Falling Star" were his three U.S. No. 1s. From 1955 to 1963 he had a popular television show, and appeared in four films.

Como's relaxed crooning of his theme song "Dream Along With Me" was the antithesis of the blossoming rock 'n' roll sound in the '50s and his hits dried up as the decade wound to a close. However, he retained a loyal live audience throughout his life and two of his best known records were '70s releases, "It's Impossible" and "And I Love You So."

Thomas Hischak

Role Recording Artist

Date 1945

Nationality USA

Why It's Key The barber who became one of the world's most-loved crooners.

Key Event Charlie Parker leads "The Greatest Jazz Session Ever"

Kansas City born Charlie Parker, known as "Yardbird" or merely "Bird," was the most influential jazz saxophonist of all time. Though he could, and often did, play at great speed, every line was logical, a gem of creation. In tandem with trumpeter Dizzy Gillespie, he is considered the founder of bebop, the new form of jazz that disdained rigid structure and stately paces for uptempo improvisation.

The session for Savoy Records that took place on November 26, 1945 – the first time that altoist Parker was actually leader on a record date – stands as a milestone both in the short career of Parker, who died aged 35, and the development of modern jazz (even if the "greatest jazz session ever" line by which it was sold was hyperbolic). It was a superstar line-up: a young Miles Davis handled most of the trumpet chores, while Dizzy Gillespie mainly filled in on piano. Curly Russell played bass and Max Roach drums. The material played, all penned by Parker, included "Billie's

Bounce," "Ko Ko," "Thrivin' On A Riff," "Meandering," and "Now's The Time" (The last-named later surfaced as the 1949 R&B hit "The Hucklebuck," though no composer credit was given Bird.) It's Parker's astonishing playing on "Ko Ko," a tune based on the chords to Ray Noble's "Cherokee," that is regarded as providing a master-class for any innovative musician, his final chorus being hailed as comprising a condensed history of bebop.

Fred Dellar

Date November 26, 1945

Country USA

Why It's Key The session that confirmed the world of jazz had changed forever.

Opposite Charlie Parker

Key Person
Mack Gordon

The hugely prolific lyricist Mack Gordon (who also sometimes composed) had one of the most impressive movie songwriting careers, earning nine Oscar nominations, including six in a row from 1940 to 1945, yet his sole win was for "You'll Never Know" (1943).

Born Morris Gittler in Poland in 1904, he wrote his first stage scores in 1925, finally hitting the jackpot with the song "Time On My Hands" in the 1930 show *Smiles*. Gordon teamed up with English émigré Harry Revel in 1931 and they went to Hollywood in 1933. Songs included "Did You Ever See A Dream Walking?", "Stay As Sweet As You Are," "You Hit the Spot," and "There's A Lull In My Life." The team broke up in 1939 and Gordon joined Harry Warren. They wrote for the Glenn Miller Orchestra vehicles *Sun Valley Serenade* (1941) and *Orchestra Wives* (1942). The latter featured "I Got A Gal In Kalamazoo," "I Had The Craziest Dream," "There Will Never Be Another You," "Chattanooga Choo Choo".

Others of their hits included "You'll Never Know" and "The More I See You." The latter, with which Harry James made the U.S. chart on May 26, 1945, is amongst Gordon's most famous songs and was covered to chart success by Chris Montez as late as 1966.

Gordon died in 1959. Considering his poor Oscars record, it's ironic that ASCAP has officially recognized Gordon's much-loved "Chattanooga Choo Choo" as the most played standard on television.
Ken Bloom

Date 1945

Role Lyricist

Nationality USA

Why it's key One of Hollywood's greatest lyricists – even if Tinseltown seemed unable to recognize it.

Key Performance *Carousel*
stage musical

From its seamlessly entwined plot, music, and choreography to its dramatically different tragic plot, *Carousel* broke the rules of musical theater and severely pushed the whole genre forward. Straight from the opening scene – without even so much as an overture – an audience could tell that *Carousel* wasn't going to be like other musicals. The whole exposition is told in that curtain raiser with neither words or singing, an intricate ballet taking place in a New England fairground telling the audience all they need to know about the characters and the plot.

The tale of young lovers Billy Bigelow (John Raitt) and Julie Jordan (Jan Clayton) and their disastrous love affair is told in *Carousel* by the combination of Oscar Hammerstein's words, Richard Rodgers' music, and Agnes de Mille's choreography. Never had all the elements of musical theater been employed to tell such a tale as here. Bigelow makes the most disagreeable of heroes, showing his true feelings in

rare occasions such as the epic eight minute song "Soliloquy," where he contemplates fatherhood in a whole range of emotions.

Based on the Hungarian play *Liliom* by Ferenc Molonar, *Carousel* was not to have a happy ending – another first for a musical. But with a slight change to Molonar's original work, Rodgers and Hammerstein gave the characters eventual peace of mind. Indeed, the most famous of the show's songs is the consoling anthem "You'll Never Walk Alone."
Leila Regan-Porter

Opening Night April 19, 1945

Country USA

Director Rouben Mamoulian

Cast John Raitt, Jan Clayton, Jean Darling

Composers Oscar Hammerstein, Richard Rogers

Why It's Key Domestic violence, single motherhood, crime, suicide – these weren't the usual themes that prevailed on Broadway.

Key Song "Let It Snow! Let It Snow! Let It Snow!"

Songwriters Jule Styne (music) and Sammy Cahn (lyric) were New Yorkers who spent much of the '40s in California scoring movie musicals. It seems to have been partly their nostalgia for East Coast winters that inspired this bouncy but still romantic song about the joy of watching the snow fall as one is snug and warm inside by the fire with a sweetheart: it was written after Cahn suggested on a very hot day that they visit the beach and Styne responded with a suggestion that they write a winter song instead.

A recording by Vaughn Monroe And His Orchestra popularized the cozy number in 1945. After hitting the charts on December 22 that year it remained on Your Hit Parade for thirteen weeks. Three successful discs were released soon after by the Boswell Sisters, Woody Herman, and Russ Morgan (vocal by Connee Boswell).

This perennial Christmas favorite is unique it that it is not about Christmas or the holiday season but about winter weather.

Yet because the number is thought of as a Yuletide song, it has been included on hundreds of seasonal albums and been featured in many television Christmas specials. Among the varied artists to make distinctive recordings were Dick Haymes, Rosemary Clooney, Dean Martin, The Temptations, Doris Day, Oscar Peterson, Judy Collins, Elaine Stritch, The Carpenters, Richochet, Boyz II Men, and Garth Brooks. Also, because of its conversational lyric, the song has lent itself to many successful duet recordings.
Thomas Hischak

Release Date 1945

Nationality USA

Composer Jule Styne, Sammy Cahn

Why It's Key The Yuletide celebration that actually isn't.

Key Event
The big band era comes to an end

For many years, big bands held sway. The Saturday night shindig at the local palais, jiving, perhaps, to a ten piece or more band was all important to everyday folk. Those in "society" togged up to foxtrot, at big hotels and restaurants. Some of the most important radio shows involved remote live band broadcasts from such venues. In Britain it could be Ambrose from The Mayfair and Lew Stone from The Monseigneur, in the United States, Glenn Miller might air from The Meadowbrook, New Jersey and records by such as Artie Shaw, Woody Herman, and Count Basie sold millions.

The dance bands proved the short cut to success. Virtually every top-line singer started life as a band vocalist: Frank Sinatra with Harry James, Billy Eckstine and Sarah Vaughan with Earl Hines, Ella Fitzgerald with Chick Webb, Bing Crosby with Paul Whiteman. But in December 1946, that world tumbled to an end when eight major bands, including those headed by Tommy Dorsey, Les Brown, and Benny Goodman, ceased

trading in the space of a few weeks. Their end had been hastened by AFM strikes and the mounting cost of touring. Most of them would actually re-form while others, like Stan Kenton's and Ted Heath's, continued to wave the flag, often playing concerts rather than dance dates. But the era of swing was essentially history as the DJ took over on radio and jukeboxes replaced small combos in the clubs and cafes.
Fred Dellar

Date December 1946

Country UK/USA

Why It's Key When suddenly the world didn't have that swing.

Key Event
George Formby is awarded an OBE

George Formby was awarded an OBE in George VI's birthday honors, in recognition of his work in World War II with scores of charity events, tours of bombed cities, performances for front line troops, and songs like "I Did What I Could With My Gas Mask."

Few were better qualified to keep the nation's morale high. The son of a music hall star, Formby (1904–1961) started out performing his deceased father's material before his adoption of the ukulele pointed him toward his own style, which solidified into that of a gormless (he was naturally "blessed" with comedy-friendly buck teeth) and decidedly Northern innocent who nonetheless sang songs packed with innuendo like "When I'm Cleaning Windows" provided to him by, among others, Noel Gay. He took this persona into motion pictures and by the late '30s was earning a staggering £100,000 (U.S. $200,000) per year. His films included *Let George Do It* (1940) and *Turned Out Nice Again* (1941; the title became his catchphrase).

In private, Formby was offended that his wife Beryl had been ignored in the honors list, partly because she had done so much to encourage his wartime activities (even if it was mainly to ensure that Formby was more prominent than his competitor in northern earthiness, Gracie Fields) and partly because it was no fun living with a slighted Beryl – a henpecked scenario that could have come straight from one of his films.

Spencer Leigh

Date June 24, 1946

Country UK

Why It's Key Turned out nice – up to a point.

Key Person
Al Jolson

Al Jolson (1886–1950) is considered to be the greatest performer of all time by those who were lucky enough to see him, and not just because his amazing egotism gave him the confidence to convince audiences of the monumental nature of his talents.

He got his start in minstrel shows and graduated to musical theater. Jolson ruled Broadway's Winter Garden Theater in a series of successful revues and musicals. His trademarks were blackface, talking to the audience, and performing down on one knee, his arms outstretched. His dynamic personality comes through in his movie performances. But although Jolson enjoyed early success in talking pictures – *The Jazz Singer* (1927) and 1928's *The Singing Fool* (the biggest money-maker in Hollywood history until *Gone With The Wind*), he seemed more comfortable with the human interaction involved in treading the boards.

Once he left the movies (or vice versa) he performed in nightclubs and on records and radio but his style of performing was thought increasingly anachronistic. However, with the release of the biopic *The Jolson Story* on October 10, 1946, he was rediscovered by a whole new generation and his career exploded again.

Bing Crosby excepted, Jolson introduced more hit songs than any other performer, among them "My Mammy," "Sonny Boy," and "April Showers." A measure of the mixed qualities of this difficult talent is that while he received credit for composing many of his hits, it's doubtful that he ever wrote any music or lyrics.

Ken Bloom

Role Recording Artist

Date 1946

Country USA

Why It's Key Billed himself as "The World's Greatest Entertainer." Many agreed.

Opposite Al Jolson

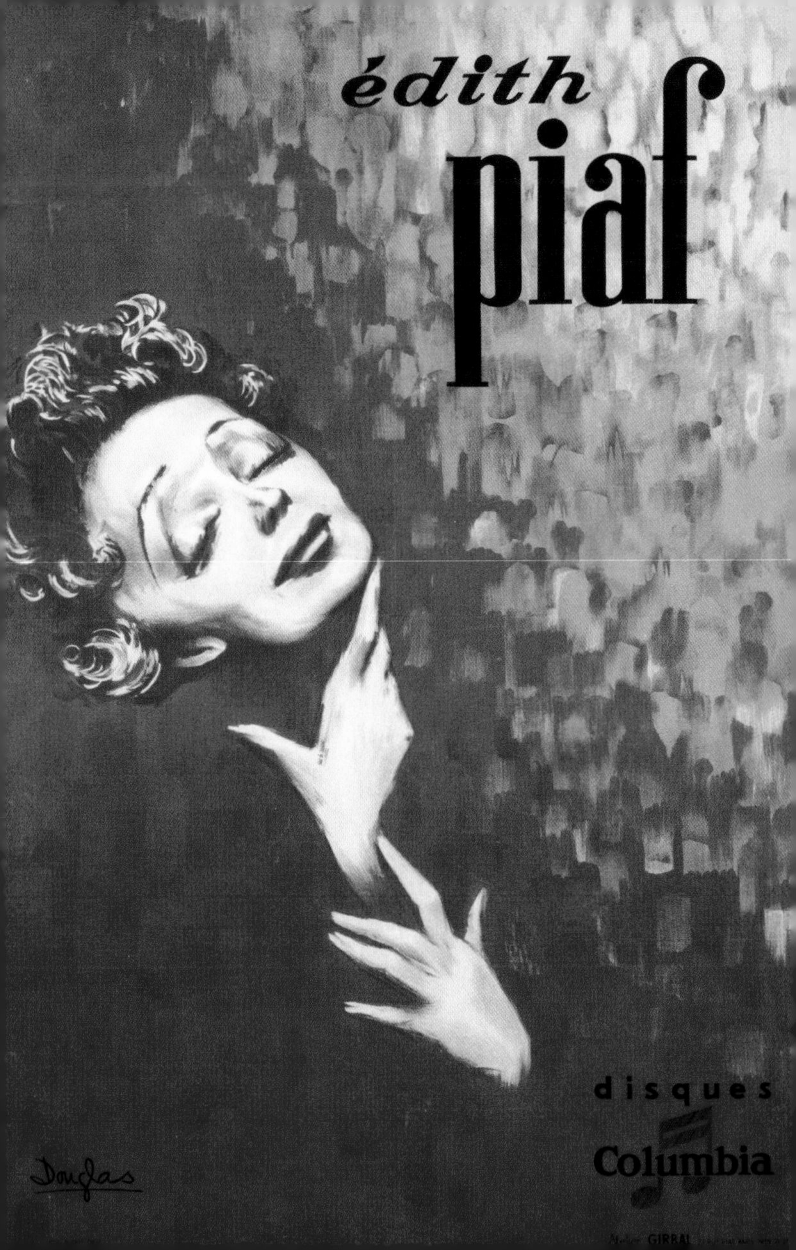
édith
piaf
disques
Columbia
Douglas
GIRBAL

Key Person
Edith Piaf

When she recorded "La Vie En Rose" in 1946, the "Little Sparrow," who was born Edith Gassion, had been singing around her native Paris for most of her 31 years. She spent part of her childhood in a brothel run by her mother and her melodramatic material often dealt with the streetwalkers' tragic destinies and mirrored her own tumultuous personal life, which included the loss of a child, three car crashes, addictions to morphine and alcohol, and numerous liaisons, most notably with the singer Yves Montand. In 1936, Piaf cut "Les Mômes De La Cloche," her first 78 and thereafter proceeded to astonish the world with the powerful voice with its dramatic *vibrato* that emanated form her petite figure.

Piaf wrote the lyric to "La Vie En Rose," with Louis Gugliemi providing the music, in 1945 but, unsure of the song's potential, she only recorded it the following year. The iconic performer, also known for "L'Hymne A L'Amour" and "Non, Je Ne Regrette Rien" (sort of a Gallic "My Way" precursor), was the first French chanson artist to appear at New York's Carnegie Hall. Piaf mentored Charles Aznavour, Gilbert Bécaud, and the vocal ensemble Les Compagnons De La Chanson but "La Vie En Rose" remains her signature song and was adapted into English by lyricist Mack David. It has been covered by Louis Armstrong, Marlene Dietrich, Madeleine Peyroux, and even done disco-style by Grace Jones and Donna Summer. Piaf died of cancer in October 1963.

Pierre Perrone

Role Recording Artist

Date 1946

Country France

Why It's Key Streetwise ambassador for French music.

Opposite **Edith Piaf**

Key Song "There's No Business Like Show Business"

Written by Irving Berlin for the musical *Annie Get Your Gun*, based on the life of sharp-shooter Annie Oakley, which opened on May 16, 1946, "There's No Business Like Show Business" is a stirring paean to "the costumes, the scenery, the makeup, the props, the audience that lifts you when you're down." Berlin composed it and the other songs in the score in a week, despite being unused to writing for a narrative. He blithely ignored the rustic setting of the show, reasoning that it was about showbusiness not "hillbilly stuff." The number doesn't actually advance the show's plot but certainly advanced the show's profits, boasting that quality of instant memorability that much great pop possesses. The syncopation of the melody drives home the delightful circular title phrase, leaving the listener as giddy and breathless as a well-worked chorus girl.

Ironically, though the song is associated with *Annie Get Your Gun* star Ethel Merman more than any other performer, the original Broadway cast recording of selections from the show does not include her rendition of the song. However, Merman sang it in the 1954 film of the same title, which showcased many Berlin hits, and she performed and recorded the song many times throughout her career – most bizarrely for her 1977 disco album. In the 1950 film version of *Annie Get Your Gun*, the anthem is sung by Betty Hutton, Keenan Wynn, Howard Keel, and Louis Calhern.

Michael Portantiere

Release Date 1946

Nationality USA

Composer Irving Berlin

Why It's Key Provided show business with an anthem.

Key Song "Zip-A-Dee-Doo-Dah"
from *Song Of The South*

In 1947, Allie Wrubel and Ray Gilbert's "Zip-A-Dee-Doo-Dah" from the Walt Disney feature *Song Of The South* (released on November 12, 1946) won the Oscar for Best Song. Doris Day, Bing Crosby, Dionne Warwick, and even The Jackson 5 have subsequently covered it.

Yet at the time of writing, it is not possible to see the song in its original context. It may be heard on the commercially available soundtrack album and those who have it on old VHS cassettes can view it but the Walt Disney Company withdrew the movie worldwide in 2001 and has never allowed a video or laser disc release in the United States.

Song Of The South is the Disney movie that the company is ashamed of. An adaptation of Joel Chandler Harris' Br'er Rabbit tales, it has been accused of conveying "Uncle Tom" images of African Americans and even romanticizing slavery. Disney has run shy of controversy by disallowing further public consumption.

In the film, the song is sung by the character Uncle Remus as he is out walking in a forest (which type of free movement defenders cite as refutation of slave assumptions). As he sings, cartoon birds and butterflies flutter around him, a then technological marvel. The song is wonderfully life-affirming, exulting in a fine morning and predicting "plenty of sunshine comin' my way."

Ironically, this clip is an iconic piece of Disney fare, still shown frequently on compilation programs.
Ken Bloom

Movie Release Date November 12, 1946

Nationality USA

Composers Allie Wrubel, Ray Gilbert

Why It's Key The classic Disney song forcibly removed from its setting.

Key Song "There But For You Go I"
David Brooks

The Broadway production *Brigadoon* opened on March 13, 1947. The Loewe/Lerner score included such future standards as "Heather On The Hill," "Come To Me, Bend To Me," "From This Day On," and "There But For You Go I." Surprisingly, all the hits from the score were ballads. As the character Tommy, David Brooks sang "There But For You Go I" to Marino Bell's Fiona – a girl from the titular mystical Highlands village which appears only once every 100 years with whom he has fallen in love. The lyric has Tommy cataloging all the lonely men he has seen (in his head, for his eyes are closed): one with his head bowed ("His heart had no place to go"), another alone with the tide at the seashore, another who had never known love, in all cases leading Tommy to conclude the title phrase. Brooks' impassioned performance on the RCA original Broadway cast recording helped make the song a hit and led to no less than Frank Sinatra recording the best known of the many cover versions.

There were three Broadway revivals of *Brigadoon*, in 1957, 1963, and 1980. There was also a 1954 film version which starred Gene Kelly. However, several songs, including amazingly "There But For You Go I," were not in the final edit. The producers felt that the song did not show off Kelly's voice very well.
Ken Bloom

Release Date 1947

Nationality USA

Composers Frederick Loewe, Alan Jay Lerner

Why It's Key Famous song from a stage musical that ultimately proved expendable.

Key Person
E. Y. "Yip" Harburg

The opening of *Finian's Rainbow* on Broadway was a triumph for lyricist-librettist E. Y. Harburg, who tackled experimental and controversial ideas in his musicals but was also the master of fantasy, satire, and passionate dreams.

He was born in 1896 in New York, the son of Russian immigrants, and began writing light verse as a student, signing his work "Yip" and getting published in various newspapers. When the Depression hit, Harburg turned to songwriting and he had an early song hit with "Brother Can You Spare a Dime?" (music by Jay Gorney) which became the unofficial anthem of the Depression years. He scored several Broadway revues, book musicals, and film musicals in the '30s, having his greatest success with the movie classic *The Wizard Of Oz* (1939) with composer Harold Arlen. Harburg took on the issues of feminism, war, slavery, Communist witch hunts, and the atom bomb in later Broadway works such as *Bloomer Girl* (1944), *Flahooley* (1951),

and *Jamaica* (1957) but his biggest hit was *Finian's Rainbow*, a fantasy about greed, racism, and poverty. Despite his serious topics, the Harburg musicals were always comedies with a whimsical but pointed tone. While "Over the Rainbow" remains his most famous song, he was also on the charts with such hits as "How Are Things in Glocca Morra?", "April in Paris," "Old Devil Moon," and "Happiness Is A Thing Called Joe." Harburg remained an outspoken liberal up to his death in 1981.

Thomas Hischak

Role Lyricist

Date 1947

Nationality USA

Why It's Key Lyricist whose talent spanned both escapism and realism.

Key Song "The Gentleman Is A Dope"
from *Allegro*

By 1947, songwriters Rodgers and Hammerstein were so popular that they could launch a hit song even from a flop show, as with this sly torch number from *Allegro*.

When *Allegro* opened on Broadway on October 10, 1947, the advance sale was phenomenal because the team's two previous musicals, *Oklahoma!* (1943) and *Carousel* (1945), were not only hits but landmarks in the development of the American musical. *Allegro* was also a landmark of sorts but it was not the same kind of hit. The highly experimental show was mostly panned by the press and only the advance sale allowed the musical to run for nine months. However, even reviewers and playgoers who thought the piece dreary perked up near the end of the second act when Lisa Kirk sang "The Gentleman Is a Dope," a sarcastic love song. The narrator talks of a man with many faults, "A clumsy Joe who wouldn't know a Rhumba from a Waltz." But the twist in Hammerstein's lyric is that the

man of whom she speaks, her boss, is in fact someone she is in love with but who is too stupid to notice the affection she holds for him. The number made Kirk a Broadway star and the song went on to several recordings and a place on the charts, Jo Stafford's early disc being the most popular.

Long a nightclub and concert favorite, the song has been recorded by, amongst others, Dinah Shore, Portia Nelson, and Bernadette Peters.

Thomas Hischak

Release Date October 1947

Nationality USA

Composers Richard Rodgers, Oscar Hammerstein

Why It's Key A pearl among swine.

Key People
Jule Styne and Sammy Cahn

In the pre-rock era, before best pals formed bands and before the general ending of the demarcation of roles between lyricist and composer, songwriting collaboration was very often a rather business-like arrangement, with people achieving success with one partner but still regularly moving onto others. An example of this pattern is the movie and Tin Pan Alley songwriting team of Styne and Cahn, whose collaborative period marked just one of several creative partnerships each of the pair had over the years.

Composer Jule Styne (1905–1994) was born in London and as a child came to America where he was a concert pianist at the age of eight, performing with the Chicago Symphony a year later. But Styne lost interest in classical music and formed his own band in 1931, ending up in Hollywood first as vocal coach for Alice Faye and then writing songs for movies in the '40s, most memorably *Anchors Aweigh* (1945) and *Romance on the High Seas* (1948). His lyricist for both

films was Sammy Cahn (1913–1993), a New York-native who wrote for Tin Pan Alley and Hollywood.

Both men wanted to be legit composers and the success of the comedy stage musical *High Button Shoes*, which opened on October 9, 1947, did it for them. Other famous Cahn and Styne collaborations included "Saturday Night Is The Loneliest Night Of The Week," "Let It Snow! Let It Snow! Let It Snow!," and Oscar-winner "Three Coins In A Fountain."

Thomas Hischak

Roles Composer (Styne) and Lyricist (Cahn)

Date 1947

Nationality USA

Why It's Key The partnership that illustrates the sometimes practical nature of songwriting.

Opposite Jules Styne

Key Event
CBS introduces the Long Player

Since the earliest days of sound recording, inventors had been seeking ways to increase playing time. The original pitiful three minute playback was determined by technological factors such as the width of the groove in the record and the strength of the recording medium. It limited the record industry to short popular songs and comic monologues and made it impossible to record classical music in its entirety. Many popular songs of the day had sections omitted in order to allow them to fit onto a record – and those amended renditions, absurdly, became the genuine versions to the public.

In the '30s long playing records had been developed for dictating machines and movie soundtracks. The Columbia company incorporated these advances into a 12-inch diameter vinyl disc with much smaller (micro) grooves which it demonstrated on June 21, 1948. Dr. Peter Goldmark led the research to improve all aspects of the system, from the stylus

that ran in the groove to the motor that turned the record at 33 ⅓ revolutions per minute.

When Columbia introduced the Long Player (as it was later called) it stacked its new discs next to the old 78s. It took an eight-foot-high stack of 78s to contain the same amount of music as a pile of LPs of only 15 inches. The LP had a significant effect on popular music and on the mass media. The main one was that it freed artists from the straightjacket of a recording time of 180 seconds.

Andre Millard

Date June 21, 1948

Country USA

Why It's Key The invention that meant music could be heard in more than small chunks.

Key Person
Doris Day

Born Doris von Kappelhoff in Cincinnati in 1924, Doris Day trained for a dancing career until a car accident forced her to turn to singing. She was a vocalist for the Les Brown and Bob Crosby bands by the early '40s and by the middle of the decade she had a successful recording career. Day's disc of the Joan Whitney-Alex Kramer song "Love Somebody" with Buddy Clark's Orchestra entered the U.S. chart on May 29, 1948 and went to the No. 1 spot just as movie audiences heard her sing "It's Magic" in *Romance on the High Seas* (1948), a film role she got as a last-minute replacement for Betty Hutton.

From that point, Day continued to make popular records but starred in many movie musicals, such as *Calamity Jane* (1953) and *The Pajama Game* (1957), films which gradually caused her to assume a pure, all-American girl image that those who remembered her unnervingly sensual singing with big bands as a 17-year-old must have been surprised by.

Day sang less and less in the later part of her career, concentrating on non-musical movies and television in the '60s and '70s. She retired from show business in the late '80s. Day's singing was characterized by clean, clear vocals of a chipper quality – best heard in her signature song "Que Sera, Sera," – but she could also deliver a torch song with power and conviction.

Thomas Hischak

Role Recording Artist

Date 1948

Nationality USA

Why It's Key The woman who seemed to become more virginal as she got older.

Opposite **Doris Day**

Key Person
Frank Loesser

Hard to believe, given his prodigious output, but Frank Loesser, born June 1910, died at 59. Young Loesser learned piano, resisting family pressure to pursue classical training, eventually becoming a lyricist contributing to a flop Broadway revue in 1936. It led, though, to several Hollywood contracts under which he collaborated with composers like Jule Styne, Hoagy Carmichael, and Burton Lane, producing dozens of standards such as "Two Sleepy People" and the Oscar-winning "Baby, It's Cold Outside." His World War II patriotic march "Praise The Lord And Pass The Ammunition" saw him composing melody as well.

As that title would suggest, Loesser's spiritual home was Broadway, back to which he went to write book musicals – first on October 11, 1948 with *Where's Charley?*, whose classic Americana was typified by the soft shoe "Once In Love With Amy." Next: the 1950 watershed *Guys And Dolls*, with high rollers and nervy dames in the patois of Runyonesque New York, the

music flavored with rhythm and jazz. *The Most Happy Fella* (1956) was another success but the only thing successful about the folk-tale-like *Greenwillow* (1960) was its hit "Never Will I Marry." However, Loesser's 1961 grand finale, *How To Succeed In Business Without Really Trying*, a virtual light operetta (its hit song "I Believe in You" originally sung by the hero to himself) won a Best Musical Tony and a Pulitzer Prize.

David Spencer

Role Songwriter

Date 1948

Nationality USA

Why It's Key The lyricist with a gift for combining irony and heart with American colloquialism.

Key Performance **"Kiss Me Kate"** stage musical

After Cole Porter suffered a crippling horse-riding accident in 1937, his success with musicals seemed to bear the same fate. As his contemporaries Rodgers and Hammerstein went on to break boundaries with highly acclaimed musicals, Porter wrote odd songs here and there, overshadowed and jealous of their abilities. After witnessing the accomplishment the aforementioned pair had with their "integrated" musical *Carousel*, Porter was anxious to do the same, but better. When writers Bella and Samuel Spewack approached Porter with the idea to do a play within a play based on Shakespeare's *Taming Of The Shrew*, the composer worried that the subject matter would be too highbrow before agreeing to write the lyrics and music.

The idea of portraying a stormy divorced couple playing opposite each other the parts of Katharina and Petruchio in a production of *Taming Of The Shrew* worked perfectly for Porter's cheeky, turbulent songs.

The naughty liveliness of "Brush Up Your Shakespeare" puts life into the classic literature, while the moody "Why Can't You Behave?" and passionate and unsettled "So In Love" brings genuine emotions to the characters of Fred (aka Petruchio, played by Alfred Drake) and Lilli (aka Kate, played by Patricia Morison).

The original Broadway show, which opened on December 30, 1948, was a huge success, both critically and publicly. That same year the cast recording became the first released on the new 33 ⅓ LP format, with just enough room for the whole score.
Leila Regan-Porter

Opening Night December 30, 1948

Country USA

Director John C. Wilson

Cast Alfred Drake, Patricia Morison, Lisa Kirk

Composer Cole Porter

Why It's Key A supposedly washed-up Cole Porter makes a spectacular comeback by taking on Shakespeare.

Key Song **" 'A' – You're Adorable (The Alphabet Song)"**

Published in 1948, "'A' – You're Adorable… " is a conceptually close relative to songs that spelled out words as their gimmicks like "M-I-S-S-I-S-S-I-P-P-I," "C-O-N-S-T-A-N-T-I-N-O-P-L-E," and 'I'll See You in C-U-B-A." This one, however, takes the idea one stage further.

When composer Sid Lippman and lyricists Buddy Kaye and Fred Wise got together to work, they would tell each other the latest jokes. One joke concerned a man who was recommending a friend for a job. He listed the man's attributes alphabetically: A – he's amiable, B – he's benevolent, etc. Thus an idea for a song was born.

The opening constitutes a little backstory, about when two young sweethearts were in grade school together. It sets up the alphabetical section that takes up the rest of the song. Adverbs are a key to lyric writing but here was a song entirely made up of adjectives and description – "adorable," "beautiful," and "cutie full of charms," all the way to "kissable" and

"lovelight in your eyes." Either because of song time limits, laziness, or because the conceit was already sagging when for "F" they could only muster a reference to the girl being a feather in the boy's arms, the team didn't even bother when it came to letters M through T. Ditto for W to Z.

Nevertheless, the idea worked beautifully and simply in a song that gave Perry Como a U.S. No. 1 in 1949 and which is well-known to this day.
Ken Bloom

Published Date 1948

Nationality USA

Composers Sid Lippman, Buddy Kaye, Fred Wise

Why It's Key A song that is an A to Z of adjectives. Well, within reason…

Key Event
First 45-rpm 7-inch record

Throughout the '30s and '40s, the big record companies sought a technology to replace the standard 78 rpm (revolutions per minute) shellac disc. Shellac was becoming more expensive and the weight and fragility of the material made transportation and storage difficult and costly. Vinyl was an ideal replacement and it allowed for smaller grooves in the record. While the Columbia company developed its 33 ⅓ rpm 12-inch diameter long playing disc, its great competitor RCA worked on a much smaller 7-inch disc that turned at 45 rpm. The smaller grooves meant that this disc could hold as much music as the old 78 rpm (initially around three minutes) while its reduced size allowed designers to produce more compact players. The 45 rpm disc, which appeared in 1949, was very light and could only be broken with effort.

Central to the new RCA record format was the introduction of autochangers in record players which stacked several discs on a spindle and dropped them one at a time onto the turntable. To facilitate this mechanism, the 45 rpm disc had a much larger cutout in the middle of the record.

Although RCA hoped that its new disc could be used for all types of music, the 45 rpm became the format of choice for popular music – whose individual songs were short – and the LP was initially employed for classical music. Nobody, of course, referred to it as the 45 rpm disc: it was the "single."

Andre Millard

Date 1949

Country USA

Why It's Key Became the currency of popular music in the '50s and '60s.

Key Person
Johnny Mercer

Johnny Mercer had his first Broadway hit with *Texas, Li'l Darlin'* a musical that opened November 25, 1949 and well represented his talent for colloquial regional phrases and a poetic Southern outlook. Remembered today primarily as a movie lyricist, Mercer was also an accomplished singer, a sometime composer, and a farsighted music businessman who co-founded Capitol Records.

He was born in Savannah, Georgia, in 1909. When he went to New York city in 1930, he was turned down for singing jobs but was engaged to write lyrics for a musical revue. Mercer was finally hired as a vocalist for Paul Whiteman's Orchestra where he met composer Hoagy Carmichael. The two collaborated on the hit song "Lazybones" in 1933 and two years later Mercer was in Hollywood working with such composers as Richard A. Whiting, Harold Arlen, Jerome Kern, and others, writing evergreens like "You Must Have Been a Beautiful Baby," "Jeepers Creepers," "Blues in the Night," "That Old Black Magic," and "Ac-Cent-Tchu-Ate the Positive." While pursuing a successful singing career on radio and records, Mercer also scored seven Broadway musicals, including the innovative *St. Louis Woman* (1946) and the satirical *Li'l Abner* (1956). He sometimes wrote or co-wrote the music for his songs ("I'm An Old Cowhand," "Something's Gotta Give.") Before his death in 1976, Mercer concentrated on writing lyrics for non-musical movies, resulting in such song standards as "Laura," "The Days Of Wine And Roses," and "Moon River."

Thomas Hischak

Role Songwriter

Date 1949

Nationality USA

Why It's Key Excelled as lyricist, singer, and music businessman.

Key Performance *South Pacific*
stage musical

The Pulitzer Prize-winning musical *South Pacific* was based on two of the early short stories of James Michener: *Fo' Dolla* (about a handsome American marine officer and the local island girl whose heart he breaks) and *Our Heroine* (about a May-December romance between a middle-aged French planter and a young American nurse). Both derive from Michener's likewise Pulitzer Prize-winning collection, *Tales Of The South Pacific* and both candidly examine the issue of racial prejudice. Because this theme is so poignantly dramatized within the show's exotic locale and tropic-drenched score, *South Pacific* is often cited as one of the best musicals ever.

That composer Richard Rodgers' collaborator, lyricist-librettist Oscar Hammerstein, was taken by the subject matter is perhaps inevitable, as the issue of racial prejudice had inspired passionate work in him years before in the form of *Show Boat (1927)*. In *South Pacific*, though, he would be even more pointed, with a song declaring that one doesn't embrace bigotry naturally but rather has to be "Carefully Taught."

That intense little lesson at the heart of a story whose complementary songs sweep ("Bali H'ai"), charm ("Cockeyed Optimist," "I'm Gonna Wash That Man Right Outta My Hair"), amuse ("There Is Nothing Like A Dame," "Happy Talk"), and flat-out soar ("Some Enchanted Evening") infused an alchemical mix that led to a five-year Broadway run starting on April 7, 1949, plus two movies, several all-star recordings, and over 25,000 subsequent productions worldwide.

David Spencer

Opening Night
April 7, 1949

Country USA

Director Joshua Logan

Cast Mary Martin, Ezio Pinza, Juanita Hall

Composers Richard Rodgers, Oscar Hammerstein

Why It's Key The classic musical that saw a baton-passing of Pulitzers from source to adaptation.

Opposite *South Pacific*

Key Song "Rudolph The Red Nosed Reindeer" Gene Autry

In 1939, the Montgomery Ward department stores asked copywriter employee Robert L. May to write a story that could be given away to customers as a Christmas present. May came up with a tale in verse entitled "Rudolph The Red-Nosed Reindeer." Denver Gillen from Ward's art department illustrated it and the book was such a success that the more than 6,000,000 copies were given away by 1949. Ward's owned the copyright but, in a remarkable example of corporate generosity, granted it to May in January 1947.

May happened to be songwriter Johnny Marks' brother-in-law and in 1947 he asked Marks to turn his story into a song. Marks gave May's alliterative reindeer poem an appropriately good-time melody, amending the words as he did. Gene Autry recorded the result and his version – which entered the U.S. charts on December 3, 1949 – sold over 30,000,000 copies, making it the world's second most successful recording after "White Christmas."

Once he hit with "Rudolph… ," Marks devoted a good deal of the rest of his career trying to equal that Yuletide-flavored success. His best-known Christmas songs include "I Heard The Bells On Christmas Day," "Rockin' Around The Christmas Tree," and "The Most Wonderful Day Of The Year."

It is "Rudolph… ," though, that has achieved almost mythic status, so much so that many people believe it to be a folk song rather than a Tin Pan Alley creation.

Ken Bloom

Release Date 1949

Nationality USA

Composer Johnny Marks

Why It's Key The song whose composition led its writer to become a Christmas song specialist.

Key Song "The Fat Man"
Fats Domino

The recording of "The Fat Man" by Fats Domino on Imperial Records resulted in – ahem – a domino falling at a key spot in a chain. More than two years earlier, Imperial Records' founder Lewis Chudd had seen bandleader/composer Dave Bartholomew perform in Houston and told him he wanted to record him. The next time they met was in late November of 1949, in New Orleans. A few days later, Bartholomew took Chudd to see a new friend and associate of his who was pulling in big crowds, named Antoine "Fats" Domino, a large, jolly black man with a stupendous if laid back piano technique. Ten days after that, Domino was signed to Imperial and at his first recording session, laying down a song called "The Fat Man" that Bartholomew had devised out of a traditional piece called "The Junker Blues." He'd worked out the lyric while writing with Domino, and thinking about the singer-pianist's nickname and a popular radio show called The Fat Man.

The idea seemed a natural fit, as it turned out not just for Bartholomew and Domino but the public as well. Issued in January of 1950, the single sold over a million copies. With its fat backbeat, thick rolling piano, and Domino's strutting persona, "The Fat Man" was also a serious contender for being the first rock 'n' roll record, in addition to providing him with a signature tune for a six-decade career.
Bruce Eder

Release Date
December 10, 1949

Nationality USA

Composer Dave Bartholomew

Why It's Key Possibly the record that kicked off the rock revolution.

Opposite Fats Domino

Key Person
Nat "King" Cole

Born Nathaniel Adams Coles [sic] in Montgomery, Alabama, Nat Cole (1919–1965) played organ in his minister father's church and piano in talent contests as a youth. He formed his own jazz group, the King Cole Trio (a reference to nursery rhyme character Old King Cole), who played in clubs and started recording in 1941. Cole started complementing his exquisite piano technique by singing a little as part of the trio's live performances.

Songwriters Jay Livingston and Ray Evans tried unsuccessfully to interest singers like Frank Sinatra and Perry Como in recording their ballad "Mona Lisa." Cole's disc hit the U.S. charts on June 10, 1950 and sold 3,000,000 copies. His reputation shifted from a jazz pianist and songwriter to a stand-up singer and song interpreter. Many other hits records followed, most memorably "Stardust," "Nature Boy," "Smile," "Route 66," and "Unforgettable." In 1955 he became the first singer to have six records on the charts at the same time. His stylistic and audience shift caused some controversy among his old jazz colleagues, who considered his new pop career a selling out. It was some of those same people who considered the elegant Cole to be an Uncle Tom. Defenders point out that Cole's status as one of the first African-Americans to have his own television series would make him revolutionary enough even without the fact that he sued hotels who refused him rooms.

Cole died of lung cancer at the age of 46.
Thomas S. Hischak

Role Recording Artist

Date 1950

Nationality USA

Why It's Key Moved from jazz to pop but remained sublime.

Key Event
The coming of the Dansette

The Dansette record player became an iconic artifact of the youth culture of the '50s and '60s, and the name became a generic term for many different makes of small record player, like "Hoover" for vacuum cleaner.

A small, portable record player became very popular at the time of World War I: its spring motor turntable and acoustic horn fitted into a suitcase. The introduction of electronic recording and reproduction via loudspeaker tethered the record player to a power outlet, and its status as a piece of furniture led to larger and more ornate machines that sat proudly in living rooms.

In 1950, Morris Margolin's British company returned to the earlier format of compact player encased in a suitcase (complete with strap-handle), with the loudspeaker incorporated into the lid. They called it the Dansette. The turntable had three speeds – 78, 45, and 33 ⅓ rpm– to suit all the records available but the growing popularity of the 7-inch 45 rpm, and the inclusion of an autochanger, made the Dansette the choice of teenagers who wanted to play their singles in the privacy of their bedrooms. The leatherette-covered Dansettes came in a variety of bright colors, which made them especially attractive to young women, and some models came with built-in transistor radios. Millions of these machines were made all over Europe and the Americas under many different names, but the Dansette name retains the aura of the '60s.
Andre Millard

Date 1950

Country UK

Why It's Key Enabled the forbidden pleasures of enjoying pop music in one's bedroom.

Key Performance *Guys And Dolls*
stage musical

In the '30s and '40s, writer Damon Runyon's colorful New York characters gained a huge following. Their exuberant, larger-than-life qualities and distinct patois also made his short stories perfect fodder for a musical (alas posthumous).

Its producers originally conceived *Guys And Dolls* as a serious-minded romance, dramatizing the relationship between gambler Sky Masterson and salvation army officer Sarah Brown as a story of class opposites akin to *South Pacific*. The show went through 11 bookwriters in search of its tone (the penultimate, Jo Swerling, still receives a contractual cocredit) before settling on Abe Burrows, who refashioned it as a Times Square comedy, drawing plot points heavily from Runyon stories "The Idyll Of Miss Sarah Brown" and "Blood Pressure," with added elements from "Pick The Winner." Although paradoxically, Burrows didn't preserve a line of Runyon's text, in brilliantly adapting its distinctive rhythms and locution style to his own original dialogue, he created the illusion of pure Runyon.

By the time Burrows was on board, composer-lyricist Frank Loesser had already fashioned most of the score, including the title song, "If I Were a Bell," "Sit Down, You're Rockin' the Boat," and the imperishable "Luck Be a Lady." In a manner that normally defies healthy book-musical gestation, he shaped the new libretto around the existing songs. The result, which debuted on November 24, 1950, proved one of the most indestructible musical comedies in history, as foolproof in a school auditorium as on a professional stage.
David Spencer

Opening Night November 24, 1950

Country USA

Director George S. Kaufman

Cast Robert Alda, Isabel Bigley, Sam Levene

Composer Frank Loesser

Why It's Key A semi-farcical genesis leads to an indestructible warhorse of a musical.

Key People
Leiber and Stoller

The duo got off to a low-key start with "That's What The Good Book Says," a single for Bobby Nunn and the Robbins in February 1951, but then they were still teenagers. Over the next decade, however, lyricist Leiber and tunesmith Stoller reigned supreme, injecting wit, satire, and social comment into an extraordinary number of vital, vibrant records, most of which they organized the recording of and selected the musicians for. They authored pretty much every major song recorded by black vocal group The Coasters, including "Poison Ivy," "Yakety Yak," and "Searchin,'" while "Love Potion No. 9" (The Clovers) and "Kansas City" (Wilbert Harrison and literally hundreds of others) were other seminal early compositions. An association with The Drifters produced a string of innovative, influential records like "There Goes My Baby" and the magnificent "On Broadway" (a cowrite with Mann and Weil), while "Stand By Me" drew a spine-tingling performance from the band's former vocalist, Ben E. King.

After covering their "Hound Dog" (written for Big Mama Thornton), Elvis Presley went on to record more than 20 Leiber-Stoller songs, including "King Creole" and the typically humorous "Jailhouse Rock." In the mid-'60s, though, the duo scaled down their activities, although one further masterpiece emerged when Peggy Lee recorded the deliciously acerbic "Is That All There Is?" in 1969.

David Wells

Role Songwriter (Leiber) and Producer (Stoller)

Date February 1951

Nationality USA

Why It's Key As producers, they were the first, as songwriters they were amongst the very best.

Key Song "Rocket 88"
Jackie Brenston And His Delta Rhythm Boys

Ike Turner, born in 1931 in Clarksdale, Mississippi, was a guitarist, pianist, bandleader, and an ex-DJ with a great ear. He had heard Joe Liggins' "Cadillac Boogie" in 1947. Two years later, he updated the song as well as rewriting it and it became "Rocket 88," named for a new model of Oldsmobile, one of the very first heavily marketed and advertised cars of the postwar era. (There'd hardly been any cars made in America since 1941.) Turner took the 88's reputation for power and added a macho strut and some sexual innuendo.

Recorded in early March 1951 with producer Sam Phillips, "Rocket 88" got five new attributes: Turner's pounding piano, drummer Willie Sims' powerful backbeat, a raw tenor sax contribution from Raymond Hill, Willie Kizart's over-amplified, distorted guitar, and Jackie Brenston's vocals. For the song's release, Turner's group, Kings of Rhythm, got rechristened Jackie Brenston And His Delta Rhythm Boys, and for financial reasons Brenston's name replaced Turner's as

composer. The single topped the *Billboard* R&B chart on June 9, 1951, and was the second-biggest selling R&B single of the year.

More than that, its mix of sexual bravado, automotive references, and thrilling, over-the-top music earned it a profoundly more important accolade. Debate raged for decades over what was rock 'n' roll's opening shot but in recent years a consensus gradually emerged on the subject. "Rocket 88" is now almost universally acknowledged as the first rock 'n' roll record ever made.

Bruce Eder

Role Recording Artist

Date 1951

Nationality USA

Why It's Key Does this song receive the hotly contested accolade of the first rock 'n' roll record ever made?

Key Event **Debut of Alan Freed's**
Moondog Rock 'n' Roll Party

Alan Freed was one of a coterie of DJs working in Ohio's largest market, Cleveland. He had arrived there in 1949 playing jazz and pop. That changed in 1951, after an encounter with Leo Mintz, who frequented the same bar that Freed did and owned the Record Rendezvous, a store that did a big business in R&B records, and where white teenagers were starting to augment the core African-American clientele. He put Freed onto the shifting popularity of R&B and on July 11, 1951 the DJ took the plunge with a new radio show devoted to the music. That night, Freed had some fun with a record called the "Moondog Symphony" and the audience reaction was so strong that he took the on-air name "Moondog." The show became Moondog's Rock 'n' Roll Party. Ironically, while "rock 'n' roll" was Freed's choice of slang to avoid the more racially charged term "rhythm and blues," "rock 'n' roll" was already slang in the black community – for sex.

But what really mattered was the music. Freed refused to play the milder white cover versions of R&B records that most white DJs favored. Teenagers listened to his show to mainline the real music, drawing a huge audience and dominating the airwaves. Unprecedentedly, he was also dividing families along generational lines in a process that soon spread across the country – along with the renamed music.
Bruce Eder

Date July 11, 1951

Country USA

Why It's Key Vehicle of legendary DJ who pushed R&B into the mainstream and gave rock 'n' roll its name.

Opposite **Alan Freed**

196

Key Person
Johnnie Ray

In an era ruled by the crooner fraternity, Johnnie Ray, born in Oregon in 1927, was so sensational, so unconventional, that Columbia Records placed his first record release on their R&B-oriented Okeh label, giving the impression that the singer was black. In so doing, the first artist of importance to cross the white/black music dividing line was created.

"Cry," his second release, provided the sucker punch. Anguish-filled and over-brimming with theatrical sobs, it entered on 24 November, 1951, and went all the way to the top of the U.S. charts. It also provided a template for the "Nabob of Sob."

When a teenage world turned to Ray for inspiration and a widening of music horizons, the media hounded him. Homosexual and the wearer of a hearing aid, he was an easy target. He even admitted he wasn't a real singer. "When you're talking about real singers, you're talking about Tony Bennett, Vic Damone, Andy Williams, people like that," he said. "They were

stand-up singers. I revolutionized all of that." And he did, lurching across the stage, clutching microphones as though he hated them, piano bashing, writhing, and weeping, all the time creating excitement, clamor, and over-the-top emotion.

When Elvis Presley came along, there was a audience already weaned on the kind of emotionally charged music he had to offer. Ironically, it was the very rock 'n' roll singers to whom he was a precursor that made him look old-fashioned, hastening his commercial decline.
Fred Dellar

Role Recording Artist

Date 1951

Nationality USA

Why It's Key The man who made Elvis Presley possible.

Key Person
Jo Stafford

When vocalist Jo Stafford's recording of "You Belong to Me" entered the U.S. chart on August 9, 1952 on its way to over 2,000,000 sales, she confirmed her place as one of the United States' most popular song stylists of the post-World War II era.

She was born in Coalinga, California, in 1920 and was on the local radio as a teenager singing with her sisters. In 1939 she joined the Pied Pipers, the only female with seven men, and when the group was reduced to a quartet in 1942, they sang on the radio and recorded with Tommy Dorsey's Orchestra, Bob Crosby, Johnny Mercer, and Frank Sinatra. Stafford went solo in 1944 and had her own radio show for a time in 1946. Among her many bestselling records were "I've Got The World On A String," "Day By Day," "Dearie," "Shrimp Boats," "Ragtime Cowboy Joe," "'A' You're Adorable" (with Gordon MacRae), and "Make Love To Me." Stafford had her own television show in 1954.

Throughout the '50s she performed frequently on the radio with her second husband Paul Weston and his orchestra. She and Weston recorded as Jonathan and Darlene Edwards, a fictional awful lounge duo whose singer couldn't sing and whose pianist was tone-deaf. Stafford never won any major award in her own name but the Edwards' album *In Paris* won a Grammy for best comedy album.

Stafford retired from showbusiness in the '60s to pursue charity activities.

Thomas Hischak

Role Recording Artist

Date 1952

Nationality USA

Why It's Key Singer who had a bizarre parallel career.

Key Performance *Singin' In The Rain*
the movie

Before 1952, Gene Kelly, Stanley Donan, and Arthur Freed had made some great films. Kelly made his mark with his "man on the street" choreography in *An American In Paris*; Donan had co-directed *On The Town* with Kelly; and Freed had produced *The Wizard Of Oz*, among others. But it was *Singin' In The Rain* – released on March 27, 1952 – that united all their individual talents – including Freed's almost-forgotten songwriting ability that shine in the early film era – and made them all legends. *Singin' In The Rain* – whose plot revolved around the movie studios' painful transition to talking pictures – proved the possibility of recycling. The soundtrack was mostly comprised of songs already previously heard in MGM musicals dating from as far back as 1929, even the immortal title track. Today, few are aware that they were not especially written for the film, which featured Freed's songs from '20s and '30s movies like the Broadway Melody series, illustrating how the songs withstood the test of time. The film also cemented Kelly and Donan's directing credibility, showcasing Kelly's now-signature choreography in a way that only a huge-budget MGM musical could.

The movie also launched the career of a young Debbie Reynolds, only 18 at the time and not trained for dancing. She saw herself as perfect for the part of the star-struck Kathy Seldon, remarking later, "I was that young, inexperienced girl you see on the screen." She trained for hours, sometimes until her feet bled, to keep up with the talents of Kelly and Donald O'Connor. Reynolds was not the only one to have such discomfort. When recording the scene for the title number, Kelly had a fever of 103 degrees. The solution? Heat up the water. The end result was possibly the most adored and iconic piece of musical movie choreography of all time.

Leila Regan-Porter

Movie Release Date March 27, 1952

Nationality USA

Director Gene Kelly, Stanley Donan

Cast Gene Kelly, Debbie Reynolds, Donald O'Connor, Jean Hagen

Composer Arthur Freed

Why It's Key When song salvage created a classic score.

Opposite *Singin' In The Rain*

Key Person
Paul Robeson

African-American singer Paul Robeson (1898–1976) lived with the courage of his convictions. A magnificent bass-baritone, he was possibly the finest vocalist of his generation and a star of Broadway and the West End. However, this interested the authorities less than the fact that he was founder of the American Crusade Against Lynching and a leading proponent of civil rights. That, and Robeson's support of the Soviet Union's non-discriminatory practices toward blacks, got him in hot water with the government. In 1950, Robeson's passport was revoked when he refused to swear an affidavit that he was not a Communist. In 1952, The Canadian Mine, Mill, and Smelter Workers asked him to address its Vancouver convention. Though no passport was necessary, the Border Patrol threatened him with a five-year jail sentence and a U.S. $10,000 fine, invoking an obscure law passed by congress during World War I. Robeson did address the convention but by telephone.

On May 18, 1952, he ingeniously and comprehensively sidestepped the authorities' attempts to stop him communicating artistically and politically with people outside his home country. From a flatbed truck parked at the edge of Washington state, he sang spirituals to the people across the border in Vancouver, British Columbia. Thirty thousand Canadians turned up to hear him and/or show solidarity with him.

These border concerts became annual events until 1955. Though Robeson's passport was returned in 1958, his recordings and films were blacklisted.
Ken Bloom

Date May 18, 1952

Country USA/Canada

Why It's Key A singer considered a radical threat thinks one step ahead of his oppressors.

Key Person **Liberace debuts on his own television show**

America in the spring of 1952 was having an impassioned romance with television, flocking to the new medium and leaving movie theaters all but empty on week nights. In the midst of that boom, on July 1, 1952, pianist and singer Wladziu Valentino Liberace, made his debut on his own television show. It quickly developed a huge audience.

Looked at today, it seems bizarre that in the button-down '50s such a flashy, flamboyant, and – yes – effeminate figure should be so popular. But his unrestrained gushing and gesturing were the very qualities that audiences loved; up to that time, most musical performers on television had seemed stiff and uncomfortable and, at best, oblivious to the viewing audience. Liberace, by contrast, came off not only as comfortable with the camera but also seemed to revel in its presence, and, by extension, that of the audience on the other side of the lens. His trademark was winking directly at the viewer.

Throughout his career, Liberace played music that was a mix of popular songs and light classical. Despite his multi-million sales and the fact that he was a gifted pianist, his music has no more survived his 1987 AIDS-related death than the novels of Barbara Cartland survived her demise: everything stemmed from the larger-than-life personality.
Bruce Eder

Role Recording Artist

Date July 1, 1952

Nationality USA

Why It's Key The first major musical star to adapt fully to the medium of television. Also pioneered the concept of the lovably camp musical star.

Key Song **"Takes Two To Tango"**
Pearl Bailey

The tango was a dance style that originated in Argentina and swept the Western world in the teen years of the twentieth century. By the '50s the tango was no longer the somber, exotic music of romance but often a tempo for more playful numbers, such as the tongue-in-cheek love song "Takes Two To Tango".

Al Hoffman and Dick Manning collaborated on the song which uses a moderate tango pattern and a sly lyric listing all the things you can do by yourself, from sailing a boat and haunting a house to going into debt, or going to pot, but concludes it takes two to "do the dance of love." The breezy, flippant implications in the lyric were brought out beautifully by Pearl Bailey, whose recording of the number with Don Redman's Orchestra entered the U.S. chart on September 27, 1952. Louis Armstrong used his own sassy way with a lyric in his early recording that also hit the charts.

The success of the song, which is sometimes listed as "It Takes Two To Tango," led to other whimsical tango numbers in the '50s, such as "Hernando's Hideaway," "Whatever Lola Wants," "Just in Time," and "The Rain in Spain." Most significantly, though, it led to a popular phrase still widely in use, "it takes two to tango" – meaning that co-operation is required in an effort or that both parties are equally culpable for something happening.

Thomas Hischak

Date September 27, 1952

Nationality USA

Composers Al Hoffman, Dick Manning

Why It's Key The song whose title metaphor has entered the language.

Key Performance *High Noon*
movie soundtrack

In the spring of 1952, movie producer Stanley Kramer had a problem with a picture called *High Noon*. The Western – an anti-McCarthy allegory – had long stretches depicting its star, Gary Cooper, walking around the increasingly empty streets of a town that test audiences found interminable.

Composer Dimitri Tiomkin recommended a song to ameliorate the problem. He and lyricist Ned Washington came up with a ballad, "High Noon (Do Not Forsake Me)," sung by Tex Ritter. Preview audiences took to it. Tiomkin provided a characteristically classy score. His music for the majority of the picture frequently quoted from the "… Do Not Forsake Me" melody using horns, cellos, basses, and percussion, and was otherwise built on thick-textured, Tchaikovsky-like (or even denser) romantic orchestral scoring, some of the most ambitious heard in a Western up to that time. "… Do Not Forsake Me" was itself used several times.

The movie was released on July 7, 1952. Its huge success was aided by two versions of the song hitting the charts, one by Ritter, the other by Frankie Laine. Ritter's version omitted the ominous drumbeat that underscored both Laine's and the film version and only made U.S. No. 12. Laine's version was a U.S. No. 5. The song won an Oscar.

Tiomkin's suggestion had been quite radical: hitherto, very few dramatic films featured songs. But from hereon in, the obvious benefits of media cross-promotion led to it becoming commonplace for movies to have theme songs, especially Westerns.

Bruce Eder

Movie Release Date July 7, 1952

Country USA

Why It's Key The start of a new role for music in movies.

Key Event
Death of Hank Williams

No one can be certain precisely when or where Hiram King "Hank" Williams died. The vocalist/guitarist was being driven on the last day of 1952 from Montgomery, Alabama, to Canton, Ohio, where he was due to perform on New Year's Day. At some point during that journey, he died in the back seat of the car of heart failure. He was just 29 years old.

He had just released the sadly prophetic (if obviously titled) "I'll Never Get Out Of This World Alive," which would become his eighth U.S. country chart-topper in under three years. He was a chronic alcoholic and drug-taker and already looked twice his age. The only thing reliable about him was his talent. A purveyor of what we might now term beautiful loser anthems, most of which he wrote, he had become the first superstar of country music and in a sense – courtesy of his iconoclastic and anarchic spirit – the first rock star, when rock did not yet exist.

His main influence of course has been as a performer and as a writer of a huge catalogue of now evergreen songs, including "Hey Good Lookin'," "Your Cheatin' Heart," and "Jambalaya." However, his tormented life and sad premature death has also served as an unhealthy template for other troubled musical souls, both talented (Jim Morrison, Janis Joplin) and talentless (Sid Vicious). Williams' impact on country music has been compared with that of Marilyn Monroe on Hollywood. Perhaps a more accurate comparison might be with James Dean.
John Tobler

Date December 31, 1952

Country USA

Why It's Key Popular music's first "cool" tragedy.

Opposite Hank Williams and family

Key Song **"Doggie In The Window"**
Patti Page

Sometimes referred to as "How Much Is That Doggie in the Window," the short number asking about the purchase price of a pooch in a pet store window was written by Bob Merrill, a lyricist who decided to compose his own tunes even though he couldn't read or write music. After banging out the melody on a toy piano, he sent the completed song to Patti Page, who recorded it because she thought it might appeal to children.

Certainly its sing-song qualities and simple lyric gives it the feel of a nursery rhyme as old as "Baa-Baa Black Sheep" or a traditional American folk song. It became perhaps the simplest and most juvenile song ever to reach the top position in the U.S. chart, which it entered on January 31, 1953. A record by Lita Roza in Britain made it a bestseller there as well. It was also recorded by Homer and Jethro, The Persuasions, Wylie Gustufson, and others.

A distinctive feature of most of the recordings is the inclusion of sound effects (usually barking and growling) at the end of each line and when sung in concerts or television programs the songs often became a participation number. As for Merrill, he would go on to compose Broadway scores (Carnival, New Girl In Town, Take Me Along etc.) of some complexity – but still never learned how to read music.
Thomas Hischak

Date 1953

Nationality USA

Composer Bob Merrill

Why It's Key A song that feels like it originates in the Middle Ages but is in fact a product of the nuclear age.

Key Person
James Van Heusen

In 1940, hitmaker of two year's standing James Van Heusen (1913–1990) moved to Hollywood and teamed up with lyricist Johnny Burke. They became the premier songwriters at Paramount and the favorites of Bing Crosby, penning most of the crooner's movie songs. Despite their dozens of hits for Crosby and Paramount, though, the duo failed to conquer Broadway twice, first with *Nellie Bly* in 1946 and then *Carnival In Flanders*. Though the latter was a flop upon its opening on September 8, 1953, it did at least yield the memorable "Here's That Rainy Day."

Jimmy Van Heusen stayed in California after breaking with Burke in 1953, and in 1955 he teamed up with a new lyricist, Sammy Cahn. By the mid-'50s Hollywood had changed and movie musicals were less in demand. So, between scores, Cahn and Van Heusen wrote title tunes for a variety of films. They also became Frank Sinatra's team of choice, most memorably devising the swinging "Come Fly With Me" and "It's Nice to Go Travellin'." The team perfectly captured Sinatra's new "ring-a-ding-ding" persona and helped, in fact, define it. Cahn and Van Heusen also dreamed of Broadway success but lucked out with 1965's *Skyscraper* and 1966's *Walking Happy*.

Other well-loved songs to which Van Heusen contributed the melodies include "Call Me Irresponsible," "High Hopes," "Polka Dots And Moonbeams," and "Swingin' On a Star."
Ken Bloom

Role Songwriter

Date 1953

Nationality USA

Why It's Key The composer for whom movie and chart hits came easy but stage hits not at all.

Key Performance *Gentlemen Prefer Blondes* the movie

1953 was the year that Norma Jean Mortensen made her leap into the role of the Blonde Bombshell that was Marilyn Monroe. She had previously had many bit parts and one starring role in the steamy drama *Niagara*, but it was *Gentlemen Prefer Blondes*, released on July 18, 1953, with screen beauty Jane Russell (as fellow lounge singer Dorothy Shaw), which launched her as an international star.

Carol Channing had played the loveable gold-digger in the original Broadway play in 1949, but Monroe's take on Lorelei Lee became the iconic version, decked out in bright, glamorous (bordering on gaudy) outfits such as the pink, silk dress from the now-legendary number, "Diamonds Are A Girl's Best Friend." That song was the work of Jule Styne and Leo Robin – Hoagy Carmichael and Harry Adamson also provided material.

Lee's get-what-I-want attitude and Shaw's do-what-I-want determination is seen by some as a precursor to women's liberation, despite both girls' main goals being to win men. A dramatic shift was surely witnessed in the raunchy scene of a fully dressed Russell dancing around the barely covered men from the American Olympic swim team (usually the women are half-naked and on display). In the end their charm and genuine likeability outshines any underlying schemes, and both girls make it to the altar with the best of intentions.

From the moment Monroe stood out on stage with Russell in that red, sequined dress, gaudy or not, beauty would never be the same again.
Leila Regan-Porter

Film Release Date July 18, 1953

Nationality USA

Director Howard Hawks

Cast Marilyn Monroe, Jane Russell, Charles Coburn

Composers Jule Styne, Leo Robin, Hoagy Carmichael, Harry Adamson

Why It's Key An early example of feminism in musicals – maybe.

Opposite *Gentlemen Prefer Blondes*

Key Song **"That's Amore"**
Dean Martin

The most popular song to emerge from the many Jerry Lewis-Dean Martin movies, pseudo-Italian ballad "That's Amore" illustrated how Americans prefer their foreign songs to be homegrown.

Just as the most beloved Irish songs in America did not come from Ireland, many Italian favorites were written by Stateside songwriters who tended to be Jewish rather than Mediterranean. Harry Warren (music) and Jack Brooks (lyric) wrote "That's Amore" for the Lewis-Martin film *The Caddy* (1953). The music bounces up and down like a concertina melody and the wry lyric describes the omens of love with contrived – sometimes nonsensical – Italian food imagery, such as the moon hitting you in the face like a pizza and stars making you drool like fazool. Still, it was clearly hardly intended to be serious: in the movie, a crooned rendition by Martin was quickly reprised by the nasal-voiced Lewis before turning into a singalong number in an Italian restaurant. Martin in fact was initially suspicious of the song, thinking that his ethnic origins were being ridiculed, and had to be persuaded to sing it.

The song is something of a satire on Italian-American ballads but Martin's solo recording seemed to be largely accepted as a straightforward love song and it became a bestseller, entering the U.S. charts on November 14, 1953. His recording was used effectively on the soundtrack of the movie *Moonstruck* (1988).
Thomas Hischak

Release Date June 1953

Nationality USA

Composers Harry Warren, Jack Brooks

Why It's Key A red, white and blue Italian anthem.

Key Event **Elvis Presley records "That's Alright (Mama)"**

"That's Alright (Mama)" had started life as "I Don't Know It," penned and recorded by bluesman Arthur "Big Boy" Crudup in 1946. In 1949, Crudup recorded the song again as "That's All Right (Mama)."

Young Memphis recording artist Elvis Presley loved the song but was only using it as a basis for an impromptu jam with guitarist Scotty Moore and drummer Bill Black during a break in his first session for Memphis' Sun Records on July 5, 1954. The trio had just completed recording "Harbor Lights" and "I Love You Because" but this was something else entirely. Crudup's original was somewhat slower and less sprightly than the trio's playful, sleek, country-inflected vamp. Producer and label owner Sam Phillips was amazed that Presley should even know a Crudup song and was excited by what he heard. He asked the trio to repeat the performance, which was then fashioned as Elvis' first A-side (although credited, like all his Sun records, as "Elvis, Scotty, and Bill").

There are many candidates for first rock 'n' roll recording. "That's Alright (Mama)" was not the first disc to meld visceral R&B with glossier country stylings, but it was certainly the most influential insofar as it set the first stone on the pathway to superstardom of rock 'n' roll's first substantial icon. Local DJ Dewey Phillips played the single 14 times on his show. Within two years, the entire world was similarly galvanized by Elvis and his sound.
Fred Dellar

Date July 5, 1954

Country USA

Why It's Key Arguably the world's most important post-war recording.

Key Song **"Mr. Sandman"**
The Chordettes

By the '50s, popular music was acquiring a simplicity that made traditionalists fume. "Mr. Sandman" with its AABB lyric pattern (and with the false rhyme of "dream" and "seen") epitomized the decline of the golden age of popular song but its catchy tune and unique arrangement made it a latter day standard.

The Chordettes first came to the public's attention when they appeared on the *American Idol* of its day, Arthur Godfrey's *Talent Scouts* in 1949. Godfrey's music director, Archie Bleyer, founded Cadence Records in 1953 and signed The Chordettes. Their first and biggest hit for the label was "Mr. Sandman," which made U.S. No. 1 on December 4, 1954. Blyer, now married to Chordette Janet Ertel, kept the accompaniment to a minimum – in some parts seeming to feature merely slapped thighs – the better to feature the girls' harmonies, including those famous ascending "bongs."

Ballard's lyric is remarkable for the audacity of its banality and contrived rhyming: it suggests that the girls' dream man would have a lonely heart like Pagliacci (whatever that means), while they also yearn for a man with wavy hair like Liberace!

The Chordettes' hit also made UK No. 11. The Four Aces also charted with the song in Britain, as did Max Bygraves. The trio of Emmylou Harris, Dolly Parton, and Linda Ronstadt recorded a particularly charming version of the song in 1978.

Gershwin this ain't, but huge fun it is.
Ken Bloom

Release Date 1954

Nationality USA

Composer Pat Ballard

Why it's key The song that illustrated a new, less sophisticated type of pop.

Key Event
Death of Johnny Ace

R&B and rock 'n' roll had a great year in 1954. John Marshall Alexander, aka Johnny Ace, had been having as good a year as anyone – after starting the decade as a pianist in B. B. King's band, he'd switched to vocals, made the band his own after King's departure, and begun making a name as Johnny Ace, signed to the Duke label in 1952, with his self-written, mostly tender fare. He'd begun occupying the top of the R&B charts from the start with "My Song" and enjoyed eight more consecutive hits, leading up to Christmas Eve of 1954 in Houston. The 24-year-old Ace was performing at the City Auditorium and had just gone backstage.

While in his dressing room, Ace began playing with a 22-caliber revolver, pointing it at his girlfriend and her friend; the gun had a single bullet in it. Next he pointed it at himself – and the bullet fired into his head, killing him instantly. That's the official story. Rumors abounded that Ace was murdered by Duke Records' Don D. Robey, with whom he was in dispute. In those days, however, investigating a black man's death was not a priority.

The public propelled Ace's final recording, "Pledging My Love," to the No. 1 spot on the R&B chart and to his first pop chart placement at U.S. No. 17. Soon after came another first for the new music, *The Johnny Ace Memorial Album*.
Bruce Eder

Date December 24, 1954

Country USA

Why It's Key The first death of a major R&B or rock 'n' roll star.

Key Event **The Fender Stratocaster goes on sale**

The Fender Stratocaster (or "Strat") was not the first electric guitar. Hawaiian and lap steel guitars had previously been fitted with electric pick-ups. Gibson was already producing their hollow-body design, and the first commercially produced Spanish solid-body guitar was Fender's simpler Telecaster, produced from 1950. But the Stratocaster, first marketed in 1954, was a major step forward in design, and became both the classic instrument of its period, and the blueprint for future electric guitars.

In the '50s the future was viewed through science-fiction lenses, and the Strat's futuristic design reflected this. The name evoked modern military aircraft such as the Boeing B-52 Stratofortress. The compact pick-ups, Fender's streamlined tremolo arm design, and the beveled cut-aways to the wooden body combined to make this the most comfortable, innovative design the world had ever seen for an electric guitar.

Early adopters included Buddy Holly, and famous Strat players form a roll call of the rock 'n' roll hall of fame. Hank Marvin, Jimi Hendrix, Buddy Guy, George Harrison, Eric Clapton, David Gilmour, Mark Knopfler, and Stevie Ray Vaughn are only a few of the great guitarists known for their use of Strats. The Strat can sound bland at times, and various changes to the design over the years haven't stopped guitarists seeking heavier or harsher sounds in other brands. But the Strat's adaptability, innovation, and longevity give it a central position in the history of guitar-based rock and pop.
Hugh Barker

Date Fall 1954

Country USA

Why It's Key The Strat was the coolest guitar ever seen.

Key Event **Invention of the transistor radio**

The transistor replaced the bulky and unreliable vacuum tube in amplification units. Transistors did the job better and were much smaller, making it possible to drastically reduce the size of radios and record players. Transistors had significantly lower power usage which meant that batteries became an option as a power source. The first transistors were used in calculators but were very quickly applied to radios. The transistor radio was announced on October 18, 1954 but they were not commonly available until 1955.

The transistor radio might not have had the sound quality of larger table-top models but it was portable and much cheaper. It was especially appealing to the young and a "tranny" became a necessary part of teenage culture in the late '50s and '60s. Transistors were also used in car radios and small tape recorders, enabling people to take their entertainment with them wherever they went.

Now that it was no longer necessary to sit still at home to enjoy music, many young people heard popular songs first on transistor radios (and AM radio as they cruised around in their cars). Transistor radio was the major outlet for rock 'n' roll and R&B. By the '60s successful record companies like Motown and hit-makers like Phil Spector were actually mixing their recordings to suit the low fidelity of these machines and thereby maximize their appeal to the kids.
Andre Millard

Date October 18, 1954

Country USA

Why It's Key Had a profound effect on consumer electronics and on the way people listened to music.

Key Song "(We're Gonna) Rock Around The Clock" Bill Haley And His Comets

Though determining which was truly the first rock 'n' roll song has long been a subject of debate, there's no doubt about the song that took rock 'n' roll into the mainstream – "(We're Gonna) Rock Around The Clock."

Written in 1952 by Max C. Freedman and Jimmy DeKnight, the song's initial recording was by Philadelphia-based Sunny Dae And The Knights in 1953. It was next released as a B-side on May 10, 1954, by Western swing band Bill Haley And His Comets. As discussed elsewhere, the flip achieved its success through being featured in the film *Blackboard Jungle*, making No. 1 in the United States and UK.

After two opening drum beats, Haley commences singing about the joys of rocking around the clock through two lively, if hardly frantic, minutes. The phrase "rock and roll" had long been used in blues songs to refer to sexual activity but Haley's bright, almost chipper vocal delivery recast the song as an ode to dancing all night, aiding its crossover success.

Haley explained the new form of music for which he had abandoned Western swing thus: "If I could take, say, a Dixieland tune and drop the first and third beats, and accentuate the second and fourth, and add a beat the listeners could clap to as well as dance, this could be what they were after." It certainly was. No longer confined to R&B radio, rock 'n' roll had finally taken center stage. World domination would follow.

Gillian G. Gaar

Release Date
May 10, 1954

Nationality USA

Composers Max C.
Freedman, Jimmy DeKnight

Why It's Key The first
major rock 'n' roll hit.

Opposite **Bill Haley And
His Comets**

Key Song "Riot In Cell Block No. 9" The Robins

When Jerry Leiber and Mike Stoller wrote "Riot in Cell Block No. 9," it was – despite its dramatic title and prison setting – a comedy/novelty affair. The song was inspired by a radio show called *Gangbusters* which opened with the sound of a machine gun, which sound effect was used on the recording of the song issued by black vocal group The Robins in June 1954. Though it sold 100,000 copies in the Los Angeles area, The Robins's recording, featuring the bass voice of Richard Berry, failed to dent the R&B listings.

The song took on a very different kind of life nearly two decades later. When the National Guard shot four students dead at Kent State University during an anti-Vietnam demonstration, Mike Love of the Beach Boys provided Leiber and Stoller's light-hearted number with a new, very serious and angry lyric and reamed it "Student Demonstration Time." It appeared on the Beach Boys *Surf's Up* album in 1971. Though Love's fury was genuine, some people found the track

fatuous, even offensive. However, it was certainly an intriguing example of a song being reimagined.

Meanwhile, "… No. 9"'s refrain "There's a riot going on" – which leads into the title phrase – appears to have entered the language. What else are we to make of the fact that when Sly Stone decided to make his 1971 album a response to *What's Going On* – Marvin Gaye's album title question – he alighted on *There's A Riot Goin' On*?

Fred Dellar

Release Date April 1954

Composers Jerry Leiber,
Mike Stoller

Nationality USA

Why It's Key A song given
a new meaning.

Key Song "Shake, Rattle, And Roll"
Bill Haley And His Comets

When Kansas blue shouter Big Joe Turner recorded "Shake, Rattle, And Roll" in 1954, no one realized that such a risqué song was destined to become a staple at family parties.

Penned by Jesse Stone (under the pseudonym Charles E. Calhoun) it was a standard 12-bar blues that, like many of its kind, came peppered with sexual references. Commencing with the line "Get out of that bed and wash your face and hands," the lyric confirmed that a couple had spent the night together. Recorded by white artist Bill Haley on June 7, 1954, the action was transformed from the bedroom to the kitchen, where the woman of the story was merely banished to get breakfast for the man in her life. The clean-up ploy would become increasingly used as white artists raided the black music charts seeking material that could be transformed into a form of rock 'n' roll palatable for white teenagers. Thus the form was popularized. Bizarrely, Haley retained the obscene line,

"I'm like a one-eyed cat peeping in the sea food store," and nobody noticed as it became a mainstream hit.

The song was also twice recorded by Elvis Presley and became a 1968 hit for Arthur Conley. Though Haley was frequently denigrated for ripping off Turner, the latter was grateful to the rocker for recording the song, providing Big Joe with both welcome publicity and a whole new audience. The two became friends and even toured Australia together in 1957.
Fred Dellar

First Released
June 7, 1954

Nationality USA

Why It's Key Raunchy blues begins transmuting into family rock.

Key People
The Ames Brothers

"The Naughty Lady Of Shady Lane" – a hit for vocal group the Ames Brothers which entered the *Billboard* Top 40 on November 20, 1954 – epitomized the clean-cut nature of the artists. What sounds like a celebration of a town slut turns out to be about a baby.

The Ames Brothers were close-harmony baritones. Joe, Gene, Vic, and Ed Ames were all born in the '20s in Malden, Massachusetts, the sons of Russian-Jewish immigrants, and first sang together in grammar school. When a single appearance at a posh Boston nightclub turned into an engagement of several months, the brothers decided to try New York where they were discovered singing at a music store and given a record contract. Their recording of "You You You (Are The One)" was a hit in 1949 and the next year the brothers' disc of "Rag Mop" sold a million copies. Despite many U.S. hits, "The Naughty Lady Of Shady Lane" was their only record to also climb the charts in the UK. The

brothers made many television appearances and had their own variety show in 1955.

In 1958, they released an album called *Destination Moon*, which contained songs exclusively related to stars and space. On the cover, they were shown standing (in tuxedos) on the moon's surface.

The attempt to imply modernity was doomed: their wholesome image and sound was already being made to look more Stone Age than Space Age by rock 'n' roll.
Thomas Hischak

Role Recording Artists

Date 1954

Nationality USA

Why It's Key A last gasp for old-style harmonizing.

Key Event **Pete Seeger refuses to talk to the House Un-American Activities Committee**

Pete Seeger's subpoenaed appearance before the American House of Representatives Committee on Un-American Activities (HUAC) on August 18, 1955, was a long time in coming.

Seeger, the son of musicologist Charles Seeger, was 36 years old when he faced the committee, and he had been active in folk music and in American radicalism – and trying to mix the two – since he dropped out of Harvard College aged 19 in 1938. By 1940, he was performing at labor rallies with such compatriots as Woody Guthrie. In 1941, he, Guthrie, and others formed the left-leaning folk group The Almanac Singers.

The Almanacs' success was hampered by their political ties, but Seeger's next group, The Weavers, formed in 1949, managed to appear apolitical at first, long enough to achieve the hit "Goodnight Irene" in 1950. Within a couple of years, however, as the Communist witch hunts of Senator Joseph McCarthy and HUAC intensified, they were forced to disband. There was never much question that, when the committee got around to him, Seeger would refuse to name names, or to answer, on principle, the question, "Are you now or have you ever been a Communist?". He was indicted for contempt of Congress and convicted. The conviction was overturned on a technicality but the hearing's effects stretched long into the future, both for Seeger personally and for the folk music movement he represented.

William Ruhlmann

Date August 18, 1955

Country USA

Why It's Key His courage helped inspire a generation of political folk musicians who followed him in the '60s.

Key Song **"Love Is A Many-Splendored Thing"** The Four Aces

Assigned to write the title song for the pseudo-poetically titled film *Love Is a Many-Splendored Thing* (1955), Sammy Fain (melody) and Paul Francis Webster (lyric) came up with an appropriately lush and mellifluous number. The music soars in an opera-like aria mode while the gushing lyric describes wandering through Hong Kong looking for the answer to where love is. The refrain answers the query, defining love as a multifaceted affair that can variously be found in nature and in the morning kiss of two lovers in the mist.

The film studio wanted the song sung by a major recording star on the soundtrack but Tony Martin, Eddie Fisher, Doris Day, Nat "King" Cole, and other big names turned it down, complaining that the ballad was too heavy-handed and old-fashioned. Finally male vocal group The Four Aces agreed and their recording made U.S. No. 1 on October 8, 1955. Dozens of discs by others followed, including notable ones by songwriter Sammy Fain, Kate Smith, Don Cornell, David Rose, The Platters, Roger Williams, Mantovanni's Orchestra, Dinah Washington, Woody Herman, The Lettermen, Jerry Vale, Little Anthony and the Imperials, and Kenny Rogers. A choral version was heard on the soundtrack of *Grease* (1978), used in a satirical way to emphasize the song's purple pretentiousness.

A last footnote: *Love Is a Many-Splendored Thing* won an Academy award for Best Song.

Thomas Hischak

Date 1955

Nationality USA

Composers Sammy Fain, Paul Francis Webster

Why It's Key A song deemed too cheesy by the big names ends up selling a million copies.

Key Person
Guy Mitchell

Guy Mitchell (1927–1999) was born Albert Cernik and recorded for King Records as "Al Grant." When he signed with Columbia Records, label president Mitch Miller rechristened him Guy Mitchell. Mitchell's break came when Frank Sinatra refused to record "My Heart Cries for You" and "The Roving Kind" for the label. Mitchell recorded them and both songs became small hits. Columbia molded Mitchell into a light pop singer, and subsequent records included "My Truly, Truly Fair" and "Ninety Nine Years (Dead Or Alive)." He also appeared in films.

When rock 'n' roll arrived, Mitchell cannily leapt onto the bandwagon. Miller was no fan but, recognizing its commercial potential, allowed Mitchell to record bowdlerized covers of rock originals. "Singing The Blues," previously recorded by Marty Robbins, therefore, had its country element toned down and gave Mitchell his first U.S. No. 1. Mitchell shamelessly used the same ploy again with "Knee Deep In The Blues," also previously a Robbins record. While not as successful, it still reached a respectable No. 16, entering the U.S. Top 40 on February 2, 1957. Another Mitchell record that tipped its hat to rock, "Rock-A-Billy," was a U.S. Top 10 in 1957, the same year Mitchell acquired his own television show. He was also particularly popular in the UK, where he had four No. 1s. Mitchell had another U.S. No. 1 in the shape of "Heartaches By The Number" (1959). By the mid-'60s he retired, though he later returned to the nostalgia circuit.
Gillian G. Gaar

Role Recording Artist

Date 1955

Nationality USA

Why It's Key A pop crooner reenergized by the rock 'n' roll era.

Key Person
Pat Boone

In the mid-'50s, Randy Wood of Dot Records, who had released his share of R&B, recognized that some rock 'n' roll songs were perfectly fine but would never get played on radio stations whose programming was aimed at middle-class audiences who considered rock 'n' roll low-brow.

Wood saw in the clean-cut collegiate look and voice of Pat Boone – a student at North Texas State University whose signing to Dot was announced in a *Billboard* ad introducing him as "a great new voice"– a chance to sell those songs to audiences that would, otherwise, never hear them. Boone was initially reluctant to record rock but his version of The Charms' "Two Hearts" completely eclipsed the group's original commercially, ditto his rendition of Fats Domino's "Ain't That A Shame" (a U.S. No. 1), and the singer saw Wood's point. The fact that Boone's singing was totally unsympathetic to the originals and the tame instrumentation behind him was almost the antithesis of rock's fervor was apparently irrelevant to those who bought him.

Boone went on to have a long career, encompassing many U.S. and UK chart hits, most notably "Love Letters In The Sand" and "Speedy Gonzales," neither remotely rock 'n' roll, a genre he left behind not long after it had jump-started his career. It's difficult to tell whether rock or Boone benefited most from his dalliance with the form but it's undeniable that both did.
Bruce Eder

Role Recording Artist

Date 1955

Nationality USA

Why It's Key Possibly the savior of rock 'n' roll. No, really.

Opposite Pat Boone

Key Song "The Yellow Rose of Texas"
Mitch Miller

When rock 'n' roll began dominating the airwaves in mid-1955, a counter-reaction materialized via the resuscitation of a song whose values were very different to rock's free and rebellious spirit.

The jaunty recording of the traditional "The Yellow Rose Of Texas" by Mitch Miller And His Orchestra And Chorus in a version adapted by songwriter Don George may have been steeped in the sort of old-world heroism that seemed hokey to kids thrilled by James Dean and Little Richard, but there were still millions of Americans who loved that sort of stuff. Released in July of 1955, it began an ascent up the U.S. charts that was as relentless as its flute-ornamented march style, culminating on September 3, when it hit No. 1.

Mitch Miller's recording marked a nationwide embrace of a song that had been kicking around for over a century. It originated about the time of the 1836 Battle of San Jacinto in the Texas War of Independence from Mexico. The original lyric referred to the legend of Emily West, who, so the legend goes, distracted the Mexican General Santa Anna, enabling the Texans to win the battle. During the Civil War it became a favorite of Confederate soldiers. Despite its traditionalism, Miller's hit recording of George's adaptation had cleaned up lyrics to go with its very different melody, designed to reflect more tolerant modern mores: references such as "No other darkie knows her" were excised.

Bruce Eder

Release Date July 1955

Nationality USA

Composer Don George (arrangement of trad. folk song)

Why it's key Proved that in popular culture as with physics, every action yields a reaction.

Opposite **Mitch Miller**

217

Key Album *Shake, Rattle, and Roll*
Bill Haley And His Comets

Bill Haley And His Comets, had been building an audience among teenagers for years, playing their own version of an R&B sound previously associated with black performers. Late in 1954, they'd finally hit with a single of their version of "Shake, Rattle, And Roll." Now it was time do something that no one had ever done before with this music – assemble a long player. Albums at this stage were such a nascent form that the LP *Shake, Rattle, And Roll*, released on May 23, 1955, was a 10-inch record with eight tracks (although it was later superseded by a 12-inch album titled *Rock Around The Clock*, which added four tracks).

It wasn't even clear that the teenagers who pushed the "Shake, Rattle, And Roll" single into the Top 10 or who'd bought 75,000 copies of their prior single, "Thirteen Women" would even notice an LP – but it was the longest sustained string of rock 'n' roll songs yet offered to the public at one time in one place, almost every one a classic, including "Dim, Dim The Lights" and a then little-known "Rock Around The Clock." In point of fact, it didn't sell well – the kids in 1955 were taking their music mostly one song at a time. But with nearly half-an-hour of great dance music and lots of attitude, the mere existence of the album showed a little bit – to teenage fans and adult skeptics alike – of just how far this new music could go.

Bruce Eder

Release Date May 23, 1955

Nationality USA

Tracklisting (We're Gonna) Rock Around The Clock, Thirteen Women, Shake, Rattle And Roll, ABC Boogie, Happy Baby, Dim, Dim The Lights (I Want Some Atmosphere), Birth Of The Boogie, Mambo Rock

Why It's Key The first rock 'n' roll album.

Key Song **"I'm A Man"**
Bo Diddley

Rock 'n' roll was just bubbling up in early 1955, sharing space on the charts with twee pop and novelty tunes; it was in the air but it wasn't yet ubiquitous, and was still a tough sell in many places. In May 1955, when guitarist/vocalist Bo Diddley and his band – Jerome Green on maracas, Roosevelt Jackson on bass, and Clifton James on drums – walked into Chess Records, their prospects didn't look too good. They'd already been thrown out of Vee Jay Records' offices, and Chess was still a blues label.

But the two sides of Bo's sound set down that day – each song as brilliant, iconic, and influential as the other and therefore impossible to separate for editorial purposes – plunged Chess into rock 'n' roll head first. Some even argue that the resultant single is the greatest of all time. One side boasted "Bo Diddley," two minutes and 43 seconds of shimmering tremolo-laden guitar, a frantic shave-and-a-haircut beat and several layers of percussion. The other blasted the gritty megalo-strut of "I'm A Man." The single, released in May, brought Bo Diddley the man and "Bo Diddley" the song to the attention of millions of young listeners, black and white alike. The record roared to the top of the R&B charts and by November Diddley was playing *The Ed Sullivan Show*, in the process becoming the first African-American performer to appear on the show, and the first rock 'n' roller to appear on national television.
Bruce Eder

Release Date May 1955

Nationality USA

Composer Ellas McDaniel

Why It's Key The greatest single of all time?

Opposite Bo Diddley

Key Person
George Jones

George Jones began his prodigious, enormously influential recording career in early 1954 with "No Money In This Deal." It flopped, but he broke through when "Why, Baby, Why" entered the U.S. country charts on October 29, 1955, eventually reaching the Top 5. After a brief flirtation with rockabilly, Jones joined the Grand Old Opry, his run of early, Nashville-recorded hits culminating in 1959 with his first country No. 1, "White Lightning."

Jones has become increasingly less prolific as a writer of songs but the consistent gift he does have is a superb, soaring voice. Frank Sinatra once described him as "The second best white male singer." A string of classics – "She Thinks I Still Care," "The Race Is On," "Walk Through This World With Me," "A Good Year For The Roses" – was graced by that voice, as Jones became increasingly ballad oriented.

With two marriages already behind him, in 1969 he wed fellow country superstar Tammy Wynette. The pair recorded together under the guidance of producer Billy Sherrill but their 1975 divorce exacerbated a debilitating lifestyle that sat in sharp relief against the gentle tone of much of his art: it included alcohol and cocaine addictions. In 1980, though, his career was revitalized by his first million-seller, "He Stopped Loving Her Today."

Though his hell-raising days appear to be in the past, Jones remains that country music archetype: the hard-living, bruised, and battered survivor.
David Wells

Role Recording Artist

Date 1955

Nationality USA

Why It's Key The country music superstar whose specialty style was a stark contrast to his turbulent private life.

Key Performance *Blackboard Jungle*
the movie

When MGM did a deal with publisher Jimmy Myers for the use of the Bill Haley And His Comets song "(We're Gonna) Rock Around The Clock" in an upcoming feature film called *The Blackboard Jungle*, the track was not very well known. It had been merely the B-side of Haley's modestly successful single "Thirteen Women" the previous spring. The film starred Glenn Ford and dealt with juvenile delinquency in American schools, then a hot new topic.

When it opened, the movie's impact was explosive. Though tame by today's standards, adults were shocked by the disobedient kids they saw. Younger viewers' reactions were often very different – in some theaters, where they weren't dancing in the aisles, they were tearing up seats and otherwise behaving abominably, worked into a frenzy by the action on the screen, which was preceded by "Rock Around The Clock" playing over the title credits. This reaction was repeated with even more violence when the movie

opened in Britain, where it had to be pulled from some theaters due to the wild behavior of "Teddy Boys." The film ended up making headlines for rock 'n' roll many times over, establishing the connection for many between this new form of music and insurrection. Not that this did "… Rock Around The Clock" any harm: re-released in June of 1955, it shot to the U.S. No. 1 spot, the first rock 'n' roll record to do that.
Bruce Eder

Opening Date
March 19, 1955

Country USA

Director Richard Brooks

Cast Glenn Ford, Vic Morrow, Sidney Poitier

Composer Willis Holman

Why It's Key Established the perceived link between rock and rebellion.

Opposite *Blackboard Jungle*

Key Performance *Artists And Models*
the movie

Artists And Models was the 14th of 16 films to star the spectacularly successful music-and-comedy team of Dean Martin and Jerry Lewis. It appeared at a time when the nearly ten-year-old partnership, which spanned nightclub work and radio and television series in addition to their movies, was suffering from strain. The goofy Lewis had always grabbed most of the attention but Martin was finally getting recognition for his singing, which encouraged him to seek a career as a solo artist.

Based on the play *Rock-a-Bye Baby!*, *Artists And Models* depicted the conflicts between artist roommates. It boasted a song score by composer Harry Warren and lyricist Jack Brooks fashioned for Martin's talents as an Italianate ballad singer. The standout selection was "Innamorata," which Martin crooned in his characteristic legato style. While his singing had long taken a backseat to Lewis' clowning, Martin had belatedly broken through to a national hit with "That's

Amore" two years earlier, and as *Artists And Models* opened in theaters on August 25, 1955, his folkish "Memories Are Made Of This" was on its way to the top of the charts. When "Innamorata" followed it into the Top 40 in early 1956, Martin could consider himself a consistent hitmaker, one who didn't need to remain yoked into a comedy team in which he felt increasingly uncomfortable. Martin and Lewis fulfilled their contractual commitments through mid-1956, after which Martin launched an equally successful career as a singer, actor, and personality.
William Ruhlmann

Opening Night
August 25 1955

Country USA

Director Frank Tashlin

Cast Jerry Lewis, Dean Martin, Shirley MacLaine

Composers Harry Warren, Jack Brooks

Why It's Key Dean Martin begins to break free.

Key Song "Cry Me A River"
Julie London

Julie London was initially an actress but put her career on hold during her first marriage. Her second husband, composer and bandleader Bobby Troup, encouraged her singing. She began performing in nightclubs and in 1955 released her first album, *Julie Is Her Name*, produced by Troup.

"Cry Me A River," written by Arthur Hamilton (a high school friend of London's), was the album's first single and the song whose title is now most readily conjured by London's name. The song is a kiss-off to a former lover who now wants to reconcile. As ever, London's voice didn't exhibit much range but was remarkably expressive; deep-throated and sultry (London described it to *Life* magazine as "oversmoked"; the album's original liner notes praised her "furry singing style"). The effect was achieved by having London sing close to the studio microphone. Heightening the intimacy was Troup's decision to have London backed solely by two musicians, who provided a restrained guitar and bass accompaniment. London's cool delivery made "Cry Me A River" seem both caustic and tinged with regret. Another arresting element was the unique rhyming of "plebian" with "through with me, and."

The composition has often been described as a torch song. This isn't strictly accurate, for the torch song is a genre in which a singer expresses an enduring affection for an absent or unobtainable lover. Whatever the style, London's record entered the U.S. chart on December 3, 1955 and made No. 9, providing a moment of calm amidst the growing rock storm.
Gillian G. Gaar

Release Date 1955

Nationality USA

Composer Arthur Hamilton

Why It's Key The torch song that wasn't.

Opposite Julie London

Key Song "Only You (And You Alone)"
The Platters

The sweet, chocolate-smooth ballad "Only You (And You Alone)" was initially credited to Buck Ram and Ande Rand. In truth, it was penned purely by Ram who admitted; "I put another name on a few things. I wrote as Ande Rand, Lynn Paul, and a few others." Oddly, Ram had problems getting anyone to record this classy song initially. But Tony Williams, lead singer with The Platters, the vocal group managed and masterminded by Ram, loved the composition, which he'd seen in songsheet form on Ram's piano.

The Platters performed the song in a smooth, hand-holding, romantic fashion, eschewing any jump or R&B traits apart from Williams' trade mark "Uh uh" and the outcome was something that was a throwback to the sound of The Ink Spots in the '40s. But the record-buying public loved what they heard and the single entered the U.S. Top 40 on October 1, 1955. It was challenged by a cover from The Hilltoppers, a white pop vocal quartet from Kentucky. Ram didn't mind in the least – he received royalties on both these and other versions by Billy Eckstine, Louis Armstrong, The Cues, Ringo Starr and others.

The Platters would still be located in the U.S. Top 20 right up to 1967, thanks in part to such other Buck Ram compositions as "The Great Pretender," "(You've Got) The Magic Touch," and "Enchanted."
Fred Dellar

Chart Entry Date October 1, 1955

Nationality USA

Composer Buck Ram

Why It's Key An echo from the past kickstarts the career of the most successful black vocal group of the early rock era.

Key Song "Sixteen Tons"
Ernie Ford

Tennessee Ernie Ford had enjoyed a six-year string of hits by 1955 but it was "Sixteen Tons" that put him on the map as a pop-culture fixture. In the process, it occupied the U.S. No. 1 slot from 1955 into 1956, becoming on January 1, 1956, the first record ever to bridge two years from that exalted vantage point. It was an improbable success for a song that had originally been only the B-side of "You Don't Have To Be A Baby To Cry."

The song first appeared on a 1947 album by its composer Merle Travis called *Folksongs Of The Hills*. "Sixteen Tons" was built on recollections of the Kentucky coalfields where Travis' father worked and made use of his dad's comment about owing his soul to the company store as well as a line Travis' brother John had written in a letter. The chorus posited the question that after loading sixteen tons what did you get, and memorably replied, "Another day older and deeper in debt." The album did well but by 1955 it was forgotten, a 78 rpm relic. Travis still performed the song, however, and Ford added it to his repertory. When the smoke cleared from his single, it was not only a new pop standard but its account of social injustice made it a subject of much discussion and analysis.

Whatever deep debt Merle Travis might have been in before was washed away by a ton of royalties.
Bruce Eder

Release Date 1955

Nationality USA

Composer Merle Travis

Why It's Key A rare workingman's anthem in the apolitical '50s.

Key Person
Little Richard

Little Richard was the originator, emancipator, and architect of rock 'n' roll. These are his words, not this writer's, but as early rock anthem "Long Tall Sally" – which entered the *Billboard* Top 40 on April 7, 1956 – was a partial template for many succeeding artists, including The Beatles, he may have a case.

Born Richard Penniman, his trademark style consisted of gibberish, often slyly obscene lyrics, breakneck instrumentation and berserk singing. "Tutti Fruitti," "Rip It Up," "Lucille," "Jenny, Jenny," and "Good Golly Miss Molly" were just some of his other, now iconic, hits most of them written by him.

Like his white piano playing rock 'n' roll counterpart Jerry Lee Lewis, Richard believed the naysayers who deemed rock the devil's music but with the additional twist that he somehow seemed to blame his homosexuality – about which he was also tormented – on his rockin'. All these things combined to make him retire from rock and switch to gospel in 1957, with predictably disastrous commercial consequences. His career subsequently has been spent mining the nostalgia circuit (he has switched back and forth in his belief in the harmful potential of rocking 'n' rolling) with one single glorious exception: in 1964 he released a comeback single, "Bama Lama Lama Loo." Far from being the pale imitation of past glories it would have been reasonable to expect, it was in fact the deliciously demented Little Richard formula to the nth degree.
Sean Egan

Role Recording Artist

Date April 7, 1956

Nationality USA

Why It's Key One of the founders of rock – even if he does say so himself.

Key Event *Rock And Roll Dance Party*
radio show first broadcast

In February 1956 both rock 'n' roll and its preeminent champion Alan Freed took a giant step with the first broadcast of CBS's *Rock And Roll Dance Party*, the first regular, nationally broadcast American radio program devoted elusively to rock.

It was officially the *Camel Rock And Roll Dance Party*, due to the sponsorship of the cigarette company, which was another sign of the music's coming of age. Camel was an unusually prescient major corporation in recognizing that rock was becoming so popular that it was worth putting up its money to bring the music – and its biggest exponent in presenter Freed – to a national audience in pursuit of advancing its own profits. Also significant, of course, was the very fact that one of the major radio networks was willing to provide Freed and the music a platform on its airwaves.

The acts on the show worked live and their performances went out to over 100 stations in the CBS network by way of transcription discs, as well as to military bases around the world, giving the music some of its best and widest exposure up to that time. And although they weren't thinking of it at the time, those transcription discs – through oversight or outright ignoring of the contractual requirement that they be destroyed after use – have yielded some of the earliest preserved live broadcast rock 'n' roll performances that we have.
Bruce Eder

Date February 1956

Country USA

Why it's key The show that ensured the reach of rock 'n' roll expanded further.

Key Song "Singin' The Blues"
Guy Mitchell

"Singin' The Blues" is remarkable because it is neither blues by genre or blue by nature, yet this highly enjoyable, perky number has bounded into the charts repeatedly over the course of half a century.

It was penned by Arkansas' Melvin Endsley, a songwriter wheelchair-bound through polio. The song explained to a woman that its narrator had never felt more like singing the blues because he had lost her love. Perhaps the "felt" was an important qualifier: he wasn't in fact singing the blues but a chunk of happy-go-lucky country-pop. Marty Robbins recorded it for Columbia Records. Guy Mitchell, also a Columbia star, talked A&R supremo Mitch Mitchell into masterminding a cover version that featured whistling by orchestra leader Ray Conniff. The result was a record that topped the U.S. chart in December 1956. Additionally, the singer's record spent two weeks at the top of the UK chart, before his version handed over that position to yet another cover of the same song, this time by Bermondsey's Tommy Steele, a toothy, wholesome British singer nonetheless influenced by Elvis – as denoted by Steele's slurred delivery of the song's opening line.

Dave Edmunds turned the song into a UK chart hit yet again in 1980, Status Quo included the song as part of their "Anniversary Waltz – Part Two" medley (1990) and in 1994 Ireland's Daniel O'Donnell once more provided the song with chart status, taking it back to its original country roots.
Fred Dellar

Release Date December 1956

Nationality USA

Composer Melvin Endsley

Why It's Key Singin' the… well, something.

Key Event
The skiffle craze

A roughshod but generally joyous form of American folk and blues, known in the '20s as spasm music, skiffle could be performed on virtually anything that came to hand: the cheapest guitar, a washboard for percussion, comb and paper for something vaguely resembling a wind instrument, and a discarded tea chest for upright bass. No money or even talent was needed, just enthusiasm and a will to entertain.

Singer/guitarist Lonnie Donegan provided the catalyst for the UK skiffle craze of the late '50s. He recorded a frenetic version of Leadbelly's "Rock Island Line" with Chris Barber's skiffle group and sparked a whole genre when the record became an unlikely but worldwide hit, first hitting the UK Top 40 on January 6, 1956.

There were other contenders, Chas McDevitt with Nancy Whiskey, The Vipers, and Johnny Duncan's Blue Grass Boys all weighing in with successful records. More importantly, the whole nation joined in, spawning many thousands of skifflers, hundreds of skiffle clubs, and even nationwide contests, creating a learning zone for young musicians whose ranks included Van Morrison, Jimmy Page, Keith Richards, John Lennon, Paul McCartney, George Harrison, Mick Jagger, Gerry Marsden, and Graham Nash among many other future superstars. This impetus to obtain and play instruments on extremely limited means was vitally important for those living in an impoverished country.

Though rock 'n' roll swiftly thereafter consolidated the achievements of skiffle, it had set the ground for the '60s British pop explosion.
Fred Dellar

Date January 6, 1956

Country UK

Why It's Key The music that told British kids they could do it too.

Key Song **"Be Bop A Lula"**
Gene Vincent

In early 1955, vocalist/guitarist Vincent Eugene Craddock was recovering from a motorcycle accident in a Virginia hospital. While waiting for his damaged leg to heal, he cowrote a song called "Be-Bop-A-Lula." Though some sources claim a fellow hospital patient named Don Graves devised the lyric, a DJ who became Craddock's manager named Sheriff Tex Davis copped the lucrative cowriter's credit.

Either way, when Craddock and his band The Virginians went into a recording studio in May 1956, "Be-Bop-A-Lula" was one of the songs they recorded. Initially it was decided that "Woman Love," another track recorded that day, was to be the debut release of Gene Vincent (the name his record company decided to give Craddock) and the Blue Caps (the name given The Virginians after their golf-style headwear). "Woman Love," however, was too suggestive for the times and "Be-Bop-A-Lula" became the hit side. Though nonsense songwords were already a tradition in rock 'n' roll's short history, this record validated their worth once and for all, courtesy of the unquestioning emotion of Craddock's imperishable vocal, which was given an additional gravitas by it being drenched in echo. The music was wonderfully smoldering and featured some stinging guitar work by Cliff Gallup. The ecstasy the song – which entered the Billboard Top 40 on June 23, 1956 – induced in the public was matched by the excitement in the studio: at one point drummer Dickie Harrell had let out a scream of delight. Vincent liked it and kept it in.
Sean Egan

Release Date June 1956

Nationality USA

Composers Tex Davis, Gene Vincent

Why It's Key Permission-granter for gibberish lyrics.

Opposite Gene Vincent

Key Event
Carl Perkins is involved in a car accident

When Sun Records owner Sam Phillips sold Elvis Presley's contract to RCA for U.S. $35,000 in 1956, he genuinely believed that he had a suitable replacement waiting in the wings in the shape of Carl Perkins. He seemed to have been vindicated when Perkins' "Blue Suede Shoes" entered the charts on the same day as Presley's "Heartbreak Hotel," not least because, unlike Presley, Perkins wrote his own material.

That Perkins was more talented than Presley is not much in doubt but there are Perkins fans who to this day will swear that their idol would actually have been the bigger star than the Memphis Flash were it not for the awful occurence on March 22, 1956. Perkins was on his way to New York to make a television appearance when his car hit a pickup truck. He was hospitalized, stopping his promotional activities in their tracks.

While recuperating, Perkins saw Presley performing "Blue Suede Shoes" on television. The track was indicative of Perkins' songwriting nous, perfectly capturing the still-new vanity afforded youth by their unprecedented prosperity to a thrillingly uptempo backing. The song went U.S. Top 3 and sold a million but by the time Perkins was fit again, his moment seemed to have passed. It was Perkins' last appearance on the *Billboard* chart.

Even so, Perkins was still much loved by other musicians. No less than John Lennon once said that the only album he had ever enjoyed from start to finish was Perkins' debut LP.

John Tobler

Date March 22, 1956

Country USA

Why It's Key Prohibited an alternate musical universe in which Carl Perkins could have been The King.

Key Album *Elvis Presley*
Elvis Presley

Though a seminal album, *Elvis Presley* (known as *Rock 'n' Roll* in the UK, where it had a slightly different tracklisting), was really a cut and paste affair. RCA had signed Elvis but didn't expect his popularity to last. Accordingly company executive Steve Sholes, who had signed Elvis to the label, pieced together what material he had around – seven RCA recordings along with five tracks recorded earlier for Sun Records – and rushed it onto the U.S. market on March 23, 1956.

Even so, the record proved sensational not only sales-wise – becoming the first rock album to top the U.S. chart and the first album to sell a million copies – but also in terms of musical quality and ambition. It contained coruscating covers of such rock classics as Carl Perkins' "Blue Suede Shoes," Ray Charles' "I Got A Woman," and Little Richard's "Tutti Frutti," and climaxed with an energetic rendition of The Drifters' hit "Money Honey," a song which Buddy Holly had taught to Elvis when the two were performing together in Texas during 1955. Additionally, there was a wide spread of material spanning country songs, pop, and even a Rodgers and Hart standard in "Blue Moon," perhaps delineating that Elvis could be all things to all people, though the album remains supreme as one of the greatest-ever rock releases.

The iconic cover, which employed a black and white stage shot counterpointed by giant day-glo lettering, has been much pastiched.

Fred Dellar

Release Date USA: March 1956, UK: November 1956

Nationality USA

Tracklisting (USA) Blue Suede Shoes, I'm Counting On You, I Got A Woman, One-Sided Love Affair, I Love You Because, Just Because, Tutti Frutti, Trying To Get To You, I'm Gonna Sit Right Down And Cry (Over You), I'll Never Let You Go (Little Darlin'), Blue Moon, Money Honey

Why It's Key The first major rock 'n' roll album.

Opposite Elvis Presley

Key Performance *Eurovision Song Contest* television show

In 1955 Marcel Bezençon, a Swiss television director, had the inspired idea to protect Western European cultural patrimony from the simultaneous threats of Soviet domination and American rock 'n' roll by taking advantage of the recently developed technology that provided the means to broadcast simultaneously to several countries. In fact Bezençon's suggestion was a contest for "amateur entertainers." Mercifully his colleagues, inspired by Italy's already popular San Remo Song Festival, had other ideas.

The first *Eurovision Song Contest* held in Lugano on May 24, 1956, was a sober affair, far removed from the insanity and inanity the contest is now loved (and hated) for. Each nation involved – Netherlands, Switzerland, Belgium, Germany, France, Luxembourg, and Italy – entered two songs and performers. The voting was secret, the ballots apparently later destroyed. The winner? "Refrain" by Lys Assia of Swizterland. Luxembourg sent no judges and asked the hosts to vote in their name, making this the first of many *Eurovision Song Contest* voting scandals. Only German Freddy Quinn's "So Geht Das Jede Nacht" even approached the emerging sound of rock 'n' roll. The show overran by ten minutes, setting an example that continues to this day.

Over 50 years later the contest has expanded hugely and is such a ratings shoo-in that America's NBC is developing its own adaptation. Despite popular belief, incidentally, no presenter has ever uttered the ungrammatical French phrase "nul points."
Steve Jelbert

Date May 24, 1956

Country Switzerland

Why It's Key The inauguration of the longest-running music television show in the world.

Key Album *My Fair Lady* original cast recording

My Fair Lady was a musical adaptation of George Bernard Shaw's play *Pygmalion* (1912) about Professor Henry Higgins who decides as an experiment to see if he can teach manners to the impoverished cockney Eliza Doolittle. Alan Jay Lerner was the librettist-lyricist and Frederick Loewe the composer of a show that started its Broadway run in March 1956.

CBS financed the Broadway production in exchange for the exclusive rights to the cast recording. The bid paid off. The album – which made U.S. No. 1 on July 14, 1956 – had many highlights. *My Fair Lady* gave Broadway newcomer Julie Andrews the chance to shine as Eliza Doolittle. Her crystal clear vocals on "I Could Have Danced All Night" contrasted with the charming yet authentic Cockney tones on "Wouldn't It Be Loverly." The musically inexperienced Rex Harrison (Higgins) had new kinds of songs created for him by Lerner and Loewe where he talks in a rhythmical style over the music such as in the brilliant "I'm An Ordinary Man."

Yet there was a postscript. Although *My Fair Lady* spent 480 weeks on the *Billboard* charts, these statistics are for two albums combined. In 1959, with the show now in London, another cast recording was made – this one in stereo, then the coming thing. Andrews was glad of this opportunity, for the mono original had been recorded in a single day. She considers the stereo version "far superior" to the first attempt.
Leila Regan-Porter

Release Date April 1956

Nationality USA

Tracklisting Overture (Orchestra, Why Can't The English?), Wouldn't It Be Loverly?, With A Little Bit Of Luck, I'm An Ordinary Man, Just You Wait, The Rain In Spain, I Could Have Danced All Night, Ascot Gavotte, On The Street Where You Live, You Did It, Show Me, Get Me To The Church On Time, A Hymn To Him, Without You, I've Grown Accustomed To Her Face

Why It's Key The hugely successful cast album that turned out to be a dry run.

Key Album *Calypso*
Harry Belafonte

No one would blink today at a recording selling a million copies. But in 1956, when Harry Belafonte's *Calypso* became the first album by a single artist to do so – ultimately spending 31 nonconsecutive weeks at the top of the *Billboard* album chart, starting on September 8, 1956 – the accomplishment was deemed even more remarkable because Belafonte was black. Never before had an African-American performer so totally charmed the popular music marketplace, let alone by purveying a genre virtually unknown to the mainstream American record-buying public: Caribbean-rooted folk songs.

Calypso originated in Trinidad at the start of the twentieth century, its history traceable to African slave songs. A few calypso artists, notably Lord Kitchener, had garnered a sizable audience outside of the islands, but it took Belafonte to introduce the style to the masses. For *Calypso*, his third album for RCA Victor, the Harlem-born, 29-year-old Belafonte, whose parents had emigrated from the Caribbean, turned largely for his source material to Irving Burgie (aka Lord Burgess), a Brooklyn-based songwriter and nightclub singer who also claimed a Caribbean heritage. Burgie is credited with co-writing eight of Calypso's 11 songs, among them the opener, "Day-O (Banana Boat Song)," which was a top five hit and has since become a classic, and "Jamaica Farewell."

Calypso became a phenomenon, and it made Belafonte a star whose reach in subsequent decades extended into the worlds of theater, film, and civil rights and humanitarian causes, as well as several other musical genres.

Jeff Tamarkin

Release Date 1956

Nationality USA

Tracklisting Day-O (Banana Boat Song), I Do Adore Her, Jamaica Farewell, Will His Love Be Like His Rum?, Dolly Dawn, Star-O, The Jack-Ass Song, Hosanna, Come Back Liza, Brown Skin Girl, Man Smart (Woman Smarter)

Why It's Key A phenomenally successful record, made when the odds were stacked against the African-American performer.

Key Person
Victor Young

Composer, violinist, and conductor Victor Young (1900–1956) was born in Chicago and was so accomplished on the violin as a child that he was sent to study at the Warsaw Conservatory in Poland, where he made his professional debut with the Warsaw Philharmonic. As an adult Young arranged and conducted orchestras on Broadway, on tour, and on the radio before going to Hollywood in the mid-'30s.

Over the next 20 years he would arrange, compose, and conduct the music for over 350 films, creating memorable soundtracks for such movies as *Golden Boy* (1939), *Reap The Wild Wind* (1942), *The Emperor Waltz* (1948), *Three Coins In The Fountain* (1952), and *Around The World In Eighty Days* (1956). The prolific Young was not thought of as a writer of song hits as much as a composer of well-known movie themes. Yet a couple of songs to which he wrote the music are his most enduring legacy. One is "Love Letters," the title theme to a 1945 movie that was later covered by artists including Elvis Presley and Alison Moyet. For the movie *One Minute To Zero* (1952), Young wrote hymn-like music for the solemn ballad "When I Fall In Love," whose lyric was by Edward Heyman. Doris Day recorded the song successfully at the time of the film's release but Nat "King" Cole's album version – recorded on December 28, 1956, the year of Young's death – is now better known.

Thomas Hischak

Role Composer

Date 1956

Nationality USA

Why It's Key An accomplished soundtrack composer now ironically best known for a pair of unusual hits.

Key Performance *The King And I* the movie

Due to the success of the movie musical *The King and I* – released in June 1956 following the original 1951 stage version – its heroine Anna Leonowens is renowned worldwide as the Court of Siam's governess. In the musical – book and lyrics by Oscar Hammerstein II, plus Eastern-tinged but otherwise Western-idiom music by Richard Rodgers – teacher Anna arrives in 1860s Siam (now Thailand) and resolves to bring "civilized" thinking to the noble but borderline-barbarian monarch and his many children of many wives.

Audiences rallied to Anna (via Deborah Kerr's person and Marni Nixon's singing voice) who'd "Whistle A Happy Tune" to mask fear and tell students in "Getting To Know You" that she was "putting it my way – but nicely"; and were amused, outraged, and finally touched by the antics of the King (Yul Brynner, recreating his 1951 Tony-winning role) bewildered by modern mores. With the ahh-inducing "March Of The

Siamese Children" and the sprightly "Shall We Dance?" dramatizing an Anna-King love affair that dare not speak its name, *The King And I* brilliantly presents tuneful history in CinemaScope.

The problem is, it ain't history. The real Leonowens was neither governess nor court figure (her memoirs are hugely fanciful); King Mongkut spoke fluent English and was technologically progressive. The film so insulted Thais that it was banned from their country on grounds of historical and cultural distortions. But why let truth get in the way of a great story?

David Spencer

Date June 1956

Nationality USA

Director Walter Lang

Cast Deborah Kerr (with Marni Nixon), Yul Brynner

Composer Oscar Hammerstein II, Richard Rodgers

Why It's Key The musical whose narrative rewrote history.

Key Performance **Elvis Presley's torso appears on *The Ed Sullivan Show***

Elvis Presley had first emerged on television before he'd ever charted a record nationally, in January of 1956 on the Dorsey brothers' television show. Ever since, the combination of his music and his television appearances had proved totally inflammable. Presley's records were provocative enough, as a white man performing a musical style that had previously been associated with black performers. But the sight of him violently gyrating his hips as he sung was one the like of which had never previously been allowed into people's homes.

It seemed likely that Presley's television career would be cut short, especially after his first two appearances on *The Ed Sullivan Show* in 1956, which had taken place after Sullivan had pledged never to allow him to appear. But he was still the biggest thing in music as 1957 opened, and it was unthinkable that the biggest impresario on television could ignore him. By the same token, Presley and his manager, Colonel Tom

Parker, had something to prove to the public – that neither their television sets nor their souls would be cast into eternal flame for brushing up against an Elvis Presley performance. On January 6, 1957, Presley got back on Sullivan, and CBS and Sullivan were able to present him in terms that the singer's worst critics could sort of cope with: from the waist up. It marked a compromise that both could live with. However, the sociological tide was in Elvis' favor.

Bruce Eder

Date January 6, 1957

Country USA

Why It's Key Demonstrated how the powers-that-be tried to corral rock's primeval power.

Opposite Elvis Presley on *The Ed Sullivan Show*

Key Event
Paul McCartney and John Lennon meet

Along with a police dog display and the crowning of a Rose Queen, the Quarry Men skiffle group were one of the attractions at a garden fete at St. Peter's, the parish church of Woolton, Liverpool, on Saturday July 6, 1957. The Quarry Men, formed in March, was led by 16-year-old vocalist and guitarist John Lennon. Its other members were Rod Davis (banjo), Eric Griffiths (guitar), Colin Hanton (drums), and Pete Shotton (washboard). Their set was culled from Lonnie Donegan's repertoire with a few Elvis songs thrown in. John added lyrics about schoolteachers from their own Quarry Bank School and rewrote the Dell-Vikings' "Come Go With Me," possibly because he didn't know the real words. Although Lennon and 15-year-old Paul McCartney had not met, they shared a friend, Ivan Vaughan, who recognized their similar interests. After the Quarry Men's set and before their evening performance, McCartney introduced himself to Lennon. He recalled, "I was a fat schoolboy and as he leaned an arm on my shoulder, I realized he was drunk." Lennon was not drunk enough to miss Paul's talent and he was impressed by his ability on the guitar – Lennon only used four strings as he had learned banjo chords from his mother – and the fact that Paul knew the lyric of Eddie Cochran's "Twenty Flight Rock."

The paths of the creative fulcrum of what would be The Beatles had bisected. The rest is hysteria.
Spencer Leigh

Date July 6, 1957

Country UK

Why It's Key The most momentous meeting in the history of popular music.

Key Person
Larry Williams

Larry Williams, born in 1935, formed his first group aged 16. When that band split, he worked for Lloyd Price and Fats Domino, then signed to Art Rupe's Specialty Records label. After recording a cover of Price's "Just Because," Williams brought in an original number for his second single, "Short Fat Fannie," in which the singer celebrated his love for the titular Fannie over a lively rock backing laid down by Little Richard's band (Williams played piano) with exuberant shouting that rivaled Richard himself. The single entered the *Billboard* Top 40 on July 8, 1957 and made No. 5.

"Bony Moronie" (tall and skinny in contrast to Fanny's characteristics), made a U.S. No. 14 but was Williams' last Top 40 hit. However, the quality of Williams' work spread his name far beyond the gaze of chart watchers. The Beatles in particular clearly had a penchant for his brand of humorous but gritty R&B, covering no fewer than three of his songs bringing him much needed income: "Dizzy Miss Lizzy" (yet another variant of compositions dedicated to Williams' apparently always unfortunately afflicted muses), the importunate "Slow Down," and the teen rebel's anthem "Bad Boy."

Something of a hellraiser, Williams continued recording, performing, and producing but only when he wasn't imprisoned for drug convictions. His last album, *Here's Larry Williams*, released in 1978, featured the modish reinvention "Bony Moronie (Disco Queen)." In 1980 he was found dead in his home of a self-inflicted gunshot wound.
Gillian G. Gaar

Role Recording Artist

Date July 8, 1957

Nationality USA

Why It's Key A man whose R&B had a twinkle in its eye.

Key Song "Whole Lotta Shakin' Goin' On"
Jerry Lee Lewis

Mothers could be convinced that Elvis was cute but when "Whole Lotta Shakin' Goin' On" entered the U.S. Top 40 on July 15, 1957 sung with lascivious abandon by a blonde-haired southerner who attacked his piano with uncontrolled fury, it was clear this was a different animal.

Jerry Lee Lewis – aka "The Killer" – was a man whose ego was, remarkably, as big as his pneumatic-fingered piano talent. Born in 1935, in Ferriday, Louisiana, he epitomized Southern torment: imposed religious faith constantly broken by the sins of flesh and booze. He alternately sought salvation and indulged in bigger than life excess. No recording represents this contradiction better than "Whole Lotta Shakin' Goin' On." Composed by white country pianist Roy Hall and black singer Dave Williams, it had been recorded in by Hall and by R&B shouter Big Maybelle. Lewis cut it at Sun Studios in Memphis with no bass – just his piano, drums, and guitar – transforming it into a sexually suggestive, relentless boogie with a wicked rhythm that made it his forever. On July 28, the singer stormed onto *The Steve Allen Show* and the whole country witnessed piano poundin', stool kickin' outrage. At the end of August, although banned by some radio stations, it hit No. 1 in both the country and R&B charts. Fuelled on Benzedrine capsules and a feverish lust for life, the God-fearing kid had taken his audience on an exhilarating trip to hell with him.
Ignacio Julia

Chart Entry Date July 15, 1957

Nationality USA

Composers Roy Hall, Dave Williams

Why It's Key Revealed rock 'n' roll's full disruptive potential.

236

Key Song "Bye Bye Love"
The Everly Brothers

Don and Phil Everly began their careers performing country music with their parents, so a strong country influence was natural when they began working as a duo in 1955.

Their first single was a flop, but their second, "Bye Bye Love," written by the husband-and-wife team of Boudleaux and Felice Bryant, entered the *Billboard* Top 40 on May 27, 1957 – the first of 27 Everly hits to do so – and eventually made No. 2. The song was a deliciously self-pitying lament about the end of a love affair, and had been rejected by a number of artists before Archie Bleyer, who signed the Everlys to his Cadence label, suggested the brothers record it.

The Everlys added a magic ingredient via their harmonies. The harmonizing of siblings always has a special, almost uncanny, synchronization not present among singers who are not blood relations and the Everlys' close harmonizing was particularly noteworthy in that each vocal line could stand on its own, giving their material an exceptional power. The rustic feel combined with a more modern, uptempo musical arrangement, resulted in a song that was a true hybrid in the development of rock 'n' roll, bringing country and rock together in a way that was at the time rare. So much so that people hardly knew how to categorize it: in addition to its success on the pop charts, it made No. 1 on the country charts and No. 5 on the R&B charts.
Gillian G. Gaar

Release Date March 1957

Country USA

Composers Boudleaux Bryant, Felice Bryant

Why It's Key Built a bridge between country and rock 'n' roll.

Key Person
Dalida

A t the time of "Bambino," her third release on the French market, Dalida embodied all the mystery of Egypt, the country where she was born in January 1933. However, even though she was crowned Miss Egypt in 1954, she had Italian blood (she was born Yolanda Christina Gigliotti) and French residency (she had moved to Paris to break into showbusiness). She sang in cabaret and had a few film parts before appearing at the Olympia as one of the "Stars Of Tomorrow" presented by impresario Bruno Coquatrix. Dalida was spotted by Eddie Barclay, who signed her to his label, and by Lucien Morisse, of radio station Europe 1, who play-listed her records and had an affair with her. With that kind of support, Dalida couldn't fail and headlined the Olympia to riotous scenes in 1956.

"Bambino," a cover of a catchy Italian hit of the day delivered in her usual endearing Italian-inflected French, achieved sales of 300, 000 copies and on September 19, 1957 secured her the first of many gold discs. Dalida became a huge star throughout continental Europe, the Middle East, and the Far East, sang in more languages than any other performer, and reinvented herself as a glamorous disco diva in the '70s.

A tragic, Callas-like figure throughout her thirty years in the public eye, Dalida was haunted by the suicides of Luigi Tenco, her fiancé, Morisse, her mentor, and Richard Chanfray, her lover, and killed herself in May 1987.

Pierre Perrone

Role Recording Artist

Date September 19, 1957

Nationality Egypt

Why It's Key Proof that success doesn't always bring happiness.

Key Performance *West Side Story*
the musical

H ard to believe now but *West Side Story* – which opened on September 26, 1957 – had great difficulties finding financial backing. Many producers didn't want to go near a project with such subject matter as gang violence and murder. It was no musical comedy: It was a musical tragedy, based on the greatest tragedy ever written, Shakespeare's *Romeo And Juliet*.

But then the members of the collaborating team were serious people. Composer Leonard Bernstein wrote jazz and loved the classics, director and choreographer Jerome Robbins did ballets, and book writer Arthur Laurents authored serious plays. Together they created a seamless masterpiece.

Using the racial divides in New York's young gangs – originally Catholic against Jewish, but updated to Puerto Rican versus white – the musical paints a vivid picture of society that still holds true today. Bernstein's music didn't tread the usual stage musical line, opting for ethnic flavors and jazz to drive the emotions conveyed by the lyrics of Stephen Sondheim deep into the hearts of the audience. "Maria" is tender and magical, "Rumble" is sharp and fierce, and the fiery "America," sung by an electrifying Chita Rivera, screams with Latin flavor. The trilling "I Feel Pretty" meanwhile is second only to "America" in fame.

The 1961 film version of the show starring Natalie Wood brought the musical to its natural youthful audience, winning a record 10 Oscars, the final affirmation that musicals no longer had to be comedies but could deal with the real, painful issues of contemporary society.

Leila Regan-Porter

Date September 26, 1957

Country USA

Director Jerome Robbins

Cast Larry Kent, Carol Lawrence, Chita Rivera

Composers Leonard Bernstein, Stephen Sondheim

Why It's Key The first streetwise musical.

Key Person
Kay Starr

The immensely versatile Kay Starr (born 1922), got her start while barely in her teens in radio. She made her first recordings with Glenn Miller's band. In 1943 she joined Wingy Manone's New Orleans Jazz Band with Charlie Barnet. She made some V-Discs and Decca Records with Barnet. In 1945, a bout of pneumonia forced her to quit singing and talking for six months.

In 1947, her voice huskier, she signed with Capitol (with whom she would provide hits such as "I'm the Lonesomest Gal in Town," "Hoop-Dee-Doo," and "Bonaparte's Retreat"). Her repertoire started inching toward a country flavor. On January 17, 1952, she recorded "Wheel Of Fortune," the biggest hit of her career. She moved to RCA in 1955 and the following year she presciently recorded "The Rock And Roll Waltz." She returned to Capitol in 1959 where she cut her first LPs, including a series of jazz recordings. In 1966, Capitol dropped her and she concentrated on nightclubs, concerts, and Las Vegas.

Starr made a 1968 album with Count Basie and a few more albums with small labels. She toured with fellow songbirds Helen O'Connell and Margaret Whiting in the late '80s and continued performing through the '90s.

The highlights of her recorded legacy are arguably, album-wise, 1957's *Losers, Weepers* and, song-wise, "Wheel of Fortune" and "The Rock And Roll Waltz." On the latter tracks, her hard-driving singing and no-nonsense emotions had momentum and a slight touch of recklessness.

Ken Bloom

Role Recording Artist

Date 1957

Country USA

Why It's Key One of the few female singers who were a link between the worlds of jazz and rock 'n' roll.

Key Album *A Swingin' Affair!*
Frank Sinatra

Since 1954, Frank Sinatra and conductor Nelson Riddle had created four brilliant concept releases ranging from jazzy ballads (*Songs For Swingin' Lovers*) to introverted lonesomeness (*In The Wee Small Hours*). Not only did these albums showcase Sinatra's ability as a performer to make the song fit his personality but they were also innovative in their cohesive collecting of songs with the same mood.

Any one of those uniformly excellent albums could have been chosen for this book. *A Swingin' Affair!*, however, is arguably the most notable Sinatra album of this era because its success illustrated that "Ol' Blue Eyes" was going to be able to survive in the new era. Rock 'n' roll, had, particularly in the year previous to its May 1957 release, taken the world by storm but Sinatra here asserted the validity of swing, that looser, more fun variant of jazz that he practiced.

Riddle's arrangements had become the most trusted vessel for Sinatra to sail his stunning voice, which by this point had matured into the instrument of an authoritative adult rather than the tool of a confident but callow adolescent that it had been. Although many consider *A Swingin' Affair!* a *Songs For Swingin' Lovers* "2", its renditions of familiar standards, such as Cole Porter's "Night And Day" and the Gershwins' "Nice Work If You Can Get It" are stronger, harsher, and more jazzy, paving the way for a sound that would become Sinatra's staple throughout the '60s.

Leila Regan-Porter

Release Date May 1957

Nationality USA

Tracklisting Night And Day, I Wish I Were In Love Again, I Got Plenty O' Nuttin', I Guess I'll Have To Change My Plans, Nice Work If You Can Get It, Stars Fell On Alabama, No One Ever Tells You, I Won't Dance, Lonesome Road, At Long Last Love, You'd Be So Nice To Come Home To, I Got It Bad (And That Ain't Good), From This Moment On, If I Had You, Oh! Look At Me Now

Why It's Key Showed that swing still had resonance.

Opposite Frank Sinatra

Key Album *Blue Train*
John Coltrane

In 1957 John Coltrane's career was at a crossroads. His heroin habit had forced trumpeter Miles Davis to fire the tenor saxophonist from his quintet. Twice. Coltrane was earning cash by recording a slew of bebop blowing sessions as a sideman for the Prestige label. But he was already 30. He knew bebop was all but blown out when hard living buried Charlie Parker in 1955. So he cleaned up his act. He rehoned his chops in pianist Thelonius Monk's quartet. He took his first tentative steps as a leader on his solo debut, *Coltrane*. Then, in December Coltrane released *Blue Train* on the prestigious Blue Note label.

It was the first record where the saxophonist proved that he was more than simply a sideman with potentially prolific chops. Presiding over a cooking cast including Lee Morgan (trumpet), Curtis Fuller (trombone), Kenny Drew (piano), Paul Chambers (bass), and "Philly" Joe Jones (drums), Coltrane showed his mastery of burnished ballad standards ("I'm Old Fashioned"). More crucial were the original compositions, including spiritual blues ("Blue Train"), inquisitively cool vamps ("Locomotion"), and complex hard bop changes ("Lazy Bird"), Trane's signature "sheets of sound."

Later albums would be more technically challenging (1959's *Giant Steps*), commercially successful (1960's *My Favorite Things*), critically-championed (1964's *A Love Supreme*), or off the map (1967's *Interstellar Space*), but it was the spiritual moment of truth echoing at the core of *Blue Train* that would inspire generations of jazz musicians to find their own flow.

Miles Keylock

Release Date December 1957

Nationality USA

Tracklisting Blue Train, Moment's Notice, Locomotion, I'm Old Fashioned, Lazy Bird

Why It's Key Saxophonist kicks drugs and kick starts his solo career.

Opposite John Coltrane

Key Performance *The Music Man*
stage musical

Teenage Mason City, Iowa musician Meredith Willson (1902–1984) left home to study flute at Juilliard, whence he was hired for the John Phillip Sousa band, and later the New York Philharmonic. Serendipitously he soon became musical director for various radio programs, plus film composer for The Little Foxes and Chaplin's first talkie, *The Great Dictator* (1940). Always full of stories about his beloved hometown, he was told by many, including songsmith Frank Loesser, that he should write a musical about it. He resisted the idea (citing his own "Iowa stubborn") until he doubted he could do it anyway, which impelled him to try ("Iowa arrogance").

Though Willson had written hits like "Iowa (It's A Beautiful Name)," acclimatizing to a musical theater score took time. However, his (and Franklin Lacey's) original story of huckster salesman Harold Hill – who comes to "River City" Iowa to sell instruments and uniforms, then decides to leave before it's discovered he can't deliver the lessons to go with them; but ultimately stays because true love with the town librarian reforms him – took Broadway root on December 19, 1957 for 1,375 performances (and two later revivals), establishing Robert Preston (Hill) as an equally definitive star, who repeated his role in the faithful 1962 film, as did director Morton da Costa.

The score includes the rousing march, "Seventy-Six Trombones," the quintessential patter song ("Ya Got Trouble"), and the gentle ballad "'Till There Was You" – later covered by The Beatles.

David Spencer

Opening Night December 19, 1957

Nationality USA

Director Morton DaCosta

Cast Robert Preston Hill, Morton da Costa

Composer Meredith Willson

Why It's Key The definitive musical of small-town Americana.

Key Song "At The Hop"
The Juniors

Even before the term rock 'n' roll was in common use, African-American teens and young adults were gathering on street corners to sing the harmonized R&B that would come to be known as doo wop. It's a measure of the lightning spread of rock 'n' roll's popularity in the mid-'50s that within just a couple of years, white teenage doo wop groups – usually of Italian-American background – were proliferating as well. One of the first was Philadelphia's Danny And The Juniors – Danny Rapp, Dave White, Frank Maffei, and Joe Terranova – whose "At The Hop" made U.S. No. 1 on January 11, 1958.

Though undeniably more clean-cut and adolescent in tone than most of the first wave of rock 'n' roll classics, the song's ascending hook, pounding piano, and impeccable evocation of high school dancing had an archetypal force that couldn't be denied. It helped, of course, that one of the song's key boosters was American Bandstand host Dick Clark, who not only plugged it on his Philadelphia-based television show but even suggested the lyrics be changed to refer to record hops before it was recorded.

Though technically not rock 'n' roll, "At The Hop" was possessed of its spirit. The Juniors subsequently hit big with another David White song "Rock And Roll Is Here To Stay." That that title is true is mainly because of the excellence of records like "At The Hop."

Richie Unterberger

Release Date 1957

Nationality USA

Composers John Madara, Arthur Singer, David White

Why It's Key Doo wop spreads from its black inner-city origins to white teenagers.

Key Song "That'll Be The Day"
Buddy Holly

The recording career of Charles Hardin Holley – known professionally as Buddy Holly – lasted just three years before his untimely death, but it is studded with iconic compositions still known and loved after half a century.

None more so than his first hit, "That'll Be The Day," an undisputed classic of the original rock 'n' roll era. It was written by Holly with Jerry Allison, drummer with The Crickets, under which group name the track was released in May 1957. Holly had actually recorded a previous version for Decca Records in 1956 but the label turned it down. In fairness, the earlier version of the song, whose title phrase came from the laconic verbal refrain of John Wayne in the movie *The Searchers* (1956), was nothing like as exciting as the brilliant performance The Crickets laid down the next year under the auspices of Norman Petty, a producer local to their Lubbock, Texas, hometown (although that hardly justifies Petty nabbing a dubious cowriter's credit). The winding, descending guitar intro, Holly's newfound hiccupping vocal gimmick, the mischievous lyric in which the narrator defies his lover to desert him and the breathless ambience all conspired to ensure that, unlike some other original rock 'n' roll standards, "That'll Be The Day" doesn't have a patina of age about it but instead sounds as vibrant and modernistic today as when it first entered the *Billboard* Top 40 on August 19, 1957.

Sean Egan

Release Date May 1957

Nationality USA

Composers Jerry Allison, Buddy Holly, Norman Petty

Why It's Key A song that went from mediocre to immortal in the space of a year.

Key Song **"Summertime Blues"**
Eddie Cochran

Despite its implicit teenage rebellion, seldom did rock 'n' roll initially directly target authority figures with the power of a bullying boss or nagging parent. Rockabilly star Eddie Cochran's "Summertime Blues," which entered the *Billboard* Top 40 on August 25, 1958, skillfully took aim at both those forbidding fixtures of late teenagers' lives.

Its empathy quotient was ratcheted up by authentic language, its everyday vernacular hitting home with any kid working a dead-end summer job or being denied the use of the family car. Its final verse, however, took things to the next level, Eddie pleading his case with his Congressman – only to be dismissed out of hand for not being the age of majority. If only in retrospect, it's a glimmer of the rebellion that would explode into rioting in song and in the streets in the '60s, with hundreds of thousands of American youth, to quote the track, "too young to vote" being sent to fight a war in Vietnam that Congress hadn't even officially declared.

The record wouldn't have meant anything, of course, without Cochran's thick, chugging slabs of power chords. Those were an immense influence on the Beach Boys, who covered it on their first album, and The Who, who upped the wattage and made "Summertime Blues" one of their concert staples in the late '60s. Blue Cheer turned up the volume yet further for their 1968 hit version.
Richie Unterberger

Release Date June 1958

Nationality USA

Composers Jerry Capehart, Eddie Cochran

Why It's Key One of the first rebellion songs to speak in the voice of white kids of humble origin.

Key Performance ***Aladdin***
television show

"I find it very exciting writing for our newest entertainment medium, television" said legendary songwriter Cole Porter before the February 21, 1958 broadcast of *Aladdin* on CBS. As his introduction made clear, television provided an intriguing new outlet for artists like him used to seeing their work on stage or in cinemas.

Aladdin was produced for the DuPont Show of the Month. The libretto of this retelling of the classic Arabian fairytale was by humorist S. J. Perleman. The show starred Sal Mineo as the title character and Anna Maria Alberghetti as the princess whose heart he captures. Cyril Ritchard played an evil magician and Basil Rathbone portrayed the emperor. Dennis King, a star of early operettas and musicals made his last appearance in the show as an astrologer who urged Aladdin to "Trust Your Destiny To A Star." The marvelous score also included the ballad, "I Adore You" and one of Cole Porter's trademark "list" songs, "Come To The

Supermarket In Old Peking." The latter achieved some renown apart from the television special when it was covered on an album by Barbra Streisand.

The musical, retrospectively, left almost the impression that Porter was trying to tell us something. Ill health meant that it was his last writing assignment, but before he departed the scene he proved his genius could translate to the medium that would in large part replace the theater world in which he had engaged so triumphantly.
Ken Bloom

Date February 21, 1958

Country USA

Why It's Key Master composer songwriter proves he can conquer yet another medium.

Key Person
Otis Blackwell

The *Billboard* Top 40 entry of "Fever" in 1958 was significant to Peggy Lee as her biggest hit. However, it was perhaps more important to its cowriter: this slinky, sensual creation was the first of many major chart successes for Otis Blackwell.

It was a something of a turnaround for a man who on Christmas Eve, 1955 sold the publishing rights to six songs for an advance of a mere U.S. $150, one of which was "Don't Be Cruel," destined to be an iconic Elvis Presley smash. "At the time you've got to remember that he was just glad to get something out there," his close friend Michael Campbell later reasoned. "He was getting money for something that came so easy to him." Amongst other Blackwell songs the King would cover were "Return To Sender" (cowritten with Winfield Scott) and "All Shook Up." Some claim an even greater influence by Blackwell on Presley: it is said that the sensual, playful singing style Presley adopted at this juncture was simply him imitating Blackwell's vocal style on his song demos.

Other notable Blackwell hit compositions were "Great Balls Of Fire" and "Breathless" (Jerry Lee Lewis), "Hey Little Girl" (Dee Clark), "Handy Man" (Jimmy Jones), and "Nine Times Out Of Ten" (Cliff Richard). Another Blackwell song covered by Presley was "Paralysed." With awful irony, Blackwell ended up in that state – and unable to speak – in 1991 after suffering a stroke. He died in 2002.

Sean Egan

Role Songwriter

Date 1958

Nationality USA

Why It's Key Great songwriter who prophesized his own sad fate.

Key Album *Buddy Holly*
Buddy Holly

Though technically the debut LP of the titular vocalist/guitarist, *Buddy Holly*, released in March 1958, could just as easily have been credited to The Crickets, the group he fronted and which included drummer Jerry Allison, bassist Joe B. Mauldin and (until three months before its issue) rhythm guitarist Niki Sullivan. Only four months earlier, the group's equally brilliant debut album, The "Chirping" Crickets, had been released, but they (and particularly Holly) were such prolific songwriters that producer Norman Petty wasted no time in cutting more tracks. (Petty's name on the songwriting credits did not accurately reflect his contribution.)

Twenty-five per cent of the album comprised cover versions of current hits: Elvis Presley's "Baby I Don't Care," Little Richard's "Ready Teddy" and Fats Domino's "Valley Of Tears." While all enjoyable, it is the originals that are the key. Both sides of the inaugural Buddy Holly single are included and sum up the breadth of Holly's genius: "Peggy Sue"'s grin-inducing *joie de vive* and brutal chopped guitar solo contrasting wonderfully with "Everyday"'s vulnerability and musical delicacy. Rocker "I'm Gonna Love You Too" and ballads "Listen To Me" and "Words of Love" are further classic originals. The berserk "Rave On," meanwhile, was a cover that Holly effortlessly made his own.

This was rock 'n' roll with a new slick veneer. The Beatles based almost their entire early sound on The Crickets. Perhaps the only negative aspect relating to this immortal masterpiece is that its total running time is less than 25 minutes.

John Tobler

Release Date March 1958

Country USA

Tracklisting I'm Gonna Love You Too, Peggy Sue, Look At Me, Listen To Me, Valley Of Tears, Ready Teddy, Everyday, Mailman, Bring Me No More Blues, Words of Love, (You're So Square) Baby I Don't Care, Rave On, Little Baby

Why It's Key The template for the Fab Four.

Opposite **Buddy Holly**

Key Song "**Rumble**"
Link Wray

"Rumble" sprang to life when Wray and his Wraymen were playing a gig in the Washington, D.C. area. Some of the kids requested the band play "The Stroll," popularized by The Diamonds. Wray didn't know it but began piecing together the gritty, full-on, down and distorted creation that comprised "Rumble." Some months later, the instrumental, originally named "Oddball," was recorded and a demo version given to Archie Bleyer of Cadence Records. Bleyer was old-school and hardly *au fait* with Wray's primeval way of things. But his teenage daughter raved about the demo and "Rumble" consequently received a full release, rewarding Cadence with one of the label's biggest hits. It hit the U.S. Top 40 in April 1958, and eventually made No. 16. Despite its popularity, however, the record was banned by many radio stations.

As an instrumental communicating no lyrical message, one would imagine that it could not offend anyone. But in an era where rock 'n' roll was still associated with gang violence, the fact of the combination of its menacing tones and that its new title was street slang for "fight" caused some to deem it a corrupting influence.

Today, the record is regarded by some as one of the starting points for heavy metal. Not a bad CV for a sound said to be created after Wray, piqued with an amplifier malfunction, kicked a hole in a speaker, then took a shine to the distorted sound that emerged from his damaged equipment.

Fred Dellar

Release Date April 1958

Nationality USA

Composers Milt Grant, Link Wray

Why It's Key Unreasonable censorship hits an all-time low.

Key Event
Jerry Lee Lewis' disastrous UK tour

Since its 1956 breakthrough, every week had seemingly brought reports of atrocities on social decorum committed in the name of rock 'n' roll. The kids who loved the music laughed at the fear it instilled in the older generation. Jerry Lee Lewis' arrival in the UK for his first tour there on May 22, 1958 however, gave even the most enthusiastic rocker pause for thought.

Mississippi's piano pounder was set to play nearly 40 dates. Among his entourage was a 13-year-old girl named Myra, Lewis' first cousin. Then the news broke that Myra and Lewis were a married couple. Additionally, Jerry Lee had initially neglected to divorce his previous wife. By the time the tour opened in Edmonton, despite a performance from Lewis that left the audience at fever pitch, he was a reviled figure. When he played Tooting the next evening, he was jeered and regaled with cries of "Go home babysnatcher." The tour organizers, reeling under the impact of bad publicity, immediately shipped Lewis home and left support band The Treniers and various other UK acts to complete the series of shows.

"We have more than enough rock 'n' roll entertainers of our own without importing them from overseas" observed one member of Parliament, and for once rock 'n' roll fans weren't too sure that this was just the voice of a fuddy duddy.

Fred Dellar

Date May 22, 1958

Country UK

Why It's Key Proved that though rock was a rebellious medium, there were limits to what the public would tolerate from their stars.

Opposite Jerry Lee Lewis

Key Album *One Dozen Berrys*
Chuck Berry

When Chuck Berry's second album was released in March 1958, it was just another rock 'n' roll product aimed at the growing teenage market. Today, it is appreciated as a turning point in the genre.

While most of rock's early singers were performing other people's titles, Berry insisted on recording his own songs, which were both so powerful and so idiosyncratic they altered the form's musical and lyrical stances. He converted the disjointed rhythms of rockabilly into the now classic 4/4 beat, and as a lyricist effortlessly played with words, creating a slang teenagers could relate to, a heightened, sympathetic portrait of their urges and troubles. He was also a unique guitar player whose liquid riffs would inspire both The Beatles and The Rolling Stones. Berry gave rock 'n' roll its vocabulary and emotional grammar with tracks like "Sweet Little Sixteen," based on a girl he saw chasing autographs and gave him, then 30, the grown-up blues; and the genre-defining, myth-making "Rock

And Roll Music," its lyric outlining forever every aspect of this raucous, life-affirming sound. Other classics included were "Oh Baby Doll," a return to the beat of Berry's breakthrough hit "Maybellene," and "Reelin' and Rockin'," inspired by the sight of Big Joe Turner in a Chicago club. Around these epochal vignettes, as usual, a mix of blues and country, ballads and instrumentals: a cornucopia of rock 'n' roll freshness and wisdom in the making.
Ignacio Julia

Release Date March 1958

Nationality USA

Tracklisting Sweet Little Sixteen, Blue Feeling, La Jaunda, Rockin' At The Philharmonic, Oh Baby Doll, Guitar Boogie, Reelin' And Rockin', In-Go, Rock 'N' Roll Music, How You've Changed, Low Feeling, It Don't Take But A Few Minutes

Why It's Key Definitive album statement from the man whom John Lennon said defined rock 'n' roll.

Key Event **Johnny Mathis releases the first "Greatest Hits" LP**

Now working with more mainstream, adult-orientated material, the singer rapidly established himself as a major new talent; his light baritone voice, with its distinctive tremolo, led to him being dubbed "The Velvet Voice." By 1957, he was turning into a considerable live draw, had appeared in two movies, and was also a familiar face on U.S. television. That year saw Mathis enjoy five more U.S. hits, including "The Twelfth Of Never" and the chart-topping "Chances Are," and his popularity briefly rivaled that of more established stars, such as Frank Sinatra.

By 1958, having scored hits in the UK (including "A Certain Smile" and "Winter Wonderland"), he released *Johnny's Greatest Hits* and topped the *Billboard* album chart in 1958. The first-ever "best-of" compilation, it went on to spend an astonishing 490 weeks – nearly 10 years – on the U.S. charts. Ironically, Mathis was not that well-known for blockbuster hits, having only gone top five twice on the *Billboard* chart

hitherto. Even more ironically, the new format was created partly out of necessity: Mathis was out of the country at the time and unable to record a scheduled album of new fresh material, so his manager simply compiled the LP from 12 prior releases. The "greatest hits" or "best of" album format is now not only a music industry staple but a mini-industry all on its own, its inherent pleasing, no-padding nature often leading to the most successful album of an artist's career.

Mathis' warm, relaxed way with a tune (television host Johnny Carson once commented: "Johnny Mathis is the best ballad singer in the world") and openness to a wide range of genres – including pop, jazz, Latin, Broadway standards, and disco – has reaped astonishing commercial rewards since then. With three Grammy Awards, 60-plus hit albums on the *Billboard* charts, and sales upwards of 180 million, he is one of the most successful recording artists of all time.
Robert Dimery

Release Date 1958

Country USA

Why It's Key After signing to Columbia in 1956, 19-year-old vocalist Johnny Mathis first made his mark with the jazzy *Johnny Mathis: A New Sound In Popular Song*. This album provides a summary of the gems of the baladeer's musical career in the two years that followed, changing the face of album release in the process.

Key Event
Stereophonic records introduced

The quest for perfect sound reproduction began the moment that Thomas Edison heard the first recorded speech from his tin-foil phonograph. Although great strides were made during the acoustic era, the playback of the talking machines would be almost unintelligible to modern ears used to digital sound. Although the electrical recording process introduced in 1925 increased the fidelity of recordings dramatically, the sound still only came from one source. Stereophonic sound was the means to reproduce music in two channels and – because our ears pick up sound from several sources – give it a spatial quality that we perceive as more realistic.

The introduction of microgrooved vinyl records in the '40s was the basis of experiments to record sound in two channels – each wall of the V-shaped groove was inscribed with a separate track. RCA introduced stereophonic LPs and 45s in 1958 and soon the rest of the industry followed. The establishment of a set of common standards was important in the smooth introduction of the new format, yet the expense of doubling-up the playback system meant that monophonic discs did not disappear for many years.

The superior reproduction of "stereo" allowed record companies to justify increasing the price of their products. High Fidelity was the marketing tool of the '60s and a new upscale market of audiophiles was developed. Stereo also helped produce the effects popular in psychedelic rock music in the '60s, with speaking-panning gleefully practiced by those who wanted to aurally recreate an LSD trip.

Andre Millard

Date 1958

Country USA

Why It's Key A major technological advance improves the quality of the listening experience.

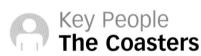

Key People
The Coasters

"Yakety Yak," which hit No. 1 on the *Billboard* chart on July 21, 1958, marked the apex of The Coasters' hit-strewn career. Carl Gardner, Leon Hughes, Billy Guy, and Bobby Nunn got together in 1955. Provided with material and production duties by Leiber and Stoller, they generated a string of comedy-tinged R&B hits, including "Searchin'" and "Young Blood," bringing them endearingly to life with their spread of different timbres. Nunn and Hughes were succeeded by Will "Dub" Jones and Cornell Gunter in late 1957, and in the spring of 1958 the group went right for the funny bone with "Yakety Yak," driven by a frantic beat, a thick King Curtis sax solo and Jones' basso hook "don't talk back." Underneath the comedy, they were speaking directly to the kids in identifying with their irritation at nagging parents.

The Coasters had a string of chart singles into the '60s, highlighted by "Along Came Jones," "Poison Ivy," and "Little Egypt" – Gunther was succeeded 1961 by ex-Cadillac Earl "Speedo" Carroll. Leiber and Stoller moved on to other projects in 1963 and the group's sales waned but their influence was felt during the British invasion, with covers of their songs by the Rolling Stones ("Poison Ivy"), the Downliners Sect ("Little Egypt"), and The Move ("Zing! Went The Strings Of My Heart"). With Gardner still there, the Coasters' last new record appeared in 1976, after which various groups using the name and associated with different members began working the oldies circuit.

Bruce Eder

Role Recording Artists

Date July 21, 1958

Nationality USA

Why It's Key The group who played R&B for laughs.

Key Person
Miles Davis

"I'll play it first and tell you what it is later," chirped trumpeter and composer Miles Davis when a critic asked him for a definition of jazz. He could almost have said jazz was whatever he was doing at the time, because for five decades Davis was at the vanguard of almost every stylistic innovation in the music.

With his all-star sextet album outing *Milestones* (1958), he pioneered a "modal" approach to improvised swing on the title track, and would continue in this vein on the genre-defining *Kind Of Blue* (1959). However, barrier-smashing occurred both before and after that. When bebop was at it peak, it was Davis' muted horn melodies that challenged Charlie Parker and Dizzy Gillespie's chord running complexity on the 1949–50 singles sides collected on *The Birth Of The Cool*. It was Davis who incorporated European classical music into the big band vernacular on the first of several collaborations with orchestral arranger Gil Evans, *Miles Ahead* (1957). Not that he ever gave a damn about jazz swinging. *In A Silent Way* (1969), *Bitches Brew* (1969), and *On The Corner* (1972) shredded the jazz rulebook, experimenting with psychedelic funk-rock and avant-garde classical dissonance to invent fusion, while his final studio album *Doo-Bop*, released in 1992, the year after his death, embraced hip-hop to define the acid jazz blueprint. It was this genre-bending impulse to constantly challenge himself, his collaborators, and his audience that made Miles Davis the king of the jazz iconoclasts.

Miles Keylock

Role Recording Artist

Date 1958

Nationality USA

Why It's Key The Pied Piper of jazz.

Opposite **Miles Davis**

Key Performance *Irma La Douce*
stage musical

According to coadapter Julian More, it was integrating such terms as *poule*, *mec*, and *grisbi* sans translation into the otherwise English text of *Irma La Douce* that provided the key to creating a linguistic equivalent of the French original, without resorting to idiomatic British slang or regional accents. The words mean, respectively, "prostitute," "pimp," and "money," which should give you some idea of the milieu of this musical, which opened in the West End on July 17, 1958.

Irma La Douce, a romantic farce, tells the story of the proverbial hooker with a heart of gold, with whom young law student Nestor falls so hopelessly in love that he assumes the guise of a rich, elderly sugar daddy who will be her only client. Meanwhile in his true identity, he wears himself so thin earning her upkeep that he finally "kills" his alter-ego, only to find himself on trial for his own murder. The show originated in Paris but the English version – which made it to the United States in 1960 with its original stars – would become even more popular, worldwide, than the French.

The music was by Marguerite Monnot, best known for having written many of Edith Piaf's songs. Alexandre Breffort's original French book and lyrics were replaced by an English book and lyrics by More, David Heneker, and Monty Norman. Generally upbeat in tone, score highlights include the title track, "Dis Donc-Dis Donc," and "Our Language of Love."

David Spencer

Opening Night July 17, 1958

Country France/UK

Director Peter Brook

Cast Keith Michell, Elizabeth Seal, Clive Revill

Composers Marguerite Monnot, Alexandre Breffort, Julian More, David Heneker, Monty Norman

Why It's Key The first hit musical adapted from an original French version.

Key Performance *Gigi*
the movie

In turn of twentieth-century Paris, bored young *bon vivant* playboy Gaston (Louis Jourdan) is tired of his mistresses, only valuing time with his uncle (Maurice Chevalier), uncle's friend, Madame Alvarez (Hermione Gingold), and her granddaughter Gigi, who gets sent away to learn how to be a famous courtesan. Gaston considers being her first patron but gradually discovers he is in love. Examined in contemporary light, the Colette novella-based story might seem distasteful but, at the time, the transformation of child to courtesan to wife of a roué was charming enough to cop *Gigi* an Academy Award for Best Picture.

MGM musicals producer Arthur Freed tapped the *My Fair Lady* team of Alan Jay Lerner (for screenplay and lyrics) and composer Frederick Loewe. The latter was reluctant, having never written directly for the screen before. Ironically, theater craftsmanship was the key: sharply defined characters and literate, properly motivated songs complemented the stylish period backdrop, lovingly recreated by Cecil Beaton (himself a veteran of *My Fair Lady*, brought on at Lerner's insistence). Connoisseurs of movie musicals assert that this release was the end of an era for the form.

Famous songs include the boulevard ditty "Thank Heaven For Little Girls"; a sweet waltz of memory romanticized, "I Remember It Well"; the appropriately bubbly "The Night They Invented Champagne"; and the rapturous title song, in which Gaston finally tweaks to what we knew all along.

David Spencer

Movie Release Date
May 15, 1958

Nationality USA

Director Vincente Minnelli

Cast Leslie Caron, Louis Jourdan, Maurice Chevalier, Hermione Gingold

Composer Alan Jay Lerner, Frederick Loewe

Why It's Key Considered by many the last great original live action film musical.

Opposite *Gigi*

Key Song **"Move It"**
Cliff Richard And The Shadows

Britain had been under the spell of rock 'n' roll since Bill Haley's 1955 success but, despite game attempts, it wasn't until "Move It" – a brilliantly exciting creation – that a UK act created an example of the form that vied in quality with American rock gems.

Guitarist Ian Samwell later recalled that he wrote the song aboard a Green Line bus while on his way to Cliff Richard's home, where The Drifters, Richard's back-up unit, of whom Samwell was a member, were rehearsing. Booked to record "Schoolboy Crush," a proposed debut single for Cliff, Samwell, together with drummer Terry Smart, entered EMI's Studio 2 at Abbey Road, London 1958, where it was decided to make "Move It" the B-side. To boost the level of musicianship on the disc, producer Norrie Paramor drafted in two established sessioners, bassist Frank Clarke and guitarist Ernie Shear, the latter providing the searing licks that gave the record a unique identity. Additionally, engineer Malcolm Addey opted to record the session at a higher level than that normally allowed at EMI's fusty studios, a ploy that ensured added power. After hearing a promo copy, Jack Good so raved about "Move It"'s potential in *Disc* magazine ("When one considers that this is the product of a 17 year-old boy from Cheshunt, Hertfordshire, the mind boggles!") that the record was flipped. "Move It" became the A-side and entered the UK chart on September 12, 1958, and the first essential British rock hit was born.

Fred Dellar

Release Date July 1958

Nationality UK

Composer Ian Samwell

Why It's Key First credible UK rock 'n' roll single.

Key Event
The Winter Dance Party plane crash

"I hope your plane crashes" said Waylon Jennings to Buddy Holly in friendly but horribly prophetic banter when the latter and fellow stars Ritchie Valens and the Big Bopper were preparing to take a private plane to the next gig on the Winter Dance Party tour.

The tour saw the above artists, Frankie Sardo, and Dion and the Belmonts traveling across the American Mid West in such awful conditions that some on their tour bus contracted frostbite. Valens was the hottest of the three properties who had hired the plane to get to the next gig early and get some laundry done. His self-written ballad "Donna" b/w the traditional, Spanish-language "La Bamba" had recently made a *Billboard* No. 2. The Big Bopper was famous for his twinkle-eyed, lustful "Chantilly Lace," a U.S. Top 10 the previous fall. The least hot was Holly, who was bewildered by his inability since the previous March to make the U.S. Top 20.

Conditions were terrible as young pilot Roger Peterson took off. Within minutes the snow and fog caused him to crash in a cornfield. All four passengers died. Said the then teenage Dion later, "We just seemed to be on top of the world the night before… I didn't know life was so fragile… "

Some moments are key for negative reasons. The event snuffed out the lives of three considerable talents and in the case of Buddy Holly almost certainly prevented rock's foremost barrier-smasher from instigating yet more innovations.
Sean Egan

Date February 3, 1959

Country USA

Why It's Key Rock 'n' roll's first major tragedy.

Key Song "Dream Lover"
Bobby Darin

Though it made U.S. No. 2 after its *Billboard* Top 40 chart entry on July 4, 1959, "Dream Lover" marked a triumph for Bobby Darin beyond merely being a smash.

Until "Dream Lover," Bobby Darin did bad rock 'n' roll, because that was what his label wanted. He'd scored his first million-seller by co-authoring and recording "Splish Splash," a goofy but catchy novelty tune about an interrupted bath.

But Darin saw himself more as a rival to Frank Sinatra than to Bill Haley or Chuck Berry and it was "Dream Lover" that both proved his point and suggested something about what rock 'n' roll could be. His lyric about a man with a fantasy woman in his head was fairly standard but cruised on a lovely melody, and the percussion-heavy, pause-punctuated bridge ("because I want.. a girl.. to call.. my own") was sublime.

His recording showed off a great set of pipes, and its success proved to his label's management that people would pay to hear him sing that way.

Additionally, "Dream Lover" not only sold several million copies in Darin's version but was widely covered by others (including his Bronx-born rival Dion). It was a sign that some of these young rock 'n' rollers were potentially very prodigious musical talents, and not only as singers.

After this, there was no stopping Darin. Subsequently, he recorded "Mack The Knife" from *The Threepenny Opera*, no less. It made U.S. No. 1.
Bruce Eder

Release Date March 1959

Nationality USA

Composer Bobby Darin

Why It's Key An artist breaks out of his straightjacket.

Opposite *Bobby Darin*

Key Song "There Goes My Baby"
The Drifters

By June 29, 1959 – on which this song first entered the *Billboard* Top 40 – Leiber and Stoller had racked up many hits for some of the biggest acts going. However, though their Elvis records were splendid and their Coasters records unusually witty, they were not really epoch-marking. However with The Drifters – a black vocal group for whom they rarely wrote, tending only to produce their records – they came up with a single that changed R&B forever.

The track shoehorned stuff into R&B that was presumed would never go. The first supposedly incongruous element was a Latin rhythm, which the pair were inspired to tackle by some Silvana Mangano music from the film *Anna* (1951). This rhythmic approach was, incidentally, massively influential on the subsequent productions of fellow composer-producer and protégé Burt Bacharach. The other innovation was classical strings, mixture of which with gritty R&B was a laughable concept until the two did it. After the phenomenal success of "There Goes My Baby" – it made a U.S. No. 2 – strings in black pop went from being unthinkable to de rigueur.

Some elements of a landmark record, though, are borne of happenstance, not inspiration. Though the strings were sweet, there was a peculiar roughness underlying the record. As Leiber later explained, "The timpani player, who was a regular drummer, didn't know how to pedal the timpani properly, so it ended up being out of tune. That created this interesting abrasive rub in the record."

Sean Egan

Release Date May 1959

Nationality USA

Composers Jerry Leiber, Mike Stoller

Why It's Key The record that changed R&B – twice over.

Key Song "Shout"
The Isley Brothers

"Shout" is, in essence, pure church. It was born on a stage as Ronald Isley sang Jackie Wilson's "Lonely Teardrops"; brothers O'Kelly and Randolph responded to Ronald's gospel routine, crying out "You make me wanna shout" in a familiar throwback to their childhood church in Cincinnati, Ohio and their successful family gospel group.

RCA signed the group on the strength of "Shout"'s abandoned, rhythmic mania, which stops just short of speaking in tongues. Others patterned secular songs on gospel standards before, but the Isleys explicitly performed like preachers, a delivery since copied by generations of rock singers. The song, released on September 21, 1959, slows, speeds up, introduces a quiet/loud dynamic, and features a church organ passage (provided by their childhood church keyboardist Professor Herman Stephens) complete with congregational clapping and ecstatic responses, although the lyrics are strictly about non-holy love.

The song is more familiar to UK residents through a 1964 UK Top Ten cover by female singer Lulu that was amazingly gutsy for a 15 year old. Since 1959, the Isley Brothers' original has sold a million copies, but it stalled at 47 on the pop charts at the time and never made the R&B chart. The Isleys remain criminally undervalued as architects of modern music but "Shout"'s lasting fame outstrips other important R&B landmarks of the time such as Ray Charles' "What'd I Say."

Chris Goodman

Release Date September 21, 1959

Nationality USA

Composer Rudolph Isley, Ronald Isley, O'Kelly Isley

Why It's Key While many R&B songs can lay claim to easing rock and soul into existence, few are, like "Shout," standards of both.

Opposite The Isley Brothers

Key Album *Time Out*
The Dave Brubeck Quartet

Although his 1959 *Time Out* album became a bigger smash hit than anyone expected, Dave Brubeck was actually no stranger to the charts prior to the late '50s. In fact, he'd dented the Top 10 *Billboard* album listings three times in 1955 alone. Nor was he shy about incorporating cerebral trimmings into his brand of cool jazz, using elements of classical music, complex harmonics, and tricky time signatures employed in few other styles of records created for the popular market, jazz or otherwise. *Time Out* was no exception in this regard, using 5/4 time (i.e. five beats in a four-bar measure) for its title track, 9/8 time for "Blue Rondo A La Turk," and other exotic rhythms elsewhere.

Though Brubeck was the pianist and leader of his quartet, and did compose most of the material on the LP, it was his alto saxophonist, Paul Desmond, who was responsible for writing the title track. That song is now not only Brubeck's signature tune but one of the most famous in all of jazz, its insinuating minor-key melody having become one of the most globally familiar jazz standards of all. It helped vault cool jazz into households and college dorms that wouldn't know a 5/4 beat from a cymbal crash. Rising to No. 2 in the pop charts, the album remained in the U.S. Top 40 for 86 weeks, and "Take Five" even becoming a Transatlantic hit single.

Richie Unterberger

Release Date 1959

Nationality USA

Tracklisting Blue Rondo A La Turk, Strange Meadowlark, Take Five, Three To Get Ready, Kathy's Waltz, Everybody's Jumpin', Pick Up Sticks

Why It's Key Brought intellectual jazz into the commercial mainstream and spread it further into college campuses.

Key Album *The Amazing Nina Simone*
Nina Simone

In her autobiography, Nina Simone wrote that for her music was "part of everyday life, as automatic as breathing." But her initial dream was to be a classical pianist, and she only began her career as a nightclub performer in order to earn money to further her studies in that direction. It was her success on the club circuit that led to a recording contract.

Simone (1933–2003, born Eunice Waymon) had developed a broad repertoire through her years of club gigs, and this versatility was fully on display on *The Amazing Nina Simone*, released in 1959 and her second proper album. There were folk songs ("Tomorrow"), traditional numbers ("Children Go Where I Send You"), show tunes ("It Might As Well Be Spring," from the Rodgers and Hammerstein musical *State Fair*), R&B ("You've Been Gone Too Long"), the theme from the film *The Middle Of The Night*, and swing ("Stompin' At The Savoy"). This album showed that it was impossible – and unnecessary – to neatly categorize her.

Simone's piano work was not highlighted; Bob Mersey's orchestral arrangements provided the musical backing. But as had been evident from her very first recording, it was Simone's voice that commanded attention, which was all the more remarkable considering that her musical training had never included singing (she only began singing when nightclub owners insisted her shows couldn't be solely instrumental). She was blessed with a breathy, feline voice that imbued everything she sang with a unique quality.

Gillian G. Gaar

Release Date 1959

Nationality USA

Tracklisting Blue Prelude, Children Go Where I Send You, Tomorrow (We Will Meet Once More), Stompin' At The Savoy, It Might As Well Be Spring, You've Been Gone Too Long, That's Him Over There, Chilly Winds Don't Blow, Theme From Middle Of The Night, Can't Get Out Of This Mood, Willow Weep for Me, Solitaire

Why It's Key A reluctant singer provides a vocal masterclass.

Opposite Nina Simone

Key Album *Let's All Sing With The Chipmunks* The Chipmunks

Years before The Archies reared their animated heads onto American television screens, The Chipmunks became countless young rockers' initial exposure to pop music.

They were the brainchild of songwriter/producer Ross Bagdasarian, who'd already made U.S. No. 1 with "The Witch Doctor" under nom-de-disc David Seville. Chipmunks Alvin, Simon, and Theodore (slyly named after three of Bagdasarian's Liberty Records bosses) topped the charts with the perennial "Chipmunk Song (Christmas Don't Be Late)" in 1958. Their helium-high voices were all that of Bagdasarian, sped-up. It was an effect so startling for the time that it helped garner the following March's album *Let's All Sing With The Chipmunks* a Grammy. The album – which boasted another highly unusual facet in being pressed on bright red vinyl – spawned several successful long-playing follow-ups (highly recommended: *The Chipmunks Sing The Beatles' Hits*, *Urban Chipmunk*, and the beyond-classic *Chipmunk Punk*), not to mention a cartoon franchise which keeps the motley trio alive and chirping on home video to this day.

While one can claim Bagdasarian's late 50's breakthrough was a brilliant reaction to, and/or parody of, the entire *Sing Along With Mitch Miller* phenomenon, *Let's All Sing With The Chipmunks*' high-fidelity carnival of frantic vocals and mock studio spats between Seville and nemesis Alvin (the Chipmunk whose "enthusiasm is boundless and despair bottomless," according to his official biography) is in retrospect truly one of the most clever, best-engineered and ultimately entertaining records of the era.

Gary Pig Gold

Release Date March 1959

Nationality USA

Tracklisting Yankee Doodle, Chipmunk Fun, The Little Dog, Old MacDonald Cha Cha Cha, Three Blind(-Folded) Mice, Alvin's Harmonica, Good Morning Song, Whistle While You Work, If You Love Me (Alouette), Ragtime Cowboy Joe, Pop Goes The Weasel, The Chipmunk Song (Christmas Don't Be Late)

Why It's Key Pioneered the concept of non-existent recording artists.

Key Album *The Genius Of Ray Charles* Ray Charles

During his career trajectory Ray Charles was primarily viewed as a singles artist. 1959's aptly titled *The Genius Of Ray Charles*, however, proved that his gifts translated to the long-playing medium.

The album was divided into two stylistically distinct halves. Side one found him backed by various Count Basie and Duke Ellington sidemen, who supplied a vibrant jazz, big-band backdrop to Charles' animated, vocally charged performances. Charles breathed new soul-stirring vitality into these Quincy Jones-arranged numbers while the big band treatment provided that extra measure of oomph to traditionally more animated fare (i.e., Irving Berlin's "Alexander's Ragtime Band" and the Louis Jordan hit "Let The Good Times Roll"). Side two found Charles in full ballad mode backed by a lush string orchestra arranged by Ralph Burns. Though the strings had the effect of muting the sound of Charles' piano, his always expressive vocals were miked squarely up front. The swelling orchestration heightened the emotional impact of beloved standards such as "Am I Blue," "Don't Let The Sun Catch You Crying," and what some consider to be the definitive version of "Come Rain Or Come Shine," a tune associated with Frank Sinatra that in Charles' hands sounded downright haunting.

A landmark recording that found the master expanding his musical palette once more beyond the R&B and soul people expected of him, *The Genius Of Ray Charles* illustrated yet again that the only thing to expect from Charles was great, richly expressive music.

Tierney Smith

Release Date November 1959

Nationality USA

Tracklisting Let The Good Times Roll, It Had To Be You, Alexander's Ragtime Band, Two Years Of Torture, When Your Lover Has Gone, Deed I Do, Just For A Thrill, You Won't Let Me Go, Tell Me You'll Wait For Me, Don't Let The Sun Catch You Cryin', Am I Blue, Come Rain Or Come Shine

Why It's Key Musical groundbreaker (pleasantly) surprises the public yet again.

Key Event
Motown Records is incorporated

Berry Gordy, a former Detroit boxer and failed jazz record-shop owner, had big hits writing R&B tunes in the '50s, including "Reet Petite" for Jackie Wilson. But frustrated with the uncertainty of getting paid by the record companies he sold them to, Gordy founded his own Tamla Records, later to become Motown, with an $800 loan from his family.

Based in a house at 2648 West Grand Boulevard, Detroit, the first release on the label – incorporated on January 12, 1959 – in the summer of 1959 was The Miracles' "Way Over There," the group headed by Motown vice-president, songwriter, and producer William "Smokey" Robinson. What followed was an extraordinary production line of rigorously quality-controlled hits from talent such as Marvin Gaye, Stevie Wonder, and The Supremes and the label was the only real indigenous competition to The Beatles' domination of the American charts in the early '60s.

That should have made Motown significant enough but in the context of America during the nascent civil rights movement, a black-owned-and-run enterprise was a new and inspiring concept in music. Motown became the most powerful African-American business in America and while its songs were rarely openly political, the fact of its "crossover" success – the result of eschewing a harder soul style to identify with black and white fans alike – was radical in itself. Vainglorious company slogan it may have been, but Motown really was the "Sound of Young America" that it proclaimed itself.
Chris Goodman

Date January 12, 1959

Nationality USA

Why It's Key A phenomenally successful African-American concern was the perfect champion for the U.S. civil rights movement.

Key Person
Marty Robbins

Born Martin Robertson in Arizona in 1925, Marty Robbins straddled the worlds of pop and country. In his own, quietly idiosyncratic way, he was very much a revolutionary.

Robbins recorded "Singing The Blues" before Guy Mitchell had a hit with it. His first big pop hit, was the self-written "A White Sport Coat (And A Pink Carnation)" (1957), which united him with pop orchestra conductor Ray Conniff. He also did well with the jaunty Bacharach and David number "The Story Of My Life."

It was his determination to fuse the buttoned-down smartness of the Conniff collaboration with a cowboy song narrative inspired by both television shows like *Gunsmoke* and his maternal grandfather's Wild West stories, that led to the creation of what became his signature song, "El Paso." After winning a battle with his A&R man to get the 4:12 song from his celebrated album *Gunfighter Ballads And Trail Songs* (1959) released as a single in an era when radio

shunned anything over three minutes, Robbins's credentials as a shrewd envelope-pusher were established: the song entered the *Billboard* Top 40 on November 30, 1959, and made U.S. No. 1.

He capitalized on this hard-won creative freedom, recording the first country song to use a guitar played through a fuzz box ("Don't Worry," 1961) and even had a hit with a calypso tune ("Devil Woman," 1962). He was inducted into the Country Music Hall of Fame a few weeks before his death in December 1982.
Angus Batey

Role Recording Artist

Date 1959

Country USA

Why It's Key Eclectic pioneer who stretched the boundaries of country.

Key Person
Ornette Coleman

For an artist whose music is generally considered "difficult," Ornette Coleman's influence has been surprisingly broad. Today, the iconoclastic Texan, born in 1930, is cited as an inspiration by musicians from the classical, jazz, hip hop, and rock worlds but from the outset, his determinedly singular music provoked extreme reactions.

Coleman was an obscure figure until his November 17, 1959, debut at New York's Five Spot made him a controversial overnight sensation. The Big Apple's jazz cognoscenti was divided. The whiff of hype led to this upstart and his plastic saxophone being greeted with intense suspicion: Coleman's music broke all be-bop's rules and led to claims that his freeform improvisation meant he didn't know what he was doing, and what some heard as tonal idiosyncrasies others felt displayed a lack of ability. Critics were enthusiastic but an enigmatic Miles Davis said Coleman's music showed he was "all screwed up

inside." Drummer Max Roach was more forthright: he punched Coleman in the face.

But the records Coleman and his quartet began making for Atlantic, including the determined mission statement *The Shape Of Jazz To Come* (1959) and 1960's entirely improvised, eight-musician *Free Jazz*, became accepted as pioneering milestones. He shared studios with Pat Metheny, Jerry Garcia, and Lou Reed and scored a David Cronenberg movie. In his seventies, he still tours and records, and his complicated theory of the interaction of harmony, melody, and rhythm – harmolodics – continues to frustrate and fascinate.

Angus Batey

Role Recording Artist

Date 1959

Nationality USA

Why It's Key The man whose innovations provoked both adoration and physical violence.

Opposite **Ornette Coleman**

Key Performance *Gypsy*
stage musical

Initially, Stephen Sondheim was engaged to write both lyrics and music for this tale, the freely adapted memoirs of celebrity stripper Gypsy Rose Lee about growing up on the road with an overbearing stage mother. But when Ethel Merman signed to portray Mama Rose, who pushes her kids to succeed on the Orpheum vaudeville circuit, living vicariously through them the opportunities she never had, Merman refused to put her trust in a first-time composer; Sondheim, not yet 30, was known only as a lyricist (for *West Side Story*). Sondheim took the assignment on the advice of his mentor, Oscar Hammerstein II, who told him the experience of writing for a star would be invaluable.

Sondheim's acquiescence was the catalyst for a classic work, his first-rate lyrics carried on melodies that showed the faultless hand of an old master. Librettist Arthur Laurents had an unusual affinity for exploring dark subject matter in the musical arena and director-choreographer Jerome Robbins was the master

of blending storytelling milieu and structure with underlying dramatic theme to create the most rich, cohesive, and resonant evening possible.

Gypsy contains more "liftable" songs (i.e. later recorded outside of dramatic context) than any Sondheim show other than *West Side Story*, including "Together," "Wherever We Go," "You'll Never Get Away From Me," and perennial variety program show-stopper "Everything's Coming Up Roses."

David Spencer

Opening Night
May 21, 1959

Nationality USA

Director Jerome Robbins

Cast Ethel Merman

Composer Stephen Sondheim, Jule Styne

Why It's Key Bracing one-time collaboration between lyricist Stephen Sondheim's next-generation sensibility and the razzmatazz of brassy Broadway-and-Hollywood tunesmith Jule Styne.

Key Song "What'd I Say"
Ray Charles

Ray Charles had already provided the blueprint for soul with 1954's "I Got A Woman" – mixing gospel and bluesy sexual suggestion for the first time with a song based on the sacred hit "It Must Be Jesus." However, it never made the *Billboard* pop charts and Charles' new sound was confined to the black "Chitlin" touring circuit and R&B charts until 1959 and "What'd I Say," which entered the *Billboard* Top 40 on July 13, 1959.

An improvised piano riff over a lascivious, abandoned call and response with his female backing singers the Raeletts, this triumph of innuendo was conceived in a nightclub near Pittsburgh when Charles found extra time to fill before the end of his set. Although Atlantic Records removed the more suggestive verses, its "shake that thing" lyrics and grunts still made it an unusually risqué presence on the Hit Parade. It hit No. 6, Charles went mainstream, and the hitherto polite pop charts, more used to white teen idols and big bands, became a growing concern for

black artists, an open floodgate filled by the likes of record companies Motown and Stax, as well as artists James Brown and Sam Cooke. "What'd I Say" became a staple for budding '60s R&B bands.

The success secured Charles a deal with major label ABC, making him a showbusiness staple. By 1961, he had the power to refuse to play segregated shows, a potent example for the burgeoning Civil Rights movement.

Chris Goodman

Release Date July 1959

Nationality USA

Composer Ray Charles

Why It's Key Suggestive R&B makes its way into the squeaky-clean pop charts.

Opposite **Ray Charles**

Key Song "The Twist"
Chubby Checker

"The Twist" dated from 1958 and was written and originally recorded by Hank Ballard. In 1959, after some effort, Ballard got a version commercially released, but only as a single B-side. Soon the record started getting "flipped" by teenagers. At one club in Philadelphia, where the owner had banned participants from touching while dancing, the kids embraced the song's beat and the suggestive moves urged by the lyrics, and it took off locally.

American Bandstand host Dick Clark got word of the song's smoldering appeal and urged the local Cameo-Parkway label to record a version. They turned to Ernest Evans, a chicken-plucker with a knack for impressions and a love of music, who'd previously cut one slightly successful single, "The Class," under his new stage name, Chubby Checker. "The Twist," released in July 1960, spawned a revolution when Checker could be seen demonstrating the titular dance's moves on television appearances. Teenagers across the country

were suddenly dancing without touching, but they were still being fiercely provocative in their moves, all swiveling their hips in a way that outraged a generation still recovering from the similarly pelvis-oriented Elvis Presley a few years before.

The Twist – which made U.S. No. 1 on September 19, 1960, and then again on January 13, 1962 – started a revolution in dancing that continues to this day whereby it is the norm for young people on a dance floor to not have bodily contact.

Bruce Eder

First Released 1959

Nationality USA

Composer Hank Ballard

Why It's Key The beginning of the cultural shift away from dancing with a partner.

Key Album *Elvis Is Back!*
Elvis Presley

When Elvis Presley reported for duty in the U.S. Army on March 14, 1958, conventional wisdom suggested that his career would suffer as he spent two years stationed in West Germany. "Out of sight, out of mind" was the – possibly reasonable – assumption of the music business, who thought fickle audiences would move on to the next new entertainer.

But Presley's manager and his record label RCA Victor managed to keep a stream of record releases coming, mostly consisting of repackagings, although the singer did get into a recording studio during his enlistment, cutting the hits "One Night" and "A Fool Such As I" on a weekend pass in June '58.

Still, the reaction to Presley's 1960 return was uncertain, especially because popular music had changed in the interim, becoming more pop-oriented. The release of an initial single, "Stuck On You," suggested he had, too. But *Elvis Is Back!*, released on April 8, 1960, stretched across the range of Presley's talent, from rockers to blues songs and ballads, pleasing not only the pop-inclined but those who had loved him for his adoption of gritty black stylings too. The highlight was an extraordinary smoldering rendition of Lowell Fulsom's "Reconsider Baby" in which saxophonist Boots Randolph was allowed to let rip on a lengthy solo.

The public's response, which kept the LP in the U.S. charts more than a year, confirmed that the album title was accurate.

William Ruhlmann

Release Date April 8, 1960

Nationality USA

Tracklisting Make Me Know It, Fever, The Girl Of My Best Friend, I Will Be Home Again, Dirty, Dirty Feeling, The Thrill Of Your Love, Soldier Boy, Such A Night, It Feels So Right, The Girl Next Door Went A'Walking, Like A Baby, Reconsider Baby

Why it's Key Demonstrated that artists could come back from the wilderness if they reemerged with a strong album.

Key Person
Eddie Cochran

On April 17, 1960, Eddie Cochran, along with Gene Vincent, Cochran's girlfriend songwriter Sharon Sheeley, and a deputizing tour manager named Patrick Thompkins were traveling in a taxi on the way to London's Heathrow Airport. Though they were leaving Britain – Vincent had some Paris dates to attend to while Cochran was planning some recording – returning was very much on the two rockers' minds. Brought over under the aegis of legendary TV producer Jack Good to appear in his latest show *Boy Meets Girl*, the pair had been minting it in a country in which they were more popular than in their native America. On their joint tour, they had been reportedly earning sums of U.S. $1,000 per week upwards each.

Thompkins drew to the driver's attention that he had taken a wrong turn. The driver, who had been traveling at high speed but probably only because he was instructed to do so, sought to change direction. He lost control of the vehicle, which crashed into a lightpost. Cochran died at 4:10 P.M., aged just 21. The others all survived, in a manner: Sheeley was obviously left distraught, Vincent suffered permanent injury to his already damaged left leg, and the cabbie received a prison sentence for dangerous driving.

It was a tragic end to a love affair between Cochran and the UK, a love sealed by the ascension of Cochran's spookily titled single "Three Steps To Heaven" to UK No. 1 in June.

Bruce Eder

Role Recording artist

Date 1960

Nationality UK

Country UK

Why It's Key The first major rock 'n' roll death in the UK.

Key Song "Shakin' All Over"
Johnny Kidd And The Pirates

One of the few perfect creations in rock, every element of Johnny Kidd And The Pirates' "Shakin' All Over" oozed primeval brilliance.

The intro, a chilling guitar figure devised and played by session man Joe Moretti, provided a signature, instantly recognizable, while Kidd's vocal, quiveringly powerful yet also somehow weary, was equally superb, the whole proving to be not just a superior rock offering but one that raised the bar and influenced countless contenders. What was even more remarkable was that it was British, lacking even the vaguest hint of pastiche that had always attended even the best of previous UK attempts at this U.S. artform.

The eye-patch wearing, cutlass wielding Kidd, who had earlier led London bands under his real name Freddie Heath, had entered Abbey Road Studios to record a version of golden oldie "Yes Sir That's My Baby." "Shakin' All Over," penned just the day before at a Soho coffee bar, was offered as a filler B-side. There'd been no real rehearsal for the song, just a brief, acoustic run though in Kidd's front room. But the recording session proved a date with alchemy. The hastily fashioned B-side was clearly an instant classic, as recognized by producer Jack Good, who promoted the release on his *Wham!* television show. The result was a UK No. 1 on August 4, 1960.

Subsequent covers have included a 1965 U.S. hit by The Guess Who and a rendition by The Who on *Live At Leeds* (1970).

Fred Dellar

Release Date
June 1960

Nationality UK

Composer Johnny Kidd

Why It's Key Milestone in British rock.

Key Event
The payola hearings

On February 8, 1960, a U.S. government sub-committee began a public hearing on the subject of "payola." The term was applied to the practice of record companies paying money in order to have their wares played in key spots on radio stations.

Many believed that the payola scandal was just another method of halting the rise of rock, *Billboard* pointing out that payola was long established in the record industry and had been in operation even before the big band era. Credence was given this argument by the fact that the impetus for the hearings was complaints from ASCAP, whose traditionalist music was losing airplay ground to R&B and rock 'n' roll, mainly represented by rivals BMI.

Though charges against 106 names were originally proposed, the listing was narrowed down to a mere two dozen DJs and program managers, attention finally being focused on just two DJs – Cleveland's Alan Freed, the DJ whose *Moondog Matinee* shows had been instrumental in introducing rock 'n' roll to teenage America, and Dick Clark. The latter avoided further investigation by selling his stake in a record company and cooperating with the authorities. Freed was later found guilty of taking bribes but was merely fined U.S. $500 and given a suspended sentence.

Rock 'n' roll survived this scandal. However, the case ruined Freed's career and he died penniless in 1965, at the age of 43. Many say the man nicknamed "Mr Rock 'n' Roll" died of a broken heart.

Fred Dellar

Date February 8, 1960

Country USA

Why It's Key The scandal that destroyed Alan Freed.

Key Album *The Sound Of Fury*
Billy Fury

The Sound Of Fury was issued by Decca in an unusual 10-inch format. It seemed to signal the album's special nature for, with it, Billy Fury (born Ronald Wycherley) not only provided the album that set the pace for homegrown UK rock in terms of authenticity, but – highly unusual for the time – he wrote every song on the record.

Like Elvis Presley's early recordings, everything was kept spare, the songs being backed by a bare-bones if superb band –Joe Brown (guitar), Reg Guest (piano), Alan Weighell (electric bass), Bill Stark (slap bass), and Andy White (drums) – the only concession to a bigger production being the employment of The Four Jays vocal group who provided a Jordanaires patina to the proceedings. Joe Brown later revealed that both the singer and producer Jack Good wanted to reproduce the feel of Presley's rockabilly-oriented sides and that his own brief was to sound as much like Scotty Moore as possible. Songwise, the record, while maintaining its pure rockabilly character throughout, was amazingly diverse. The stuttering "Turn My Back On You" proving to be music for the hop, "Phone Call" stemming from the blues, while "That's Love," the album's Top 20 single, was country, albeit with a hard beat. Fury's insistence on writing his own material was vindicated when the album entered the UK albums charts in May 1960. Fury's early death at 42 was commemorated by a bronze statue in his home city of Liverpool.

Fred Dellar

Release Date May 1960

Nationality UK

Tracklisting That's Love, My Advice, Phone Call, You Don't Know, Turn My Back On You, Don't Say It's Over, Since You've Been Gone, It's You I Need, Alright Goodbye, Don't Leave Me This Way

Why It's Key Britain's first true rock album.

Opposite Billy Fury

Key Person
Connie Francis

Concetta Rosa Maria Franconero (aka Connie Francis) started recording for MGM Records at the age of 16 in 1955 but she didn't score her first big hit, a revival of the stately, vengeful 1923 song "Who's Sorry Now," until 1958.

Francis, a native of Newark, New Jersey, got her start as a child performer playing the accordion on a local television show. Her strong voice, attractive appearance, and domineering stage father combined to bring her to the attention of record companies. Another TV break, on DJ Dick Clark's weekday afternoon teen dance show *American Bandstand*, made her a star. She was as surprised as anyone when Clark played "Who's Sorry Now," a song her father had insisted she record.

Having gotten her break, however, Francis took advantage of it. In 1959, she was the most successful pop singles artist of the year in the United States. The following year, on June 21, she topped the U.S. charts for the first time with "Everybody's Somebody's Fool."

It was the first time a solo female singer had hit number one since Debbie Reynolds' "Tammy" three years before. Three months later, Francis was back in pole position with "My Heart Has A Mind Of Its Own."

Other notable recordings of hers are her 1963 JFK tribute "In The Summer Of His Years" whose profits were donated to relatives of shot policemen and – of all the ironies – "Where The Boys Are."

William Ruhlmann

Role Recording Artist

Date 1960

Nationality USA

Why It's Key Paved the way for women in pop.

Key Song "Apache"
The Shadows

Quartet The Shadows were perceived as merely the backing band for UK pop idol Cliff Richard until shortly after composer Jerry Lordan played them the atmospheric instrumental "Apache" on his ukulele during their spring 1960 UK tour. Lordan warned them that guitar virtuoso Bert Weedon had already recorded it.

The "Shads" laid down their Fender Stratocaster-powered version complete with Cliff pounding away on Chinese drums. When Weedon found out, he called his label, Top Rank, telling them to release his version immediately and began appearing on television and radio to plug the tune. Disastrously, his plan backfired because Top Rank didn't get the single into the shops. "There I was promoting Apache," he fumed later, "and anybody asking for it in a record shop was offered The Shadows' version!" On August 25, The Shadows knocked their guv'nor, Cliff, off the top of the UK chart. It was the first of two dozen Shadows hits, all without vocals, proving that a rock group could sustain a career with a type of record normally associated with the novelty market.

"Apache" inspired innumerable future axmeisters, including Eric Clapton and Mark Knopfler to save their pocket money for a Fender Strat. It also became so associated with native Americans that the sonorous, reverberating riff played by Shadows lead guitarist Hank B. Marvin was latter alluded to by Adam And The Ants when they wanted a musical shorthand for "red Indian" on *Kings Of The Wild Frontier* (1980).
Gavin Michie

Release Date July 1960

Nationality UK

Composer Jerry Lordan

Why It's Key The record that inspired countless guitarists and popularized the Stratocaster.

Key Event **The Kingston Trio have four albums in the *Billboard* Top Ten**

The Kingston Trio have never exactly been hip. Their natty striped shirts, scrubbed clean-cut look, and wholesomely innocuous (if immaculately harmonized) brand of commercial folk music have been lampooned as by-products of a cornier era. Yet it's often forgotten just how huge the group were. On December 12, 1960, they had four albums in the *Billboard* Top 10 at once – all four of which reached No. 1 at some point. That's Beatlemania-strength sales, and while no one would claim them to be innovators on a par with the Fab Four, certainly they were striking a chord among huge segments of the record-buying audience, especially on college campuses.

Additionally, the musical skills of the three guitarist/vocalists – Nick Reynolds, Bob Shane, and Dave Guard – were far from negligible. Smooth and sophisticated though their harmonies might have been, they were responsible for bringing American folk music to a wider listenership than ever before, starting with their No. 1 hit single "Tom Dooley," an adaptation of an Appalachian folk ballad. They also had hits with songs by Pete Seeger and Hoyt Axton, as well as their own material. Nor were they bereft of a social conscience, refusing to play to segregated audiences. And while earthier singer-songwriters that followed in their wake were far more creative and enduring, The Kingston Trio were crucial in forming the listener base for the very performers who superseded them, a fellow named Dylan included.
Richie Unterberger

Date December 12, 1960

Country USA

Why It's Key The apex of their massive influence on the revitalization of folk in America.

Opposite The Kingston Trio

Key Song "Battle Hymm Of The Republic"
The Mormom Tabernacle Choir

"The Battle Hymn of the Republic" had its lyric written in 1861 by Julia Ward Howe to a tune devised in 1855 by William Steffe that had been given various words in the interim. Howe's marching song for union soldiers battling to end slavery with its rousing chorus of "Glory, glory Hallelujah" was first published on the front page of *The Atlantic Monthly* of February 1862.

The new song was an instantaneous success and has lasted over 100 years as one of the country's best-loved patriotic songs. The Republican Party appropriated the song as its own and the Reverend Martin Luther King often evoked the song in speeches and sermons. His last public words were its first line: "Mine eyes have seen the glory of the coming of the Lord," given in a sermon in Memphis the night before he was assassinated.

In 1959, the 375-strong Mormon Tabernacle Choir had a U.S. Top 20 hit with a recording of the song which won the 1960 Grammy Award for Best Performance by a Vocal Group or Chorus. It has been posited that the great success of this version is linked to the upbeat, patriotic feeling in the country after the election of John F. Kennedy. As if reflecting the new optimism of "Camelot," the choir's recording replaced the line "Let us die to make men free" with "Let us live to make men free."

Ken Bloom

Release Date 1960

Nationality USA

Composers William Steffe, Julia Ward Howe

Why It's Key A new age of optimism sees the revival of a stirring Civil War anthem.

Key Album *The Explosive Freddy Cannon*
Freddy Cannon

Freddy Cannon's maiden hit, 1959's "Tallahassee Lassie," rocked out with real if somewhat crude raunch. When its follow-up fell short of the U.S. Top 40, however, Swan Records' Bernie Binnick hit upon the idea of Cannon reviving the relatively ancient "Way Down Yonder In New Orleans," inspired by watching Al Jolson perform the number in a movie. Recast as a rock 'n' roll song, it dragged the singer out of one-hit-wonderland by making U.S. No. 3.

From rock 'n' roll's inception, its performers had sometimes looked to non-rock standards for material, sometimes even scoring big hits, as The Flamingos did with the classic "I Only Have Eyes For You." It was something else, however, to stuff nearly an album's worth onto an LP, as *The Explosive Freddy Cannon* did, especially considering Cannon was still a teenager himself. "Sweet Georgia Brown," "St. Louis Blues," "California Here I Come," "Deep In The Heart Of Texas," and "Chattanooga Shoe Shine Boy" (the last a follow-up single to "Way Down Yonder… ") all got the Freddy "Boom-Boom" Cannon treatment.

The album didn't crack the U.S. Top 40, but somewhat surprisingly, it went all the way to No. 1 in the UK upon its 1960 release. Cannon briefly toyed with making a career out of the shtick but when his adaptation of "Muskrat Ramble" stalled at No. 54, it was back to teen idol rock 'n' roll, his "Palisades Park" becoming a smash in 1962.

Richie Unterberger

Release Date 1960

Nationality USA

Tracklisting Boston My Home Town, Kansas City, Sweet Georgia Brown, Way Down Yonder In New Orleans, St Louis Blues, Indiana, Chattanooga Shoe Shine Boy, Deep In The Heart Of Texas, California Here I Come, Okefenokee, Carolina In The Morning, Tallahassie Lassie

Why It's Key An LP almost utterly dominated by rock 'n' roll arrangements of pre-rock pop standards.

Key Person
Miriam Makeba

She may not be as globally well-known as, say, Madonna but over a career spanning five decades the singer, sometime songwriter, actress, and political activist Miriam Makeba has performed for John F. Kennedy, Fidel Castro, Haile Selassie, and Nelson Mandela. She's even had three private audiences with the Pope.

Makeba was born in 1932. After initial successes with South African doo-wop pioneers The Manhattan Brothers and her own girl group The Skylarks in the '50s, starring roles in the seminal black jazz opera *King Kong* and anti-apartheid documentary *Come Back Africa* permitted her to advance her career, albeit in exile. In 1960 she released her eponymous debut album. The "exotic" timbres of her bewitching Xhosa vocals on Afro-pop-jazz hits like "The Click Song" had *Time* magazine hailing Makeba as "the most exciting new singing talent to appear in many years." In 1966, her album with Harry Belafonte, *An Evening With*

Belafonte/Makeba (1965), made her the first African artist to win a Grammy. But it wasn't just her music that earned Makeba the status of "Mama Afrika." It was also her politics. Her marriage to Black Panther activist Stokely Carmichael in 1968 resulted in U.S. blacklisting but that didn't stop Makeba spending the next 22 years promoting the cause of African liberation as Guinea's UN delegate and a member of Paul Simon's worldwide *Graceland* tour of 1987/8, before her triumphant homecoming to a post-apartheid South African in 1990.

Miles Keylock

Role Recording Artist

Date 1960

Nationality South Africa

Why It's Key The most influential African diva of the twentieth century.

Key Person
Joan Baez

The American folk revival was already picking up momentum by the time Joan Baez's debut album was released in 1960, particularly in liberal cities and college campuses. She was the first commercial star of the American folk revival movement, however, who truly reflected the young counter-cultural crowd that gathered to hear folk music in coffeehouses. Her long flowing hair, omnipresent acoustic guitar, and casual wardrobe marked her out as "one of us". While her repertoire was at the outset traditional – and she rarely wrote material – she sang those ageless songs with an angelic, if austere, reverence that impressed her generation as more honest and authentic than the smooth harmonizing folk groups The Kingston Trio had spawned.

At the same time, Baez's commercial success was considerable, her first half a dozen albums reaching the Top 15, and the singer even landing on the cover of *Time* magazine. Her impact broadened beyond the

music world when she began to perform contemporary topical songs and via her championing and interpretation of a still-emerging protest songwriter named Bob Dylan. Baez backed up her words with action, throwing herself into civil rights and anti-war activism, immersing herself into those causes even more heavily after Dylan abandoned protest music. It would be no exaggeration to state that Baez influenced hundreds of other recording artists in covering and writing socially conscious anthems of dissent.

Richie Unterberger

Role Recording Artist

Date 1960

Nationality USA

Why It's Key The launch of a career that encouraged many listeners to put their dissenting views into action.

Key Song "Runaway"
Del Shannon

On a Friday evening in October 1960, Del Shannon and his band were performing their regular stint at the Hi-Lo Club in Battle Ground, Michigan, when keyboardist Max Crook began improvising on the piano. The rest of the band quickly joined in the impromptu jam, and the next morning, Shannon developed a song out of the jam's main riff. Shannon debuted the song with his band that very night, and three months later, he and Crook headed to New York city to record it. By April 24, 1961, the song, "Runaway," was U.S. No. 1. It also topped the UK chart.

The song was a melancholy look back at a failed relationship. There were two elements that made it stand out; Shannon's vocals and Crook's keyboard part. Shannon was one of the first white artists to sing falsetto, having been inspired by artists like The Ink Spots and Dion And The Belmonts. His vocal was also sped up, giving the song a more urgent feel, especially in the chorus, with its immortal descending "Wah-wah-wah-wah-wonder" plea. This was matched by Crook's unearthly keyboard line, created on an instrument he called a "Musitron," a proto-synthesizer he fashioned out of a Clavioline that was modified with television tubes, appliance parts, and other items. It was the first time such a device had been used on a pop record and it made "Runaway" sound unlike anything else currently in the charts. It was the sound of the future.
Gillian G. Gaar

Release Date
February 1961

Nationality USA

Composers Del Shannon, Max Crook

Why It's Key Synthesizers are introduced to rock 'n' roll.

Key Song "Wimoweh (The Lion Sleeps Tonight)"

When The Tokens took "The Lion Sleeps Tonight" to the top of the U.S. charts on December 18, 1961, the song already had a considerable history. It started life as "Mbube," a Zulu song recorded in 1939 and popularized by its composer Solomon Linda and his group The Evening Birds. A hit in South Africa, the composition was later heard by American folk song collector Alan Lomax who played it to The Weavers.

Released under the title "Wimoweh" and employing a sensational orchestral arrangement by Gordon Jenkins, The Weavers' rendition headed into the U.S. Top 20 during 1952, its traditional chanting and talk of jungle animals providing a taste of the exotic for Americans. The Tokens' even more successful revamped, retitled version employed Jay Siegel's extraordinary high-voice lead. There seemed to be no end to the song's travels. A year later, as "Wimoweh" once more, it crossed the Atlantic to become a UK Top 10 hit for Scot Karl Denver. After which, in one form or another "Wimoweh"/"The Lion Sleeps Tonight" provided hits for Dave Newman (UK), Tight Fit (UK), Robert John (USA), and finally, for The Tokens again during 1994 when the song clambered back into the U.S. Hot 100 following its appearance as part of the soundtrack to the movie *The Lion King*.

Not that Solomon Linda benefited from such success. He died a pauper in 1962 and was buried in a grave without a headstone.
Fred Dellar

U.S. No. 1 Date
December 18, 1961

First Released 1952

Nationality South Africa

Composers Hugo Peretti, Albert Stanton, Luigi Creatore, Paul Campbell, George Weiss, Roy Ilene

Why It's Key Brought a taste of Africa to the West.

Opposite The Weavers

THE ROOSEVELT HOSPITA

Key Event
Jackie Wilson is shot

When on February 15, 1961, Jackie Wilson was shot by one of his alleged lovers, Juanita Jones, it was somehow symbolic of the career of a man who possessed all the talent in the world but none of his rightful share of luck.

Wilson, born in 1934, started out as a clone of Clyde McPhatter but soon developed his own style as both a vocalist and a performer. His talent in the former department is shown to its full glorious extent in "Reet Petite," a 1956 single in which Wilson rolled his "r"s to awe-making lengths. In the latter department he showed it in every spinning, leg-splitting, sweat-drenched concert. But Wilson, a non-writer, was at the mercy of others for material and it is probably this that ensured that – to his distress – contemporary Sam Cooke had the greater credibility, even though they had both introduced the passion of gospel into R&B and thereby helped to pioneer the creation of soul.

He released other worthy records, notably "I Get The Sweetest Feeling," but the shooting was later compounded by the seizure of his home by the IRS and the killing of his teenaged son.

It seems par for the course that when in 1986 "Reet Petite," on the back of its use in a television advert, belatedly made the top spot in Britain, Wilson was in no position to appreciate it: he had been left brain damaged in 1975 following a fall on stage. He died in 1984.

Sean Egan

Date February 15, 1961
Country USA
Why It's Key One of the founders of soul music.

Opposite Jackie Wilson

Key People
Gerry Goffin and Carole King

Having met as college students in 1958, Gerry Goffin and Carole King married the following year. Though also a singer, King elected to concentrate on writing; both worked with other partners, but there was an indefinable magic when they came together. In 1960 they coauthored "Will You Love Me Tomorrow," intending to pitch it at Johnny Mathis. However, the song's will-you-still-respect-me-in-the-morning undertow made it ideal for a female voice, and, when paired with girl group The Shirelles, it provided the Goffin-King partnership with their first U.S. No. 1 on January 30, 1961.

The duo's complementary talents – Gerry's sensitive lyrics, Carole's melodic flair and grasp of song construction – made them an unbeatable combination as they helped define the Brill Building era with innumerable hits including "Take Good Care Of My Baby" (a U.S./UK chart-topper for Bobby Vee), "Halfway To Paradise" (Tony Orlando, Billy Fury), "Up On The Roof" (The Drifters), "One Fine Day" (The Chiffons), "I'm Into Something Good" (Earl-Jean, Herman's Hermits), and "Chains" (The Cookies, but also recorded by The Beatles, who were massive fans). They even supplied their babysitter, Little Eva, with a U.S. No. 1 in "The Loco-Motion," while King herself was successful with "It Might As Well Rain Until September," initially meant for Bobby Vee.

Later "questioning" material like "Goin' Back" (Dusty Springfield, The Byrds) and The Monkees' "Pleasant Valley Sunday" indicated an ability to adapt their writing style for the changing times, but this was rendered irrelevant when their personal and professional relationship collapsed in 1968.

David Wells

Role Lyricist (Goffin), Composer (King)
Date 1961
Nationality USA
Why It's Key When married bliss led to a creative and commercial rapture.

Key Album *Judy At Carnegie Hall*
Judy Garland

On November 18, 1959, Judy Garland started a stint at Doctor's Hospital in New York. After being diagnosed with hepatitis and finishing a long treatment, Garland's doctors told her she'd better get used to taking it easy and not working another day in her life. Yet after six months off, the recently divorced Garland started the next stage in her career and her life. After playing Europe, she started a North American tour. The last stop was New York, April 23, 1961, at Carnegie Hall.

When the petite singer walked out on stage, the applause for the recently stricken signer and actress was so stupendous it "stalled the song fest for several moments," reported *Variety*. The performance that followed deserved all that reception and more. With genuine affection emitting from both the stage and the audience, chatty Garland had her fans glowing with adoration. Songs old ("The Trolley Song," "Over The Rainbow") and new ("How Long Has This Been Going On?") shone right to the back of the over-capacity theater and showed that Garland's voice could still pack a wallop, despite being told her career was over.

On July 10 that year, Capitol released the recording of the event as a double album. *Judy At Carnegie Hall* stayed at No. 1 for 13 weeks. The album won five Grammy Awards, including Best Female Vocal Performance and – first time for a woman – Album Of The Year.

Leila Regan-Porter

Release Date July 10, 1961

Nationality USA

Tracklisting When You're Smiling, Do It Again, You Go To My Head, Alone Together, Who Cares?, Puttin' On The Ritz, How Long Has This Been Going On, Just You Just Me, The Man That Got Away, San Francisco, That's Entertainment!, I Can't Give You Anything But Love, Come Rain Or Come Shine, You're Nearer, A Foggy Day, If Love Were All, Zing! Went The Strings Of My Heart, Stormy Weather, Rock-A-Bye Your Baby With A Dixie Melody, Over The Rainbow, Swanee, After You've Gone, Chicago (plus medleys)

Why It's Key Showed that Judy could still wow 'em.

Opposite Judy Garland

Key Song **"Quarter To Three"**
Gary "U.S." Bonds

Gary "U.S." Bonds (born Gary Anderson) had a string of – mostly local – U.S. hits between 1960 and 1964. All were compelling and accessible versions of what might best be called "party rock," in his case a very energetic brand of the New Orleans sound. Just one, "Quarter To Three," made it to No. 1.

The record was a unique convergence of ideas and production technique. The Church Street Five, the house band used by Bonds' producer Frank Guida, had done an instrumental called "A Nite With Daddy G," the latter a reference to tenor saxman Gene Barge. Bonds turned it into a vocal number and under Guida's production approach – combining vocal and instrumental parts with party ambience layer-on-layer to a mono tape, losing a generation with each addition but leaving Bonds' voice and Barge's sax at the top of the "mix" – created a perfect faux-live performance.

The single, released on Guida's Legrand label in the spring of 1961, made U.S. No. 1 on June 26 and was all over the radio that summer, and circulated for years after, well past the advent of the British invasion that had rather overtaken American musicians not long after its release. It stayed in the repertories of hundreds of frat-bands and, in the '70s, it got a new boost when Bruce Springsteen made it a regular part of his stage performances. Springsteen later produced two albums for his boyhood hero.

Bruce Eder

Release Date 1961

Nationality USA

Composers Frank J. Guida, Joseph F. Royster, Gene Barge, Gary L. Anderson

Why It's Key The ultimate party music artist creates his quintessential record by faking a party.

Key Person
Willie Nelson

Though his multifaceted career encompasses political activism, acting, and even pop standards (the hugely successful 1978 album *Stardust*), it's his seismic contribution to the country music landscape that ensures Willie Nelson's legendary status.

Born (in 1933) and raised in Texas, he released his first, self-financed single in 1956, but only hit his stride after his composition "Family Bible" was a 1960 hit for Claude Gray. Moving to Nashville, he penned a string of classics with which others hit big: "Night Life" (Ray Price), "Funny How Time Slips Away" (Billy Walker), "Pretty Paper" (Roy Orbison), "Hello Walls" (Faron Young). On November 6, 1961, Patsy Cline took what is now probably his most famous composition, the immortal "Crazy," into the *Billboard* Top 40. He duly relaunched his solo career, but, by 1970, a disillusioned Nelson had retired to run a pig farm.

Back in countercultural Texas, he regained his musical appetite. Rejecting the Nashville establishment's suffocating conservatism, he adopted a rebellious, long-haired hippie image while developing a brand of country that incorporated rock, folk, and western swing. By the mid-'70s he was at the forefront of country music's outlaw movement, scoring his first U.S. country No. 1 with "Blue Eyes Crying In The Rain," while *Wanted! The Outlaws* (1976) – an adroitly marketed set based around old recordings by Nelson and kindred spirit Waylon Jennings – became the first country album to sell a million. After two decades in the business, the iconoclastic, astonishingly durable Nelson was finally about to become a household name.
David Wells

Role Recording Artist

Date 1961

Nationality USA

Why It's Key The hippie country superstar.

Opposite **Willie Nelson**

Key Event **Mick Jagger and Keith Richards meet at Dartford railway station**

On the morning they bumped into each other at Dartford railway station in October 1961, Mick Jagger and Keith Richards were each on their way to their places of higher education, Jagger to the prestigious London School Of Economics, Richards to Sidcup Art College. Born at the same hospital in 1943, they had lived a street apart when younger but Richards' family had moved away when he was about eleven.

Like many British musicians of his generation, Richards was only going to art school as a holding action, using the state subsidized breathing space to improve his chops on guitar. He was surprised and delighted to see that under his arm, his childhood playmate was clutching albums by Chuck Berry, Little Walters, and Muddy Waters. As they fell into conversation, Jagger not only confirmed that he shared Richards' passion for R&B but revealed that he sang in an amateur R&B group called Little Boy Blue and the Blue Boys. Richards promptly joined.

When he did, Jagger's mother began to worry, for it was at this juncture that she noticed Jagger beginning to think of playing the music he loved not as a mere hobby but as something more vocational. She had no way of knowing, of course, that the pair would ultimately form the songwriting axis of one of the most celebrated and successful rock ensembles of all time, The Rolling Stones.
Sean Egan

Date October 1961

Country UK

Why It's Key A friendship is rekindled and the '60s' second greatest songwriting team is born.

Key Album *Showcase*
Patsy Cline

In 1961, country artist Patsy Cline's one national hit "Walkin' After Midnight" was an increasingly distant memory and her recording contract had expired. A new direction was required.

With her long-term producer, Owen Bradley, she rethought her style. The first fruit was a single, "I Fall To Pieces," released under a new contract with Decca, which reached the top of the country charts in August 1961. For its recording, Bradley hired The Jordanaires, the backing singers famed for their creamy work with Elvis Presley, slowed the tempo down and added the sort of strings more normally associated with pop orchestras than country hoedowns. "… Pieces" was followed in September 1961 by the album *Showcase*, recorded in the same manner, which included a new version of "Walkin'… " and "Crazy," the Willie Nelson-penned hit that became Cline's signature song.

Showcase was as vital a part of the history of what became known as the Nashville Sound as it was in establishing Cline's formidable reputation. Over the years, the smooth country style Bradley and Cline helped pioneer here would become synonymous with all that was wrong with country music and by the '80s was so roundly derided that the country establishment had to invent New Country as a means of revitalizing a genre mired in string-drenched schmaltz.

It should not be forgotten that Cline was not responsible for the misuse of her style and that *Showcase* is a truly fine album.

Angus Batey

Release Date
September 1961

Nationality USA

Tracklisting I Fall To Pieces, Foolin' Around, The Wayward Wind, South Of The Border, I Love You So Much It Hurts, Seven Lonely Days, Crazy, San Antonio Rose, True Love, Walkin' After Midnight, A Poor Man's Roses (Or A Rich Man's Gold), Have You Ever Been Lonely (Have You Ever Been Blue)

Why It's Key Pivotal in creating the Nashville Sound – but that shouldn't count against it.

Key Person
Dion

Although Dion DiMucci (born in 1939) came from a tough New York neighborhood, singing on street corners was commonplace when he was a kid and this was the way in which he developed his vocal technique. Signed to Laurie Records at the age of 18, he and vocal group The Belmonts made the U.S. Top 40 seven times in the period spanning 1958 to 1960, most notably with "I Wonder Why" and "A Teenager In Love."

DiMucci, though, grew tired of the clean sound of the Belmonts' records. "I started writing about what I knew," he later recalled. "People in my neighborhood, people that seemed bigger than life: Donna the Prima Donna, and Runaround Sue." The latter faithless character inspired a song of the same name written by DiMucci with Ernie Maresca. It was DiMucci's second hit under the new professional name of simply "Dion" and made a deserved U.S. No. 1 on October 23, 1961. Though only a No. 2, possibly even more significant was follow-up, Maresca's "The Wanderer," an ostensible piece of braggadocio undermined by the eyebrow raising line, "With my two fists of iron, I'm going nowhere."

Despite his success, DiMucci spent the mid-'60s in what he termed "hell on earth" due to the worsening of his long-term drug use. He subsequently replaced heroin with God and swapped his old image(s) for that of a folkie, making waves in 1968 with martyr's anthem "Abraham, Martin, And John," his last hit to date.

Sean Egan

Role Recording Artist

Date 1961

Nationality USA

Why It's Key Star who reinvented himself twice.

Opposite Dion

Key Song *Stranger On The Shore*
Acker Bilk

Received wisdom says Acker Bilk's serenely haunting clarinet instrumental "Stranger On The Shore" was written as the theme tune for a successful BBC TV show and that this regular exposure propelled it to UK No. 1.

When Bilk – a long-term luminary of British trad jazz – knocked it up in the back of a London taxi cab, it was called "Jenny," after one of his children. It was only when the BBC asked him if he had anything suitable for an upcoming series that he changed the title. Nor did television rocket it to the top of the charts. In fact, the short-lived series ran for just five episodes and was finished by mid-October, a good six weeks before Bilk's sublime melody entered the lower reaches of Britain's chart. No, it was good old-fashioned radio airplay and the audience's ability to know a good tune when they heard it that sent Mr. Acker Bilk With The Leon Young String Chorale, as they were billed, to No. 2 with the recording.

"Stranger On The Shore" did even better in America (where the television show was never broadcast), peaking at No. 1 in *Billboard* on May 26, 1962, sparking off a string of almost-forgotten covers. It was Bilk's greatest achievement. Despite his trademark bowler hat and loud waistcoats, Bilk had little of the charisma of the soon to emerge British beat groups yet he had just become the first Briton to top the U.S. chart.

Johnny Black

Release Date November 1961

Nationality UK

Composer Bernard "Acker" Bilk

Why It's Key The story attending the song was myth but its achievement very real.

Opposite **Acker Bilk**

Key Person
Joe Meek

When "Telstar" by the Tornadoes topped the *Billboard* chart on December 22, 1962, the then very rare Atlantic-spanning success of a British record emphasized the extraordinary abilities of the man who produced the record, Joe Meek, the UK's equivalent of Phil Spector.

Born in 1929, Meek graduated from being an RAF radio technician to an engineer at London's IBC studios, and then Lansdowne Studios. He honed his craft on records by the likes of Frankie Vaughan, Petula Clark, and Lonnie Donegan. The people he recorded when he set up his own studio, RGM Sound, in 1960 were less stellar but the exceptional sonic qualities he conferred on their records ensured hit parade triumphs. "Johnny Remember Me" was a record that – sung as it was by a soap star called John Leyton – was ostensibly pure novelty but its surreal and breathless ambience gave it the status of classic. "Telstar" was an instrumental that – courtesy of some pioneering in the manipulation of tape – sounded as futuristic as the inaugural communications satellite – launched in July 1962 – to which its title referred. Amazingly, such sonic experiments – and Meek's innovations in overdubbing, echo, and reverb – were produced from Meek's own flat, whose walls were lined with equipment and whose every room played host to performing musicians. Surreally, his downstairs landlord would complain about the noise.

Tormented by his homosexuality and by declining chart fortunes, Meek committed suicide in 1967 after murdering his landlady.

Sean Egan

Role Producer

Date 1962

Nationality UK

Why It's Key A genius at creating inspired and sometimes unparalleled recorded sounds.

Key Song
"The Stripper"

If you want to evoke the milieu of a circus, a square dance, or a church service, there are many musical selections that you might choose to employ. But if your goal is for people to think "striptease," there's only one real option: David Rose's "The Stripper."

The late Rose, born 1910, achieved significant success as a composer, arranger, and conductor; "Holiday For Strings," "Calypso Melody," and music for such TV series as *Bonanza* and *Little House On The Prairie* featuring on his resume. He also served as musical director for *The Red Skelton Show*. Yet "The Stripper," originally written in 1958 for a television program called *Burlesque*, only saw commercial release because MGM needed something to use as the flip of his single "Ebb Tide." On July 7, 1962, the B-side made U.S. No. 1.

With its scorching, jazzy melody and orchestration – the central brass part seeming almost to leer – this amazingly sleazy-sounding instrumental piece of music has become firmly associated with the art of the ecdysiast, overshadowing "Let Me Entertain You" (from *Gypsy*) and easily holding off late contender "You Can Leave Your Hat On," which is anyway a male stripper's song. "The Stripper" has been used in countless films, television shows, cartoons, and commercials, the first and only port of call for any editor needing sonic ambience for a voluptuous female character or simply an atmosphere of tawdry sex.

Michael Portantiere

U.S. No. 1 Date
July 7, 1962

Nationality USA

Composer David Rose

Why Its Key No other piece of music is so uniquely associated with a particular act.

Key Performance
James Brown plays The Apollo

James Brown was first voted America's Number 1 R&B star in 1962. Not one to rest on his laurels, when on October 24, 1962 he bounded onstage at Harlem's Apollo Theatre, he was clearly determined to prove he merited the accolade. He proceeded to showcase his mastery of crowd control, proving an audience is as important to a gig as a performer and that the performer does not need to be a matinee idol to wreck the joint. Working up his soulful screams before opting for a velvety growl, he continually took his audience to the edge and back again, women exploding with screams and hollered responses to his rhetorical calls for answers. An 11-minute rendition of "Lost Someone" gradually turned up the pressure before Brown's band, the Famous Flames, blared into his plaintive hit "Please Please Please" releasing the valve and engendering near riot.

It was the apex of Southern soul's gospel dramatics in a secular nightclub.

Luckily for those of us who were not present, the event was recorded for posterity. Few had made live albums before this, least of all in R&B where hardly anyone even bought studio albums. The technological limitations and a perceived lack of demand meant that Brown had to finance the recording himself.

The number two *Billboard* chart placing and pop chart tenure of 14 months of the resultant *James Brown Live At The Apollo* convinced the industry that live albums and R&B LPs had a place in the future.

Chris Goodman

Date October 24, 1962

Venue Apollo Theatre, New York, New York

Country USA

Why It's Key A show that summed up why James Brown was the biggest live attraction in soul.

Opposite James Brown fans

Key Person
Ray Charles

G iven that Ray Charles (1930–2004) grew up listening to an array of musical styles including gospel, blues, jazz, country, and big band, it's really no surprise that his career would be defined by a knack for stamping his own inimitable style on whatever genre he chose to tackle at that moment.

It didn't quite begin that way, however. Charles' earliest recordings found him consciously imitating the smoother pop stylings of his idol Nat "King" Cole. Charles' move to Atlantic in 1952 coincided with the development of what would turn out to be his signature style, what he once called "this spiritual and churchy, this religious or gospel sound." By infusing secular R&B with a gospel-fueled fervor Charles created a driving new sound: soul. But eclecticism marked his career. Charles made forays into mainstream jazz in the 1950s, culminating in 1961's critically lauded, Quincy Jones-arranged *Genius + Soul = Jazz*. For all his versatility Charles surprised nearly everybody by bringing a soulful charge to the country idiom on the landmark album *Modern Sounds In Country And Western Music* (1962), a commercial smash that featured his galvanizing take on such country chestnuts as "I Can't Stop Loving You" and "You Don't Know Me."

Though Charles' post-'60s output with its emphasis on a softer pop sound disappointed many, and his abandonment of his songwriting for cover jobs dismayed even more, he will be forever remembered as a true musical revolutionary.
Tierney Smith

Role Recording Artist

Date 1962

Nationality USA

Why It's Key The man who revolutionized R&B – among other things.

Key Person
Phil Spector

P hil Spector started as a songwriter but was destined to become the '60s – and arguably history's – top producer. The young Jewish prodigy had already scored as a member of The Teddy Bears, whose 1958 U.S. No. 1 "To Know Him Is To Love Him" he wrote and arranged but his first significant record as a producer was "He's Rebel" by girl-group The Crystals. It made U.S. No. 1 on November 3, 1962, heralding the arrival of the passionate, spectacular teen symphonies whose monumental presence the eccentric genius dubbed The Wall of Sound.

This sound – The Crystals' demented but somehow elegant 1963 hit "Da Doo Ron Ron" being its first perfect example – was one maniacally concocted at Hollywood's Goldstar Studios with scores of session musicians playing double-up guitars, strings, horns, and percussion in original, dramatic orchestrations that belied the almost simplistic lyrics they provided a bed for. On his own label Philles, Spector launched girl groups like the Ronettes ("Be My Baby," 1963) and blue-eyed soul duo The Righteous Brothers ("You've Lost That Lovin' Feelin'," 1964). These international smashes started a wave of much-copied recordings that had him reigning as star producer until 1966. That year, the failure of what he saw as his masterpiece, Ike and Tina Turner's "River Deep, Mountain High" emphasized the eccentric side of his genius, sending him into a reclusion he would only leave to help out the final Beatles recordings, a career hiccup he has never really recovered from.
Ignacio Julia

Role Producer

Date 1962

Nationality USA

Why It's Key Propelled rock 'n' roll to a new grandiosity.

Key People
Barry Mann and Cynthia Weil

Husband and wife duo Barry Mann and Cynthia Weil met while working for music publishers Aldon. They married in August 1961, just as Tony Orlando's recording of "Bless You" gave them their first joint songwriting hit.

A series of three-minute masterpieces ensued, including the magnificently neurotic "You've Lost That Lovin' Feelin'," co-written with Phil Spector and a UK/U.S. chart-topper for The Righteous Brothers. But while the duo had a knack for penning superlative love songs, Weil's lyrics often brought social comment and urban realism to the teen pop market, a notable example being "Uptown" (The Crystals) which entered the *Billboard* Top 40 on April 28, 1962 and examined the humiliations endured by an unskilled worker. Their gritty, streetwise approach also resulted in a garage band classic, the cautionary drugs tale "Kicks" (Paul Revere And The Raiders), and the equally hard-hitting "We've Gotta Get Out Of This Place" (The Animals). They also co-wrote The Drifters' "On Broadway" with Leiber and Stoller.

Unlike many of their '60s contemporaries, the Mann/Weil team would also prosper in subsequent decades: "Here You Come Again" (1977) took country superstar Dolly Parton into the pop mainstream, "Don't Know Much" (1989) reignited the careers of Aaron Neville and Linda Ronstadt, while the theme song for 1987's *An American Tail*, "Somewhere Out There," won two Grammy Awards. In 1997 the duo proved their durability and versatility yet again by penning the U.S. Top 10 single "I Will Come To You" with teen idols Hanson.

David Wells

Role Songwriters

Date 1962

Nationality USA

Why It's Key The Brill Building pop gets a socio-political conscience.

Key Event
The opening of the Ealing Club

It was so wet that [they] had to put a horrible sheet over the bandstand so that the condensation didn't drip directly onto you," Mick Jagger once recalled of the the Ealing Club, West London which opened its doors to fellow blues and R&B enthusiasts on March 17, 1962. Hardly a ringing endorsement but the club's effect on the early '60s UK R&B boom, and by extension, '60s rock, is incalculable.

The founder of the club was guitarist-singer Alexis Korner who, along with singer-harmonica player Cyril Davies, headed Blues Incorporated. Just a month after the club's opening date, Alexis Korner introduced Mick Jagger and Brian Jones, an event that led to the formation of The Rolling Stones. That alone would make the venue important but a list of the people who got their first significant exposure and/or chance to hone their craft at Ealing is a Who's Who of '60s rock superstardom: Ginger Baker, Jack Bruce (both Cream), Eric Burdon (The Animals), Paul Jones (Manfred Mann), and Rod Stewart among them. The Stones played the club on a regular basis, making their final appearance there in March 1963. Lesser names who were nonetheless highly influential on that important British blues scene who were Ealing club regulars included Graham Bond and Long John Baldry.

Today, the venue is a club called The Red Room.

Fred Dellar

Date March 17, 1962

Country UK

Why It's Key The venue that served as boot camp for '60s rock stars.

Key Song **"Wipe Out"**
The Surfaris

There was nothing that could unite a lunchroom full of radio-fueled grade school students in the '60s – not to mention enrage their minders – than a barrage of pre-teen fists pounding out the tribal beat of The Surfaris' "Wipe Out" in unison atop the nearest handy surface. While rock 'n' roll had always inflamed the old and conservative types for its rebellion-inspiring properties, few could have predicted this: an instrumental deemed subversive.

This moronically brilliant gem, which along with "Louie Louie" by The Kingsmen would become one of the keystones of American garage rock, was actually written and recorded by the young Surfaris in a mere ten minutes flat, simply to provide a throwaway B-side for their showcase "Surfer Joe." Yet amazingly, it was "Wipe Out," not "Surfer Joe," that entered the *Billboard* Top 40 on July 6, 1963, peaking just behind Little Stevie Wonder's "Fingertips" at chart top five weeks later.

A percussive tribute to Surfari drummer Ron Wilson's high school marching band, decorated with a melodramtic picked guitar riff and prefaced with a menacing cackle, this pervasive record's primitive strum und thump reappeared in the Beatle and Motown-dominated Top Twenty of 1966, gave the Fat Boys and Beach Boys an unlikely duet hit in 1987, and has been hailed by no less than Daniel Lanois as the reason he became a record producer. But perhaps most telling of all, the song which decades earlier could so galvanize rebellious young schoolyard snackers became the only instrumental recording to make Clear Channel Communication's post-9/11 red list of "Songs with Questionable Lyrics."

Gary Pig Gold

Release Date
December 1962

Nationality USA

Composer Bob Berryhill, Patrick Connolly, Jim Fuller, Ron Wilson

Why It's Key No lyric, but deemed a threat nonetheless.

Key Song **"Green Onions"**
Booker T And The M.G.s

"Green Onions" is perhaps the most famous instrumental hit of all time. Booker T And The M.G.s were the house band at Memphis' Stax records, the grittier Southern Soul counterpart to Detroit's smoother Motown. The track was the B-side to another instrumental, "Behave Yourself," recorded one Sunday when rockabilly singer Billy Lee Riley failed to show for a session. Radio DJs unanimously favored the flip, an irresistible blues boogie based around Booker T. Jones' hip organ motif and Steve Cropper's stabbing guitar.

It made the *Billboard* Top 40 on September 1, 1962, peaking at No. 3. It would also become a belated UK Top 10 in 1979 when it was featured on the soundtrack to the movie *Quadrophenia*.

The very make-up of the M.G.s (Memphis Group) was quite a statement in a still segregated South. Jones, bassist Lewis Steinberg, and drummer Al Jackson were black while Cropper was white. Later,

when Donald "Duck" Dunn replaced Steinberg, the 50-50 color split provided an even stronger symbol.

The label and Cropper had already achieved an instrumental pop hit with 1961's "Last Night" by the Mar-Keys, but the company was called Satellite then. "Green Onions" was the first hit on the renamed Stax, setting it on the on the way to recording Otis Redding, Sam and Dave, and other soul greats, a lot of whom were backed by this very group.

Chris Goodman

Release Date August 1962

Nationality USA

Composers Steve Cropper, Al Jackson Jr., Booker T. Jones, Lewis Steinberg

Why It's Key Demonstrated the racial cooperation possible via music as well as proving the viability of songs without lyrics to rock and soul audiences.

Key Album *Let's Face The Music*
Shirley Bassey

Already established as a star by virtue of strident, big-voiced romps through the likes of "Kiss Me, Honey Honey, Kiss Me" and "As Long As He Needs Me," in 1962 Shirley Bassey embarked upon a ten-day British tour in the company of leading American arranger/conductor Nelson Riddle. Famous for his work with Judy Garland, Nat King Cole and, in particular, Frank Sinatra, Riddle was available to work with Bassey as a result of Sinatra's label move to Reprise, which meant that the singer and arranger (who was under contract to Sinatra's former label, Capitol) were unable to continue their partnership.

Bassey and Riddle hit it off so well that they quickly hatched plans for a studio collaboration: days after the tour ended, they started recording the album *Let's Face The Music*. Despite the speed at which they worked (the arrangement for "What Now My Love?" was written by Riddle on the morning of the recording, with parts of the orchestral score arriving midway through the session), the American's sympathetic, understated arrangements brought out the best in the singer, who discovered a new vocal subtlety for masterful interpretations of such standards as "Let's Fall In Love," "I Get A Kick Out Of You," and the title song. Preceded by the release of Top 5 single "What Now My Love?," *Let's Face The Music* was a major success when issued in December 1962, and remains an enduring peak of Bassey's lengthy career.

David Wells

Release Date
December 1962

Nationality UK

Tracklisting Let's Face The Music And Dance, I Should Care, Let's Fall In Love, Second Time Around, Imagination, All The Things You Are, I Get A Kick Out Of You, Everything I Have Is Yours, Spring Is Here, All Of Me, I Can't Get You Out Of My Mind, What Now My Love?

Why It's Key Sinatra arranger coaxes the performance of a lifetime out of the Welsh diva.

Key Album *Howlin' Wolf*
Howlin' Wolf

Although it was actually a collection of 1957–'61 singles, the *Howlin' Wolf* LP – informally nicknamed "the rocking chair album" in honor of its cover illustration – is considered by many the defintive Chicago electric blues album. Much of its brutal power was due to the Wolf's (real name Chester Burnett) commanding earthquake tremor of a voice. Give just as much credit, however, to the incendiary guitar playing, which put a newly threatening, even scary cast on the classic '50s Chicago electric blues format. It might have been marketed by record company Chess as blues, but the axwork in particular had an adventurous, reckless quality. Perhaps unconsciously, it was crossing blues with rock when the term blues-rock had yet to be invented.

While none of these songs were hits (even in the R&B charts), the LP had an influence that none of its creators could have foreseen. Across the Atlantic, young British groups breeding electric blues with amped-up guitar pyrotechnics were captivated by the record. Two of the numbers were made into standards via astronomically successful covers, the first being "The Red Rooster," taken by The Rolling Stones to the top of the British charts in 1964 (under the title "Little Red Rooster") with spine-chilling slide guitar by Brian Jones. Cream likewise brought "Spoonful" to international audiences, Eric Clapton heaping special praise on Wolf's guitarist Hubert Sumlin in *Guitar Player*: "He did some things that freaked me out when I was picking up the guitar… He is truly amazing."

Richie Unterberger

Release Date 1962

Nationality USA

Tracklisting Shake For Me, The Red Rooster, You'll Be Mine, Who's Been Talkin', Wang Dang Doodle, Little Baby, Spoonful, Going Down Slow, Down In The Bottom, Back Door Man, Howlin' For My Baby, Tell Me

Why It's Key The Chicago Blues album whose contents had unexpected resonance across the Atlantic.

Key Performance *Ready Steady Go!*
television show

"The weekend starts here" was the slogan of *Ready Steady Go!*, the British pop television show whose first Friday night broadcast was on August 9, 1963. And for millions, this was no hype.

Originally only broadcast in the London region, it was networked by 1964. What gave the program real impetus was the way the informality of the audience reflected modern young people: instead of being seated, they danced. The squareness the producers were setting their face against was perhaps illustrated by the viewer who complained of the dancers "one of them was even wearing a hat!" Also chiming with the intended audience was "gear bird" teenage presenter Cathy McGowan, who was recruited following magazine ads. (More conventional fellow presenter Keith Fordyce was a steady hand on the tiller.) From the opening title music – Manfred Mann's countdown-like "5-4-3-2-1" – the show oozed vitality.

It last aired on December 23, 1966, victim of more progressive fashions but during its heyday was ultra hip, certainly more so than rivals like *Top Of The Pops*. The show broke talent (e.g. Donovan, Jimi Hendrix), played songs full-length, and even spurned lip-synching completely by 1965.

The show epitomized Swinging Britain and became the one in which every worthwhile act had to take part – The Beatles, Stones, Dusty Springfield, James Brown to name but a few. But, as The Tremeloes' Brian Poole said, "The main thing about *Ready Steady Go!* was always the audience. And we simply took part in it."
Fred Dellar

Date August 9, 1963

Country UK

Why It's Key The most important UK television pop show of the '60s.

Key Song **"She Loves You"**
The Beatles

By summer 1963, The Beatles had racked up three successful, self-written singles, a unique image (those moptops were shockingly long for the time), modest innovation (the descending bridge of "From Me To You"), and a fine debut album. However, there was nothing thus far that suggested a potential for musical and social phenomenon rather than merely adept pop group. "She Loves You," was the record that changed that.

Their fourth UK single, it was a delightful concoction that almost seemed tailor-made to sum up The Beatles' singular appeal, from John Lennon and Paul McCartney's unison vocals to the way that the relentless sizzle of drummer Ringo Starr's hi-hat gave opportunity for camera close-ups of his see-sawing, grinning head to the joyous "Whooh!" with which McCartney and lead guitarist George Harrison jointly climaxed each verse. However it was far more than that, possessing a gleefulness of spirit, an informality

of tone (McCartney's father was somewhat put out that the famous refrain was "Yeah, yeah, yeah!" rather than "Yes, yes, yes"), and the breakneck pace befitting a generation impatient to create a brave new world. The innovation of making the narrative a second-person one – the lyric petitioning a friend to apologize to the lover he has wronged – itself epitomized the barrier-smashing gestalt.

In discussion of records that summed up the '60s, this one is rarely mentioned but just about everything about it encapsulates the young, fresh, optimistic, and insurgent zeitgeist of that tumultuous decade.
Sean Egan

Release Date August 1963

Nationality UK

Composers John Lennon, Paul McCartney

Why It's Key The record that *really* sums up the '60s.

Opposite **George Harrison, Paul McCartney, and John Lennon**

Key Event **Influential folk acts attend Luther King's "I Have a Dream" speech**

The March on Washington on August 28, 1963, was an extraordinary peak of the early-'60s American Civil Rights Movement, with a quarter of a million people demonstrating in the nation's capital against segregation and for racial equality. The soundbite most likely to be quoted from the day's events is Martin Luther King's "I Have a Dream" speech, not just the most celebrated oratory in the history of the Civil Rights Movement, but one of the most famous declarations of the twentieth century. The day also marked, if only in hindsight, the apogee of the folk revival's involvement in the movement, which had been intensifying ever since the election of President John F. Kennedy at the beginning of the decade. The three most popular and influential folk acts of the time performed at the march, including its most beloved solo performer (Joan Baez), its most commercially successful group (Peter, Paul, And Mary), and its most admired socially conscious protest singer-songwriter (Bob Dylan).

But as the times they were a-changing, so they would change again. Though Baez and Peter, Paul, and Mary, would continue to champion social causes, they gradually faded in popularity; African-American demands for civil rights would grow more militant, and less inclined to accommodate sympathetic whites in their organizational efforts; and Dylan would abandon protest songs, go electric, and see his popularity soar. But a precedent had been set for popular musicians to endorse liberal and progressive agendas, echoing down the decades in events such as Live Aid and innumerable benefit concerts.
Richie Unterberger

Date August 28, 1963

Country USA

Why It's Key The apex of the intertwining of folk music and political activism.

Opposite **Bob Dylan and Joan Baez**

Key Album *The Barbra Streisand Album*
Barbra Streisand

Considering the hard work that the title artist put in to get signed to Columbia Records – the first fruit of which was *The Barbra Streisand Album* – it's amazing that she would seem to have inaugurated that career as a recording artist, only to use it as a stepping stone to her other careers as actress and director.

Previously, despite the attention she was garnering on the legitimate stage and in nightclubs, Columbia President Goddard Lieberson felt that she was "too special" to sell records. Finally, though, he gave in. It was a wise decision. Peter Matz arranged and conducted the music, which included some of the standout numbers from Streisand's nightclub act, such as her slowed-down version of the Depression anthem "Happy Days Are Here Again," her powerful appropriation of Julie London's signature song "Cry Me A River," and her seductive reading of "A Sleepin' Bee" from the musical *House Of Flowers*. Streisand's voice was beautiful, clear, strong, and versatile throughout.

The LP hit the U.S. Top 10, stayed in the charts nearly two years, went gold, and won the Grammy Award for Album of the Year. When it was released Streisand was not yet 21 years old but judging by her subsequent career she already had her sights set on different disciplines, none of which – arguably – she excelled in as much as that of recording artist.
William Ruhlmann

Release Date February 25, 1963

Nationality USA

Tracklisting Cry Me A River, My Honey's Lovin' Arms, I'll Tell The Man In The Street, A Taste Of Honey, Who's Afraid Of The Big Bad Wolf?, Soon It's Gonna Rain, Happy Days Are Here Again, Keepin' Out Of Mischief Now, Much More, Come To The Supermarket In Old Peking, A Sleepin' Bee

Why It's Key Proved an artist didn't necessarily know what she was good at.

Key Event
Death of Patsy Cline

The deaths of Brian Jones, Jimi Hendrix, Jim Morrison, and Tupac Shakur were so clouded by rumors and conspiracy theories that the notion a pop star could simply die in a tragic accident eventually came to seem almost bizarre. Yet when country legend Patsy Cline was killed in a plane crash on March 5, 1963, these sorts of belief were still comparatively rare.

Following a near-fatal motor accident in 1961, Cline told friends that she feared an early death. That was more than enough for some to conclude that her demise was a little eerie, something underlined by the fact that country star Jack Anglin died in a car crash on the way to Cline's funeral. Such views in later years gained even greater currency. In the '90s, the song "Blue," one Cline was reportedly due to sing in what would have been her next session had she lived, was recorded by a teenage LeAnn Rimes. Rimes' voice bore a striking similarity to Cline's, and a story that the song was somehow so "cursed," that others had shied away from recording "Cline's lost song," was widely reported. Yet at least three other singers had recorded it before Rimes, and evidence Cline planned to record it is scant.

The great pity of these myths is that they obscure the fact that a great talent was cut down in her prime, aged just 30, with the best music of her career possibly yet to come.

Angus Batey

Date March 5, 1963

Country USA

Why It's Key Among the first popular music deaths to generate a myth culture.

Key People
The 4 Seasons

There had been Little Richard "Woo!"s, the keening high singing in Gene Chandler's "Duke Of Earl," and the surf harmonies of The Beach Boys. No one, however, sang as high or melodramatically as The Four Seasons' Frankie Valli. For many listeners, his falsetto crossed the line from high to shrill and to such detractors the fact that he sang "Walk Like A Man" like, in fact, a girl provoked guffaws. However, many listeners bore the falsetto with pleasure: in reaching U.S. No. 1 on March 2, 1963, "Walk Like A Man" became the group's third chart topper, following 1962's "Sherry" and "Big Girls Don't Cry."

Though sometimes dismissed as a gimmick, Valli's falsetto was but one feature of The 4 Seasons, whose songs – usually cowritten by the group's Bob Gaudio and producer Bob Crewe – also employed sympathetic backup harmonies, damned catchy (if somewhat innocuously) upbeat tunes, and imaginative and rich musical arrangements. Not even the British Invasion could throw a wrench in the Seasons' phenomenal success, for a couple of years at any rate, with smashes like "Rag Doll," "Dawn," and "Let's Hang On" hovering at or near the No. 1 position in 1964 and '65.

However, though they tried to keep up with the subsequent musical evolutionary steps led by The Beatles, it seemed the Seasons' audience wanted them to remain a simple chart act: *Genuine Imitation Life Gazette*, their brave concept album, was not a success.

Richie Unterberger

Role Recording Artists

Date 1963

Nationality USA

Why It's Key Showcased the most stratospherically high, operatic falsetto yet heard in pop.

Key Song "Can't Get Used To Losing You"
Andy Williams

Andy Williams' first U.S. No. 1 was an uptempo Presley-style rocker, "Butterfly," in 1956, during the heyday of rock 'n' roll. Having established a chart presence somewhat by subterfuge, however, Williams soon reverted to more mainstream fare better suited to his smooth vocals and considerable interpretative powers. Typical of this material was "Can't Get Used To Losing You," which entered the *Billboard* Top 40 on March 23, 1963, eventually climbing to No. 2 – a rare singles success for this album-oriented artist.

Written by legendary songwriting partnership Doc Pomus and Mort Shuman, this easy-listening classic is a charming paean to lost love, characterized by lyrics both wistful and wry (Williams asserts he'll find somebody to love, before appending, "Who am I kiddin'? Only me… "). Williams double-tracked the vocal (he was one of the first artists to employ the technique), harmonizing with his own melody line on the chorus. Pizzicato on the offbeat of the verse emphasizes the song's distinctive stop-start hook, while the chorus sees a seamless blend of female backing vocals and smooth strings.

Williams initially thought the song "dumb" and was reluctant to perform it on his popular television show, but its yearning charm has exerted a lasting appeal down the decades, attracting cover versions by Percy Faith and Bobby Darin among others. More surprisingly, UK group The (English) Beat picked up on the underlying ska element in the track's trademark syncopated riff to score their biggest hit, a UK No. 3, in 1983.
Robert Dimery

Release Date
March 1963

Nationality USA

Composers Doc Pomus, Mort Shuman

Why It's Key One of the definitive classics of lounge music.

Key People
Ellie Greenwich and Jeff Barry

Jeff Barry recorded in his own right before success as a composer – Ricky Valance topped the UK charts with his "Tell Laura I Love Her" – led to a change of emphasis in his career. In October 1962 he married Ellie Greenwich, a fellow singer and writer with whom he had previously collaborated, and they resolved to concentrate exclusively on their writing partnership.

Although they teamed up as The Raindrops and also issued solo singles, it was their backroom work for others which established them as one of the leading lights of New York's legendary Brill Building scene: the term that referred to the proliferation of freelance, chart-making songwriters working at publishers' offices based in and around that New York structure in the early '60s. With collaborator Phil Spector, they defined the girl group sound courtesy of such magnificent creations as "Da Doo Ron Ron" (which, on May 11, 1963, became the first Greenwich-Barry *Billboard* Top 40 entry), "Then He Kissed Me," "Be My Baby," and "Baby I Love You." Also employed by Leiber-Stoller as writers/producers for the Red Bird label, this liaison produced a further batch of classics, including the sweet "Chapel Of Love" (The Dixie Cups) and the melodramatic and then-scandalous "Leader Of The Pack" (The Shangri-Las).

Divorcing in late 1965, they briefly continued to write together, with classics "River Deep, Mountain High" and "I Can Hear Music" both coming from this traumatic period. However, the strain quickly proved too great, and the Greenwich-Barry writing partnership was dissolved.
David Wells

Role Songwriters

Date 1963

Nationality USA

Why It's Key The team who characterized Brill Building pop and epitomized the girl group.

Key Song "Louie, Louie"
The Kingsmen

At first glance, "Louie, Louie" is nothing more than a garage band anthem and quintessential party song of the '60s. Yet the FCC and the FBI viewed it as something more sinister.

It started out as a B-side to a record made by Richard Berry and the Pharoahs in 1957. Its easy chords and primitive rhythm made it a perfect song for start-up groups to learn and it was recorded by over 300 different artists, many in the American Northwest, which in the '60s was a bastion of garage bands (amateur groups who formed in the wake of The Beatles) and independent labels. The ferociously exciting version cut by The Kingsmen of Portland, Oregon that entered the *Billboard* Top 40 on November 30, 1963 was the best, despite an inferior recording that made the vocals of Jack Ely even more unintelligible. (His unfamiliarity with the words and the Jamaican patois they were bizarrely written to be sing in were the first hurdle for the listener.)

The youthful audience, as is their wont, imagined decadent messages in the lilting tale of a man telling the titular bartender how much he is looking forward to visiting his woman. It's not known how many hours the Feds consequently spent spinning their copy of the disc before concluding that it was impossible to discern any obscenities but it took them 31 months to do so.

Andre Millard

Release Date
1963

Nationality USA

Composer Richard Berry

Why It's Key The song that launched a thousand garage bands – and an investigation by the authorities.

Key Album *The Freewheelin' Bob Dylan*
Bob Dylan

Having commenced sessions for his proposed second album (which bore the working title *Bob Dylan's Blues*) in April 1962, Dylan considered it to have been completed when he journeyed to England in December. However, the artist's exposure to the British folk club scene inspired him to pen "Girl From The North Country" and "Bob Dylan's Dream," which were based around guitarist/singer Martin Carthy's arrangements of traditional English songs "Scarborough Fair" and "Lady Franklin's Lament" respectively.

Returning home, Dylan decided that he had outgrown some of the songs that he had cut for the album, and revamped it to incorporate newer material. Recording sessions were eventually concluded in April 1963 and *The Freewheelin' Bob Dylan* (as it was now entitled) was duly issued the following month. It represented an astonishing artistic advance from Dylan's little-noticed, self-titled debut, which had featured only a couple of original songs but more

importantly it showed a spiritual progression. In place of songs as old as the hills were compositions which addressed the concerns of the increasingly disaffected age. Built around such epic, cornerstone creations as the raging "Masters Of War," the apocalyptic "A Hard Rain's A-Gonna Fall," and "Blowin' In The Wind" – a pop hit a month or two later for Peter, Paul, And Mary, and the song that, more than any other, made its writer a household name – *The Freewheelin' Bob Dylan* unveiled a major new voice in what became known as protest music. Dylan was about to be cast as spokesman for a generation.

David Wells

Release Date May 1963

Nationality USA

Tracklisting Blowin' In The Wind, Girl From The North Country, Masters Of War, Down The Highway, Bob Dylan's Blues, A Hard Rain's A-Gonna Fall, Don't Think Twice It's Alright, Bob Dylan's Dream, Oxford Town, Talkin' World War III Blues, Corrina Corrina, Honey Just Allow Me One More Chance, I Shall Be Free

Why It's Key The album that addressed the issues of that concerned the young.

Opposite Bob Dylan

Key Album *Night Beat*
Sam Cooke

By 1963, Sam Cooke had established a career as a hitmaker, taking his singular mix of gospel, R&B, and pop to the charts' upper echelons with the likes of "You Send Me," "Cupid," and "Twistin' The Night Away." However, there was greater depth to this singer-songwriter than the simple formulas ordained by the Hit Parade and in September 1963, a little more than a year before his unexpected violent death, he proved it with the album *Night Beat*.

Though not quite the early concept album it's sometimes described as, *Night Beat* boasts songs that uniformly fit a late-night mood, apart from the closing jump blues cover of "Shake, Rattle, And Roll." It's also one of the few early soul albums crafted as a stand-alone LP rather than a slapdash affair built around a hit single or two with miscellaneous other tracks appended. Though it was cut over the course of just three nights in February 1963, *Night Beat* felt solid and considered.

Cooke also seemed to take the opportunity to sink his teeth into rather bluesier material and more keyboard-based arrangements than usual. He also revisited his gospel roots with "Mean Old World" and "You Gotta Move." For all that, however, the best track was the one that turned out to be a hit single: his strutting adaptation of Howlin' Wolf's "Little Red Rooster," pushed along by a juicy midtempo groove and some inspired devilish organ by a teenage Billy Preston.
Richie Unterberger

Release Date
September 1963

Nationality USA

Tracklisting Nobody Knows The Trouble I've Seen, Lost And Lookin', Mean Old World, Please Don't Drive Me Away, I Lost Everything, Get Yourself Another Fool, Little Red Rooster, Laughin' And Clownin', Trouble Blues, You Gotta Move, Fool's Paradise, Shake, Rattle, And Roll

Why It's Key One of the first quality soul albums.

Key Album *Little Deuce Coupe*
The Beach Boys

Undertaking a workload that would constitute many a band's entire career, The Beach Boys' 21-year-old bassist and songwriter Brian Wilson composed or cocomposed, arranged, performed on, and produced a whopping three full-length albums during 1963 alone, while still finding time to partake in seven concert tours as well as writing (and ghost-singing on) a No. 1 record for his pals Jan and Dean.

Thankfully, the young miracle man was afforded a sliver of breathing room when Capitol Records demanded only eight new masters to fill out their first of many Christmastime Beach Boys LPs. *Little Deuce Coupe*, reprised four previously available tracks alongside a clutch of freshly written numbers. The latter were all concerned with affairs of the drag strip and drive-up root beer stand in a canny attempt to hook those landlocked listeners without access to surfboards, surfer girls, or either U.S. coastline and who therefore couldn't relate to the previous Beach Boys hits.

Tear- and grease-stained odes to broken-down jalopies and car-crazed cuties abound, and an a cappella tribute to teenage America's greatest fallen hot-rodder James Dean brings *Little Deuce Coupe* to a melancholy head. The album went top five. This four-wheeled formula was soon refined to even greater success on "I Get Around" and the T-Bird powered "Fun Fun Fun," but even then Wilson, ever restless, already had his sights on more profound artistic territory.
Gary Pig Gold

Release Date
October 21, 1963

Nationality USA

Tracklisting Little Deuce Coupe, Ballad Of Ole' Betsy, Be True To Your School, Car Crazy Cutie, Cherry Cherry Coupe, 409, Shut Down, Spirit Of America, Our Car Club, No-Go Showboat, A Young Man Is Gone, Custom Machine

Why It's Key The Beach Boys cannily side-step ghettoization as a surfer's band, paving the way for a long career.

Opposite The Beach Boys

Key Performance *Half A Sixpence* stage musical

In the '50s Larry Parnes was Britain's leading rock 'n' roll impresario, overseeing the careers of, among other UK rockers, Tommy Steele, Marty Wilde, Vince Eager, and Billy Fury. However, Parnes was not convinced rock would last and his ambition was to transform his best performers into all-round entertainers.

In 1962, the composer David Heneker, who had written the West End musical, *Expresso Bongo* (1958), told Parnes that he was adapting H. G. Wells' 1905 novel *Kipps, The Story Of A Simple Soul* into a musical and wanted Steele to star. Steele, who was Britain's first rock 'n' roll star by dint of the fairly execrable "Rock With The Caveman" (1956), had already begun to accept Parnes' mainstream remoulding via the 1959 movie *Tommy The Toreador*. He knew that *Half A Sixpence* – the tale of an irrepressible working class lad who makes a fortune but realises true wealth is back home – was for him. It opened to excellent notices at the Cambridge Theatre on March 21, 1963, Steele's

romantic costar Marti Webb. The score included the engaging title song, "If The Rain's Got To Fall" and the show-stopping photography anthem "Flash, Bang, Wallop." The musical – with Steele – transferred to Broadway and then celluloid.

Steele did indeed become the wholesome family entertainer his pearly white teeth had always suggested was his destiny. The demise of rock that Parnes had feared, though, has still not quite come about.

Spencer Leigh

Opening Night
March 21, 1963

Country UK

Directors Bob Weston, Bert Lee

Cast Tommy Steele, Marti Webb, Anna Barry

Composer David Heneker

Why It's Key The vehicle by which Britain's first rocker bailed out of a supposedly sinking ship.

Key Event **Gerry And The Pacemakers' achieve a historic treble**

In the beginning, quartet Gerry and the Pacemakers, led by the irrepressibly chirpy Gerry Marsden, outdid The Beatles at every turn. Although they were signed up by manager Brian Epstein after he'd signed The Beatles, they scored a UK No. 1 with "How Do You Do It" before The Beatles reached the top with "From Me To You." Their second single, "I Like It," put them into the record books as the first act in pop history to score British chart-toppers with their first two releases. "You'll Never Walk Alone," a Rodgers and Hammerstein tear-jerker from the 1945 musical *Carousel*, seemed an unlikely choice for their third release but when it too reached the summit on November 2, 1963, the Pacemakers' position at the top of the Scouse tree seemed unassailable.

"What began as a healthy artistic rivalry before 1963," revealed The Beatles' publicist Tony Barrow some years later, "became more bitter as time went by. The Beatles were as jealous of Gerry as he was of

them." Unfortunately, The Pacemakers lacked The Beatles' charisma and didn't have a prolific on-board writing team like Lennon and McCartney. While the Pacemakers' momentum shortly flagged, The Beatles just kept getting better.

Even so, The Pacemakers' record-busting achievement of three No. 1s with their first three singles would not be matched until another Liverpool group Frankie Goes To Hollywood equalled it in 1984 with "Relax," "Two Tribes," and "The Power Of Love."

Johnny Black

Date November 2, 1963

Country UK

Why It's Key Fellow Liverpudlians have The Beatles genuinely worried by making chart history twice in the space of months.

Key Event **The Beatles occupy the top five spots on the *Billboard* Hot 100**

For the first quarter of 1964, The Beatles had dominated American press coverage of rock 'n' roll – but much of that coverage was just reporters exploiting a story about frenzied teens. On April 4, 1964, however, the group's impact on American popular culture was eternally quantified. The top five of Billboard's Hot 100 that week read thus: No. 5: "Please Please Me"; No. 4: "I Want To Hold Your Hand"; No. 3: "She Loves You"; No. 2: "Twist And Shout"; No. 1: "Can't Buy Me Love." All were by The Beatles, who also had seven other Top 100 singles, plus the top two LP spots. Even Bing Crosby, Frank Sinatra, and Elvis Presley had never come close to this kind of achievement.

The irony of this was that it wasn't planned – indeed, had The Beatles' U.S. parent label, Capitol Records, had its way, only "I Want To Hold Your Hand" and "Can't Buy Me Love" would have been there. But Capitol had been so uninterested in the English band in 1963 that it had sub-licensed the other three singles to the Swan and Vee Jay labels, which were now flooding the marketplace – and fulfilling a demand that Capitol hadn't foreseen.

In the liner note to the UK Beatles album *Beatles For Sale*, released that December, Derek Taylor described The Beatles as "the biggest attraction the world has ever known." The above statistics – which will surely never be replicated – prove him right.
Bruce Eder

Date April 4, 1964

Country USA

Why It's Key Sales figures and a cultural domination never seen before or since.

Key People
The Supremes

Three years after signing to the Motown Label in 1961, black vocal group The Supremes had only had one minor U.S. chart hit. It wasn't until labelmates The Marvelettes rejected the song "Where Did Our Love Go?" as "childish" that the trio enjoyed the first of a string of smashes. Their version made U.S. No. 1 on August 22, 1964, the first of ten chart-toppers in four years.

The Supremes – Florence Ballard, Mary Wilson, and Diane (later Diana) Ross – celebrated a succession of musical milestones. With that same year's "Baby Love" they became the first all-female group to have a chart topper in Britain and, back home, became the first group in *Billboard* history to enjoy three No. 1 hits from an album.

With their elegant gowns and meticulous choreography, The Supremes epitomized glamour. Lead singer Ross' breathless, crystalline vocals proved to be the perfect vehicle for songs written and produced by Motown's principal production team, Holland-Dozier-Holland; classic hits such as "Come See About Me," "Stop! In The Name of Love," and "You Can't Hurry Love" blended pop with soul and doo-wop, sustaining the group's chart success throughout the '60s. Eventually, the group's famously demanding, ambitious lead singer established herself as the undisputed frontwoman: the band were officially renamed "Diana Ross And The Supremes" in early 1967, the same year that Ballard was replaced with Cindy Birdsong, over which there has subsequently been much controversy. Ross left to go solo in 1970.
Melissa Blease

Role Recording Artists

Date 1964

Nationality USA

Why It's Key The most successful and iconic girl group ever.

Key Performance **The Beatles on *The Ed Sullivan Show***

As Beatlemania swept Britain in November 1963, Beatles manager Brian Epstein made a deal with CBS-TV in America for the band to make three February 1964 appearances on the prime-time entertainment showcase, *The Ed Sullivan Show*.

By February 1, The Beatles were at U.S. No. 1 with "I Want To Hold Your Hand" but only a short British performance clip had aired on U.S. television, so, to see the band properly for the first time, you had to tune into Sullivan on February 9, 1964. The show's 73,700,000 Nielsen ratings made it by far the largest television audience to date and meant that one in three of the 191,000,000 population had watched.

In 13-and-a-half minutes the United States heard five songs. Meanwhile, what they saw (by McCartney's later admission, then more important) was amazingly shaggy hair for the time set off surprisingly by smart suits, a snazzy band logo with a dropped "T," a symmetrical front line (left-handed Paul's bass pointing out on one end, right-handed Lennon's guitar the other) over which sat a grinning Ringo on his riser, and a sweet collective bow. The whole thing was deliciously exotic, exuberant, and fresh.

In the wake of President Kennedy's assassination the previous November, grief had been succeeded by a nationwide desire to be cheered up. This broadcast proved to young and old alike that The Beatles were exactly the youthful, unusual but exuberantly pro-American tonic the country needed.

Mat Snow

Date February 9, 1964

Country USA

Why It's Key The TV broadcast that turned The Beatles from mere pop story to pan-generational phenomenon.

Opposite The Beatles on *The Ed Sullivan Show*.

Key Performance ***Top Of The Pops* television show first transmitted**

Producer Tony Visconti once bitterly complained about the unique power of BBC TV's weekly *Top Of The Pops* to destroy a promising new act in the UK by not granting it airwave time.

To be fair to the producers of the program, first transmitted on January 1, 1964 from a converted church in Manchester, *Top Of The Pops* merely did precisely what it said on the label: it provided a chart rundown and broadcast performances of the records going up in said chart, or at least of those whose artists were prepared to appear on the program. (Promotional films/videos were only allowed if the artist was genuinely indisposed.) And while the show was criticized by purists for allowing lip-synching, most acts did not actually want their meticulous studio craft ruined by imperfect live performance, while the kids couldn't care less. The program's heyday was the early 1970s when a massive teenage demographic, sexy dancers Pan's People, and a desire by glam rock acts to be more outrageous by the week made it a family viewing staple.

The virtual monopoly that conferred its unique power was gradually eaten away by the emergence of MTV, the proliferation of national pop radio stations, and internet technology that made a week-long wait for a chart rundown obsolete. Its cancelation was announced in June 2006, only two years after celebrations of its fortieth anniversary.

Though oft criticized, it is undeniable that *Top Of The Pops* memorably charted the childhoods of several generations of British teenagers.

Sean Egan

Date January 1, 1964

Country UK

Why It's Key The program with the power to make or break acts.

Key Performance *A Hard Day's Night* the movie

Named after a Ringo malapropism, The Beatles' first film, *A Hard Day's Night*, was rushed out because United Artists doubted that Beatlemania would last much longer. Ironically, the movie's rushed nature, black and white stock and cost-conscious cinéma vérité style gave it an appealing urgency. With camera images cut to the beat of the music, outdoor sequences like "Can't Buy Me Love" can be seen as a precursor to the modern pop video. Its box-office success inspired U.S. TV executives to commission a small-screen series concerning the madcap adventures of another bunch of loveable mop-tops, pre-Fab Four The Monkees.

Perhaps most importantly though, the film illustrated The Beatles' effortless capacity to side-step the bog standard in anything they did. *A Hard Day's Night* captured a day in the increasingly surreal, goldfish-bowl lives of The Beatles, giving it a mock-documentary feel in which their individual, intelligent

personalities shone. Reviews were hugely favorable, New York's *Village Voice* describing it as "the *Citizen Kane* of jukebox musicals." They were ably assisted by a sharp script from Alun Owen, Richard Lester as director, and a fine supporting cast of British character actors (Wilfrid Brambell, Norman Rossington, John Junkin, Victor Spinetti).

However, the likes of the breathless title track and the affecting "I Should Have Known Better" were overlooked for Best Song at the Oscars, the prize going to the Mary Poppins selection "Chim Chim Cheree"…
David Wells

Movie Release Date
July 6, 1964

Nationality UK

Director Richard Lester

Cast The Beatles, Wilfrid Brambell, Norman Rossington

Composers John Lennon, Paul McCartney

Why It's Key The Fab Four revolutionize rock film just as they had rock music.

Key Song "The House Of The Rising Sun" The Animals

By the '60s, "The House Of The Rising Sun" – in which a woman tells of her descent into prostitution in New Orleans – was a "traditional" song, i.e. one so old that its authorship is unknown.

First recorded in the '30s, it was subsequently given a new arrangement by New York folk scenester Dave Van Ronk. A baby-faced newcomer named Bob Dylan impertinently recorded Van Ronk's version on his 1962 debut album. Over in England, R&B combo The Animals were so impressed with Dylan's version of the song that they decided to cover it for their second single. Their recording was utterly original however, boasting hypnotic winding guitar arpeggios and dazzling organ work – as well as a change of the risqué subject matter to gain airplay. Not only did a classic record and Transatlantic No. 1 ensue – it made UK No. 1 on July 11, 1964 – but the way the record used electric backing to purvey a traditional flavor is almost certainly what convinced Dylan himself that he could

turn from folkie to rock artist, a move which itself had seismic consequences. Recalled The Animals' drummer John Steel, "He said he was driving along in his car and ["House… "] came on the radio and he pulled the car over and stopped and listened to it and he jumped out of the car and he banged on the bonnet. That gave him the connection… "
Sean Egan

Release Date
June 1964

Nationality USA/UK

Composer Alan Price, Traditional

Why It's Key Illustrates how widely the ripples of a pebble dropped in the musical pond can spread.

Opposite Eric Burdon of The Animals

Key Person
Jim Reeves

"Gentleman" Jim Reeves was one of the earliest and most successful country music stars to enjoy major success as a pop artist. A non-appearance by Hank Williams at a Louisiana Hayride broadcast in 1952 gave Reeves his lucky break. Following a successful performance, he was swiftly signed to Abbott Records, and promptly notched up a country No. 1 with "Mexican Joe" – the first of 40 country hits.

RCA soon picked up Reeves' contract, and his first hit with them was the self-penned "Yonder Comes A Sucker" in 1955. With the new deal a new sound emerged, with the help of producer Chet Atkins: out went country fiddles and steel guitar; in came richly orchestrated arrangements (the "Nashville Sound") that helped introduce country to a broader audience. Abandoning the raucous vocal style hitherto typical of the genre, Reeves crooned intimately in a smooth baritone – inspiring the epithet "Gentleman" – imbuing country's characteristic melancholy with a radio-friendly warmth. The result was a string of hit country-pop ballads, including country No. 1s with "Four Walls" (1957) and "He'll Have To Go" (1960).

On July 31, 1964, Reeves was killed when the light aircraft he was piloting crashed in a storm near Nashville. Not even death could slow his record sales. "Distant Drums" topped the UK singles chart in 1966 and he racked up six further U.S. country No. 1s (more than he had scored alive). Incredibly, his run of chart entries continued well into the '80s.

Robert Dimery

Role Recording Artist

Date 1964

Nationality USA

Why It's Key The man whose sophisticated style helped country music cross over.

Key Performance *Mary Poppins*
the movie

Despite its success and reputation, P. L. Travers resisted the advances of the Walt Disney Corporation for more than 20 years after it first approached her with the proposition of adapting her much-loved children's book *Mary Poppins* for the big screen. Eventually, she capitulated, on the provision of script approval.

By this time, Disney had already started combining live action with animation, the most notable early example of which was *Song Of The South*. Mary Poppins was the film that showed that this technique could produce a result that had the same fantastical imprimatur and rosy-cheeked charm as a cartoon. Julie Andrews, star of the stage version of *My Fair Lady*, was perfect casting as quintessential English rose Poppins, even if she was a somewhat more saintly nanny than depicted in the book. Dick Van Dyke was then the darling of television audiences Stateside and his casting as Poppins' chimney sweep pal Bert was an astute America-oriented commercial move, even if his cockney accent was atrocious. The Sherman brothers provided the score, arguably the first major one of their great career with Disney in a film that is surprisingly leftist (pro-suffragette, anti-work ethic). Fondly remembered musical highlights include the entreaty to take foul-tasting medicine "A Spoonful Of Sugar," the superlative-coining "Supercalifragilisticexpialidocious" and Bert's theme, the Oscar winning "Chim Chim Cher-ee." Another Oscar winner was Andrews for Best Actress.

Sean Egan

Movie Release Date June 26, 1964

Country USA

Director Robert Stevenson

Cast Julie Andrews, Dick Van Dyke, David Tomlinson

Composer Robert B. Sherman, Richard M. Sherman

Why It's Key The film that showed the magic of Disney could transfer to live action.

Opposite Julie Andrews in *Mary Poppins*

Key Song **"Walk On By"**
Dionne Warwick

Burt Bacharach and Hal David's evergreen "Walk On By" needs to be sung by a woman and no woman ever sung it with more impassioned articulacy than the composers' preferred muse and the song's original hitmaker Dionne Warwick. Entering the U.S. Hit Parade on May 9, 1964, Warwick's definitive adaptation is a veritable solitaire of stoical acquiescence. It is delicate, dignified, and private. The briefest of eye contact. The unobtrusive tears. The "no looking back." Bacharach's string arrangements welter like waves of grief and even the flugelhorn sounds friendless. It's lonesome but it's proud. And it's feminine.

Other notable renditions by usually admirable artists like Isaac Hayes (1969) and The Stranglers (1978) are hamstrung by obtrusive masculinity. Isaac Hayes' libidinous soul gymnastics and blazing brass lacks reticence, striding down the road past the narrative's former lover for 12 long minutes as inconspicuously as a carnival procession while The Stranglers' psychedelic-punk recasting carries an undercurrent of reprisal, loitering injuriously on the other side of the street hoping for confrontation and bearing a face like thunder.

Perhaps it took the virtue of social conscience to come close to Warwick. In one of the musical finales of the UK TV puppet satire show *Spitting Image* (1984-1996), the song was coopted to highlight the plight of the homeless, whom the more fortunate "walk on by." It was a reinvention that made for an unexpectedly haunting experience.
Kevin Maidment

Date April 1964

Nationality USA

Composer Burt Bacharach, Hal David

Why It's Key A Bacharach/David classic. Much covered. Often misconstrued. Never equaled.

Opposite **Dionne Warwick**

Key Person
Roy Orbison

Texan Roy Orbison was bound for melodrama both in song and real life. Starting as another Sun rockabilly singer out of Memphis, in 1960 his smash record "Only The Lonely" heralded a string of fifteen Top 40 U.S. hits. Most of them were haunted and overwhelming mini-operas that took the classic tear-soaked ballad to new emotional heights with a far-reaching voice and theatrical arrangements. With songs like the paranoid U.S. No. 1 "Running Scared," the haunting "In Dreams," and the self-explanatory "Crying," the odd-looking, dark-spectacled singer embraced a rock 'n' roll loser persona. These dramas were balanced by bluesy material such as "Candy Man" and the immortal "Oh! Pretty Woman," which on September 26, 1964, took him to the U.S. top spot again. The latter record was infused with the usual Orbison melancholy but had a perky rhythm and a tom-cattish undercoat – summed up in his much imitated feline growl – and deservedly sold more copies in its first ten days than any other 45 rpm in history thus far. But Orbison's career would decay after he left the Monument label for MGM in 1965. In 1966, real life caught up with his tragic aura when wife Claudette died in a motorcycle accident. Two years later, he lost two sons when his house burned down while he was on tour.

A heart attack claimed Orbison's life in December 1988, the same year he had teamed-up with Bob Dylan, George Harrison, Jeff Lynne, and Tom Petty in The Traveling Wilburys.
Ignacio Julia

Role Recording Artist

Date 1964

Nationality USA

Why It's Key Took rock into untrammeled areas of darkness.

Key Album *A Love Supreme*
John Coltrane

Ask most people to name the first concept album and the LPs most likely to be cited are The Beatles' *Sgt. Pepper's Lonely Hearts Club Band* (even though it didn't have a narrative) and The Who's *Tommy*. While John Coltrane's *A Love Supreme* – recorded on December 9, 1964 and released considerably before either of those records – is roundly acknowledged as a modern jazz classic, few people know or remember that it was a concept work of sorts. In part that's because the record is almost wholly instrumental, save for some chanting of the title phrase.

However, Coltrane himself implied a heavy-duty concept in his liner notes, where he declared *A Love Supreme* as a "humble offering" to a God who was responsible for his spiritual awakening. The concept is reflected by the organization of the record into four parts, implying a journey toward that awakening, those sections being "Acknowledgment," "Resolution," "Pursuance," and "A Love Supreme." If it seems like a bit of a stretch to see this as a concept album or ancestor thereof, the instrumental evocation of a heavy-duty metaphysical progression by Coltrane's quartet was certainly taken to heart by other jazz and rock musicians: Dick Taylor of The Pretty Things once cited it as an influence on their decision to record the themed LP *S.F. Sorrow*.

Either way, *A Love Supreme* is a glorious, rich, and challenging work.

Richie Unterberger

Release Date February 1965

Nationality USA

Tracklisting Part 1: Acknowledgment, Part 2: Resolution, Part 3: Pursuance, Part 4: Psalm

Why It's Key A jazz classic that was also one of the earliest examples of a concept album in any genre.

1960-1969

313

Key People
The Hollies

Music lovers are frequently amazed to find that the answer to the rock and pop trivia question "Which British chart act had the most number of '60s UK hits behind the Beatles?" is not "The Rolling Stones" but "The Hollies."

That the band – who hailed from Manchester, England – should hold that accolade should not really come as a surprise. Their second album, *In The Hollies Style*, released in November 1964, was mostly composed by singer Allan Clarke and guitarists Tony Hicks and Graham Nash (under the "L. Ransford" collective pseudonym) at a time when only The Beatles were so self-reliant. The Hollies' image suffered because of the fact that they were never cool or trailblazers and that they were just as prepared to release covers as singles. Explained Hicks, "We were always happy to record the best songs that were there at any given time, whether it be our songs or anyone else's."

Their hits ranged from the breathless pop of "Just One Look" and "I'm Alive" through the surrealism of "Stop! Stop! Stop!" and "King Midas In Reverse" through the grandeur of "He Ain't Heavy, He's My Brother" through the sensuality of "The Air That I Breathe" through the brawny rock of "Long Cool Woman In A Black Dress." Despite line-up upheavals, their polished, three-part harmonizing ws a constant.

The band still carry on, despite the retirement of Clarke and the death of his replacement Carl Wayne.

Sean Egan

Role Recording Artists

Date November 1964

Country UK

Why It's Key The band who racked up a phenomenal run of hits while no one was looking.

Opposite **The Hollies**

Key Song **"You've Lost That Lovin' Feelin'"**
The Righteous Brothers

Celebrated songwriting duo Barry Mann and Cynthia Weil started "You've Lost That Lovin' Feelin'," an anguished tale of a man who can see his relationship disintegrating before his eyes. But it was their belated collaborator in the writing process who turned a significant smouldering ballad into something altogether more grandiose: producer Phil Spector applied his "Wall Of Sound," marshalling the session musicians, the beautiful string arrangement of Jack Nitzsche and Gene Page, and the voices of the "brothers" to create a mesmerizing concoction.

As it that wasn't enough, the warm baritone of Bill Medley and the high tenor harmonies of Bobby Hatfield kicked off a revolution of their own, something that the critics defined as "blue-eyed soul": R&B and soul played and sung by white musicians. Though Mann and Weil were surprised by this description, they also conceded that the song was inspired by "Baby I Need Your Loving," a recent hit for black vocal group The Four Tops. Spector came in on the writing when they had devised two verses and the chorus. Amongst the producer's important additions was the unforgettable "'Gone, gone, gone – whoa-oh-ohhh" part that ended each chorus. The other unforgettable vocal refrain was Mann's opener: "You never close your eyes anymore when I kiss your lips."

The song made No. 1 in both the UK and United States on February 6, 1965. It is officially the most broadcast song of the twentieth century.
Giancarlo Susanna

Release Date November 1964

Nationality USA

Composers Barry Mann, Cynthia Weil, Phil Spector

Why It's Key The song that invented blue-eyed soul.

Key Event
The first Mellotron is released

The Mellotron is a machine that simulates other instruments by playing recordings of them that are activated through a keyboard – in essence the first analog sampler. Its invention followed the introduction of magnetic recording tape in the '40s and the ability to store many different sounds in a compact and convenient form. The American inventor Harry Chamberlin was the first to construct such an instrument, which basically stored and retrieved a small number of drum loops. In 1960 Chamberlin began to sell his first models but had little success until he joined with an English tape recording company who developed the capabilities of the instrument and gave it its name.

Leslie Bradley and his brothers increased the number of sounds that the Mellotron could produce and made it into a practical instrument that could be used by musicians in performances. Their machine had two keyboards, one accessed "lead" sounds such as strings and horns and the other produced rudimentary rhythms. They perfected mass production of Mellotrons and successfully marketed them to rock musicians. Mike Pinder was an employee in their Birmingham factory and left to join the Moody Blues, who featured the Mellotron in several hit recordings. Once The Beatles used a Mellotron (the flute sound in "Strawberry Fields Forever") its future was assured and many was the rock musician over the next decade who would make it provide him with wind, brass, or even orchestra sounds beyond his own abilities or budget.
Andre Millard

Date 1964

Country UK

Why It's Key Opened up new horizons for rock musicians.

Key Performance *Hello, Dolly!*
stage musical

At an intimidating meeting, producer David Merrick expressed uncertainty that Jerry Herman was American enough for a musical based on Thornton Wilder's romantic farce *The Matchmaker*. Jerry Herman retreated to the one-room walkup on East 10th Street he was still living in despite modest Broadway success with *Milk And Honey* for an intense weekend of furious writing on spec to prove otherwise. Armed with a mimeographed treatment of material by librettist Michael Stewart, Herman blasted out three songs that would not only secure him the gig, but remain in the show right through opening night: delightfully meddlesome Dolly Levi's I Am song, "I Put My Hand In," the traveling song about youthful adventure "Put On Your Sunday Clothes," and the waltz "Dancing."

Opening on January 16, 1964, *Hello, Dolly!* – as it was titled – was one of the sturdiest musical comedies in history, its plot about romantic entanglements in 1890s New York all artfully negotiated by the lead character, who would become the equally sturdy vehicle for many a star. Broadway Dollys include Ginger Rogers, Betty Grable, Dorothy Lamour, and Ethel Merman, although many consider none surpassed the role's originator, Carol Channing.

The title song virtually defined the pageantry of star entrances, "Before The Parade Passes By" became the anthemic march for second chances at life and *Hello Dolly!* would not close until breaking the existing record for longest running Broadway musical ever, at 2,844 performances.

David Spencer

Opening Night
January 16, 1964

Country USA

Director Gower Champion

Cast Carol Channing, David Burns, Eileen Brennan

Composer Jerry Herman

Why It's Key The musical propelled by a young composer's burning desire to prove himself.

1960-1969

315

Key Song **"The Leader Of The Pack"**
The Shangri-Las

Melodramatic death songs were a vogue of sorts in rock'n'roll in the late 1950s and early 1960s, when such shameless weepers as Jody Reynolds' "Endless Sleep", Mark Dinning's "Teen Angel" and Ray Peterson's "Tell Laura I Love Her" became massive smashes. Even in late 1964, ridiculously contrived teen death tales still made an occasional impact, as J. Frank Wilson did with "Last Kiss". Hot on its heels, however, was a sign of changing times, a record that was not an elegiac farewell but a virtual play-by-play of the gruesome road death of a motorcycle hoodlum, complete with "Look out look out!" screams, screeching tires and shattering glass.

The narrative of the Shangri-Las' "Leader Of The Pack", which made U.S. No.1 on November 28, 1964, seemed the ultimate parents' nightmare, one in which their lovely daughter was captivated by the meanest gang leader on the block (even if his horrific end validated their fearful warnings). The teens weren't scared, though: sales were massive, aided by the Shangri-Las' fairly authentic New York street-tough image. It also helped that the song was written by top Brill Building tunesmiths Jeff Barry and Ellie Greenwich with Shadow Morton. Morton (whose love of bikes inspired the composition) and Barry co-produced the track with appropriate drama. Camp as it was, it was an instant classic, lifted high by the Shangri-Las' heartfelt mournful vocals and a multi-part construction that made it sound like an opera in miniature.

Richie Unterberger

Release Date 1964

Nationality USA

Composers Jeff Barry, Ellie Greenwich, Shadow Morton

Why It's Key The most blatantly violent teenage death disc hit.

Key Song **"In The Midnight Hour"**
Wilson Pickett

Wilson Pickett was signed to Atlantic Records by A&R man Jerry Wexler in 1964, having already written a soul standard, "If You Need Me" (Solomon Burke).

After early flops, Wexler sent Pickett to Stax Records in Memphis, an up-and-coming label distributed by Atlantic. Steve Cropper, guitarist with house band the M.G.s, had heard Pickett's Atlantic debut "I'm Gonna Cry" in which Pickett sings "late in the midnight hour" and suggested it be appropriated for a title. Left with a bottle of Jack Daniels whiskey in the Lorraine Motel across the road from Stax, Cropper and Pickett wrote the song in two hours. Wexler advised basing the rhythm on the contemporary "Jerk" dance craze, demonstrating the dance step right there in the studio, explaining, "push the second beat while holding back the fourth." Wexler and Dowd's visit refined the Stax sound, leaving a strong impression on the Memphians as to how to make a major hit from their instinctive R&B. It entered the *Billboard* Top 40 on August 15, 1965. Although its final position was only No. 21 (and No. 12 in the UK), it has become recognized as a solid-gold soul classic.

A notoriously volatile character, Pickett later claimed that he was the sole writer, something Cropper vehemently denies. But its success convinced Wexler to try other acts on Stax and by December he sent Florida duo Sam and Dave to Memphis too, cementing the hard gospel style of Southern soul in the pop charts.
Chris Goodman

Release Date July 1965

Nationality USA

Composer Steve Cropper, Wilson Pickett

Why It's Key Established Stax Records as a soul hit factory.

Key Performance
The Beatles at Shea Stadium

The Beatles' first concerts in America were promoted by impresario Sid Bernstein. It was Bernstein who had the novel concept of accommodating the unprecedented scale of demand for concert tickets The Beatles had caused by featuring them at the home of baseball's New York Mets, the William A. Shea Stadium in Queens. With an audience of over 55,000 and ticket prices around U.S. $5, it was a rock concert on a previously unimagined scale.

The Beatles, wearing beige-colored, military-cut jackets, traveled by helicopter, landed on a nearby roof and made their journey to Shea in a security truck. Following half a dozen support acts, The Beatles were introduced by Ed Sullivan and launched into "Twist And Shout." John Lennon seemed to be almost feverish with the excitement of the event, speaking into the microphone in tongues and virtually assaulting the keyboard. As Paul announced the last song of the evening, "I'm Down," he glanced at his watch as though it was getting late but in fact The Beatles had only played for 30 minutes. The music was perfunctory and the relaying of sound primitive by today's standards. Few cared: the crowd were ecstatic, the event the height of Beatlemania. Because of the intensity of the screaming, some music was overdubbed for the TV special of the concert, which was shown by the BBC in March 1966. The Beatles took home $160,000. George Harrison promised they would be back the following year, and they were.
Spencer Leigh

Date August 15, 1965

Country USA

Venue William A. Shea Stadium, New York, New York, USA

Why It's Key The event that redefined the parameters of the rock concert.

Opposite Fans of The Beatles at Shea Stadium

Key Event
The folk rock explosion

When The Turtles entered the *Billboard* Top 40 on August 21, 1965 with a cover of "It Ain't Me Babe" that turned Bob Dylan's hip put-down into a cheery pop tune and then proceeded to go Top Ten with it, it confirmed a revolution that had been building throughout 1965: the marriage of two forms hitherto thought irreconcilable.

In 1963, folk was considered authentic, adult music, and rock largely fun for teenagers. Yet by 1965, the styles had merged to bring both folk and rock to a place that neither could have reached on its own steam. The Byrds had launched folk-rock as a craze by marrying The Beatles and Bob Dylan with their chart-topping cover of Dylan's enigmatic "Mr. Tambourine Man" in mid-1965. Dozens of folkies subsequently scampered to go electric, even if it meant grafting electric guitar and drums onto a previously released acoustic track, as producer Tom Wilson did for Simon And Garfunkel's brooding "The Sound Of Silence." Most

monumentally, Dylan himself went electric, first on record, then in concert, inciting howls of outrage from purists who wanted their folk "uncontaminated." Now a pop icon, Dylan's songs for a brief time in late 1965 were as popular to cover as even Lennon-McCartney's.

Folk-rock's most important legacy, however, was introducing a newly sophisticated intelligence into rock music lyrics, whether in socially conscious songs, surrealistic landscapes, or probes into the workings of the inner psyche. Soon those traits would spread beyond folk-rock into all of rock music, dragging its audience into adulthood on the way.
Richie Unterberger

Date August 21, 1965

Country USA

Why It's Key Folk and rock join hands to produce a new genre.

Opposite The Turtles

Key Album *Highway 61 Revisited*
Bob Dylan

Having already crossed the boundary between acoustic folk and amplified rock, Bob Dylan recorded one of his most enduringly revered albums of all. Released by Columbia *Highway 61 Revisited* gave Dylan his first U.S. top ten single; "Like A Rolling Stone" reached No. 2 and No. 4 respectively on the U.S. and UK charts, with the album peaking at No. 3 and No. 4.

But the cultural resonance of *Highway 61 Revisited* amounts to much more than mere chart success. Dylan turned inspirations gleaned from a road trip through the heartland of America into an album that amalgamates disturbing compositions with carnival rhythms, Biblical apocrypha with family sing-a-long melodies and brutal anti-capitalist diatribes with vaudeville waltzes. The music was alternately beautiful and coruscating but it was the words that sealed the deal; poetic, intellectual, and penetrating like only an ex-folkie's lyrics would be, but in truth a step above the

best folk lyrics ever written. His records were now being bought by Beatles and Stones fans (and spurned by many Woody Guthrie and Pete Seeger advocates) and one can only imagine what these new disciples thought of something like the eleven-minute, utterly absorbing album closer "Desolation Row," a street-as-world metaphor that touched all bases in its dissection of the human condition.

Dylan himself had stated a year earlier that the times they were a-changin'. *Highway 61 Revisited* was the agent of a change in pop never imagined.
Melissa Blease

Release Date August 30, 1965

Nationality USA

Tracklisting Like A Rolling Stone, Tombstone Blues, It Takes A Lot To Laugh It Takes A Train To Cry, From A Buick 6, Ballad Of A Thin Man, Queen Jane Approximately, Highway 61 Revisited, Just Like Tom Thumb's Blues, Desolation Row

Why It's Key Established the role of socio-political commentary in popular – as opposed to folk – music.

Key Performance *The Sound Of Music*
the movie

The Sound Of Music, which opened on March 2, 1965, was massively successful, and it had to be to avoid being eclipsed by the popularity of the original stage version. The work had its start when theater legend Mary Martin saw a German film based on the autobiography of Maria von Trapp, which told the story of a young Austrian postulant sent by her convent to be the governess to the children of Captain von Trapp, shortly before the Nazi annexation forced the family to flee to their homeland.

Martin brought in Broadway's premier songwriting team, Richard Rodgers and Oscar Hammerstein. Six years after the start of that Broadway musical's 1,443 performance run came the film. Songs like "My Favorite Things," "Do-Re-Mi," and the title track (with iconic choreography of Julie Andrews spinning against a vast grass backdrop) were squeaky clean but had a radiant charm. A charmed public ensured the movie surpassed *Gone With The Wind* as the highest grossing film ever.

Hollywood took this to mean that people still wanted to see lavish movie musicals and many expensive ones went into production. In fact, *The Sound Of Music* was a last hurrah for its sort of entertainment. The big movie musicals that followed it lost oceans of money, and, for the most part, albums of show music stopped selling in significant numbers.
William Ruhlmann

Movie Release Date
March 2, 1965

Nationality USA

Director Robert Wise

Cast Julie Andrews, Christopher Plummer, Eleanor Parker

Composers Richard Rodgers, Oscar Hammerstein

Why It's Key A watershed in the history of movie musicals and show music, although the meaning of that watershed was misinterpreted at the time.

Key Song "Downtown"
Petula Clark

A tribute to the bright lights of the big city inspired by British songwriter Tony Hatch's first visit to New York, "Downtown" was more Broadway show tune than rock anthem but when making U.S. No. 1 on January 23, 1965, it became the first song by a female British artist to do so.

Its elements – Petula Clark's voice dancing over a jaunty piano riff, rising with huge orchestral crescendos, lyrics name-checking "gentle bossa nova" and jazzy brass – were all reminiscent of the Brill Building songwriting era of the late '50s and early '60s. The song resounded with showbusiness panache and reserved a place for that glitzy approach amongst the new earthy rock scene. Hatch had originally intended "Downtown" for The Drifters. However, Clark heard the unfinished tune and urged him to write the lyric for her. A smash hit in Europe in 1964, "Downtown"'s success in America the following year made Clark a pioneer for British women in America.

The song's stylishness was something of a contrast to Hatch's lightweight pop for The Searchers ("Sugar And Spice"), and his later theme tunes to the soap operas *Crossroads* and *Neighbours*. Clark has meanwhile had a chart career spanning half a century, as well as writing for the movies and becoming engaged in television production and presentation.

Strangely, "Downtown" won a Grammy for Best Rock 'n' Roll Record, an indication of how much the American industry still mistrusted actual rock in 1965.
Chris Goodman

U.S. No. 1 Date
January 23, 1965

Nationality Uk

Composer Tony Hatch

Why It's Key Led the way for the British distaff side in America.

Key Song "(I Can't Get No) Satisfaction"
The Rolling Stones

The Rolling Stones had already notched a couple of American Top 10 hits ("Time Is On My Side" and "The Last Time"), but it was "(I Can't Get No) Satisfaction" – which topped the charts for four weeks starting on July 10, 1965 – that first separated them from their British Invasion compatriots. Not released in Britain until late August, the song had been conceived, completed, and recorded during the band's third American tour. The killer guitar riff and then-risqué title phrase came to Keith Richards during the night: despite his misgivings that the melody was too similar to Martha and the Vandellas' hit "Dancing In The Street," he played it to the rest of the band at their next recording session.

After Mick Jagger had penned a raging, alienated lyric about the myriad frustrations and all-pervasive commercialism of modern life, the group cut a semi-acoustic version at Chicago's Chess Studios on May 10, 1965. It was rejected, but the band nailed the song to their liking over the next couple of days at Hollywood's RCA Studios, with Richards playing the riff on his newly-acquired Gibson Maestro fuzzbox. Released on May 27, "(I Can't Get No) Satisfaction" elevated the band into superstars, its snarling sonic ambience and yowled, snotty lyric seeming to encapsulate their rebel image. "It was the song that really made the Rolling Stones," Jagger once claimed. "It changed us from just another band to a huge, monster band."

David Wells

Release Date
May 27, 1965

Nationality UK

Composers Mick Jagger, Keith Richards

Why It's Key The song that turned the Stones into legends.

Key Performance
Bob Dylan at Newport

By July 25, 1965, Bob Dylan was a much loved fixture at the Newport Folk Festival. However, just four days before he was due to make this, his third appearance at the event, he had released the rockin' "Like A Rolling Stone," which was folk only in its streetwise lyric.

What happened next has gone down in lore – even if it is shrouded in confusion. A leather-jacketed Dylan took to the stage and launched into "Maggie's Farm" only to be met with a crescendo of boos. Whether the audience were reacting to the accompaniment of the rock band Dylan had, surprisingly, got up with, an inadequate sound system, or merely MC Peter Yarrow's introductory announcement that Dylan would only be playing a short set is still unclear, but, after playing two more songs with his band, a severely shaken Dylan left the stage, returning only to perform solo renditions of "It's All Over Now Baby Blue" and "Mr. Tambourine Man." The electric set-up may or may not have prompted the booing but it certainly informed the fury of diehard folk purists like Ewan MacColl in their response to the performance. "Only a non-critical audience, nourished on the watery pap of pop music, could have fallen for such tenth-rate drivel," he wrote, outraged by Dylan's "betrayal" of genuine music for the supposedly empty flash and sensation of rock 'n' roll. It was obvious from such rhetoric that a crossroads had been reached. History has shown that Dylan took the right turning and his critics entered a cul-de-sac.

David Wells

Date July 25, 1965

Venue Newport Folk Festival, Newport, Rhode Island, USA

Nationality USA

Why It's Key The moment that revealed – and deepened – the fissures between folk and rock.

Key People
Sonny and Cher

Songwriter Salvatore "Sonny" Bono and his 19-year-old girlfriend Cherilyn "Cher" Sarkisian made No. 1 in the *Billboard* pop charts on August 14, 1965 with "I Got You Babe." Bono may have borrowed the hipster term "babe" from Bob Dylan's "It Ain't Me, Babe," a recent hit for The Turtles, but their songs were mid-tempo ballads and Sonny and Cher became the acceptable face of hippy culture. Sonny and Cher had the language, the uniform – all bangs, stripy trousers, and boas, clothes which still got you kicked out of restaurants in '65 – and the love anthem with none of the anarchism associated with "freaks" in the news around and shortly after this time like Ken Kesey and Timothy Leary. The fact that Bono was already 30 and that they were a married couple singing traditional love songs helped them seem less "dangerous" to the mainstream.

Until 1967, they could not miss but the hits then stopped until the couple won their own variety television show in 1972. Their stage act translated perfectly to the screen – Cher playing the witty intellectual and Bono her stooge. The hits returned, with Cher's parallel solo career proving as popular as the duo. The two even briefly revived their television show after their divorce in 1975.

Cher went on to 40 years of pop and film superstardom and Bono became a politician before a skiing accident took his life in 1998.

Chris Goodman

Role Recording Artists

Date August 14, 1965

Nationality USA

Why It's Key Took hippies and freaks into the living rooms of America.

Key Event **Three of The Rolling Stones are fined for "insulting behaviour"**

On the same day that Russian cosmonaut Alexei Leonov took a 20-minute walk in space, three British cultural icons made a different kind of history altogether.

Already controversial chart toppers, The Rolling Stones were fast gaining a reputation for outrageous behavior both on and off stage: "Would you let your daughter marry a Rolling Stone?", the tabloid headlines screamed in indignation at their casual dress (unheard of in showbusiness), long hair, and louche demeanors. Increasing numbers of Stones followers emulated the band's attitude, whose rebelliousness was intoxicating in a very strait-laced and snobbish culture. Their music was infused with the same flavor: a blend of menacing blues and rock across which Mick Jagger veritably yowled.

Jagger, guitarist Brian Jones, and bassist Bill Wyman were the subject of a private prosecution for urinating on the wall of an East London petrol station and supposedly telling the pompous forecourt attendant who'd refused them permission to use the garage facilities "we piss anywhere, man." Tame stuff now but, again, very uncommon for celebrities of the day.

Although the relatively petty charge of insulting behavior (which resulted in a fine of five pounds each on March 18, 1965) became inconsequential as further Stones-related crimes and misdemeanors made the headlines, the garage wall incident confirmed the outlaw chic surrounding the first band to put the shock into rock 'n' roll.

Melissa Blease

Date March 18, 1965

Country UK

Why It's Key Earned the Stones their first official medal of dishonor, confirming their rebel credentials and setting the standard for rock 'n' roll's code of misconduct.

Opposite **The Rolling Stones**

Key Song **"Yesterday"**
The Beatles

The Beatles were already an unprecedented worldwide pop culture phenomenon when "Yesterday" was recorded in June 1965 but it would elevate them yet higher, commercially and artistically.

Composed by Paul McCartney the previous year as a paean to girlfriend Jane Asher and provisionally titled "Scrambled Eggs," he fooled around with the tune for months. Obsessed with it, he played it constantly when a piano was at hand, greatly boring his fellow Beatles, Harrison commenting that Paul was starting to think he was Beethoven. When producer George Martin made the novel suggestion of bringing in a classical chamber quartet for accompaniment, "Yesterday" became the perfect Beatles ballad: sad and melancholy but not gloomy or maudlin.

The evocative simplicity of lyric and music made it the trademark Beatles cover for all kind of artists in all kind of styles. It became the most recorded song ever: around three thousand versions exist. Sung and played by McCartney alone, with the sweet strains of the string quartet emerging on the second verse, it appeared on the non-soundtrack side of the UK *Help!* album (1965), just as if it were filler. But in the United States, Capitol issued it as a single that made No. 1 on October 9, 1965 and stayed there for a month. Even if "Here, There and Everywhere" or "Eleanor Rigby" might arguably be better McCartney ballads, no Beatles composition sounds so universally resonant.
Ignacio Julia

Date 1965

Nationality UK

Composers John Lennon, Paul McCartney

Why It's Key Brought chamber music into mainstream pop.

Key Event **Jim Morrison and Ray Manzarek have a chance meeting**

Jim Morrison and Ray Manzarek had known each other as film students at the University of California but keyboardist Manzarek had no idea that non-player Morrison harbored musical ambitions. By chance, the pair ran into each other on L.A.'s Venice Beach in mid-August 1965, shortly after Morrison's graduation. When Ray asked Jim what he was up to, the latter admitted he'd been writing LSD-inspired songs, though he had to be pressed by Manzarek to sing a few couplets of "Moonlight Drive."

Manzarek, who'd already done obscure recordings as part of Rick And The Ravens, later said, "When he sang those lines, "Let's swim to the moon/Let's climb through the tide/Penetrate the evening/That the city sleeps to hide," I said, "That's it"... " Manzarek instantly concluded that if he and Morrison formed a group they could make a million, not least because Morrison's chiseled, tousle haired beauty put him in mind of Michelangelo's David.

It took a few line-up adjustments but with the addition of drummer John Densmore and guitarist Robby Krieger, The Doors were in place. The initially shy Morrison would become not just a full-throated crooner of tales of sex, mysticism, and psychological confrontation but the preeminent sex symbol of American rock. A bumpy five-year ride through superstardom took in classics like "Light My Fire," "People Are Strange," and "Riders On The Storm" but ended with Morrison's mysterious death at the age of 27.
Richie Unterberger

Date August 1965

Country USA

Why It's Key A happenstance meeting sparks the birth of one of America's most controversial and celebrated bands.

Opposite **The Doors**

Key Album *September Of My Years*
Frank Sinatra

Approaching his 50th birthday, Frank Sinatra shook off his carefree, playboy image with an album playing heavily on themes of autumn, aging wines, and loneliness. Unlike his previous themed albums, this one involved no acting.

Teaming up with arranger and composer Gordon Jenkins over a decade after their last collaboration was just what the somber subject matter needed. Jenkins' heavy strings and melancholy orchestrations were a perfect backdrop to Sinatra's mordant enunciation of lyrics of lost love and misspent youth. *September Of My Years* was the first time Sinatra trusted an arranger so thoroughly as to perform two songs written by him: the pensive "How Old Am I" and the oddly romantic "This Is All I Ask." Perhaps slightly shockingingly considering his love for classic standards, Sinatra chose "It Was A Very Good Year," previously sung by folk outfit The Kingston Trio, as the album's core track. But this album takes a marvelous mix of the traditional romantic ballad and contemporary folk song and gives them a sincere coating of Sinatra's apparently real despair, making *September Of My Years*, released on Reprise in August 1965, one of his darkest albums.

Sinatra may have been down in the dumps at his half century but the very intimations of mortality that informed this album are what made it a milestone and what made Sinatra a relevant artist again. The record won Grammys for Best Album and Best Solo Vocal.
Leila Regan-Porter

Release Date August 1965

Nationality USA

Tracklisting The September Of My Years, How Old Am I?, Don't Wait Too Long, It Gets Lonely Early, This Is All I Ask, Last Night When We Were Young, The Man In The Looking Glass, It Was A Very Good Year, When The Wind Was Green, Hello Young Lovers, I See It Now, Once Upon A Time, September Song

Why It's Key An artist who had traded on youthful beauty reinvents himself as an elder statesman.

Key Person
Graham Gouldman

"For Your Love," which entered the UK Top 75 on March 18, 1965, transformed The Yardbirds from club band to chart sensations. It had an equally dramatic effect on its composer Graham Gouldman.

Up in his native Manchester, Gouldman was working by day in a shop while fronting his own semi-pro group, The Mockingbirds, at evenings and weekends. Signing with EMI, they had recorded his "For Your Love" as their debut single, only for it to be rejected by the label. A publisher managed to place the song with The Yardbirds.

Its UK Top Three success engendered a strange situation. While The Mockingbirds struggled to make any impact, their leader enjoyed a golden two-year period as a freelance songwriter, penning a string of hits for The Yardbirds ("Heart Full Of Soul," "Evil Hearted You"), The Hollies ("Bus Stop," "Look Through Any Window"), Herman's Hermits ("Listen People," "No Milk Today," "East West") and Wayne Fontana ("Pamela Pamela"). Many of these songs, like "For Your Love," had a surprisingly haunting quality for Hit Parade material. Gouldman tended to employ minor chords, the result, he believed, of his Jewish upbringing and the type of music he heard in the synagogue when young. After Jeff Beck sneaked into the Top 30 in the summer of 1967 with "Tallyman," the hits dried up. However, some five years later Gouldman was to gain a long-overdue second wind as a member of the highly successful 10cc.
David Wells

Role Songwriter

Date 1965

Nationality UK

Why It's Key The songwriter whose signature sound revealed his Jewish roots.

Key Event **The Kinks are banished from the United States for four years**

The Kinks' first U.S. tour was an unmitigated disaster. Their U.S. debut gig, which saw them billed as "The Kings," set the tone for three weeks of mayhem. Running battles with promoters over money (or lack of same) led to the group truncating some performances and canceling others – a state of affairs that led to them being reported to the American Federation of Musicians. Equally damagingly, group vocalist, guitarist, and songwriter Ray Davies, on July 2, 1965, after refusing to sign a union contract, became involved in a backstage fist-fight with an official from the American Federation of Television and Radio Artists union, who allegedly retaliated by threatening to have The Kinks banned from playing in the United States.

They received no formal acknowledgment of a ban, but subsequent applications for visas were refused and The Kinks wouldn't return to the States until October 1969. Though raging at the unjustness of it all, Davies used the situation to find his own creative voice. His writing began to explore the cultural identity and heritage of the North London backyard that was the subject of his enforced observation. With a trademark combination of sly wit, social comment, sepia-tinted nostalgia, and character vignette, Davies authored a remarkable body of songs that concerned such decidedly non-rock 'n' roll subject matter as London bridges, Carnaby Street dandies, village greens and rheumatic gardeners. By the time the Americans allowed the band back in, this very Englishness made them love The Kinks all the more.

David Wells

Date July 2, 1965

Country UK

Why It's Key Provided the impetus for Ray Davies' uniquely English songs.

Key Event **Pete Townshend is inspired to write "My Generation"**

The late Queen Mother was not especially known for inspiring rock classics. She was, however, partly the impetus for a song that would both confirm that The Who's Pete Townshend was the composing equal of contemporaries like Lennon and McCartney and Bob Dylan, and sum up the seething discontent of a generation.

To be more precise the discontent of kids in Britain who not only came from poor backgrounds but had the additional grievance of a system that conspired to keep them in their place. The hierarchical nature of British society was underlined for guitarist/songwriter Townshend by the way that the Queen Mother imperiously had his beloved Packard Hearse car removed from outside his home in London's Chesham Place, next to Buckingham Palace, in 1965. Townshend later said, "Her husband had been buried in a similar vehicle and it reminded her of him." Townshend's blood also had reason to boil when, out driving at around the same time, a snooty lady in the car next to his asked him if he was driving his mummy's vehicle. The young guitarist vented his spleen over these two incidents in a song whose first verse climaxed with the spat line, "Hope I die before I get old!" That kind of rage and spite was precisely the kind of thing not often heard in a society where the lower orders had become accustomed to keeping their grievances to themselves in public.

Sean Egan

Date 1965

Country UK

Why It's Key Illustrates how rage can lead to great music.

Key Song
"Gloria"

Van Morrison was singing with the Belfast R&B group Them when he wrote "Gloria." His blues influences are clear in Them's recording, particularly its menacing beat and earthy lyrics. Its tempo starts slowly but gradually speeds up, culminating in a climax where the singer shouts out the letters of his girlfriend's name. This and the sublime winding guitar riff give the song a real sense of drama and sexual excitement.

Them's recording was actually only a B-side in the UK but is much better known in the United States. The three-chord structure of the song was easy to learn and its power to galvanize an audience soon made it a garage band favorite almost on the level of "Louie, Louie." Obscure garage rockers The Gants were the first of countless to cover it. A version by The Shadows Of Knight, though tepid by the original's standards, entered the *Billboard* Top 40 on April 16, 1966, and made No. 10. A live cover version by The Doors released posthumously on *Alive She Cried* (1983) was much closer to the original: this was clearly a song that perfectly suited the sexuality and confrontation that was at the heart of Jim Morrison's performances. Patti Smith's rewrite of "Gloria" as a lesbian anthem on *Horses* (1975) meanwhile proved that one could inject new life into a song now done so many times that it had seemed every last drop had already been squeezed from it.

Andre Millard

U.S. Chart Entry Date
April 16, 1966

Nationality UK

Composer Van Morrison

Why It's Key The flipside that launched a thousand cover jobs.

Key Song "Eight Miles High"
The Byrds

Merging the revivalism of the new folk movement with the fresh pop/rock hybrids that dominated the charts, Byrd-song like "Mr. Tambourine Man" and "Turn! Turn! Turn!" initially seemed like a jangly, more serene variant of Beatle-sound.

But when the L.A .band's fifth single entered the *Billboard* Top 40 on April 30, 1966, a seminal new chapter in rock 'n' roll was opened. On "Eight Miles High," as Gene Clark's ethereal subject matter merged with the startling liquid fretwork of Jim McGuinn's 12-string guitar, Chris Hillman's rumbling basslines, David Crosby's immaculate rhythm guitar chords, Michael Clarke's widespan drum explorations, and the band's haunting vocal harmonies, they were purveying a sound that defied definition. Some tried to give it one, especially when it became known that McGuinn was trying to emulate (surprisingly close to successfully) a saxophone with his Rickenbacker, but "jazz-rock" still didn't seem adequate. Whatever the tag, every artist in the world now had permission to test the boundaries as a consequence of it.

Widely misinterpreted as a paean to drug use, "Eight Miles High" was actually inspired by The Byrds' first trip to London in 1965. Main song lyricist Gene Clark originally called it "Six Miles High," referring to the cruising altitude of a Transatlantic airliner, but the band decided "Eight" sounded more poetic. Ironically, Clark quit The Byrds shortly after the single's success, citing fear of flying as the reason for his departure.

Melissa Blease

Release Date
March 1966

Nationality USA

Composer Gene Clark David Crosby, Jim McGuinn

Why It's Key Pop had never sounded either so adventurous or so unearthly.

Opposite The Byrds

Key Album *Aftermath*
The Rolling Stones

When The Rolling Stones started out in 1962, they intended to be a blues group that played covers of songs exclusively by American artists. But their manager, Andrew Loog Oldham, believing that they would have to come up with original material if they were to have a long-term career, cajoled Mick Jagger and Keith Richards into writing together. A year later, they'd devised the classic "Satisfaction."

The first Rolling Stones LP to consist entirely of Jagger/Richards songs was *Aftermath*, released on Decca in the UK on April 15, 1966. Recorded in seven days at RCA Studios, Hollywood with their favored engineer Dave Hassinger, it was a brilliant collection, seeing Richards devise fine melodies and licks graced by Jagger's inspired lyrics. Many of the latter were Dylan-influenced putdowns ("Mother's Little Helper," "Stupid Girl," "Under My Thumb") that sealed the Stones' status as a rebellious counterpoint to the more respectful Beatles. Even so, they proffered the tender

Chaucerian ballad "Lady Jane." Daringly, "Goin' Home" was an 11-minute blues jam. Though increasingly isolated, multi-instrumentalist Brain Jones ratcheted up the interest level of several songs with exotic decoration (marimbas, dulcimer, sitar) while bassist Bill Wyman and drummer Charlie Watts continued proving they were arguably the greatest rhythm section of all time.

As was common practice at the time, the U.S. version trimmed and altered the tracklisting but the songs were still all originals, and the album's quality and international success sealed the Stones' future.
William Ruhlmann

Release Date
April 15, 1966

Nationality UK

Tracklisting (UK) Mother's Little Helper, Stupid Girl, Lady Jane, Under My Thumb, Doncha Bother Me, Goin' Home, Flight 505, High And Dry, Out Of Time, It's Not Easy, I Am Waiting, Take It Or Leave It, Think, What To Do

Why It's Key A manager's nagging pays off, big-time.

Key Person
Herb Alpert

Though received wisdom suggests that the mid-'60s were dominated by cutting-edge rock music, it was also a boom period for easy listening. The proof of this is that in 1966, Los Angeles bandleader and trumpet player Herb Alpert and his Tijuana Brass sold twice as many records as The Beatles, holding down the No. 1 position in the *Billboard* album charts for an astonishing 18 weeks. Indeed, on April 2, 1966, Alpert had an astonishing four albums simultaneously in the *Billboard* Top 10.

Alpert had already coproduced Jan And Dean's inaugural hit "Baby Talk" and cowritten "Wonderful World" for Sam Cooke when, in 1962, he heard a mariachi band play at a bullfight in Tijuana, Mexico. He was inspired to record "The Lonely Bull," which became a U.S. Top 10 hit and the first release on A&M, a label he founded with business partner Jerry Moss. A succession of best-selling Tijuana Brass singles and albums followed, including *Whipped Cream And Other*

Delights (1965) and *Going Places* (1965), the latter featuring "Spanish Flea," a UK Top 3 single. The band's tuneful Latin sound inspired numerous other acts, even impacting on Love's classic *Forever Changes* (1967), but Alpert's biggest singles success was a rare vocal performance of the Bacharach/David ballad "This Guy's In Love With You," which topped the U.S. charts for four weeks and reached No. 3 in the UK. Subsequently disbanding the Tijuana Brass, Alpert achieved a further U.S. No. 1 in 1979 with the instrumental "Rise," later sampled by rapper Notorious B.I.G.
David Wells

Role Recording Artist

Date 1966

Nationality USA

Why It's Key Introduced the Latin sound to the pop/rock mainstream.

Opposite Herb Alpert and Jerry Moss

Key People
Cream

The word "supergroup" was yet to be coined but Cream would have merited it. All three members, Eric Clapton, Jack Bruce, and Ginger Baker, were unmatched virtuosi in their own fields. Clapton reigned supreme as England's premier ax hero. The cognoscenti's opinion of his astounding blues-rock fretsmanship in The Yardbirds and John Mayall's Bluesbreakers was famously trumpeted on a wall in The Angel, Islington London underground station in the much-photographed graffiti, "Clapton Is God." Seated at God's right hand in rock's new holy trinity was Jack Bruce, a gifted songwriter and vocalist whose bass-playing had been a vital feature of two seminal British blues outfits, Graham Bond's Organisation and Alexis Korner's Blues Incorporated, both percussively powered by Baker. Without peer in the British blues elite, Baker augmented his style with jazz and African music flourishes. After Baker sat in at a Bluesbreakers gig in the summer of 1966, he and Clapton hatched a

scheme to form their own band and Bruce was the natural choice for bassist. They played their first gig on July 29, 1966. Initially visualized, according to Clapton as "a Dada group… experimental and funny," they soon evolved into a blues trio and finally, the first rock band to compose, play, and improvize with the virtuosity of the revered blues and jazz masters, leaving contemporaries slack-jawed with awe. As Nick Mason of Pink Floyd recalls, "Cream was a whole new approach to what was possible… a real turning point."

Johnny Black

Role Recording Artists

Date 1966

Nationality UK

Why It's Key The band with an immodest moniker.

Key Performance *On The Flip Side*
television show

ABC Stage 67 was a weekly television series showcasing both original and adapted one-hour plays. *On The Flip Side*, written by Robert Emmett, was a music business satire broadcast in that programming strand on December 7, 1966 that featured a story involving a teen idol named Carlos O'Connor helped out of a career slump by a group of angels, taking a break from the "Big Pearly" (heaven) to boost Carlos back to the top of the charts on Earth. Starring as Carlos was a real life former chart idol, Rick (nee Ricky) Nelson.

Flimsy though this storyline might sound, however you boil it down the project constituted a foray into the concept of advancing a storyline though rock and pop song – the world first, either on screen or record.

The producers secured a coup by whom they managed to commission to write the score to their rock opera: Bacharach and David. Numbers penned by the celebrated hitmaking team included the downbeat

"It Doesn't Matter Anymore," the satirical "Fender Mender," "The Celestials" (imagining what life is like as a rock star), "Juanita's Place" (an ode to a hip boutique), and "They're Gonna Love It" (a heavy-handed fashion sales pitch).

The show has rarely been seen since its original airdate, but a commercially released soundtrack album at least stands as some testament to Bacharach and David's claim for an accolade that has always been afforded The Who, The Pretty Things, and various others.

Gillian G. Gaar

Date December 7, 1966

Country USA

Why It's Key The rock opera is born – although not many noticed.

Key Event
Jimmy Page joins The Yardbirds

When Yardbirds bassist Paul Samwell-Smith quit the band in spring 1966, nobody expected Jimmy Page to replace him. One of the busiest session guitarists in the country, Page had already turned down one previous Yardbirds invitation – to replace Eric Clapton back in 1965. He recommended his best friend, Jeff Beck, for the vacancy instead. Two years on, however, Page was hungry to throw himself back into band life, offering to hook up with the group on June 18, 1966. Initially it was as The Yardbirds' bass player, but second guitarist soon enough.

The result was stunning, as two of the hottest guitarists in the land joined forces to unleash a barrage of sound unlike that produced by any other band on the planet. Certainly movie director Michelangelo Antonioni was impressed – he hired the twin guitar Yardbirds to play in his new movie *Blow Up*, and was rewarded with one of celluloid's most incendiary performances. Audiences, too, went wild for the new combination, although they were a bit too ahead of their time for the more staid to appreciate them: the *NME* complained that the "outrageous cacophony… completely drowned out Keith Relf's voice."

The band would record just one single before Beck upped and left, the manic coupling of "Happenings Ten Years Time Ago"/"Psycho Daisies," and that, too, reverberates with the earth-shaking power of the partnership… a power that Page – alone with his guitar, but surrounded by the best new studio technology – would harness again with Led Zeppelin, just two years later.

Dave Thompson

Date June 18, 1966

Nationality UK

Why It's Key Shapes of Zeppelin-like things to come.

Key Song **"These Boots Are Made For Walkin'"** Nancy Sinatra

Although Nancy Sinatra had been singing on television since 1957 and had a record deal, in the mid-'60s she was still considered nothing more than Frank Sinatra's daughter. Even her association with Reprise Records was due to her father, with the inescapable fact of his owning the record label. She'd had almost a dozen flops and no successes when producer/songwriter Lee Hazlewood declared that in one session with Nancy he would create a hit.

The first attempt, "So Long, Babe" made a small dent, but it was the follow-up "These Boots Are Made For Walkin'" that made Nancy Sinatra a star – and sex symbol – on her own terms. It shot to No. 1 on the UK charts on February 19, 1966, a week before a similar chart-topping feat in her home country.

Hazlewood dictated that his composition be sung "like a 16-year-old girl who's been dating a 40-year-old man." The song – particularly it's immortal line "One of these days these boots are gonna walk all over you!" – gave Nancy a new image, one of a strong, sexy woman in a daring miniskirt and hip go-go boots. In fact, the image was so trendy and the result so successful that it was said to have inspired Frank to update his own image.

What followed was a debut album, *Boots*, which in turn went gold, cementing Nancy's international fame and doing no harm whatsoever to then-unknown Lee Hazlewood either.

Leila Regan-Porter

Release Date February 1966

Nationality USA

Composer Lee Hazlewood

Why It's Key A daughter finally moves out of her father's shadow.

Key Performance **Jimi Hendrix at Café Wha?**

Jobbing guitarist Jimmy Hendrix, 23, was living in New York's Greenwich Village. He and his band, The Blue Flames, played five sets a night at Café Wha? for U.S. $60 split four ways.

Though Jimmy had no game-plan, Lady Luck intervened in the shape of English model Linda Keith, who met and started a friendship with Hendrix. Enthralled by his abilities, Linda determined to get him discovered. But Stones manager, Andrew Loog Oldham, was not impressed when Linda took him to see Hendrix nor, later in June 1966, was record producer Seymour Stein. It was third time lucky, though, with Chas Chandler, bassist of The Animals, then on the brink of splitting, who wanted to go into production.

When she took Chandler to see Hendrix at the Café Wha?, the Animals man was, as she had been, blown away by his astonishing quicksilver fretboard abilities and galvanizing showmanship. Serendipitously, that night Hendrix opened his set with a cover of the menacing Tim Rose record "Hey Joe," which had already impressed Chandler so much that he hoped to produce a hit version in the UK.

"To me he was fantastic," Chandler later said." I thought there must be a catch somewhere. Why hadn't anyone else discovered him?" Chandler became not just Hendrix's producer but his manager, taking him to Britain and renaming him "Jimi." Only a matter of months later, Hendrix was revolutionizing both rock and the guitar forever with material like "Purple Haze."

Mat Snow

Date July 5, 1966

Nationality USA

Why It's Key Fate works overtime to clear the path for an astonishing guitar talent.

Opposite Jimi Hendrix

Key Person **Chip Taylor**

Chip Taylor was born James Wesley Voight in 1940. He initially considered becoming a golfer (hence the name "Chip"). However, he was also precocious musically, his group cutting a record when he was 15 (for which event the supposedly more attractive "Taylor" name was devised). A wrist injury solved his dilemma and when Chet Atkins enthused over his songs – then mainly country – he started to get noticed by publishers. Taylor began having minor country hits as well as a couple of placings on the UK pop chart, where Cliff Richard covered his "On My Word" and The Hollies his cowrite "I Can't Let Go." However, it was The Troggs' Transatlantic success with "Wild Thing" – a hard riffing lust-fest with an incongruously delicate ocarina break – that, to use Taylor's phrase, "changed everything." It made U.S. No. 1 on July 30, 1966.

Over the next few years, Taylor came up with classics like the much covered "Angel Of The Morning," "Any Way That You Want Me" (The Troggs), and "Try (Just A Little Bit Harder)," the latter a soulful hit for Janis Joplin. He also moved into recording himself.

Taylor's disgust with record company politics led to him retiring from music for around 15 years from 1980, him making his living by gambling. He has since returned to the business and in some senses obtained a new lease of life, engaging in the live work he had previously disdained.

Sean Egan

Date 1966

Nationality USA

Why It's Key A would-be golfer, a sometime gambler, but mainly a great songwriter.

Key Album *Freak Out!*
The Mothers Of Invention

Avant-garde rock/classical composer Frank Zappa might not have had a recording career if jazz label Verve had not moved into rock by engaging famed Dylan producer Tom Wilson, who quickly located two unusual, vaguely folk-rock acts, The Velvet Underground and The Mothers Of Invention.

Zappa, the leader of The Mothers (as they were called originally), was a sophisticated musician whose eclectic tastes ran from Edgard Varèse to doo-wop, and he indulged all those interests in his group. He also sang a Dylanish song called "Trouble Every Day" that caught Wilson's ear. The producer set Zappa loose in the studio to do largely as he liked, and the result was the astonishing *Freak Out!*, a double-LP debut set issued at a time when only Dylan, on the just-released *Blonde On Blonde*, had been allowed to spread across two discs. Zappa used the extra time to make his first important musical statement, a combination of serious contemporary composition and bizarre humor. Though

it was infused with a street argot uncommon in records then, it also boasted tracks like "Go Cry On Somebody Else's Shoulder," which resembled straight doo-wop, though considering Zappa's scabrous tone throughout it seemed safe to assume he was being sarcastic. After the melodic first disc came a challenging second disc. Some find its contents, like the side-long "The Return Of The Son Of Monster Magnet," unlistenable. The record made an impact though. Paul McCartney later described *Sgt. Pepper's…* as "our *Freak Out!*"

William Ruhlman

Release Date July 1966

Nationality USA

Tracklisting Hungry Freaks Daddy, I Ain't Got No Heart, Who Are The Brain Police?, Go Cry On Somebody Else's Shoulder, Motherly Love, How Could I Be Such A Fool?, Wowie Zowie, You Didn't Try To Call Me, Any Way The Wind Blows, I'm Not Satisfied, You're Probably Wondering Why I'm Here, Trouble Every Day, Help I'm A Rock, It Can't Happen Here, The Return Of The Son Of Monster Magnet

Why It's Key Satire comes to pop.

Key Event **George Harrison meets Ravi Shankar**

Rubber Soul (1965) was the pivotal album that confirmed that The Beatles were growing as musicians and songwriters, and perhaps no song on that recording offered greater proof than John Lennon's "Norwegian Wood." The lead instrumentation was provided, as usual, by George Harrison, but this time he was not playing a guitar but rather the multi-stringed Indian sitar – its first appearance on a rock record. Harrison had first encountered the sitar as a prop on the set of the group's film *Help!*. Shortly thereafter, The Byrds' David Crosby introduced Harrison to the music of Ravi Shankar, the acknowledged master of the instrument. Harrison became enamored with the sitar and vowed to study it intently.

Harrison did not initially push for a meeting with Shankar because he feared the musician would feel exploited, but when an acquaintance offered to arrange for the two to lunch at Harrison's home in June 1966, the Beatle jumped at the chance. Harrison

subsequently spent six weeks in India as Shankar's student, and later applied what he'd learnt to such Beatles tracks as "Within You, Without You" and "The Inner Light." But Harrison eventually abandoned the sitar upon realizing that it would take a lifetime to learn properly. Nonetheless, he had made the instrument instantly recognizable to Western eyes and ears. The sitar became a feature on many '60s rock albums and pop singles, even spawning a briefly lived subgenre known as raga-rock.

Jeff Tamarkin

Date June 1966

Nationality UK

Why It's Key The meeting that made Western music embrace Eastern.

Opposite George Harrison and Ravi Shankar

Key Event **John Lennon declares The Beatles "more popular than Jesus"**

Early in 1966, journalist Maureen Cleave wrote a series on The Beatles for London's *Evening Standard*. She had a leisurely conversation with John Lennon, a personal friend, at his home in Weybridge. Inspired by a reading of the controversial Christ-debunking *The Passover Plot* by Hugh Schonfield, he said "Christianity will go. It will vanish and shrink. We're more popular than Jesus now. I don't know which will go first – rock 'n' roll or Christianity. Jesus was all right but his disciples were thick and ordinary." The outrage the comments, published on March 4, 1966, provoked in the UK was restricted to things like a cartoon in the satirical *Private Eye* magazine depicting Lennon as Jesus. This lack of fury was not just due to the more muted British national character: Lennon's comment was arguably true. As Cleave herself said in the piece, "The Beatles' fame is beyond question… They are famous in the way the Queen is famous."

America was a different matter. In August 1966, the U.S. teen magazine, *Datebook*, carried excerpts from the interview, emphasizing the "more popular than Jesus" quote. The Bible Belt was horrified and Beatle records were publicly destroyed. Brian Epstein considered canceling The Beatles' imminent U.S. tour. After a semi-apology from Lennon, the tour went ahead but it was the band's first taste of being a lightning rod for people's passions, the increasing prevalence of which would ultimately lead to them ceasing to play live.

Spencer Leigh

Date March 4, 1966

Country UK

Why It's Key The Beatles discover there are limits to the world's adoration.

Key Song **"The Sun Ain't Gonna Shine Anymore"** The Walker Brothers

Frankie Valli may have been the unmistakable voice of The Four Seasons but producer Bob Crewe and group member Bob Gaudio were the brains behind the operation, writing such hits as "Big Girls Don't Cry," "Walk Like A Man," and "Rag Doll." In 1965 they attempted to capitalize on the band's success by launching Valli as a solo act. Far more solemn than the writing duo's usual fare, "The Sun Ain't Gonna Shine Anymore" was an epic, lavishly arranged ballad that drew a typically fine performance from the singer but it stalled outside *Billboard*'s Top 100.

Though Valli's effort didn't even gain a release in the UK, the song attracted the attention of U.S. expatriates The Walker Brothers, who had recently topped the UK charts with the similarly magisterial "Make It Easy On Yourself." Producer Johnny Franz and arranger Ivor Raymonde provided the Spector-esque Wall of Sound backdrop but "The Sun Ain't Gonna Shine Anymore" was elevated to classic status by Scott

Walker, whose brooding, angst-filled persona and sonorous baritone were tailor-made for the deep, regal gloom of lines like "Loneliness is the cloak you wear." On March 19, 1966, The Walkers' cover version was UK No. 1. It remained that way for four weeks. The record also went Top 20 in the United States.

Featuring prominently in the 1991 British movie *Truly Madly Deeply*, the much-covered "The Sun Ain't Gonna Shine Anymore" was also a UK Top 30 hit for Cher in 1996.

David Wells

UK No. 1 Date March 19, 1966

Nationality USA

Composers Bob Crewe, Bob Gaudio

Why It's Key A U.S. flop is imported into Britain and transformed into a pop classic.

Key Album *Pet Sounds*
The Beach Boys

Beach Boys leader/producer Brian Wilson had already graduated from surf music to symphonic pop by the time he started work on the group's *Pet Sounds*. Inspired by the achievements of The Beatles, however, this marked the first time he tried to make an album work as a piece consistent in mood, tone, and esthetic quality, rather than just producing a collection of great, good, and so-so songs. The result was a lushly orchestrated brand of pop music that owed debts to the likes of Phil Spector and brought harmonized California rock into an almost neo-classical state of grandeur. The songs might have been about love's ecstasy gone gradually sour, but the settings were as meticulous, multi-layered, harmonically sophisticated, and nuanced as those of the great classical composers. *Pet Sounds* was a big step toward changing rock from kids' music into genuine art.

Pet Sounds' magnificence was immediately recognized in the UK, where the album was a best-seller and Paul McCartney anointed its lovely "God Only Knows" as the greatest song ever written. Eric Clapton was similarly impressed, considering it "one of the greatest pop LPs to ever be released." Sadly, the record wasn't nearly as successful in the band's native United States, where it reached No. 10 for just one week. In time, however, it came to be viewed as one of rock's core masterpieces, much-imitated by numerous artists in subsequent decades in search of the perfect piece of pop auteurism.

Richie Unterberger

Release Date
May 1966

Nationality USA

Tracklisting Wouldn't It Be Nice, You Still Believe In Me, That's Not Me, Don't Talk (Put Your Head On My Shoulder), I'm Waiting For The Day, Let's Go Away For A While, Sloop John B, God Only Knows, I Know There's An Answer, Here Today, I Just Wasn't Made For These Times, Pet Sounds, Caroline No

Why It's Key Surf boards and hot rods give way to melancholy and splendour on this masterpiece.

Key Song "When A Man Loves A Woman"
Percy Sledge

"When A Man Loves A Woman" was the one pop hit for Percy Sledge, a hospital orderly from Alabama and a part-time star on the local R&B scene. Cut with musicians and producers from the celebrated Fame studio in Muscle Shoals, Alabama, but recorded at Quinvy, a local satellite studio, the song was based on Sledge's own "Why Did You Leave Me?" The words were changed and the record passed on to Rick Hall, owner of Fame, who then alerted Jerry Wexler at the legendary Atlantic Records in New York who signed Sledge up. The song reached the top in the United States on May 28, 1966.

Sledge's pleading, uninhibited vocal, Fame keyboardist's Spooner Oldham's mournful church-like organ and the backing harmony reminiscent of a church choir were all sublime but those gospel elements and the blaring brass section had all been developed before at Stax in Memphis, by James Brown or in Muscle Shoals itself. Yet none had risen so high and the song brought raw soul to a mass audience.

And Wexler, who had previously sent his artists south to Memphis to develop their sound, now switched to Muscle Shoals and Fame. Wilson Pickett was the first success, but significantly in 1967 Aretha Franklin recorded her first Atlantic album *I Never Loved A Man (The Way I Love You)* at Fame, the dawn of another musical legacy.

Chris Goodman

Release Date March 1966

Nationality USA

Composer Calvin Lewis, Andrew Wright

Why It's Key The first Southern soul record to hit No. 1 in the U.S. pop charts.

Key Song "Reach Out I'll Be There"
The Four Tops

Levi Stubbs, Abdul "Duke" Fakir, Lawrence Payton, and Renaldo "Obie" Benson were old hands by the time they signed to Motown Records in 1963 and spent some time as backing singers on the label's early hits until paired with songwriting team Holland-Dozier-Holland. Their first hit as The Four Tops, "Baby I Need Your Loving," came in 1964 and succeeding hits followed its fine but standard soul template. With "Reach Out I'll Be There," though, the Tops and H-D-H threw everything at their disposal at a mini symphony. Stubbs' rasping vocal begs, almost shouts against a maelstrom of crashing drums, epic harmonies, an oboe, and a flute, producing an echoing storm through which the singer fights his way to love, backed by a fair proportion of the Detroit Symphony Orchestra.

In a Motown quality control meeting, a company employee said the record wouldn't sell because it was "too different." Motown head Berry Gordy declared that the difference was what he liked about it and sanctioned its release. Perhaps the apex of Motown's longest-running recording stars, their most successful songwriting team, and of the label itself, the record topped the U.S. chart on October 15, 1966 and also hit No. 1 in the UK. The success of the song positioned Motown as more than just a danceable pop label. In the ultimate compliment on the record's grandeur, Wall of Sound producer himself Phil Spector called the track "black Dylan."
Chris Goodman

Release Date August 1966

Nationality USA

Composer Lamont Dozier, Brian Holland, Eddie Holland

Why It's Key Motown goes baroque.

Opposite The Four Tops

Key Song "96 Tears"
"?," And The Mysterians

The droning Vox organ that introduced "96 Tears" gave it another dimension in the guitar-dominated scene of '60s rock 'n' roll, making it sound like it was from another world. This no doubt suited the science-fiction aspirations of its composer, "?," the lead singer of The Mysterians who claimed to be born on Mars. Although there is doubt about the identity of the mysterious "?," it was probably Rudy Martinez, the founder of this group of Texans of Mexican descent, who recorded the song after moving to Michigan. The band's achievement in topping the U.S. charts with it on October 29, 1966 would have been a milestone in Latino rock if their background had been publicized.

The song is unapologetically dumb, from its primitive arrangement to its apparently arbitrary choice of the number of tears that the narrator will make his ex-lover cry when he gets even with her. The gruff, amateurish vocals and the unusual sound of the record attracted the attention of the New Wave and made it part of the rock canon favored by punk rockers in the '70s and '80s, keeping the song alive and giving the Mysterians an opportunity for a comeback. The superlatives critics have showered on the record, among them "proto-punk" and "post-modern", have assured that it will not be dismissed as just a one-hit-wonder by an obscure garage band.
Andre Millard

Release Date August 1966

Nationality USA

Composer Rudy Martinez

Why It's Key Further proof that though most garage bands had one great song in them, that great song was often immortal.

Key Album *Complete And Unbelieveable: The Otis Redding Dictionary Of Soul*

Otis Redding had started as another Little Richard imitator but, in 1962, had the chance to record his smoldering composition "These Arms Of Mine." Within a couple of years, he was the ethos of Southern soul.

Despite the title, *...Dictionary Of Soul*, released on October 15, 1966, was actually a step away from his string of soul hits like "Mr. Pitiful" and "Respect" and proof that Redding was aiming at the pop market way before his breakthrough appearance at the Monterey Pop Festival in 1967. His fifth studio album, it was the last he would complete before his early death.

His rugged voice and passionate delivery, set against the M.G.s' rhythm section's earthy but epic sound, bouyed by The Memphis Horns' brassy arrangements, as ever made for an exhilarating concoction. Though at this point his leanings toward the pop market were limited to covering, not writing, pop, so emotional and boldly personal was his approach, everything here sounds unquestionably Otis.

His own compositions – "Fa-Fa-Fa-Fa-Fa (Sad Song)," "My Lover's Prayer," "She Put The Hurt On Me" – were the usual classy Redding soul while he also demonstrated that a black singer – or at least one with his talent and commitment – could make a country tune ("Tennessee Waltz"), a Beatles single ("Day Tripper"), or a Tin Pan alley standard ("Try A Little Tenderness") totally his own. Redding's crossover potential was nowhere better represented than on this joyous album.

Ignacio Julià

Release Date
October 15, 1966

Nationality USA

Tracklisting Fa-Fa-Fa-Fa-Fa (Sad Song), I'm Sick Y'all, Tennessee Waltz, Sweet Lorene, Try A Little Tenderness, Day Tripper, My Lover's Prayer, She Put The Hurt On Me, Ton Of Joy, You're Still My Baby, Hawg For You, Love Have Mercy

Why It's Key A transitional album that sadly transpired to be Otis Redding's last.

1960-1969

343

Key Performance *The Monkees* television show

"Madness!!" promised the *Variety* audition ad. Though it is a part of the Monkees myth, only one of the eventual Monkees applied as a consequence of this call for "Running parts for four insane boys." However that wording accurately described the nature of the project: an American television version of the Beatles movie *A Hard Day's Night* (1964) in which giddy pop alternated with madcap action.

Hard as it is to believe today, it was a radical concept for the time. As Monkee Micky Dolenz later observed, "The only time you saw long hair on kids [on TV] was when they were being arrested." Dolenz was one of the shaggy-haired quartet ultimately chosen for instant stardom. His colleagues were Davy Jones, Mike Nesmith, and Peter Tork. Though the latter pair were trained musicians and Dolenz had learned drums, session musicians played on the songs featured in the show, which themselves were mainly written by top-rank freelance composers.

The Monkees, first broadcast on September 12, 1966, was not that big initially but became a ratings success partly through the phenomenal performance of the records associated with it. The fact that The Monkees did not initially play on their records caused more knowing music fans to sneer but The Monkees would obtain endorsement of the ultimate kind: John Lennon so loved their Marx Brothers-type humor that he – unprecedentedly – gave permission for the use of a Beatles song ("Good Morning, Good Morning") in an episode.

Sean Egan

Date September 12, 1966

Country USA

Why It's Key Middle America finds the longhairs invading its parlors.

Opposite Micky Dolenz, Davy Jones, and Mike Nesmith of The Monkees

Key People
The Association

The Association are never mentioned in the same breath as The Byrds or The Beach Boys, two other Los Angeles groups whose stock-in-trades were sophisticated multi-part harmonies of breathtaking beauty. For a brief time in 1966 and 1967, however, The Association were selling more records than The Byrds, The Beach Boys, and indeed almost anyone. After hitting No. 1 in the United States on September 24, 1966, "Cherish" held down the top spot for the first three weeks of that autumn; the following summer, "Windy" claimed the pole position for most of July. While "Never My Love" stalled at No. 2 later in 1967, both it and "Cherish" are among the most covered songs of the twentieth century.

The image of the sextet (later a seven piece) was wholesome, and this and their clean-cut harmonies and pretty wind-instrument decorative touches made them big in Middle America. However, they were also pretty hip. Their first hit, "Along Comes Mary," was widely suspected of referring to marijuana, and they opened the Monterey Pop Festival in June 1967, the quintessential counterculture event.

Their albums were inconsistent and the hit singles dried up after 1968 but they were at or near the pinnacle of what we now call California '60s the "sunshine pop" sound.

Richie Unterberger

Role Recording Artists

Date 1966

Nationality USA

Why It's Key On their huge pop-rock hits, The Association crafted gorgeous harmonies that rendered the group harmless to the middle-aged, but still managed to be hip.

Key Performance *The Good, The Bad, And The Ugly* the movie

In the '60s, the revitalization of American musical idioms abroad was not limited to British pop groups. In Italy, Ennio Morricone was doing the same thing via a strand of a supposedly distinctly American type of cinema through the scores he wrote for director Sergio Leone's so-called "Spaghetti Westerns."

The movies initially looked slightly comical because of the dubbing done into English but were beautifully shot. Morricone's music colored the oft-cheesy onscreen action with a genuine exotic menace, embellishing the prototype of the Western soundtrack – forlorn strumming guitars – with all manners of haunting choral voices, sweeping orchestration, and literal bells and whistles. There was also reverberating electric guitar that, while in keeping with the Western motifs, owed distinct debts to early instrumental rock 'n' roll stars like Duane Eddy, The Shadows, and The Ventures.

Morricone had actually been scoring spaghetti westerns for a few years before working on the soundtrack of *The Good, The Bad, And The Ugly* in 1966. This film, the last in a trilogy featuring Clint Eastwood as a nameless, poncho-draped gunslinger, contained the usual twangy guitars plus an almost psychedelic sense of effectively juxtaposing incongruent styles. The theme song would be the composer's international breakthrough, with its unforgettable lonesome whistling, voices that bristled like coyotes scampering through the tumbleweed, trumpet fanfares fighting it out with gunfire, and ominously galloping fretwork. Hugo Montenegro took a more bombastic version to No. 2 in the United States.

Richie Unterberger

Movie Release Date 1966

Nationality Italy

Director Sergio Leone

Cast Clint Eastwood, Eli Wallach, Lee Van Cleef

Composer Ennio Morricone

Why It's Key Brought a rock sensibility to often staid Western scores.

Key Performance *Blow-Up*
the movie

The inclusion of "Rock Around The Clock" on the soundtrack of the 1955 generation gap movie *Blackboard Jungle* alerted the entertainment business to the dramatic boost that hip young music could provide to box office receipts and record sales. Cue a flood of low-budget youth-oriented movies liberally sprinkled with sanitized rock 'n' roll. *Blow-Up*, directed by Italian auteur Michaelangelo Antonioni and released on December 14, 1966, bucked the trend. Starring David Hemmings, it exploited the hipness of London's mod fashion scene but, with its enigmatic murder plot, dreamlike ambience, and exploration of the desensitizing effects of the Sixties youthquake, it represented a quantum leap beyond teen movie norms. Appropriately, the bulk of the soundtrack is timelessly cool, dark, and melancholic jazz from keyboardist Herbie Hancock, best-known then as a Miles Davis sideman. The spark of genius, however, was including one performance by The Yardbirds, during the fleeting period when their line-up boasted both Jeff Beck and Jimmy Page. Antonioni originally wanted The Who, so in a meticulous Elstree Studios' recreation of Windsor's famous Rieky Tick club, The Yardbirds obligingly executed a dramatic guitar-smashing routine, à la Townshend's mob. Antonioni had also wanted them to perform "Train Kept A-Rollin'" but because of copyright problems, The Yardbirds rewrote it as "Stroll On." The wrong band playing the wrong song it may have been, but it nevertheless transformed a highly effective soundtrack into one that pointed the way ahead to an era in which the music could almost rival in importance the movie it accompanied.

Johnny Black

Movie Release Date December 14, 1966

Nationality UK

Director Michaelangelo Antonioni

Cast David Hemmings, Vanessa Redgrave, Sarah Miles

Composers Herbie Hancock, Jeff Beck, Chris Dreja, Jim McCarty, Jimmy Page, Keith Relf

Why It's Key The first truly cool teen movie.

Key Event
The Lovin' Spoonful drug scandal

In the '60s, drug use was often not only considered groundbreaking and risk-taking – it was also often viewed as a badge of coolness. But sometimes the heat got too hot, as The Lovin' Spoonful discovered when guitarist Zal Yanovsky and bassist Steve Boone were busted for marijuana possession on May 19, 1966.

With Yanovsky facing possible deportation to his native Canada, their dealer was named to the authorities. The musicians avoided serving time, but the ultimate outcome was about the next-worst-option. When the case hit the headlines the next year, the band's credibility with the very counterculture that had helped sustain their good-time folk-rock stardom plummeted, Lillian Roxon writing in her *Rock Encyclopedia* that "in San Francisco in 1967 their name was mud, their albums were used as doormats, groupies were urged not to ball them." Band friend and future member Jerry Yester later claimed that the intention had been for their lawyer to then represent the man they had ratted on. In the mid-'80s, chief Spoonful singer-songwriter John Sebastian was still smarting, telling author Edward Kersh that the counterculture "just deserted us... fans were all too quick to believe the worst."

The atmosphere was never the same again within the band. Yanovsky left the group, Sebastian followed not long afterward, and, soon enough, the Spoonful were finished. For mirroring the actions of the very audience they were representing, the group had paid a very dear price.

Richie Unterberger

Date May 19, 1966

Country USA

Why It's Key Showed that flirting with outlawdom could boomerang against pop and rock bands thumbing their noses at the establishment.

Key Song **"Sweet Soul Music"**
Arthur Conley

A song based on Sam Cooke's "Yeah Man," adapted by Otis Redding and Arthur Conley (a signing to Redding's own Jotis imprint), "Sweet Soul Music" is a user manual for soul.

Atlantic Record's Jerry Wexler, who recorded most defining soul and R&B stars, thought both genres the same, soul being a mere development. But this song highlights that progression. At its core, it retains the blues-with-a-backbeat essence of R&B but soul's emphasis on emotion above all, is highlighted by Conley intoning, "I got to get the feeling," with evangelical preacher's zeal, pointing to soul's roots in church gospel. R&B was always a distinctly earthly pursuit in the blues tradition.

The song builds and builds, existing on a knife-edge of tension, never quite overflowing – unlike R&B, typified by the likes of Little Richard, where the hollering rarely lets up. The brass section sharply punching through the rhythm is also typical of Southern soul as personified by the Stax studio in Memphis. The lyric namechecks the main movers on the '60s soul scene – Lou Rawls, Sam and Dave, Wilson Pickett, Redding himself, and James Brown ("The king of them all, y'all"), all originating from the American South, the geographical home of soul even if some of the artists were no longer based there.

The song entered the *Billboard* pop chart on April 1, 1967 and reached No. 2 and went Top 10 across Europe, a measure of soul's appeal by 1967.
Chris Goodman

Release Date March 1967

Nationality USA

Composer Arthur Conley, Sam Cooke, Otis Redding

Why It's Key Codified the essence of soul.

346

Key Event
Death of Otis Redding

Until Otis Redding's tragic death, none of the 26 year old's singles had climbed higher than No. 21 on the *Billboard* pop chart, despite his status among soul fans as the centerpiece of the Stax label through smoldering self-written anthems like "I've Been Loving You Too Long" and "Respect."

But an appearance at the Monterey Pop Festival in June 1967, had stunned the "love crowd" – as Redding referred to them – and in turn inspired a new Redding direction in the shape of "(Sittin' On) The Dock Of The Bay." A mournful ballad, it would appeal to the mainstream like never before. He finished the song on December 7 at Stax, flew to Cleveland on Saturday 9, and then took off for Madison, Wisconsin for a gig on Sunday 10.

His twin-engined plane crashed just outside Madison into Lake Monona. The cause remains mysterious although there was a storm and sole survivor, musician Ben Cauley, remembered waking up to hear bandmate Phalon Jones exclaim "Oh no!". Cauley unbuckled his seat belt, later allowing him to rise to the freezing lake's surface while Redding and the six others remained strapped in below and perished.

4,500 people attended Redding's funeral, with a litany of soul stars in attendance, from James Brown to Solomon Burke. "…Dock Of The Bay"'s rise to the U.S. No. 1 spot in early 1968 underlined a stellar career cut short.
Chris Goodman

Date December 10, 1967

Country USA

Why It's Key Soul's greatest star is killed just as he is about to cross over to a mass audience.

Opposite Otis Redding

Key Person
Aretha Franklin

Superstar preacher Rev. C. L. Franklin schooled his daughter, Aretha, born in 1942, in the sacred from birth and when in 1960 she joined Columbia Records, the future "Lady Soul" struggled for 12 mixed albums whose lack of grit almost seemed to imply a feeling that to get down and dirty in her music would be sacrilegious. In fact, it was probably due to the record company perceiving her as a family entertainer.

However, in 1966, Atlantic Records' A&R Jerry Wexler signed her, determined to mine her deeper soul. The sublime album *I Never Loved A Man (The Way I Love You)* resulted, a good proportion of it written by the artist herself. The lead track, "Respect," recorded on February 14, 1967, was a cover of an Otis Redding hit, a plea for reverence from a woman.

Franklin turned it into an ecstatic demand, possibly as a comment on her turbulent marriage, publicly interpreted as a feminist and civil rights anthem. It hit No. 1 in the *Billboard* pop chart and made Franklin an international star and proud symbol of black America. *Ebony* magazine declared 1967 the year of "Retha, Rap, and Revolt." An avalanche of hits followed, including the beautiful "A Natural Woman" and the moving "I Say A Little Prayer."

Her subsequent career has been patchy but always simply Aretha. Her voice, whether mastering gospel or duetting with George Michael in the '80s, has resounded as the premier female expression in soul music.

Chris Goodman

Role Recording Artist

Date 1967

Nationality USA

Why It's Key The first lady of soul.

Key Song "For What It's Worth (Stop, Hey What's That Sound)" Buffalo Springfield

On November 12, 1966, a riot occurred in the Crescent Heights neighborhood of Los Angeles on the Sunset Strip. The commercially zoned area was in transition between established stores and clubs that attracted an older, conservative clientele and new clubs like Pandora's Box that catered to young people, who swarmed the street at night, slowing traffic. Police efforts to enforce a curfew were heavy handed, the result of their antipathy to kids whose hair was of a length that they equated with communism, homosexuality, or both. Violent confrontation resulted, which was the inspiration for Buffalo Springfield's song "For What It's Worth (Stop, Hey What's That Sound)."

The L.A.-based band were actually on tour in San Francisco the night of the riot but songwriter Stephen Stills quickly heard about it from friends. His lyric was in the voice of one of the young people, but without polemic and more a sense of observation on the confusion and conflict welling up between generations.

No marching anthem, the overall mood conjured by the keening guitar notes and the refrain of "Stop, hey, what's that sound?" was one of regret more than anger.

The song entered the *Billboard* Top 40 on February 18, 1967, on its way to a peak of No. 7, and has gone on to become a touchstone of its era, frequently used in films to suggest the mood of America in those turbulent times.

William Ruhlmann

Release Date January 1967

Nationality USA

Composer Stephen Stills

Why It's Key Showed how popular song could act as a state of the union address.

Opposite Buffalo Springfield

Key Song "I Had Too Much To Dream (Last Night)" The Electric Prunes

Over on the West Coast of the United States, some big musical experimentation was going on. But it was still all very much under the radar, with records being bought but not played on air or heard by the general population. So far nothing had made the mainstream leap from familiar rock to psychedelia, an umbrella title for music whose effects-enhanced surrealism sonically resembled a trip on hippie stimulant LSD.

When The Electric Prunes' "I Had Too Much To Dream (Last Night)" hit the *Billboard* Top 40 on January 21, 1967, it became the tune that broke psychedelia overground. The song's limbo between hard-pumping garage rock and hippie tripping gave the music industry something familiar to latch onto amidst the weirdness. A new trend was born.

For all its apparent street cred, however, the record had origins similar to most pop, being written by outside songwriters, in this case the versatile and eclectic Annette Tucker and Nancie Mantz. Intentionally or not, their song's title and its surreal ambience perfectly captured the fish-eyed landscape much of turned-on Western youth were currently wandering through, as did the production tricks of producer Dave Hassinger, including oscillation and a startling opening buzz effect that grew from barely audible to ear-splitting. The record made a U.S. No. 11.

Unfortunately, with line-up changes and dubious attempts at classical music, The Electric Prunes' later albums sound pompous and dated. Luckily though, the early releases of the band still stand the test of time.
Leila Regan-Porter

Chart Entry Date
January 21, 1967

Nationality USA

Composers Nancie Mantz, Annette Tucker

Why It's Key Psychedelic music reaches the masses.

Key Performance The Beatles' "Penny Lane" and "Strawberry Fields Forever"

Prior to 1967, promotional films for records featured the artists lip-synching to the song on stage, usually with none of the instruments plugged in. The Swedish director, Peter Goldmann, devised storyboards for the promos of "Penny Lane" and "Strawberry Fields Forever," The Beatles' double-sided single, where the sequences would capture the feel of the record and even enhance the songs, yet with barely a trace of mouthing to the words or affecting instrument playing.

The "Strawberry Fields Forever" promo was utterly surrealistic, featuring disorienting visual effects like jump-cuts, X-ray simulation, and tape reverse. It was filmed, not in the grounds of the Liverpool children's home Strawberry Field in which Lennon had played as a child, but in Knole Park, Sevenoaks, Kent with the colorfully dressed Beatles confronting a broken piano in a tree. Similarly, The Beatles did not have the inclination to visit the real-life Penny Lane in Allerton, Liverpool after which that song was named but Goldmann did film the namechecked barber's shop and shelter in the middle of the roundabout. Instead, John Lennon walked down Angel Lane, Stratford, London and joined the other Beatles for a ride on horseback. The air of newness about both the films and the songs they were selling was completed by the fact that The Beatles were being seen with their new moustaches in an official product for the first time.

Many think that pop videos started with Queen's "Bohemian Rhapsody" but, once again, The Beatles were there first.
Spencer Leigh

Date February 13, 1967

Country UK

Director Peter Goldmann

Why It's Key Pioneering promotional films.

Key Album *Sgt. Pepper's Lonely Hearts Club Band* The Beatles

The first Beatles album to be recorded after their decision to quit touring, *Sgt. Pepper's Lonely Hearts Club Band*, released on June 1, 1967, took the studio experimentation of their *Revolver* (1966) to giddy new heights. A dazzlingly innovative, incredibly ambitious offering, it effectively established the LP record as an artform. It also set new standards for artwork and production, inspired a raft of concept albums (it was presented as though a performance by the fictional band of the title), popularized the gatefold sleeve, and brought avant-garde influences into mainstream popular music.

Sgt. Pepper… was greeted as the word: prominent critic/playwright Kenneth Tynan inadvertently captured the hyperbole surrounding the release when he claimed it to be "a decisive moment in the history of Western civilization." Some 40 years later, however, opinion on the merits of *Sgt. Pepper…* is rather more polarized. Although it was adjudged by *Rolling Stone*

magazine in 2003 to be the greatest album of all time, non-believers consider it to be a triumph of form over content and a long way from being even the best Beatles LP, even if few doubt that eerie album closer "A Day In The Life" represents a Fabs high watermark. Nevertheless, for many admirers it remains not only the apotheosis of the psychedelic era but of rock music per se. It has also entered the language as shorthand for an act's most ambitious, defining offering.

David Wells

Release Date June 1, 1967

Nationality UK

Tracklisting Sgt. Pepper's Lonely Hearts Club Band, With A Little Help From My Friends, Lucy In The Sky With Diamonds, Getting Better, Fixing A Hole, She's Leaving Home, Being For The Benefit Of Mr. Kite!, Within You Without You, When I'm Sixty-Four, Lovely Rita, Good Morning Good Morning, Sgt. Pepper's Lonely Hearts Club Band (reprise), A Day In The Life

Why It's Key Arguably the greatest album ever.

Key Song "White Rabbit" Jefferson Airplane

Jazz and blues songs had long included allusions to drugs but when it began to be suspected in the '60s that artists with much younger constituencies were slipping drug references into their lyrics, all hell broke loose.

Songs as innocent as "Puff The Magic Dragon" came under scrutiny for hidden meanings. The Byrds were censured for "Eight Miles High," even though it was about an airplane flight. A more "deserving" target was The Smoke's "My Friend Jack" from 1967, banned by the BBC because the line "My friend Jack eats sugar lumps" referenced a method of consuming LSD. So was The Beatles' "Lucy In The Sky With Diamonds," on the grounds that its title reduced to the acronym "LSD", although the mid-June 1967 admission of acid consumption by Paul McCartney was what led to that witch-hunt.

Ironically when Jefferson Airplane's atmospheric, bolero-driven "White Rabbit" entered the U.S. singles

chart on July 1, 1967, the LSD allusions ("One pill makes you larger and one pill makes you small… ") were inescapable but it was not banned. This was probably because every reference in its lyric came directly from the much-loved children's classic *Alice's Adventures In Wonderland*: everything in "White Rabbit" was frequently read to millions of children by their parents. "Alice takes mushrooms," mischievously pointed out Grace Slick, frontwoman of this San Francisco group and song composer, "smokes a hookah, bites some kind of stuff that's around, like a big pill."

Johnny Black

Release Date June 1967

Nationality USA

Composer Grace Slick

Why It's Key The first Top 10 hit to include undenied drug references.

Key Song "A Whiter Shade Of Pale"
Procul Harum

With its Bach-influenced Hammond organ and enigmatic lyric, "A Whiter Shade Of Pale" – which reached No. 1 on the UK charts on June 10, 1967 – has a good claim to be the song that invented classical pop. It was certainly a perfect record for the summer of love, its chart topping success occurring almost simultaneously with the release of The Beatles' *Sgt. Pepper…* , which also had previous critics of post-Elvis popular music grudgingly (sometimes ecstatically) acknowledging that the form could aspire to the same melodic and intellectual heights of Beethoven and Mozart.

Sextet Procul Harum recorded "A Whiter Shade Of Pale" in the spring of 1967. The songwords of Keith Reid – the band's lyricist but a non-perfoming member – were dazzling, talking of skipping the light fandango, millers telling tales, and sixteen vestal virgins. The title phrase, though, had more prosaic origins, being a British term for a state of drunkenness. The air of surrealism was heightened by the stately melody of vocalist/pianist Gary Brooker, which used Bach's "Air On A G String" as a springboard. The record also went Top 5 in the United States.

Though it was never in dispute that the haunting organ work of Matthew Fisher was key to the record's brilliance, few expected the suit he filed decades later against Gary Brooker and his publisher, claiming that he cowrote its music. In December 2006, Fisher was awarded a 40 per cent share of "A Whiter Shade Of Pale" but denied past royalties.

Giancarlo Susanna

Release Date May 1967

Nationality UK

Composers Gary Brooker, Keith Reid, Matthew Fisher

Why It's Key A summer of love anthem whose story ended in enmity.

Opposite Gary Brooker of Procul Harum

Key Event
Monterey International Pop Festival

Rock scribe Robert Christgau summed it up as "the first pow-wow of the Love Crowd" but Monterey Pop's real claim to fame was not as the first music festival nor even the first rock festival. It rode the coat-tails of, to name a few, the Newport Folk Festival, the Windsor Jazz and Blues Festival and, of course, the Monterey Jazz Festival. Closest in spirit to Monterey Pop, however, the Fantasy Faire and Magic Mountain Music Fest, featuring Jefferson Airplane, The Doors, Smokey Robinson, The Byrds, and others had recently drawn 15,000 flower-powered revelers to Mount Tamalpais, north of San Francisco.

Organized largely by John Phillips of The Mamas And The Papas along with producer/mogul Lou Adler, the three-day event of Monterey Pop – which began on June 16, 1967 – made the quantum leap by thinking globally. First, they sourced acts from all over the world – Otis Redding and Janis Joplin from the United States, The Jimi Hendrix Experience and The Who from the UK, Ravi Shankar from India, and Hugh Masekela from South Africa. Second they mixed the musical styles, with rock, pop, blues, soul, folk, and much more represented by acts including Simon and Garfunkel, Booker T, The Byrds, Lou Rawls, The Association, Canned Heat, Buffalo Springfield, and Butterfield Blues Band – all of them playing for free. Finally, they marketed the entire event with a movie (originally planned as a TV special) that took the legend to a mass audience. The Monterey template enabled Woodstock, Glastonbury, and the rest to put full-blown, inclusive festivals firmly onto the international map.

Johnny Black

Date June 16, 1967

Country USA

Why It's Key The first popular music festival as modern audiences define the concept.

Key Song "Society's Child (Baby I've Been Thinking)" Janis Ian

A troubled teenager's savage indictment of what she saw as America's racism and hypocrisy, "Society's Child (Baby I've Been Thinking)" became a U.S. Top 20 hit during the summer of love.

Written by 15-year-old Janis Ian as she waited to see her school guidance counselor, the song's recording was financed by black music specialists Atlantic Records, but, apparently losing their nerve, the company returned the master tape to Ian. Instead, "Society's Child… " – produced by Shangri-Las mentor and melodrama maestro George "Shadow" Morton – was released in mid-1966 by Verve Forecast. It flopped, but the label believed they had a major record on their hands, and they reissued it a couple of times.

When Leonard Bernstein featured "Society's Child… " on his April 1967 television special *Inside Pop: The Rock Revolution*, the song's shocking lyrical thrust – an interracial relationship forbidden by the white girl's mother and frowned upon by her peers and teachers – caused a sensation. It entered the U.S. Top 40 on June 17, 1967, making No. 14, but was banned by many radio stations as subversive, particularly at a time of so much civil rights unrest. DJs who broadcast it ran the risk of being fired or attacked by outraged members of the public: indeed, one Louisiana DJ was allegedly murdered after playing it on air. The song failed to provoke the same furore in Britain, where it was given a powerful, Vanilla Fudge-style hard rock treatment by Spooky Tooth.

David Wells

Release Date August 1966

Nationality USA

Composer Janis Ian

Why It's Key Teenager lambasts her "elders and betters."

Key Event
Two Rolling Stones go down

On February 5, 1967, British Sunday newspaper *The News Of The World* alleged that their reporter had seen Mick Jagger take LSD at a party (obviously not a Stones fan, the journalist had actually confused Jagger with Brian Jones). Jagger immediately denied the story and announced his intention to sue the paper for defamation of character – an ill-advised decision, considering Jagger was hardly an abstainer, drug-wise. A week later, the drug squad acted on a *News Of The World* tip-off and raided Keith Richards' country house. Jagger was charged with possession of four pep pills, Richards with allowing his home to be used for the consumption of illegal drugs.

In late June, their trial began. As expected, both were found guilty, but the severity of the sentences – 12 months imprisonment for Richards, three for Jagger – caused a public outcry. Such a flagrant abuse of the judicial system shocked even pro-establishment figures. *The Times* weighed in with the now-legendary editorial "Who Breaks A Butterfly On A Wheel?" (not the result of some blinding acid, but a quotation from eighteenth-century poet, Alexander Pope). An appeal was duly lodged, and, on July 31, Jagger's sentence was reduced to probation and Richards' conviction was quashed. Another Stone, Brian Jones, also spent a night in jail that year before a drug-related prison sentence was quashed but harassment of the band – clearly considered upstarts needing crushing – would continue.

David Wells

Date June 29, 1967

Country UK

Why It's Key The law fought rock 'n' roll – and rock 'n' roll won.

Opposite **Mick Jagger**

Key Person
Engelbert Humperdinck

Though the double-whammy magnificence of The Beatles' single "Penny Lane/Strawberry Fields Forever" is today disputed by few, the weirdness of the band's single of February 1967 was difficult for some Fab Four devotees to get to grips with and it became the first Beatles single to fail to make No. 1 in their home country for four years. When on March 4, 1967, "Release Me" by Engelbert Humperdinck beat it to the top spot, it conformed the opinions of those who thought The Beatles had gone a step too far.

An Anglo-Indian crooner, born in Madras in 1936 and schooled in the clubs of Leicester, England, Arnold George Dorsey was an unlikely titan toppler. But "Release Me" – a desperate plea for divorce which also made No. 4 in America – was the quintessence of his old-fashioned but popular style. Dorsey had been renamed Engelbert Humperdinck after a German composer by manager Gordon Mills. His overwrought, Johnnie Ray-esque '50s revival of an Esther Phillips hit became the UK's biggest single in 1967, the year we now remember as that of the hippie summer of love, psychedelia, and *Sgt. Pepper*… but Humperdinck's success was based on housewives' taste for emotional ballads and conservatively presented masculinity, not trendy youth culture. Seven straight Top 5 hits followed but he later concentrated on hugely profitable touring. Billed as the "King Of Romance," he conquered Las Vegas alongside friend Elvis Presley and Tom Jones. Although he is a byword for cheesy excess, to date he has sold over 130 million records.

Chris Goodman

Role Recording Artist

Date 1967

Nationality India/UK

Why It's Key The man who beat The Beatles.

Key Album *The Velvet Underground and Nico* The Velvet Underground and Nico

One of the most influential recordings in history, *The Velvet Underground and Nico* was totally overlooked when originally released in March 1967. Seen then as another Andy Warhol gimmick – the artist nominally produced the album (with Tom Wilson) and designed its crassly phallic peelable banana cover – its impact continues to be felt on popular music.

The product of an antagonistic creative fulcrum – songwriter and guitarist Lou Reed, viola player and sound explorer John Cale – its music juxtaposed rock 'n' roll with the avant garde, American roots, and the European tradition (Reed was a New Yorker, Cale a Welshman). Reed's lyrics meanwhile tackled themes never before addressed in rock. The icy voice of German model Nico (interpolated at the insistence of Warhol) broadened the texture on three tracks. Maureen Tucker provided drums and Sterling Morrison rhythm guitar.

A record that started with the hangover feeling of "Sunday Morning" and ended on the epic distorted rant "European Son" clearly knew no boundaries. In between, the darker side of life was explored, whether it be the junkie's lot ("I'm Waiting For The Man," "Heroin"), misogyny ("There She Goes Again," "Femme Fatale"), or sadomasochism ("Venus in Furs"). Even Dylan had draped his stretching of rock's boundaries in simile and metaphor. *The Velvet Underground And Nico* told it like it was, bluntly and baldly, and thereby announced that rock could be an artform as encompassing and concerned with the contradictions of humanity as a great novel, play, or film.

Ignacio Julià

Release Date March 1967

Nationality USA

Tracklisting Sunday Morning, I'm Waiting For The Man, Femme Fatale, Venus In Furs, Run Run Run, All Tomorrow's Parties, Heroin, There She Goes Again, I'll Be Your Mirror, The Black Angel's Death Song, European Son

Why It's Key Brought a new depth to rock.

Opposite Nico

Key Song **"Painter Man"**
The Creation

The Creation had two modest chart entries in their native UK before imploding. Not, one might imagine, the credentials of a band who made much impact on the music scene but The Creation are notable for the quite extraordinary breadth of the posthumous influence of their small catalog of recordings.

They were superstars in West Germany, the only country at the time to recognize their brilliance: May 15, 1967, marks the point at which "Painter Man" reached its peak of No. 2 in the country's chart. Kenny Pickett (vocals), Eddie Phillips (guitar), Bob Garner (bass), and Jack Jones (drums) debuted in June 1966 with the fiery "Making Time," a class warfare anthem featuring Phillips' trademark of a bowed electric guitar. "Painter Man" was even better, an anthemic lament of an ungainfully unemployed art school graduate. While Pickett complained "Who would be a painter man?" Phillips attacked his guitar strings with complete abandon, producing with the bow a sound like a

revving buzzsaw. The record failed to make the UK Top 20 but the song's empathic beat appealed to the Teutonic taste for rigid rhythms.

Despite personnel changes, even more startling mixtures of pop and the avant garde emerged from the Creation camp before their dissolution in 1968. Pickett became a roadie and Phillips a bus conductor. German record producer Frank Farian provided a fairytale ending to the story when his mega-successful charges Boney M covered "Painter Man" in 1978.

Sean Egan

Date May 15, 1967

Nationality UK

Composers Kenny Pickett, Eddie Phillips

Why It's Key An innovative classic – but only big in Germany.

Key Person
Jacques Brel

Singer-songwriter Jacques Brel never placed an album on the U.S. charts but his songs were recorded by a staggering array of artists ranging from Frank Sinatra to Joan Baez to Scott Walker to David Bowie (whose version of the sleazy "Amsterdam" was the B-side of his UK hit "Sorrow"). From Belgium originally, Brel was born in 1929 but it wasn't until his 1954 move to Paris that he began inching toward stardom, building his reputation in the city's cabarets. His break came in 1956 when his song "Quand On N'A Pas Que L'Amour" became a hit.

By the early '60s, Brel had become an internationally regarded singer and writer despite doing that singing and writing almost exclusively in French. His success in America, however, came largely via other singers interpreting his music, particularly Terry Jacks' translated cover of "Le Moribond," which became "Seasons In the Sun." Many Brel aficionados, though, consider English translations

of his songs to be ridiculously prosaic compared to their poetic splendor in the original.

When he played what he insisted would be his final concert on May 16, 1967, his fans were shocked, and the long-running off-Broadway production *Jacques Brel Is Alive And Living In Paris* (1968) pondered Brel's reasons for giving up live performance while also presenting many of his songs in new translations. He continued to record sporadically and worked in film and theater, dying of cancer in 1978.

Jeff Tamarkin

Role Recording Artist

Date 1967

Nationality Belgium

Why It's Key One of the most popular and imaginative musical artists Belgium or France has ever produced.

Opposite Jacques Brel

Key People
The Rascals

"Blue-eyed soul" was a phrase devised to describe the product of white acts whose vocalists emoted like – and copied the stylistic tricks of – black singers. A spate of them sprang up in the mid-'60s but The Rascals were by far the most significant.

The first hit of keyboardist Felix Cavaliere, guitarist Gene Cornish, vocalist Eddie Brigati, and drummer Dino Danelli was the frantic cover "Good Lovin'," released, like all their early records, under the name The Young Rascals. They were soon writing their own singles.

When "Groovin'" – a gorgeous, languid paean to the joys of lovemaking on a summer's afternoon – made U.S. No. 1 on May 20, 1967, it was their first self-written U.S. chart topper. Other hits included the tremulous "How Can I Be Sure" (which David Cassidy took a cover of to the top in the UK in 1972) and the lovely "It's A Beautiful Morning." The record that probably summed up the band, though, in their spiritual and musical bridging of racial divides (they refused to play on segregated bills) was "People Got To Be Free," an anthemic, horn-punctuated call for global unity.

This was the second single released under their shortened sobriquet The Rascals. This desire to be seen to have matured was reflected in the increasingly adult, freeform nature of some of their album tracks on pretentiously named opuses like *Freedom Suite* (1969), which, truth be told, was a tedious development. Their heart, though, was always in the right place.
Sean Egan

Role Recording Artists

Date 1967

Country USA

Why It's Key Trailblazers in "blue-eyed soul."

Opposite **The Rascals**

Key Event
The launch of *Rolling Stone* magazine

There has been rock 'n' roll journalism at least since the music seemed important enough to cover as news. But it was the work of outsiders – writers and editors who weren't part of the music's audience and who often had contempt for it. Meanwhile, the mid-'60s fan magazines covered rock and pop mostly in a contrived, gossip-driven manner, and that probably suited most musicians of the period.

By 1967, however, rock musicians were a different breed, not only socially conscious but aware of their power in shaping the perceptions of their young but decidedly not dumb audience. The music and its fans had grown up. And that's when Jann Wenner and Ralph J. Gleason brought out *Rolling Stone* magazine. Named partly after a Dylan song, party after The Rolling Stones, and partly after a Muddy Waters number, it debuted on November 9, 1967. It grew out of the hippie culture in San Francisco but applied serious journalistic standards to the writing and editing. *Rolling Stone* kept the record labels at arm's length and in its original incarnation never even acknowledged publicists. It covered rock the way the best jazz journals treated jazz, with the added bonus that rock had a social relevance to dissect that jazz did not, hence the articles about political issues perceived to be associated with rock.

Meaningful youth culture had clearly arrived.
Bruce Eder

Date November 9, 1967

Country USA

Why It's Key The first publication to try explaining both the "how" and the "why" of rock music and its listeners.

Key Album *Forever Changes*
Love

For all the lush string arrangements, *Forever Changes*, Love's magnum opus from November 1967, was filled with dark songs asking awkward questions. Southern California's Love had made their name as a raucous electric band, and though the album is built around acoustic instruments, an underlying toughness prevails (it was once described as "punk with strings").

Flamenco-tinged opener "Alone Again Or," with its distinctive mariachi horns, sets a deceptively light atmosphere immediately dispelled by "A House Is Not A Motel" (sample lyric: "The bells from the school of war will be ringing"), a caustic reflection on civil unrest capped off by a vicious guitar solo. A sense of simmering threat purveys the album ("The Red Telephone" is named for the Cold War-era hotline between America and the USSR) created primarily by main songwriter Arthur Lee, though the deft orchestration throughout – and guitarist Bryan MacLean's quieter, poignant songs – provide temporary respite. At the time, Lee was convinced he would soon die (he lived until 2006), and though "You Set The Scene" offers a bright, brass-driven coda to the album, it is his darker visions that characterize the overall mood of the work.

Although it only made No. 154 on *Billboard* (although in the UK it got as high as No. 24), this understated, carefully crafted, beautifully played album has remained a critics' favorite for decades, an unsettling psychedelic gem, a brooding masterpiece, and the definitive statement of Lee's mercurial talent.
Robert Dimery

Release Date
November 1967

Nationality USA

Tracklisting Alone Again Or, A House Is Not A Motel, Andmoreagain, The Daily Planet, Old Man, The Red Telephone, Maybe The People Would Be The Times Or Between Clark And Hilldale, Live And Let Live, The Good Humor Man He Sees Everything Like This, Bummer In The Summer, You Set The Scene

Why It's Key An album that addressed the uncertainty and strife underlying the sunny '60s.

Key Event
The Move versus Harold Wilson

When in 1965 British Prime Minister Harold Wilson made The Beatles Members of the British Empire for their services to their country's industry, he was clearly and shamelessly courting the youth vote.

However, in 1967, Wilson learnt that pop stars were not puppets to be easily manipulated. Rumors had long swirled in Britain of an affair between Wilson and his redoubtable secretary Marcia Falkender. In August of that year, pop group The Move – an ensemble whose style was hard-pop inflected with classical influences and whose creative director was future Wizzard leader Roy Wood (future ELO leader Jeff Lynne would later hook up with the group) – released their third single, "Flowers In The Rain." They produced a postcard to promote the single which featured a cartoon of Wilson and Falkender in bed together. Wilson sued. In today's climate, the band might have contested the writ but in 1967, taking on the government of the country in the courts was unthinkable. On October 11, The Move's lawyers apologized in court for the libel. They were forced to pay costs and to donate all the royalties from the record (a UK No. 2) in perpetuity to charities of Wilson's choice. Though The Move emerged both bowed and defeated, the case provided a salutary lesson to Wilson and all other politicians who thought that pop might be a force they could easily harness to their own advantage. Far from being cowed by this case, from hereon, pop would only get more irreverent and anti-establishment.
Sean Egan

Date October 11, 1967

Country UK

Why It's Key Pop takes on the establishment and loses – for now.

Key Performance *Hair*
stage musical

In 1967, the razzmatazz of Broadway and the reality of modern headbanned, bead-bedecked, hirsute youth were worlds apart. Hence the rejections experienced by the creators of *Hair* – book authors/lyric writers James Rado and Jerome Ragni and melody manufacturer Galt MacDermot – when they hawked around the project that aimed to bridge that gap.

Hair, a musical about hippies facing being sent to Vietnam, reached Broadway at exactly the right time. Though it caught the tail-end of the year of the summer of love by opening off-Broadway on October 17, 1967, by the time an expanded and revised version reached Broadway the following April (the first instance of such a graduation), America was experiencing its most divided, fractious year since the Civil War.

The creators held nothing back in the show, which featured theater's first full frontal nudity and the sort of profanity rare on Broadway. Song topics were also deliberately provocative ("Colored Spade," "Hashish," "Sodomy"). The project would have died a death, though, were there not both strength in storyline (with a surprisingly realistic, downbeat ending) and song (of which there were an unusually high number), the most famous of which being the anthemic title number, the Zodiac referencing "Aquarius," and the litany-like "Ain't Got No" (a hit for Nina Simone).

So much so, that subsequent revivals and tours have proven it has a resonance for generations with no living memory of long hair as a symbol of rebellion.
Sean Egan

Opening Night
October 17, 1967

Country USA

Director Tom O'Horgan

Cast James Rado, Gerome Ragni, Shelly Plimpton

Composer Galt MacDermot, James Rado, Gerome Ragni

Why It's Key The voice of the counterculture comes to mainstream musical theater.

Key Performance *The Jungle Book*
the movie

The Jungle Book is an (of course loose) adaptation of Rudyard Kipling's stories about the feral child Mowgli. In the film, he is raised by a wolf as her own. A few years later, it is learned that a ferocious man-eating tiger has returned to the jungle and Mowgli's animal friends realize he must be escorted to the human village where he and his kind can be protected. But playful Mowgli likes the jungle too much and breaks free of his guardians, which leads to comic and suspenseful complications.

Songwriter Terry Gilkyson, who had written many Disney numbers (most prodigiously for the anthology television series *The Wonderful World Of Disney*) was originally commissioned to write the score. After his delivery of several completed songs, though, Walt Disney deemed them too dark and – only in Hollywood, folks – "too Kipling." The Sherman Brothers, who had written the feelgood score to Mary Poppins, were called in and engaged on condition that – only in Hollywood, folks – they not read Kipling's book. Ironically, when *The Jungle Book* was released on October 18, 1967, it was Gilkyson's one surviving song, a bouncy number for the friendly grizzly Baloo, his punningly titled "The Bare Necessities," that was nominated for an Oscar. Other popular numbers include the sinuous "Trust in Me" for Kaa the viper, the barbershop stylings of "That's What Friends Are For" (the villains in close harmony), and the orangutan rag, "I Wanna Be Like You."
David Spencer

Movie Release Date
October 18, 1967

Nationality USA

Director Wolfgang Reitherman

Cast The voices of Phil Harris, Sebastian Cabot, Louis Prima

Composers Richard M. Sherman, Robert B. Sherman, Terry Gilkyson

Why It's Key A philistine and farcical creative process but a wonderful result.

Key Album *Born Under A Bad Sign*
Albert King

Blues and soul had dovetailed on occasion ever since soul music began to truly take shape in the early '60s, with the blues-soul concoctions of the three Kings – B. B., Freddie, and Albert – wielding the most enduring influence, if only because their guitar-oriented sounds had a far bigger impact on mainstream rock music. Albert King might not be as well known as B. B., but his influence certainly traveled far and wide in both the R&B and British rock scenes, particularly with the material on the 1967 album *Born Under A Bad Sign*. Its commercial impact was modest but its consistent support by Stax Records house band Booker T. And The M.G.s and the brass of the Memphis Horns was a bridge builder.

The LP was actually a collection of material (some previously released on singles) cut at five sessions between March 1966 and June 1967, rather than recorded specifically as an album. But *Born Under A Bad Sign* hung together well, and King's stinging guitar and assured vocal style found particularly receptive ears among British rock groups, with Cream making "Born Under A Bad Sign" into one of their signature tunes, Eric Clapton's guitar in particular owing debts to King's searing sustained tones. Less famously, John Mayall's Bluesbreakers (with a young Mick Taylor on lead guitar) soon covered the LP's "Oh, Pretty Woman," with Free tackling "The Hunter" and Santana "As The Years Go Passing By."

Richie Unterberger

Release Date 1967

Nationality USA

Tracklisting Born Under A Bad Sign, Crosscut Saw, Kansas City, Oh Pretty Woman, Down Don't Bother Me, The Hunter, I Almost Lost My Mind, Personal Manager, Laundromat Blues, As The Years Go Passing By, The Very Thought Of You

Why It's Key A landmark in paving the way for soul-blues-rock crossover appeal.

Key Event **Country Joe McDonald is attacked by Vietnam Vets**

The 1968 Democratic convention was seen by some of the more radical elements of the U.S. Left as a chance to get their voices truly heard. The Vietnam War was raging, and not enough progress was being made toward peace and social justice. The Youth International Party (Yippies), spearheaded by Abbie Hoffman and Jerry Rubin, were hoping hundreds of thousands of demonstrators would come to Chicago – augmented, ideally, by a phalanx of top rock bands – to protest the reigning Democratic administration's policies, and perhaps even influence their election platform.

Ultimately, however, just a few thousand demonstrators traveled there, where they were overwhelmed by the well-prepared police, who clubbed and bloodied protesters on national television. Frightened by the prospect of violence, most of the rock bands stayed away as well, though a few of the most countercultural acts – including Phil Ochs, The Fugs, and The MC5 – did show up. On August 24, 1968, Country Joe McDonald, leader of Country Joe And The Fish, suffered blows from some veterans of the very conflict he was protesting. They seemed strangely unmoved by his "I Feel Like I'm Fixin' To Die," considered by many the classic Vietnam War protest rocker. The clashes at the convention dealt yet deeper blows to the idealism of the peace movement and the faith in nonviolence to effect social change, both within and without the musical community.

Richie Unterberger

Date August 24, 1968

Country USA

Why It's Key Showed that rock artists' social conscience was not always appreciated by those whom they sought to help.

Opposite Country Joe McDonald

Key Song **"Hey Jude"**
The Beatles

"Hey Jude," released in the UK on August 26, 1968, constituted a poetic corresponding bookend to "She Loves You," the quintessential early Beatles record. Like that composition, "Hey Jude" is a song in the third person directed at a male friend who is not showing the dedication he should in pursuing the love of his life. (The song famously started out as "Hey Jules," an attempt by McCartney to comfort Julian Lennon, son of John, on his parents' separation but that is not its subject.) However, that The Beatles had grown immeasurably since the appearance of "She Loves You" – even though it was just five years previously – is indicated by the utter contrast of everything else about the two records.

Though the Beatle imprimatur of three-part harmonies remained – albeit measured here, as opposed to giddy on "She Loves You" – the tight pop patterns of "She Loves You" are nowhere to be seen in a track with a frequently opaque lyric, a running time of over seven minutes, and a chanting coda longer than the "main" part of the song.

The inaugural release of The Beatles' Apple record company, the record was actually the biggest-selling Beatles product to date. That such a quasi avant garde single should come to seem mainstream is testament to the way that the Fab Four's perennial wonderful craftsmanship could mesmerize the world into going along with their every innovation.

Sean Egan

Release Date
August 26, 1968

Nationality UK

Composers John Lennon, Paul McCartney

Why It's Key The measure of the startling artistic changes that The Beatles hurtled through in their career.

Key Song **"Born To Be Wild"**
Steppenwolf

In 1968, rock 'n' roll was becoming harder and more urgent, reflecting the uncertainty and danger of the times – and Steppenwolf's "Born To Be Wild," which entered the *Billboard* Top 40 on July 20, 1968, sealed the band's legacy in the annals of an angry counterculture with its loud guitar riffs, dense drumming, and outlaw lyrics.

Written by Mars Bonfire (aka Dennis Edmonton), the song's second verse references "heavy metal thunder," the first time the phrase "heavy metal" appeared in song. Steppenwolf's use of the term, first used colloquially by Beat poets Herman Hesse and Williams S. Burroughs, coined the name of the emerging genre – one that dominated the U.S. charts throughout the '70s.

As Steppenwolf singer John Kay commented, "Our philosophy was to hit 'em hard, make your point, and move on." With its aggressive guitar riffs and lyrics that challenged both mainstream and counterculture values and prized individual freedom above all else, "Born To Be Wild," from the album *Steppenwolf* (1968), paved the way for bands like Led Zeppelin and Black Sabbath, and even now, for bands like the atmospherically heavy HIM. It also provided the perfect sonic complement to the influential Dennis Hopper/Peter Fonda biker flick *Easy Rider* (1969).

Sara Farr

Release Date July 1968

Nationality USA

Composer Mars Bonfire

Why It's Key The song that gave Heavy Metal its name.

Opposite **Steppenwolf**

Key Song "I Heard It Through The Grapevine" Marvin Gaye

A tour de force by Motown producer Norman Whitfield and songwriter Barrett Strong, this had already been a U.S. No. 2 for Gladys Knight and the Pips in 1967 but Marvin Gaye's version went all the way to the top in the United States on December 14, 1968, in a radical reinterpretation.

A minor-key drama, with Motown legend James Jamerson laying down a particularly doomy bass under horror movie strings, Gaye's recording contrasts sharply with Knight's more bombastic interpretation. Gaye agonizes that his lover has returned to her ex-boyfriend and worse, he has found out only through local gossip. Recorded in a key just above Gaye's range, it sees him always reaching for the high notes, creating a perpetual anguish complemented by sympathetic female backing harmonies. The tapped bongos and electric piano seem to taunt him and, trapped in a world of paranoia, Gaye sounds like a man desperately trying to keep his emotions under control, occasionally hitting an anguished word before resigning himself to his fate. After this haunted performance, there was no doubting the song was forever Gaye's. Rock critic Dave Marsh went as far as to state in a 1989 book that it was the greatest single ever made.

The song reached No. 1 in Britain in 1969 but is now better known in that country for soundtracking a famous 1985 Levis jeans commercial in which model Nick Kamen strips off in a launderette. The advert returned the song to the UK Top 10.

Chris Goodman

U.S. No. 1 Date
December 14, 1968

Nationality USA

Composer Barrett Strong, Norman Whitfield

Why It's Key Showed how a song can be appropriated.

Key Album *Ogden's Nut Gone Flake* The Small Faces

They'd scored massive UK hits with the likes of "Sha La La La Lee" and the chart-topping "All Or Nothing" but, by the end of 1966, soul-pop merchants The Small Faces were growing increasingly dissatisfied with their reputation as a teenybopper act. Craving artistic freedom and critical respect, they left Decca in favor of Rolling Stones manager Andrew Oldham's own, rather more hip label, Immediate. With unlimited studio time at their disposal, they pieced together *Ogden's Nut Gone Flake*, an album whose second side revolved around a storyline of Happiness Stan's search for the "missing" half of the moon. The storyline was thin – or an inchoate allegory – but it was rock's first.

An archetypal period piece, *Ogden's...* gleefully smashed all the trappings of the era into one glorious, amorphous musical stew, with proto-heavy metal riffing ("Song Of A Baker," "Rollin' Over") and music hall pastiche ("Happydaystoytown," the ribald "Rene") existing cheek-by-jowl. Bolstered by an aggressive marketing campaign, comedian Stanley Unwin's trademark gobbledegook patter (which provided suitably surreal links on the narrative side of the album), and an attention-grabbing, award-winning circular sleeve design (inspired by a rectangular Victorian tobacco tin for Ogden's Nut Brown Flake), *Ogden's...* was hailed as the group's magnum opus, topping the UK charts on June 29, 1968, and siring a major hit single in the riotous, cockney-fied "Lazy Sunday." Ironically, the album was The Small Faces' last. They split at the beginning of the following year.

David Wells

UK No. 1 Date
June 29, 1968

Nationality UK

Tracklisting Ogdens' Nut Gone Flake, Afterglow, Long Agos And Worlds Apart, Rene, Song Of A Baker, Lazy Sunday, Happiness Stan, Rollin' Over, The Hungry Intruder, The Journey, Mad John, Happydaystoytown

Why It's Key First album whose songs were linked by narrative.

Key Album *In-A-Gadda-Da-Vida*
Iron Butterfly

The Animals started it, driving "The House of the Rising Sun" towards the five-minute mark. Dylan shattered that with "Like A Rolling Stone," The Stones broke ten minutes with the epic "Goin' Home." Dylan reclaimed his crown with "Desolation Row." Both Love and Dylan then covered a whole LP-side with "Revelation" and "Sad Eyed Lady Of The Lowlands" respectively, but it was only when you checked your watch that you realized just how short Dylan's LP side was – 11:20.

Enter Iron Butterfly, an L.A. quartet whose debut album, *Heavy*, had already established them among the loudest, hardest bands around. Now they were chasing records as well, following Dylan's lead by devoting one full side of their sophomore album, released in July 1968 on Atco, to its title track.

Five short rockers preluded the monster, and "Termination," "My Mirage," and so on were great, Butterfly-business-as-usual. Today, however, they are on nobody's lips except those of Butterfly aficionados. They were simply the appetizer. "In-A-Gadda-Da-Vida" was a mystical incantation that went on… and on… and on, through shifting movements and behemothic convolutions, sometimes riffing, sometimes howling, but always coming back to that growling title chant, reputedly derived from a mishearing of its intended title, "In The Garden Of Eden."

At 17:05, it finally ceased. Even back then nobody was claiming esthetic brilliance for a piece of acid rock that began to date as quickly as it was made. Nonetheless, Iron Butterfly's place in history as pioneers of song length was assured.

Dave Thompson

Release Date July 1968

Nationality USA

Tracklisting Most Anything You Want, Flowers And Beads, My Mirage, Termination, Are You Happy, In A Gadda Da Vida

Why It's Key Goodbye to the three-minute pop song.

Key People
Family

A sheep in heat. A tortured cat. A drowning opera star. Nobody who came away from a Family concert could fail to have their own mental image of what singer Roger Chapman sounded like, but all were agreed on one point: Chapman sounded different.

But so did Family themselves. The Leicester-based five-piece had been around for a couple of years before they ventured down to London, and they blitzed the capital's braincells with music and lyrics that were a seething blend of pre-*Clockwork Orange* ultra-violence shot through with moments of beguiling calm and bewitching fragility. Even the unconverted confessed that Family ranked among the most original bands on the scene.

Music In A Doll's House, Family's first album from July 1968, was a Top 40 hit, and, though it's acknowledged as the band's masterpiece, was just the beginning. Over the next five years, before they split in 1973, Family retained their adventurousness, with each successive album sounding different. They were also uncategorizable: nobody was sure whether to label them hard rock or progressive. Unlike Dylan, who could overcome his shortcomings with venom ("Like A Rolling Stone") or warmth ("Lay Lady Lay"), Chapman could never make his voice approach orthodoxy but that didn't stop Family scoring some hit singles. But they, and their singer, still sounded like nothing else on earth.

Dave Thompson

Role Recording Artists

Date July 1968

Nationality UK

Why It's Key Vocalist Roger Chapman proved that a conventional singing voice was no longer a prerequisite for success.

Key Performance **Elvis Presley's "Comeback Special"** television show

It's hard to conceive of a time when Elvis Presley was considered anything less than an icon of popular culture. By late 1968, however, both his commercial and critical stock were at all-time lows. He hadn't made the U.S. Top 20 for more than two years and he'd been grinding out bad movies for so long that most of his fans had stopped going to see them. While there were occasional good singles and album tracks, his recorded output was similarly underachieving and unhip.

Even diehards weren't expecting his December 3, 1968, television special on the NBC network to be much more than a banal Christmas season celebration. Instead, miraculously, they saw the Elvis they wanted to see: a leather-clad rocker, singing with real guts and conviction and even performing songs with a couple of the musicians (guitarist Scotty Moore and drummer D. J. Fontana) who'd played on the seminal '50s recordings that made him, and rock, what it was.

Actually formally titled *Elvis*, the program is now, significantly, merely referred to as the "Comeback Special." It gave Presley's career a second wind that saw him return to his roots for several big hit singles and superior albums, as well as abandon movies for a return to the concert stage. In turn, it helped restore all of early rock 'n' roll to critical favor, a status it's never since lost.

Richie Unterberger

Date December 3, 1968

Country USA

Why It's Key The biggest rock 'n' roll star goes from has-been to contemporary artist with one broadcast.

Opposite **Elvis Presley**

Key Song **"Cinderella Rockefella"** Esther Abi Ofarim

No doubt there will be some who find it a shame that the first significant international success of Israeli pop should be the trans-European smash "Cinderella Rockefella." Such national embarrassment is misplaced.

"Cinderella Rockefella" was written in 1966 by Texan songwriter Mason Williams with Nancy Ames. The song's composers sang the song on a 1967 Smothers Brothers television show. It was the latter comedy team who provided the connection to Israeli husband and wife musical act Esther and Abi Ofarim, who supported the Smothers on a tour. The Ofarims – previously successful in West Germany and Israel – were the first to record the song and it broke them internationally.

The lyric – sung as a duet between an adoring couple – is based around one good joke (the observation that "You're the lady" sung in a colloquial manner sounds a bit like a Swiss yodel) and one pretty

feeble one (that "You're the fella that rocks me" can be turned into an allusion to the then-famous, now-slipping-into-history American oil baron and philanthropist John D. Rockefeller).

Deliberately reminiscent of the twinkle-eyed duet style of the old days of Tin Pan Alley and punctuated by regular blasts of tuba, the song said nothing but did it so engagingly that it made the top of the UK chart on March 2, 1968 and stayed there for three weeks.

Sean Egan

U.K. No. 1 Date March 2, 1968

Nationality Israel

Composer Mason Williams, Nancy Ames

Why It's Key Showed that the Middle East could provide delightfully mindless chart material as good as anything the West had to offer.

Key Person
Joey Levine

When "Yummy Yummy Yummy" by Ohio Express entered the *Billboard* Top 40 on May 18, 1968, nobody seemed to notice as it sailed to a U.S. No. 4 that the group's singer Doug Grassel sounded in concert nothing like he did on the record's vocal track. This was because said lead vocal was sung by Joey Levine, the song's composer. In deciding that the kids at whom the sing-song was aimed – a younger demographic than pop had ever previously sought – were not going to agonize about such things, nor the fact that session men played the instrumentation, Levine's producers Kasenetz and Katz had invented a new genre: bubblegum music.

A Long Island native born in 1947, Levine tended to cowrite with seasoned songsmith Art Resnick or Resnick's wife Kris. He milked the formula with follow-ups like "Chewy Chewy" and "Sweeter Than Sugar." However, "Gimme Gimme Good Lovin'," a driving rocker credited to fictional group Crazy Elephant, showed Levine had some musical gravitas, as did Levine and Art Resnick's joyous travelogue "Montego Bay," a hit for Bobby Bloom.

The collapse of Levine's friendship with Art Resnick caused a bit of a crisis in his career. It was resolved when an advertising executive asked him if he would like to write some jingles, a profession he continues in very successfully to this day. The unkind might equate Levine's bubblegum songs themselves to jingles but, like a good jingle, once heard they are indelible.
Sean Egan

Role Songwriter

Date May 18, 1968

Nationality USA

Why It's Key Both songwriter and bubblegum dispenser.

Key Person
Jimmy Webb

Born in Oklahoma, in 1964 the teenaged Jimmy Webb moved to California, where he worked briefly for Motown's publishing arm, Jobete Music. He then came to the attention of Johnny Rivers, who paired him with harmony group The Fifth Dimension. The joyous "Up, Up, And Away" gave Webb his first writing hit, but he inadvertently found his most notable interpreter when Glen Campbell cut a superb version of a song that he'd written for Rivers, "By The Time I Get To Phoenix."

That song is considered part of a spare, haunting Campbell-Webb trilogy along with "Wichita Lineman" (which entered the U.S. Top 40 on November 16, 1968) and "Galveston." "Where's The Playground Susie" was another uncanny pop masterpiece for the pair but Webb's most notorious composition during this golden period came with the outlandish imagery and epic arrangement of "MacArthur Park," a UK and U.S. Top Five hit for actor Richard Harris that introduced the seven-minute single several months before "Hey Jude."

Webb never quite achieved those heights again, yet, recording sporadically in his own right, he arranged and provided the songs for mostly excellent albums by Glen Campbell (the 1974 release *Reunion*) and Art Garfunkel (1978's *Watermark*, featuring the sumptuous "Crying In My Sleep") and was rediscovered in the '90s by a new generation of admirers, including R.E.M.; Jimmy Webb was the inspiration behind their "All The Way To Reno (You're Gonna Be A Star)."
David Wells

Role Songwriter

Date November 16, 1968

Nationality USA

Why It's Key The man who wrote instant standards that at the same time sounded anything like conventional hits.

Opposite Jimmy Webb

Key Performance *Zorbà*
stage musical

It was star Herschel Bernardi's impulse to musicalize the Nikos Kazantzakis novel *Zorbà The Greek*. Having established his Broadway draw, Tevye, as a favorite in *Fiddler On The Roof*, he'd been looking to create a role of his own, and galvanized by the popular 1964 film adaptation, got *Fiddler ...* librettist Joseph Stein on board. Together they approached *Fiddler...* producer Harold Prince to direct.

Prince was hesitant, though taken with the story's "embrace life, even its bleakness" philosophy, wondering if a musical version could establish a distinct identity, against the blockbuster movie. But upon a trip to Greece, he had the notion of a commenting Greek chorus, telling the tale in a café. His unique "way in" found, he signed John Kander (music) and Fred Ebb (lyrics), the celebrated songwriting team who had worked with him on *Cabaret*, another musical that employed similar storytelling techniques.

Despite a rousing score and positive notices, audiences seemed not prepared for the darkness of the show that opened at the Imperial Theater on November 17, 1968 – nor, ironically, for Bernardi to be so different from Tevye. Sales fell off, curtailing the run at 305 performances. In 1983, a revival opened with a lighter tone (the opening "Life is what you do" lyric was changed from "while you're waiting to die" to "'til the moment you die"), faring better on Broadway and on tour – but then, its commercial pull was the original film's stars, Anthony Quinn and Lila Kedrova.
David Spencer

Opening Night
November 17, 1968

Nationality USA

Director Harold Prince

Cast Herschel Bernardi, Maria Karnilova, John Cunningham

Composer John Kander, Fred Ebb

Why It's Key A musical whose dark heart audiences baulked at.

Key Album *Astral Weeks*
Van Morrison

It took 33 years after its November 1968 release to sell enough copies to merit a Gold award but long before then Van Morrison's first solo album proper had been ranked alongside Beatles, Beach Boys, and Bob Dylan classics as one of rock's greatest masterpieces.

A suite of eight songs, whose higlights are "Madame George" (possibly about a transvestite) and "Ballerina," *Astral Weeks* links to form a seamless whole of visionary intensity. Yet its creation proceeded from a sequence of working problems and experimental solutions that could not be guessed from the music's free-spirited craftsmanship – a blend of Van's voice and guitar, upright bass, vibraphone, flute, drums, and overdubbed strings, horns, and occasional drums – and mood of serene but ecstatic transcendence.

A music-steeped, working-class R&B singer from Belfast, Northern Ireland, Van Morrison had enjoyed success with Them, but had split the band in 1966 for solo independence. Yet by 1968 he was in legal dispute with a music publisher, only extricating himself by agreeing to include two old songs on his next album, which furthermore was to be made, by order of his record company, with a producer and musicians from the New York jazz world, none of whom he'd heard of, nor they of him. And they had three days to make the album. Yet this recipe for mutual misunderstanding under extreme time pressure gelled to create a sense of fervor and tranquility in perfect equipoise with time itself suspended.
Mat Snow

Release Date
November 1968

Nationality Ireland

Tracklisting Astral Weeks, Beside You, Sweet Thing, Cyprus Avenue, The Way Young Lovers Do, Madame George, Ballerina, Slim Slow Slider

Why It's Key Poetry, folk, jazz, and blue-eyed soul fused to innovative and ecstatic effect.

Key People
Holland Dozier Holland

When Motown sued songwriting trio Holland-Dozier-Holland for breach of contract on October 2, 1968 after they'd decided to leave it, it was an indication of how vital their talents had been to the label throughout the 1960s.

Lamont Dozier (born 1941) met Motown founder Berry Gordy in the late 1950s, when Gordy's sister's label, Anna Records, released his first solo single. Brothers Edward and Brian Holland (born 1939 and 1941 respectively) had enjoyed minor chart successes in their own right too, but it wasn't until 1962 – when Gordy incorporated the trio into his self-styled "hit making machine"– that they became a crucial element of the Motown Sound.

Dozier and Brian composed and produced the songs, while Eddie concentrated on writing lyrics and arranging vocals, with enduring classics from The Supremes ("Where Did Our Love Go?" and "Baby Love"), The Four Tops ("I Can't Help Myself") and Marvin Gaye ("How Sweet It Is") encapsulating the trademark carefree melodies, lush chord structures and graceful harmonies that the multi-talented threesome habitually created, resulting in dozens of chart hits. Their streamlined technique was itself a microcosm of the Motown factory method. Peculiarly, they were billed "Holland-Dozier-Holland", then later "H-D-H", but the familiarity that billing acquired from its presence on the labels of countless hit records soon made it seem natural.

The bitter lawsuit – H-D-H countersued Motown – was eventually settled out of court. Neither Motown nor H-D-H (who would soon splinter) were ever the same forces again.

Melissa Blease

Role Lyricist (Eddie Holland), Composers, Producers (Brian Holland and Lamont Dozier)

Date 1968

Nationality USA

Why It's Key A hit factory within a hit factory.

Key Song **"On The Road Again"**
Canned Heat

Though the blues originated in the United States, and there were a few credible American blues-rockers (such as The Paul Butterfield Blues Band and Captain Beefheart's early groups), the genre was dominated by UK stars like The Rolling Stones, Cream, Fleetwood Mac, and the Jeff Beck Group. At the very point where all those acts were at their peak, Canned Heat rushed into the Top 40 on September 7, 1968 with "On The Road Again," adapted from a little-known record by Floyd Jones.

Based in Southern California, far from the blues' southern Delta origins, Canned Heat demonstrated with this single that a young American white band could both play the blues credibly and add enough of a psychedelic rock sheen to make it relevant in the late '60s. The modern touches were supplied by a solid rock beat and a pseudo-Eastern tamboura drone, though Al Wilson's eerie high vocal sounded literally out of this world. Canned Heat were dedicated record collectors and folklorists as well as musicians; Wilson had even helped teach legendary Delta bluesman Son House how to play guitar again when House made a comeback on the '60s folk circuit. So it was little surprise they reached all the way back to the '20s for their next hit, "Going Up the Country," which adapted elements from country bluesman Henry Thomas' "Bull Doze Blues."

Richie Unterberger

Release Date 1968

Nationality USA

Composers Floyd Jones, Alan Wilson

Why It's Key Brought American blues-rock to the airwaves at a time when the form was dominated by British bands.

Key Album *Switched-On Bach*
Walter Carlos

Switched-On Bach was the first album to truly explore and popularize the synthesizer. A selection of works by classical composer J. S. Bach, it was performed using a Moog Modular synthesizer system. There was no MIDI technology or sequencing at the time, so Bach's notoriously complex and overlapping countermelodies were painstakingly translated and overdubbed onto an 8-track Ampex tape machine. The synthesizers were far harder to use than later models, and by thus creating a listenable and even enjoyable artificially generated version of Bach, Carlos achieved something astonishing.

Some found it twee, irreverent, or merely novelty but the release of this baroque, classical electronica had a great impact on the imagination of Carlos' contemporaries. While others would go on to record better pop and rock music using synthesizers, this was a breakthrough moment. Released on Columbia in 1968, the album entered the *Billboard* Top 40 on March 1, 1969, and eventually went platinum – the first classical album to do so.

Walter Carlos had a gender change in 1972 and future releases would be under the name Wendy Carlos. She worked on further classical reinterpretations as well as film soundtracks including *A Clockwork Orange* (for which she created the famous recording of "Beethoven's Ninth") and Disney's *Tron*. Her later work continued to break new ground in the use of synthesizers, but it was *Switched-On Bach* that made both her reputation and that of the synth as a viable musical instrument.
Hugh Barker

Release Date 1968

Nationality USA

Tracklisting Sinfonia To Cantata No. 29, Air On A G String, Orchestral Suite No. 3, Two-Part Invention In F Major/B Flat Major, Two-Part Invention In D Minor, Jesu, Joy Of Man's Desiring, Prelude And Fugue No. 7 In E Flat Major, Prelude And Fugue No. 2 In C Minor, Chorale Prelude, Wachet Auf, Brandenburg Concerto No. 3 In G Major – Allegro/Adagio/Allegro

Why It's Key The album that demonstrated the possibilities of the new synthesizer technology.

Opposite Walter Carlos

Key Event **Jeff Beck is reduced to tears by Jimmy Page's new band**

The Jeff Beck Group had been performing Willie Dixon's "You Shook Me" for a year before they recorded it on their debut LP *Truth*. Rewired, restructured, and decibel-boosted, a familiar old blues song was transformed into something else entirely. In years to come critics would credit Beck with inventing heavy metal, and "You Shook Me" was at the forefront of the novel alchemy.

But it was Led Zeppelin who perfected the infant sound. Beck admitted he shed "tears of rage" the first time he heard a demo of the same song, which would highlight Zeppelin's eponymous debut album, in November 1968, and confirm the new group's mastery of the genre: "I looked at [Jimmy Page] and said 'Jim… what?' and the tears were coming out with anger. I thought 'This is a piss-take, it's got to be.' I mean, there was *Truth* still spinning on everybody's turntable… Then I realized it was serious." Zeppelin's Page pleaded innocence, even after he was reminded that Zep's own John Paul Jones played organ on Beck's version. "It was a total freak accident," he insisted. "[Jones] probably didn't know it was the same number."

Besides, Beck himself insists the alleged theft was probably for the best. Mercurial in his tastes, never keen to repeat himself, he admits that he could never have developed the new genre with the single-mindedness that Zeppelin displayed; that having done it once, he'd never want to revisit it again. Page and co. did, repeatedly – and became the band of the '70s.
Dave Thompson

Date Late 1968

Country UK

Why It's Key The accuser says his sound was stolen; the accused says it was just his thunder.

Key Event **Crosby Stills and Nash** sing together for the first time

Rock 'n' roll has many legends. The only verifiable fact about this one is that the three voices of ex-Byrd David Crosby, ex-Buffalo Springfield member Stephen Stills and current Hollies member Graham Nash did come together in a living room in Laurel Canyon for the first time in the summer of 1968.

But whose living room? Crosby has always said it all happened at Joni Mitchell's place. Stills remembered it at first as John Sebastian's, then decided it was Cass Elliott's. Nash vacillated between Elliott's and Mitchell's, then decided it was Elliott's. Producer Paul Rothchild says it was Sebastian's. Songwriter Bill Chadwick says it was club owner Doug Weston's. Mitchell's manager Elliott Roberts remembers it as Mitchell's. Who's right? Joni Mitchell enigmatically says "They're all right." Wherever it was, it seems that Crosby and Stills were singing together in the company of Nash, Mitchell, Elliott, Sebastian, Chadwick and Rothchild. As Crosby and Stills harmonized on a Stills' song, "You Don't Have

To Cry", Nash quietly listened. Then he asked them to sing it again. And again. On the third time, he joined them with a perfect high part harmony. Driving home, Crosby and Stills begged Nash to form a band with them. Nash said yes and left not only The Hollies but England too. It was the birth of a great trio, Crosby, Stills and Nash, possibly the only ensemble to ever live up to the tag "supergroup".
Giancarlo Susanna

Date Summer 1968

Country USA

Why It's Key An exhilarating singing session results in one of the biggest groups of the '70s

Key Person
Donovan

When "Goo Goo Barabajagal (Love Is Hot)" entered the UK Top 40 on July 9, 1969, it marked the end of a run of hits that had seen the public perception of guitarist and singer Donovan gradually transformed: once pigeonholed as an opportunist Dylan clone, he was now an artist whom a heavyweight act like the Jeff Beck Group – his collaborators on the record – were happy to work with.

There was always more substance to the man born Donovan Leitch in 1946 than glutinous early folk-pop hits like "Catch The Wind" suggested. Donovan's most important musical contribution came with his synthesis of bohemian acoustic folk, poetic lyrics, and jazz-inflected backdrops (with producer Mickie Most and arranger John Cameron providing vital support). But, no matter how impressive and innovative, psychedelic folk creations like "Sunshine Superman," the unusually visceral "Hurdy Gurdy Man," and the mystical "Atlantis" were essentially

products of the era and as the '60s ended, so Donovan found a world less receptive to music infused with the sensibility described in the title of his 1968 double-LP opus *A Gift From A Flower To A Garden*.

In 1973 he briefly threatened an artistic renaissance with the impressive *Cosmic Wheels* (on which he was, perhaps significantly, reunited with Mickie Most), but quickly lapsed back into self-indulgence and irrelevance once again. There have been mini-revivals since, with Rick Rubin overseeing *Sutras* (1996) and some surprisingly modern tones on his stylish 2004 album *Beat Café*.
David Wells

Role Recording Artist

Date 1969

Nationality UK

Why It's Key Artist who quickly evolved from imitator to innovator.

Opposite Donovan

Key Performance *Oliver!* the movie

Charles Dickens' depiction of the lives of Victorian orphans had already been the subject of many dramatizations since its publication in 1838. However, the triumph of director Carol Reed's version was that it proved that such grim subject matter could translate to the genre of the musical with no loss of pathos.

Lionel Bart wrote all of the songs for *Oliver!*, the script of which was based on his play. Bart had previously tasted West End success with *Fings Ain't Wot They Used T'Be* (1960), (which shared a proliferation of Cockneyisms with *Oliver!*) and chart success with UK pop stars Cliff Richard and Tommy Steele. The casting of *Oliver!* was inspired – particularly Jack Wild as the impish Artful Dodger, Ron Moody as Fagin, and Oliver Reed as the villainous Bill Sikes – but no more so than the music. *Oliver!* Is simply bursting with famous songs: the outraged title track ("Never before/Has a boy asked for more!"), "Food Glorious Food," the Dodger's initiation anthem "Consider

Yourself," Fagin's manifesto "You've Got To Pick A Pocket Or Two," the chin-up "It's A Fine Life," the devotional "I'd Do Anything," the beerbarrel singalong "Oom-Pah-Pah," "Who Will Buy?" – a celebration of a fine morning with a stunning set-piece of dancing workmen and women – and Fagin's hand wringing finale "Reviewing The Situation." Rare is the musical where it is quicker to list its songs that are not immediately recognizable to the public but such was *Oliver!*.

Sean Egan

Movie Release Date September 26, 1968

Country UK

Director Carol Reed

Cast Mark Lester, Jack Wild, Ron Moody

Composer Lionel Bart

Why It's Key Poverty, robbery, violence, death... Remarkably, the result is bliss.

Key Event **The Pretty Things try to explain** *S.F. Sorrow* **to their record company**

The Pretty Things had begun as a straightahead R&B group but evolved quickly. Though the claims for television show *On The Flip Side* are dealt with elsewhere in this book and though The Who's *Tommy* was imminent, by 1968 the Pretties had recently completed what could be posited as the first full length pop song cycle.

S.F. Sorrow told the story of the titular individual through vignettes of his life from birth to lonely old age, taking in adolescent masturbation, first love, drug experimentations, and bereavement on the way. A rich and powerful work, the highpoint was the stunning air disaster scenario "This Balloon Burning."

Pretties vocalist Phil May later explained, "We knew when we did it there was nothing like it. It needed a bit more than just being put out. It needed marketing." Realizing that their label EMI would have to have it explained, the band and their producer Norman Smith arranged a demonstration in late 1968. May: "We

had a light show and the record playing and Norman stopping and reading the next part of the story... We did the whole works on them. They all sat there and when the lights came up you could see this look of twitching bewilderment. You know [posh voice]: 'Very interesting chaps'."

Released by the befuddled "suits" as simply the band's latest product instead of the groundbreaking masterpiece it was, *S.F. Sorrow* failed to make the charts and The Pretty Things saw The Who be given the credit for pioneering the rock opera.

Sean Egan

Date November 1968

Country UK

Why It's Key When the potential of a masterpiece was destroyed by the "straights".

Key Event
The Altamont free concert

The spirit of the '60s had seemed to be summed up by the peace and love vibes at large gatherings like Monterey and Woodstock. The Rolling Stones decided to climax their "comeback" 1969 U.S. tour with such a large, multi-artist bill, one to which entry would be free. Staged at the Altamont Raceway track on December 6, 1969, it boasted a line-up that, as well as the Stones, included the Flying Burrito Brothers, The Grateful Dead, Santana, Jefferson Airplane, and Crosby, Stills, Nash, And Young and therefore had all the potential to be a wonderful occasion and the perfect capstone to the decade.

However, the decision to use Hell's Angels as security put paid to that, although that wasn't the sole reason for the chaos that followed. Mick Jagger was punched in the face by a crowd member as soon as he arrived and the Dead backed out of the event when they felt the bad vibes in the air. The fractiousness of the crowd was worsened by the inadequate facilities and the Stones' late show. By the end of the event, four people were dead, including a man stabbed by the Angels, allegedly in self-defense. Something began a slow death that day too: the belief that the baby boomers were a new breed of human being, able to raise themselves above petty disputes in their pursuit of a fairer society.

Maybe it was the perfect capstone to the decade after all.

Sean Egan

Date December 6, 1969

Country USA

Why It's Key The dreams of the '60s end in nightmare.

Key Album *Liege & Lief*
Fairport Convention

With its predilection for sex, violence, and the supernatural, the olde folk music of the UK embodied the spirit of rock 'n' roll centuries before the genre was invented. Fairport Convention were the first to notice. Reconvening in a rented Hampshire mansion following the road crash that claimed the life of drummer Martin Lamble, the remaining band members – singer Sandy Denny, guitarists Richard Thompson and Simon Nicol, and bassist Ashley Hutchings together with new arrivals Dave Swarbrick on fiddle and Dave Mattacks on drums – sought a new beginning in "the old ways" on their fourth album, *Liege & Lief*, released in December 1969. Denny's love of traditional British music inspired bass player Ashley Hutchings to undertake diligent research into old folk material, granting Fairport the liberty of breaking new ground with modernist transformations of salacious Scottish fairy tale "Tam Lin" and English crime passionnel classic "Matty Groves" while enhancing the newly created folk-rock canon with amplified reels and originals like the invocational "Come All Ye," and the enigmatic Thompson/Swarbrick composition "Crazy Man Michael."

Blasphemous to some roots aficionados, *Liege & Lief* rescued traditional music from finger-in-ear folk club decay and made it cool. Destined to remain peerless in perpetuity *Liege & Lief* was voted Most Influential Folk Album Of All Time by the public in the 2006 BBC Radio 2 Folk Awards.

Kevin Maidment

Release Date December 1969

Nationality UK

Tracklisting Come All Ye, Reynardine, Matty Groves, Farewell Farewell, The Deserter, Medley: The Lark In The Morning/Rakish Paddy/Foxhunter's Jig/Toss The Feathers, Tam Lin, Crazy Man Michael

Why It's Key An album that has become as venerated as the very heritage it set out to celebrate.

Key People
Jethro Tull

Named after an eighteenth century agriculturalist, Jethro Tull recorded a one-off single that unfortunately appeared under the name "Jethro Toe" before building a reputation on the club and university circuit in the U.K. Incorporating rock, blues, folk, and jazz elements, their excellent 1968 debut album *This Was* reached the UK Top 10. Their second set, *Stand Up*, released on August 1, 1969, was Tull's only British chart-topper. The contagious "Living In The Past" was a Transatlantic hit.

Firmly installed at the forefront of the burgeoning progressive rock scene, Tull were the first rock band of note to feature the flute as lead instrument. Yet in direct contrast to the introverted appearance that instrument might suggest, they possessed a strong visual image thanks to the onstage antics of their leader, singer, chief songwriter, and flautist Ian Anderson, whose persona can best be described as that of a hopping, bug-eyed tramp. The cover of 1971 release *Aqualung* partially conveyed that. As the '70s progressed, the Tull became more popular in America than at home, with *Thick As A Brick* (1972) and *A Passion Play* (1973) both topping the U.S. album charts.

An erratic, wilfully perverse band, Tull have also embraced folk rock, hard rock, and world music at various stages in their lengthy career. Indeed, that refusal to be categorized led to an unlikely triumph in the late '80s, when their album *Crest Of A Knave* saw off Metallica to win a Grammy for Best Hard Rock/Metal Performance.
David Wells

Role Recording Artists

Date 1969

Nationality UK

Why It's Key Iconoclasts who established the flute as a rock instrument.

Opposite Jethro Tull

1960–1969

383

Key Event **The MC5 place an incendiary advertisement**

Signed by Elektra after the label had visited Detroit in mid-1968 on a scouting mission, rock revolutionaries MC5 debuted with the uncompromising 1969 live set *Kick Out The Jams*. As soon as the album appeared, however, it ran into problems. The rallying cry "Kick out the jams, motherfuckers!" would subsequently be diluted to the less controversial "Kick out the jams, brothers and sisters!", but Detroit-based department store Hudson's refused to stock the album on obscenity grounds. The outraged band, and their manager John Sinclair, took out full-page advertisements in the *Ann Arbor Argus* and *Fifth Estate* on February 13, 1969 that contained the inflammatory message "Fuck Hudson's!" alongside an unauthorized reproduction of the Elektra logo. Hudson's promptly banned not only the MC5 album but all Elektra product, while Sinclair rubbed salt into the wounds by sending the bill for the ad to the record company.

A furious Elektra cancelled the MC5's contract. That and Sinclair's subsequent imprisonment for drug possession forced the band to take stock. They signed with Atlantic, hooking up with rock critic turned producer Jon Landau for a second album, *Back In The USA* (1970). Streamlining their sound, the MC5 fused proto-punk rawness with a vintage rock 'n' roll sensibility on a clutch of tough, lean, and short numbers that constituted one of the most vital, influential rock albums of the early '70s, especially on punk. (The Clash shamelessly used it as a template). Instead of crushing them, the fall-out from the Hudson's incident had ultimately served to galvanize the band.
David Wells

Date February 13, 1969

Country USA

Why It's Key A publicity stunt that went awry – but ultimately reaped dividends.

Key Event **Johnny Cash at San Quentin prison**

Johnny Cash had been playing to convicts since 1957 and in 1968 had performed at Folsom Prison, a gig that had produced a live album. However, it is his prison concert on February 24, 1969, that has had the most cultural resonance, partly because California's San Quentin was a prominent name in penal infamy and partly because a British TV crew preserved it on film.

Cash headed west with his usual touring band: Marshall Grant (bass), W. S. Holland (drums), Carl Perkins and Bob Wootton (guitars), and the Carter Family. The inmates included sex offenders, murderers, and other assorted bad-asses. Black Panther George Jackson was a prisoner at the time along with future country star Merle Haggard, who was serving a sentence for armed robbery. Though he'd only ever spent a day in jail, Cash was firmly on the inmates' side; he wore the same color as the prisoners, bantered with the guards, and famously sang a new song about the institution which included the well-received line "San Quentin, I hate every inch of you." Other sympathetic tunes included "Wanted Man," "Starkville City Jail," and "Folsom Prison Blues." He also performed signature songs "I Walk The Line" and "Ring of Fire."

The original LP released from this show contained just half of the songs performed that day, while later editions showcased more of the concert and spawned a surprise hit single, "A Boy Named Sue."

Rob Jovanovic

Date February 24, 1969

Country USA

Why It's Key The gig that cemented the outlaw image of the "Man In Black."

Key Album *Dusty In Memphis*
Dusty Springfield

Briton Dusty Springfield had long been a fan of Motown acts and other soul/R&B artists and, following a run of 14 UK and seven U.S. Top 40 hits, she was thrilled to sign to Atlantic Records, home of another Springfield favorite, Aretha Franklin. Her first Atlantic album was *Dusty In Memphis*. Ironically, though Springfield attended the sessions at Memphis' American Studios, her final vocals were recorded in New York city.

A number of the album's songs were from celebrated songwriters (Goffin and King, Bacharach and David, Mann and Weil, Randy Newman) but it was "Son Of A Preacher Man," a contribution from lesser known composers John Hurley and Ronnie Wilkins, that made the biggest splash. The funky song about a love affair with a preacher's progeny had been unsuccessfully offered to Aretha Franklin; Springfield's version would hit the U.S. Top 10. A down-home feel also permeated tracks like "Just A Little Lovin'" and "Breakfast In Bed"; others, like "Don't Forget About Me," were pop songs given a soulful delivery, while material like "The Windmills Of Your Mind," was highly-sophisticated, pop balladry.

Astonishingly considering its reputation as a masterpiece and a classic, after its release on January 13, 1969, *Dusty In Memphis* peaked at U.S. No. 99. Among the several reasons for its enduring high reputation is Springfield's smoky, emotional performance. As co-producer Arif Mardin said in the liner notes of the album's reissue on CD, "Her voice contains the essence of soul."

Gillian G. Gaar

Release Date January 13, 1969

Nationality UK

Tracklisting Just A Little Lovin', So Much Love, Son Of A Preacher Man, I Don't Want To Hear It Anymore, Don't Forget About Me, Breakfast In Bed, Just One Smile, The Windmills Of Your Mind, In The Land Of Make Believe, No Easy Way Down, I Can't Make It Alone

Why It's Key The best female white soul album – ever.

Opposite Dusty Springfield

Key Song "Something In The Air"
Thunderclap Newman

When Thunderclap Newman made UK No. 1 on July 5, 1969, during the last summer of the '60s, their song "Something In The Air" almost seemed like a hymn to the Sixties' revolutionary spirit. By 2000, its composer, John "Speedy" Keen, had sanctioned the track's use in a way the idealistic young man who wrote it would have been horrified by back in 1969: as background music in a commercial for the ultimate corporate airline British Airways.

The trio who formed Thunderclap Newman – drummer/vocalist Keen, conservative-looking barrelhouse pianist Andy Newman, and a precocious 15-year-old guitarist named Jimmy McCulloch – were originally recruited by The Who's Pete Townshend for a movie soundtrack. That this ad hoc group was mismatched was illustrated by the fact that their one album *Hollywood Dream* (1969) contained some good songs which collectively never seemed to gel. Even on "Something In The Air," Keen's ethereal, floating melody was interrupted by an incongruous Newman honky-tonk piano break. However, on this track at least it worked and Keen's plaintive, reedy voice forewarning that the revolution was imminent and intoning the rousing refrain "We have got to get it together – now!" was all over the airwaves upon the record's release.

Little did Keen and his colleagues know that the song was really one last act of defiance by their generation before their ideals died with the start of a new, more cynical decade.

Sean Egan

Release Date June 1969

Nationality UK

Composer John "Speedy" Keen

Why It's Key Underlined the way rock turned from a revolutionary force into a commodity.

Key Song "In The Year 2525 (Exordium And Terminus)" Zager And Evans

Denny Zager had been playing since forming his first band in Nebraska during the early '60s. He and Rick Evans had worked together in the mid-'60s, went their separate ways, and got back together in 1968 as a folk-pop duo.

Overnight success came for them when Evans dug out "In The Year 2525," a futuristic cautionary song with a relentless but compelling tone, which he'd written four years earlier. Zager didn't like the song but audiences responded better to its talk of food in pills and test tube babies than anything else they did, and the pair pressed up 1,000 copies to sell at their shows and send to radio stations. One of those singles made its way to RCA Records, who signed Zager And Evans. On July 12, 1969, "In The Year 2525" topped the U.S. chart. (It would also make a UK No. 1.) In an example of good timing, the song's science-fiction ambience seemed to fit the zeitgeist surrounding the first lunar landing, which took place a week later. Five million sales later, Zager And Evans were permanently ingrained in the public consciousness.

But they were never able to follow it up with anything remotely as popular, not "Mr. Turnkey" – a prison song – or anything else they tried. Within a year, Zager had left the duo, ensuring their permanent status as one-hit wonders.

Bruce Eder

Release Date June 1969

Nationality USA

Composer Rick Evans

Why It's Key The song that was totally in tune with the times – a seizing of the zeitgeist its creators were never able to recapture.

Key Performance
Blind Faith play Hyde Park

When Eric Clapton, ex-Spencer Davis Group and Traffic singer/keyboardist Steve Winwood, ex-Cream drummer Ginger Baker, and ex-Family bassist Ric Grech coalesced as Blind Faith in mid 1969, only one word applied to this band made up of already acclaimed musicians: supergroup. Such was the buzz surrounding the band that they made their live debut before no fewer than 100,000 people at London's Hyde Park on June 7, 1969, although entry was admittedly free.

In the scorching heat, the musicians attempted to concentrate on showcasing new material like Winwood's wistful "Can't Find My Way Home" and Clapton's elegiac "Presence Of The Lord" alongside covers of Buddy Holly's "Well, All Right," The Rolling Stones' "Under My Thumb," and Mississippi bluesman Sam Myers' "Sleeping In The Ground." Somehow, though, the gig never really took off. The PA system was inadequate and all were nervous. Baker was bewildered at Clapton's understated playing, which may have been to do with Clapton's – unfortunately unspoken – desire for this band to be a more low-key venture than Cream. Clapton later said, "I came off stage shaking like a leaf because I felt… that I'd let people down."

Blind Faith went on to headline arenas throughout the United States and to release an album that effortlessly made a Transatlantic No. 1 but nobody was kidding themselves: despite their stellar lineup, the band simply didn't work. By October 1969, they were history.
Pierre Perrone

Date June 7, 1969

Country UK

Why It's Key The debut gig that was as good as it got for the quintessential supergroup.

Key Event
The Woodstock Festival

Woodstock wasn't planned as the largest gathering of people to hear music that had ever been organized. When the three-day event began on August 15, 1969, it was intended as just another of the big rock festivals mushrooming all over the United States and UK at the end of the '60s.

An unprecedented throng of half a million young people set upon the space in New York state, however, making worldwide headlines as traffic snarled for miles and rainstorms caused near-disaster-like conditions. Despite the apparently bad omens though, the weekend passed without major calamities and Woodstock became an iconic symbol for the best cooperative behavior of the peace-and-love generation.

There was a lot of good music made at Woodstock, too. The lineup was about as talent-studded as any rock concert ever staged, including The Who, Janis Joplin, The Band, Creedence Clearwater Revival, Crosby, Stills, Nash, And Young, Santana, Jefferson Airplane, Sly And The Family Stone, and, closing the event just after dawn, Jimi Hendrix. The latter provided a senses-shredding, Vietnam-informed desecration of "The Star Spangled Banner" that was poetically appropriate for an event that would in retrospect be seen as the event that encapsulated Sixties dissent, over which war was a keystone. Much of the best of the music was preserved on the Woodstock film and the soundtrack album, both of which kept the mystique of the festival going strong for years after the dust had settled.
Richie Unterberger

Date August 15, 1969

Country USA

Why It's Key The ultimate rock festival of the '60s and the quintessence of the spirit of the decade.

Key People
Creedence Clearwater Revival

The music of Creedence Clearwater Revival – a sinewy mixture of R&B and rock 'n' roll with a pinch of soul – was always scruffy, often doom-laden, implicitly (later explicitly) proletarian, and rarely romantic. Such glamor-free art is not usually the stuff of which chart sensations are made, but when the band entered the *Billboard* Top 40 with a self-written single for the first time on February 8, 1969, with "Proud Mary," it was the start of a run that would see them rack up a dozen Top 40 U.S. hits, including five No. 2s.

The success, however, is testament to the band's visceral power and songwords dripping with verisimilitude. "Proud Mary" was a case in point of the latter, the lyric of composer, guitarist, and vocalist John Fogerty movingly telling of a man who exchanges his stultifying job in the city for the simple pleasures of a life on steamboats and the kindness of the people peripheral to them.

If Fogerty and cohorts – brother Tom on rhythm guitar, Stu Cook on bass, and Doug Clifford on drums – had a fault it was an over-prolificness (in 1969 alone they released three albums) which they could profitably have exchanged for honing what often sounded like under-rehearsed material.

The dissolution of the group came in October 1972 after – according to the others – John Fogerty inexplicably insisted his bandmates contribute equally to album *Mardi Gras*, with predictably disastrous critical results.

Sean Egan

Role Recording Artists

Date 1969

Nationality USA

Why It's Key Brought uncommon lack of artifice to the Hit Parade.

Key Song "Je T'aime… Moi Non Plus"
Serge Gainsbourg

The steamy "Je T'aime… Moi Non Plus" was not the first song to be banned by the BBC. That honor probably goes to Lonnie Donegan's innuendo-pumped 1956 single "Digging My Potatoes." However, "Je T'aime…" created a new template whereby the notoriety a record gained via a BBC ban propelled it to the top of the charts.

French songwriter/singer/director/actor Serge Gainsbourg's original recording of his lascivious composition originally had him trading sex-noises with his current fling Brigitte Bardot, but concerned that the tune's eroticism might anger her new husband, the Gallic actress begged Gainsbourg to pull it from release. Instead, Gainsbourg enticed the young English actress Jane Birkin to add her breathy, ingénue voice to what he declared the "ultimate love song." Against an actually quite competent organ-driven pop backdrop unfurls an almost comically intense French lyric. Translation unveils such raunchy non-sequiteurs as

"I come and I go between your kidneys…, " and the song builds to a crescendo of orgasmic purrs. As Birkin and Gainsbourg's relationship flourished, so did rumors that the gasps and sighs were recordings of the pair's own heated love-making.

The song provoked outrage in the establishment and was banned from radios in seven European countries. The Vatican was even moved to publicly denounce the single. Consequently, "Je T'aime…" became imbibed with a rebellious, pornographic glamor and on October 11, 1969 the single provided Gainsbourg with his only UK No. 1.

David McNamee

UK No. 1 Date October 11, 1969

Nationality France

Composers Jane Birkin and Serge Gainsbourg

Why It's Key The first record banned by the BBC to reach No. 1.

Opposite Serge Gainsbourg and Jane Birkin

Key Song "Is That All There Is?"
Peggy Lee

Singer/composer Peggy Lee had already enjoyed considerable success by the time she recorded "Is That All There Is?" but it was still a surprise that this world-weary anthem by an artist who was nearly 50 hit big in 1969, the year of the Woodstock festival, *Abbey Road*, and "Honky Tonk Women."

The song was by legendary songwriting team Leiber and Stoller. Inspired by Thomas Mann's novella *Disillusionment*, Leiber's lyric had the narrator looking at events in her life – a house fire, a trip to the circus, falling in love – and registering her disappointment that each failed to live up to the hype. Her jaded view is such that even death, she suspects, won't be all it's talked up to be. That being the case, she concludes with resignation, "Let's break out the booze and have a ball …"

Lee identified strongly with the song, and recorded it In January 1969. She moved easily between the spoken word verses and sung chorus, expertly creating a bittersweet and poignant mood. But Lee's label was initially reluctant to release it. Perhaps understandably: this was the voice of age in an era where youth was made out to be everything. Yet though it might have seemed out of step with the rest of the U.S. Top 40, it entered the chart on October 11, 1969 on its way to a peak of No. 11, proving that craftsmanship can sometimes be more powerful than the zeitgeist.
Gillian G. Gaar

Release Date
September 1969

Nationality USA

Composers Jerry Leiber, Mike Stoller

Why It's Key Ennui finds an unexpected place on the pop charts.

Key People
Burt Bacharach and Hal David

An omnipresent feature of '60s and early '70s pop radio, the sophisticated, often elegant, pop of the legendary songwriting team of Burt Bacharach and Hal David (who met in the famous Brill Building) seemed a throwback to a prerock era of popular song, flourishing during a musical landscape of British Invasion, psychedelia, and folk rock.

Bacharach's unconventional melodies, characterized by their offbeat time signatures, ingenious chord changes, and striking rhythmic patterns were a perfect fit for the eloquent romanticism of Hal David's poetic lyrics. David has often been treated as an irrelevance by critics but theirs was a classic case of lyricist and music composer coming together in perfect synergy. As David once described his lyrical technique, "I search for believability, simplicity, and emotional impact."

Dionne Warwick would become the most celebrated interpreter of the Bacharach/David oeuvre, but they also wrote hits for the likes of Jackie DeShannon ("What The World Needs Now Is Love"), Dusty Springfield ("Wishin' And Hopin'"), Tom Jones ("What's New, Pussycat?"), Herb Alpert ("This Guy's In Love With You"), and B. J. Thomas (the Oscar-winning "Raindrops Keep Falling On My Head," from the western *Butch Cassidy And The Sundance Kid*, released on September 24, 1969).

The strain of their disastrous 1972 film musical *Lost Horizon* eventually broke them apart but time has only enhanced the stature of their songs which stood thrillingly apart during the golden age of AM rock radio.
Tierney Smith

Role Composer (Bacharach), Lyricist (David)

Date 1969

Nationality USA

Why It's Key Proved that success on the pop charts did not preclude unusual and sophisticated intervals, phrase-lengths and rhythms.

Opposite Burt Bacharach and Hal David

Key Album *In The Court Of The Crimson King* King Crimson

An implausibly grandiose outfit formed from the wreckage of the folk-psych trio Giles, Giles and Fripp, from the moment King Crimson set foot onstage, at the Speakeasy on April 9, 1969, some of the most influential names in rock and rock journalism flocked to their side.

Classically minded musicians who loved getting down and dirty, they quickly became the most talked-about band of the year. But *In The Court Of The Crimson King*, released on Island Records, still exceeded all expectations: pure poetry draped in atmosphere and art, music that was drawn from the intellect, not the gut, but which had the power to suck you in and draw you along regardless. Their ability to not over-egg the pudding by over-playing was the icing on the cake.

"Epitaph" haunted, the title track mystified, "21st Century Schizoid Man" terrified. Greg Lake, two years away from ELP, sang with shimmering darkness, and flute and timpani danced around the Mellotron. One review compared the album to shards of light filtering through the windows of a Gothic cathedral, and the description still suits, even after three further decades of Frippertronic observations have proven that the Crimson King was simply taking baby steps back then. Other of the band's albums are, musically and lyrically, far more impressive than this. But none can recapture the sheer earthquake delight of its novelty.
Dave Thompson

Release Date
October 1969

Nationality UK

Tracklisting 21st Century Schizoid Man, I Talk To The Wind, Epitaph, Moonchild, In The Court Of The Crimson King

Why It's Key The album that revealed that rare breed: virtuosos who didn't feel the need to prove their ability with every note they played.

Key Album *The Band*
The Band

Even more accomplished and transcendental than their debut album *Music From Big Pink*, The Band's self-titled second album – released on September 22, 1969 – firmly sealed their status as a musical legend.

Formed mainly by Canadians, except for Arkansan drummer Levon Helm, The Band were to rescue the old South, the forgotten soul of the real America, from the dismissive hands of the counterculture. Educated on the road as rocker Ronnie Hawkins' backing band, introduced to folk, and folklore, by their second employer Bob Dylan, they were a modern rock 'n' roll band who came to personify the wisdom and mystique of the olde worlde. Most of *The Band* was written by lead guitar player Robbie Robertson, but every member had a voice – Helm, bassist Rick Danko, keyboardist Richard Manuel all mixed leads with harmonies – or a musical personality embedded in the final product, a stately and musty mixture of folk, blues, gospel, R&B, rock 'n' roll, and classical (keyboardist Garth Hudson was a classically trained musician) that made their sound utterly distinctive in an age of rampant psychedelia and strutting rock. Songs like "King Harvest (Has Surely Come)," the much covered "The Night They Drove Old Dixie Down" (written from the perspective of a Confederate), "Rag Mama Rag," and "Up On Cripple Creek" are unique entries in the rock canon, then or now. Although always consistent until their demise in 1976, The Band would never recapture the brilliance of this timeless album.
Ignacio Julià

Release Date
September 22, 1969

Nationality USA

Tracklisting Across The Great Divide, Rag Mama Rag, The Night They Drove Old Dixie Down, When You Awake, Up On Cripple Creek, Whispering Pines, Jemima Surrender, Rockin' Chair, Look Out Cleveland, Jawbone, The Unfaithful Servant, King Harvest (Has Surely Come)

Why It's Key The sound of Americana.

Key Album *Led Zeppelin II*
Led Zeppelin

Having released their acclaimed and best selling eponymous debut album in January 1969, Led Zeppelin refined their formula to a fine "T" on follow-up *Led Zeppelin II*, released on October 22, 1969. But while few doubt its artistic merits, it is also one of the most contentiously influential albums in rock.

Jimmy Page's galvanizing guitar riffs, the extended instrumental breaks, and lead singer Robert Plant's cosmically orgasmic vocals on U.S. Top 5 hit "Whole Lotta Love" were certainly not bog-standard chart fare – but what about the fact that the lyric, melody, and much-lauded lead riff are noticeably similar to Muddy Waters' rendition of Willie Dixon's "You Need Love"? Or that the prelude and coda of "Bring It On Home" quotes an identically titled Dixon song recorded by Sonny Boy Williamson? Or that "The Lemon Song" clearly borrows its sexual blues swagger from Howlin' Wolf's "Killing Floor"?

After being sued for copyright infringement the band were forced to come clean. They settled with Wolf's publishers in the early '70s, and in 1985 finally gave Dixon his due, damages, and credit.

Ultimately though the punters couldn't care less about such matters. *Led Zeppelin II* topped the charts on both sides of the Atlantic. The album's unabashedly heavy overhaul of the blues proved a seminal influence on countless hard rock bands to come, ranging from Deep Purple and Guns N' Roses to The White Stripes and The Mars Volta.

Miles Keylock

Release Date
October 22, 1969

Nationality UK

Tracklisting Whole Lotta Love, What Is And What Should Never Be, The Lemon Song, Thank You, Heartbreaker, Living Loving Maid (She's Just A Woman), Ramble On, Moby Dick, Bring It On Home

Why It's Key An album that was certainly innovative, if not exactly original.

1960-1969

393

Key Event
The third Isle of Wight Festival

The Isle Of Wight Festival achieved something that neither Monterey Pop nor Woodstock managed in establishing itself as the first ongoing brand-name rock festival. Initiated purely to raise funds for the island's Swimming Pool Association, the first Isle Of Wight Festival was headlined by Jefferson Airplane, and the coup of securing Bob Dylan for 1969 massively boosted its international profile. Best-remembered, however, was the third event, which started on August 26, 1970, and boasted a line-up that blew everybody else out of the water – Jimi Hendrix, The Who, The Doors, and Joni Mitchell to name just a handful.

Logically, the Isle of Wight looked set to become the world leader for the foreseeable future but... no. Trucks were set ablaze, stalls were ransacked, and a protest festival was staged nearby to demand that the event should be free. Intolerant boos and jeers greeted Joni Mitchell, Joan Baez, and Kris Kristofferson. Observed Jethro Tull's Ian Anderson of the hippie ethos,

"This was where the whole thing imploded." When protesters started tearing down the perimeter fences, organizer Rikki Farr capitulated and declared it a free festival. Though it probably wasn't related, it was at least fitting when a stoned, depressed Hendrix climaxed the final night with one of his least exciting performances ever. Festival-goer Mary Drysdale summed it up, saying, "I could have heard better music on my stereo. Don't tell me there was any kindness or sharing or love at this festival. It was cold, man."

Johnny Black

Date August 26, 1970

Country UK

Why It's Key The end of the hippie ideal.

Key Event
The Beatles split up

Picking a day when The Beatles ended isn't easy. A case could be made for the day when John Lennon told his stunned colleagues at a business meeting on September 20, 1969 that he was leaving the group, even if he was persuaded to keep it quiet while they renegotiated their royalty deal. Maybe it was the day John met Yoko. Or when Paul McCartney announced he was quitting the group on April 10, 1970. Most pundits, however, will settle for December 31, 1970, when a writ was issued on behalf of McCartney by the High Court, London. It formally began the process that would result in the dissolution of The Beatles as a legal entity.

An entire generation had grown up with The Beatles, watching them transform modern popular music from a giddy adolescent medium into high art. The band had reflected the Sixties youth counter-cultural values and by dint of their global, literally unprecedented popularity even molded them. Suddenly the world was faced with the ill-tempered and starchly formal proceedings designed to dismantle a worldwide corporate business entity and the verities and values of the love, peace, and brotherhood generation seemed to be being left in the dust as the world entered a new, grimmer decade.

The Beatles' public divorce began in the High Court on January 19, 1971. It would be long, messy, humiliating, and final. The Beatles were the best friends we'd never known, and now they were gone.
Johnny Black

Date December 31, 1970

Country UK

Why it's Key The dream is over.

Key Performance
The Who play Leeds

With their objective a live album, The Who rocked Leeds University on February 14, 1970, and Hull City Hall the following day. As it transpired, the Hull tapes were made unusable by a technical fault, leaving the Valentine's Day tapes as the only record for posterity of the band at possibly their stage peak.

The refectory of Leeds Uni provided somewhat more intimate environs than The Who had latterly become used to but they still gave it their all for the mere 2000 in attendance: Pete Townshend leaping and windmilling his arm and slashing at his guitar strings, the buckskin jacketed Roger Daltrey twirling his microphone lead and tossing his golden mane, and Keith Moon bulging his cheeks as he worked with blazing immaculacy his giant-sized kit. Yet despite their attention to the visuals, the resultant tape was stunning, incendiary hard rock – replete with breathtaking fluid guitar parts by Townshend. But then this ability to mix spectacle and rock solid musicianship is what made The Who probably the greatest live act in music history. John Entwistle represented the calm in the eye of this hurricane, playing blank-faced some of the most innovative and interesting bass lines in rock.

Only a fraction of the 33 songs The Who performed on the day could be squeezed onto a single LP (their performance of their rock opera *Tommy* was one sacrifice) but the resultant *Live At Leeds* quickly became the definitive in-concert album.
Sean Egan

Date February 14, 1970

Country UK

Why It's Key Best live act of all time in their pomp.

Opposite Pete Townshend

Key Song "Spirit In The Sky"
Norman Greenbaum

Norman Greenbaum scored a global smash with this pop oddity, a striking reflection on mortality and the afterlife set to a rockin' beat. The lyrics have a traditional, old-time religion ring ("Gonna go to the place that's the best"… "I have a friend in Jesus") more typical of gospel, and unusual for the charts in the radicalized climate of 1970. (The Jewish Greenbaum stated that he intended the song to be a broad statement of faith in general, rather than an endorsement of Christianity in particular.) But combined with hard-rock elements (the bluesy chug of the main riff, eerie snatches of distorted guitar that swoop across each verse like a bird of prey, and a vibrant solo) they create a captivating hybrid that sold 2,000,000 copies. Released late 1969, it topped the UK charts on May 2, 1970 (U.S. No. 3). In a *Rolling Stone* interview of the time, ex-Beatle John Lennon name-checked the song as one of his current favorites, praising its simplicity.

Greenbaum may be a one-hit wonder but that hit has staying power. In 1986, a cover version by Dr And The Medics returned the song to No. 1 in the UK (a feat repeated when it was released as a charity single in 2003); it has also featured in a host of films (including *Apollo 13* and *Miami Blues*) and a Nike commercial, all of which has guaranteed its author a modest income to this day.

Robert Dimery

UK No. 1 Date
May 2, 1970

Nationality USA

Composer Norman Greenbaum

Why It's Key Canny combination of religion and hard rock makes for one of rock's most distinctive hits.

Key Album *Bridge Over Troubled Water*
Simon And Garfunkel

During the '60s, every Simon And Garfunkel album – even their mediocre first effort – outsold every Rolling Stones album. It is a startling fact, for while Jagger and co. epitomized the hedonistic and anti-authoritarian Sixties, Simon And Garfunkel had pretty much the same outlook as the Stones but none of their swaggering charisma. The diminutive songwriter Paul Simon and the curls-sprouting vocalist Art Garfunkel had an over-serious manner. Their music could also tend toward preciousness.

Yet Simon's melodies were gorgeous, the pair harmonized beautifully and their then-unusual leisurely recording methods ensured lustrous production. On its release in January 1970, *Bridge Over Troubled Water*, the duo's fifth album, seemed the pinnacle of this approach. Not only was it their grandest-sounding record yet but it was choc-ful of instantly memorable songs: "El Condor Pasa" was an early foray into world music, "Cecelia," "Baby Driver" and "Why Don't You Write Me" giddy fun, "The Only Living Boy In New York" sensual bliss, and the elegant ballad of a title track an instant standard.

The Middle American homes into which the Stones' records were not allowed but which welcomed Simon And Garfunkel unequivocally lapped *Bridge…* up – it sold a staggering 5,000,000 copies. Though Garfunkel's effective vetoing of the inclusion of "Cuba Si, Nixon No" made this a Simon And Garfunkel album unusually bereft of social commentary, the album's success still ensured the pair's alternative outlook seeped into places Jagger's mob couldn't reach. This album marked the point where the counterculture went mainstream.

Sean Egan

Release Date January 1970

Nationality USA

Tracklisting Bridge Over Troubled Water, El Condor Pasa (If I Could), Cecelia, Keep The Customer Satisfied, So Long, Frank Lloyd Wright, The Boxer, Baby Driver, The Only Living Boy In New York, Why Don't You Write Me, Bye Bye Love, Song For The Asking

Why It's Key The counter-culture goes mainstream.

Key Event
The Minimoog Synthesizer goes on sale

Robert Moog's synthesizers used electronically modulated oscillators to produce a wide range of artificial sounds. They were bulky, extremely complex devices that were operated by university researchers or composers of experimental music. The introduction of the Minimoog on January 24, 1970, brought this technology to musicians at an affordable price and in a live performance-friendly package.

The Moog synthesizer used a mass of patches and electronic components that had to be assembled to suit whatever sounds were desired. The Minimoog came as one complete unit with a keyboard and built-in electronic modules replacing the mass of patch chords. To the left of the keyboard was the pitch wheel, which enabled musicians to bend pitch and add *vibrato*. These "rollers" were a unique feature of the Minimoog that endeared them to musicians, especially to progressive rock musicians in the '70s who rushed to buy them. The success of the Minimoog made the synthesizer a staple of '80s popular music with many companies (notably Roland and Korg) manufacturing them. So ubiquitous was the synthesizer sound that rock traditionalists began a movement to return to the authentic sound of real instruments. It was in vain. By the early '80s, the guitar was clearly fighting a losing battle to remain the preferred instrument of popular musicians and the whole idea of a musical group began to seem silly when all a band's parts could be produced by a synth.

Andre Millard

Date January 24, 1970

Country USA

Why It's Key Changed the sound of pop and the format of its artists.

Key Album *Workingman's Dead*
The Grateful Dead

San Francisco's Grateful Dead, after nearly five years together, had virtually invented the psychedelic jam, but the acid high was wearing off. Lead guitarist Jerry Garcia, solidifying his songwriting partnership with non-performing band member Robert Hunter, set about penning new material that drew more directly from classic American roots music: country, folk, blues. Out came the acoustic guitars and the pedal steel, a new Garcia obsession, and, utilizing tips from their friends Crosby, Stills, And Nash, vocal structures took on a new prominence.

Workingman's Dead, marked the point where this consummate live band learned how to make proper use of the recording studio. Taking its title from country star Merle Haggard's "Workingman's Blues," it was shorn of the lengthy improvisations that had characterized the Dead's past two studio albums, focusing instead on concise, character-driven songs, some sporting rather dark lyrical themes. There was still plenty of electricity ("Easy Wind," "Casey Jones," the Altamont-inspired cautionary tale "New Speedway Boogie") but the heart of the album lay in its easy-going acoustic tracks ("Uncle John's Band," "High Time," "Black Peter," "Dire Wolf"). The bluegrass-esque "Cumberland Blues" featured guitar from David Nelson, of the Dead-affiliated country-rock band New Riders Of The Purple Sage.

With *Workingman's Dead* and its similar sequel, *American Beauty* (1970), the Dead put a new spin on their penchant for experimentalism: they demonstrated that a band could utterly (if temporarily) change their sonic nature – and retain their fanbase intact.

Jeff Tamarkin

Release Date June 1970

Nationality USA

Tracklisting Uncle John's Band, High Time, Dire Wolf New Speedway Boogie, Cumberland Blues, Black Peter, Easy Wind, Casey Jones

Why It's Key Brought a country sensibility to psychedelic rock.

Key Song "(They Long To Be) Close To You"
The Carpenters

The Carpenters' exquisite "(They Long To Be) Close To You" became their first U.S. No. 1 on the date above, and showed there was room for tranquility after the turmoil of the '60s.

The song, written by Bacharach and David, had previously been recorded without success by actor Richard Chamberlain and Dionne Warwick. In 1970, the number was cut by trumpet player Herb Alpert, who also provided a rare vocal for the track. But he decided not to release it, and instead passed it on to an act he'd signed to his A&M label the previous year – The Carpenters.

Karen and Richard Carpenter were siblings. Richard was the act's pianist, vocalist, and arranger, Karen lead vocalist and (at that time) drummer. Richard provided a new arrangement for the song, opening with the piano playing solo, climaxing with a cascade of layered harmonies from the two. But it was Karen's warm contralto that gave The Carpenters their distinctive sound, with a haunting quality that gave even the most upbeat material a touch of melancholy – as in "... Close To You." Though ostensibly a love song, a careful listen reveals that the singer's desire is unrequited; all she hopes for is to be "close to" him. A recurring pretty little piano triplet served to distract from the ambiguity.

An early Carpenters press release perfectly summed up the duo's adult oriented soft rock as "bringing back the 3 H's – hope, happiness, and harmony."

Gillian G. Gaar

Release Date May 1970

Nationality USA

Composers Burt Bacharach, Hal David

Why It's Key Sunshine proves it can find room in the charts.

Key Event The First Maxi Single "In The Summertime" by Mungo Jerry

Mungo Jerry's charismatic frontman and songwriter, Ray Dorset was still working in a Timex factory when their sun-drenched jug-band anthem "In The Summertime" took the charts by storm. "I had to ask my boss for the afternoon off to do Top Of The Pops," he recalled. Virtually unknown, they had been the surprise smash of the UK's Hollywood Rock Festival, outshining headliners including the Grateful Dead and Black Sabbath. Four days later the song entered the UK Top 20, reaching No. 1 on June 13, 1970.

Undeniably a classic slab of good-time rock, "In The Summertim"'s live rootsy down-home banjo-driven vibe provided welcome relief from the era's sophisticated prog-rock and manufactured pop. Great records, however, aren't always major hits. "In The Summertime" was kick-started by huge numbers of Hollywood Festival-goers buying it en masse, but there was also an astute marketing gimmick involved by Dawn Records. It was the first maxi-single: offering three tracks for the usual price of two. Those who went to the record stores specifically to buy "In The Summertime" didn't need that extra incentive but the value-for-money option swayed many who might otherwise have bought the current No. 1, "Yellow River" by Christie. The music industry sat up and took notice and "In The Summertime" heralded the onslaught of the marketing format wars in which extra tracks, colored vinyl, picture discs, limited editions, and more were employed to give new releases that extra edge when the traditional payola system just wasn't enough.

Johnny Black

Date June 13, 1970

Country UK

Why It's Key A milestone in marketing gimmicks.

Key Album *Paranoid*
Black Sabbath

Faced with the challenge of capitalizing on a successful first album, Black Sabbath responded with the soundtrack for an urban nightmare. Sabbath – bassist Terry "Geezer" Butler, guitarist Tony Iommi, drummer Bill Ward, and vocalist John "Ozzy" Osbourne – specialized in dark, bluesy power chords and a grinding sense of doom. Though common currency for today's heavy rockers, this sounded like nothing less than the Devil's playlist to listeners still grappling with the demise of The Beatles.

Sabbath's heaviness was distinct from Led Zeppelin's. The latter's music revolved around sex. Sabbath talked of anything but. On *Paranoid*, they addressed militarism ("War Pigs"), heroin abuse ("Hand Of Doom"), comic book rumbles ("Iron Man"), and the aftermath of nuclear war ("Electric Funeral"). For a great many record buyers, however, *Paranoid*'s most relevant numbers evoked horrors closer to home. On the title track, the band – at loggerheads with management, reeling from an exhaustive tour schedule – may have been speaking from the heart or simply posturing. Either way, the song – an unexpected hit single and one so unusually uptempo as to make one think it was by their speedier metal rivals Deep Purple – remains one of rock's most harrowing depictions of mental anguish ("People think I'm insane because I am frowning all the time").

Their eponymous debut of the previous February was the album that for many kick-started the whole heavy metal genre but *Paranoid* is Black Sabbath's masterpiece.

Ralph Heibutzki

Release Date
September 18, 1970

Nationality UK

Tracklisting War Pigs (including Luke's Wall), Paranoid, Planet Caravan, Iron Man, Electric Funeral, Hand Of Doom, Rat Salad, Fairies Wear Boots (including Jack The Stripper)

Why It's Key Heavy metal, heavy subjects.

Opposite **Black Sabbath**

Key Song "Love Grows (Where My Rosemary Grows)" Edison Lighthouse

By late 1969, such was the proven hit-making record of songwriter Tony Macaulay that several record labels, including Motown, had tried to woo him. He decided to go with Bell Records, who were offering a $1m advance, payable over four years.

Working on a ballad with fellow writer Barry Mason one day, Macaulay – his nose for hit potential now very refined – abandoned the proceedings when he realised that what they were concocting was not chart-bound. An hour later, the pair had completed a giddy, uptempo song of romantic devotion called "Love Grows (Where My Rosemary Goes)". "I was absolutely certain it was number one", Macaulay recalled.

Because he was new at Bell, Macaulay didn't have an act to place the song with. He booked a group called Greenfield Hammer and an orchestra. On the morning of the studio session, a twangy guitar riff came to him while he was shaving and he would use that to open the record. Two takes of the track were completed before time ran out. A backing singer on the track named Tony Burrows was overdubbed on lead vocals and the record put out under the name Edison Lighthouse. On January 31, 1970, it did indeed sail to a UK number one, also making a US No.. 5. Though there were other records attributed to the fictional band, Macaulay played no part in them, bailing out so as not to sully the magic of the song. That $1 advance, by the way, was earned back by '..Rosemary..' alone.

Sean Egan

Release Date January 1970

Nationality UK

Composers Tony Macaulay, Barry Mason

Why It's Key The song that constituted a million-dollar hour.

Key Person
Janis Joplin

Janis Joplin's flame illuminated the Sixties' cultural revolution, presenting a new, liberated female archetype to the masses, but her quest for intoxication was to suffocate the fire too early.

Born in Port Arthur, Texas, in 1943, Janis Lyn Joplin was a shy, unpretty girl who would suffer the scorn of school classmates and find refuge in painting and the recordings of blues greats Bessie Smith and Big Mama Thornton. In 1963, already a rebellious personality whose adopted image was inspired by her blues heroines, she left Texas for San Francisco. The new, stimulant-drenched environment increased her use of drugs and alcohol. These were a means to overcome her insecurity – but then so was her powerful, rasping singing style. In 1966, she joined Haight-Ashbury band Big Brother And The Holding Company. After an eponymous first album in 1967, and her spectacular performance at the Monterey Pop Festival, Joplin became an international star. A second, acclaimed album, *Cheap Thrills* (1968), featured the pain-wracked hit "Piece Of My Heart." Her solo career started with *I Got Dem Ol' Kozmic Blues Again Mama!* (1969).

But however bigger than life her persona, she was doomed; Janis Joplin died on October 4, 1970, aged 27, of a heroin and whiskey overdose, while recording a new album in Los Angeles. The posthumously released *Pearl* (1971) was to be her most successful, with hits "Me And Bobby McGee" and the whimsical *a cappella* "Mercedes Benz."

Ignacio Julià

Role Recording Artist

Date 1970

Nationality USA

Why It's Key A true icon of female liberation, an unforgettable voice.

Opposite Janis Joplin and the Full Tilt Boogie Band, her final band

Key Event **Kris Kristofferson's Double-whammy**

Given the conservative nature of the Nashville music establishment in the late '60s, it was only a matter of time before someone came along to buck the system. Former Rhodes and Oxford scholar Kris Kristofferson was that man. Taking part of his inspiration from the Greenwich Village poets, Kristofferson brought a new lyrical depth and sexual frankness to country music, plus a political liberalism epitomized by his bogeyman denunciation "Blame It On The Stones."

The turn of the '70s saw him write two remarkable songs. "For The Good Times" was as searingly poignant as country music gets in its depiction of one last night together between parting lovers with its heart-rending entreaty "Make believe you love me one more time." "Sunday Morning Coming Down" engendered some controversy for its drug reference but as a meditation on the loss of innocence it was no less moving, its alienated protagonist observing idyllic Sunday scenes playing before him while yearning for the "disappearing dreams of yesterday."

No matter how conservative the country establishment was, they couldn't deny Kristofferson's talent. In 1970, "For The Good Times" (recorded by Ray Price) nabbed the Academy of Country Music's Song of the Year. Later that year, Johnny Cash's version of "Sunday Morning Coming Down" won the same accolade from the Country Music Association. This double feat remains unequaled to this day.

Over 30 years after that early triumph, Kristofferson's songwriting still stands for country at its most bracingly authentic.

Tierney Smith

Date 1970

Country USA

Why It's Key Conformist country music unequivocally opens its arms to a maverick.

Key Event
The first Glastonbury Festival

In June 1970, an English West Country farmer and his wife snuck through a hedge into the Bath Festival Of Blues And Progressive Rock. "We fell in love with the idea," remembered Glastonbury founder Michael Eavis. Just three months later, Eavis had pulled together the Pilton Pop, Folk And Blues Festival, convincing a mere 1,500 fans to part with £1 each. This princely sum entitled them to sit in a field while the pre-electric and pre-abbreviated Tyrannosaurus Rex, the twinkling Al Stewart, and sundry dwarf stars including Steamhammer and Quintessence, performed on a scaffolding and plywood stage knocked together by a local carpenter. "The price of the ticket included free milk from the farm," pointed out Eavis, who renamed it Glastonbury Fayre for the second event a year later.

After a six-year absence, it returned in 1977, finally becoming the Glastonbury Festival in 1981. Despite ups and downs including violence in 1990 and the immolation of the famed Pyramid Stage in 1994, the event has grown exponentially. Almost every significant rock artist on the planet has played Glastonbury, but it usually sells out before headliners are announced. By 2005, it sprawled over 900 acres, thrilling 150,000 devotees with over 385 live performances including dance, comedy, theater, and circus as well as music. Officially, it was now the Glastonbury Festival Of Contemporary Performing Arts but to those in love with its persevering informality and social conscience it remains "Glasto."

Johnny Black

Date September 19, 1970

Country UK

Why It's Key An event that has become more important than the acts appearing.

Key Performance *Company*
stage musical

A shockingly modern musical when it first opened and still remarkably insightful if a little dyspeptic, *Company* explores the games, angst, loneliness, and badinage of late-twentieth century relationships in an alternately brittle and heartfelt manner.

Company is really a "revusical"; that is, a string of non-linear scenes around a single theme. Howard Dietz invented the concept with his productions *At Home Abroad* (1935) and *Inside USA* (1948), shows that featured a theme and through-characters but that were revues otherwise. When it first burst upon the scene, *Company* was revolutionary with its take-no-prisoners attitude. No chorus, no leggy chorines (save Donna McKechnie's "Tick Tock"), no salve for the tired businessman. All it could boast was Stephen Sondheim's brilliant metropolitan score, Jonathan Tunick's incomparable, metallic orchestrations, Boris Aronson's antiseptically urban set, George Furth's cagey and revealing book, and Hal Prince's sparse, knowing staging.

Company (the first real Sondheim score) was the show that introduced us to the Sondheim/Prince/Aronson/Tunick team that would wrenchingly change the course of musical theater – and lead to a hundred second-rate imitations by Sondheim wannabes. With the electric current of the nervy, ultra-modern sound of *Company*, Sondheim embarked with Hal Prince on an odyssey of shows, including *Follies* (1971), *A Little Night Music* (1973), *Pacific Overtures* (1976), and *Sweeney Todd* (1979), which if not always financial hits, can all be categorized as successes in that they undeniably made waves in musical theater with their brave forward strides.

Ken Bloom

Opening Night April 26, 1970

Country USA

Director Harold Prince

Cast Dean Jones, Elaine Stritch, Donna McKechnie

Composer Stephen Sondheim

Why It's Key Introduced modern audiences to the "revusical."

Key Song "Knock Three Times"
Dawn featuring Tony Orlando

Not since Tchaikovsky introduced real cannons into the finale of the *1812 Overture* had a percussive sound effect stirred the public imagination as much as the immortal mime-conducive "ting ting" accompanying the words "twice on the pipe" in Tony Orlando's "Knock Three Times."

Essentially a demo vocalist who happened to be possessed of a classic blue-eyed soul voice, Tony Orlando had achieved early stardom when his 1961 demo "Halfway To Paradise" was deemed good enough for commercial release, securing him a *Billboard* Top 40 hit but, a year later, he was regarded as washed-up. He worked as a CBS Records general manager until 1970 when he was asked to overdub his lead vocal onto the song "Candida" by the non-existent group Dawn. That song's million-selling success was followed by "Knock Three Times," continuing "Candida"'s refreshingly light pop-dance style with a mildly saucy tale of lust in an apartment block. In his efforts to seduce a lonely downstairs neighbor, a man suggests a sex code – three knocks on the ceiling if she's receptive, two on the pipe if not.

Exactly what makes people love a record enough to propel it to No. 1 – which "Knock Three Times" achieved on January 23, 1971, in the United States – is never entirely clear, but one magic ingredient here, that double metallic clank, had many, many households singing back their own vocal "ting ting" in what amounted to a worldwide call and response.
Johnny Black

Release Date
November 1970

Nationality USA

Composer Tony Orlando

Why It's Key Confirmed that sound effects can constitute as powerful a hook as lyrics or riffs.

Key Song "I'd Like To Teach The World To Sing" The New Seekers

When it reached No. 1 in the UK on January 8, 1972, "I'd Like To Teach The World To Sing" – which also went Top Ten in the United States – was still being referred to by many people as "I'd Like To Buy The World A Coke." The erroneous reference was the result of the place where people had first come across the song and testament to the powerful cross-fertilization of promotion its makers had stumbled upon.

The song had originally been intended as nothing more than a new way to push Coca-Cola's latest catchphrase, "It's the real thing." Following some problems on an airplane flight, advertising man Bill Backer was impressed when he saw some previously at-odds airline passengers sharing a joke over bottles of Coke. He hit upon the idea to portray the drink as "a tiny bit of commonality between all peoples." Already equipped with the last line: "I'd like to buy the world a Coke and keep it company," he bashed the song out with fellow composers Billy Davis and Rogers Cook and Greenaway. What sounds like hands-across-the-water fatuousness became powerful when portrayed as sung by 500 children on an Italian hillside in what became one of history's most famous television commercials. The public were soon asking radio stations to play the feel-good tune they were hearing several times per evening. The New Seekers rerecorded the song without the Coca-Cola references, secure in the knowledge that few artists have about a record before its release: guaranteed chart success.
Sean Egan

Release Date
December 1971

Nationality UK

Composer William Backer, Roger Cook, B. B. Davis, Roger Greenaway

Why It's Key The ultimate media cross-fertilization.

Key People
Sly And The Family Stone

Formed by Sylvester "Sly Stone" Stewart, a DJ, songwriter, and producer, in the San Francisco Bay Area, Sly And The Family Stone were all about unity. Their members were black, white, male, female – devotees of and experts in pop, soul, rock, and jazz. They provided black audiences with a gateway into rock and white listeners with a means of figuring out funk, and their influence extended far beyond even their huge commercial success.

Their life-affirming hits included "Dance To The Music," "Everyday People," and "Hot Fun In The Summertime." The zenith of the Family Stone's career came with the release of the magnificent 1969 album *Stand!* and their performance at Woodstock. Here was music that fused style, content, and innovation in a euphoric, genuinely revolutionary burst of sound that connected directly with the hearts and minds of their disparate audience. The band's album swansong *There's A Riot Goin' On* (1971) was also a classic but it was uncharacteristically dark and brooding music that was mainly the work of a solo Stewart, holed up in an L.A. mansion, strung out on chemicals and paranoia.

That that album's "Family Affair" – Stone's wracked, cracked voice eulogizing the end of the group – should have been the last of their three U.S. No. 1s on December 4, 1971, is in one sense fitting, but its downbeat tone has overshadowed the joy and hope that characterized their greatest work.

Angus Batey

Role Recording Artists

Date 1971

Nationality USA

Why It's Key A band whose hybrid styles and rainbow-nation line-up chimed perfectly with the late-Sixties vibe of love, peace, and togetherness.

Key Event Fire at Montreux Casino where Deep Purple album is to be recorded

When heavy metallers Deep Purple arrived at the Montreux Casino, Switzerland, they were planning to record their album, *Machine Head*, in its concert area. On the eve of the recording session, Frank Zappa And The Mothers Of Invention were performing at the venue, where a concertgoer – later dubbed "some stupid" in "Smoke On The Water" – let off a flare gun, igniting a fire that burnt the casino to the ground.

The fire started small, but after part of the ceiling collapsed, Zappa ordered the audience out of the hall. He later recalled in an interview, "The auditorium filled with smoke and shortly after, the band had to escape through the backstage tunnel, [and] the heating system exploded, blowing several people through the window." Though no one was killed, Deep Purple were forced to find alternate recording space with the help of Claude Nobs, founder of the Montreux Jazz Festival and one of the heroes of that night, who pulled several kids from the fire, which destroyed Zappa's equipment and put the venue out of commission until 1975.

Deep Purple's "Smoke On The Water," which chronicles the events of that night, "came to me in a dream one or two mornings after the fire," bassist Roger Glover once said. Meanwhile, guitarist Ritchie Blackmore did justice to the drama of the event by adorning the lyric with a menacing four-note blues lick that is now probably the most famous riff in hard rock history.

Sara Farr

Date December 4, 1971

Country Switzerland

Why It's Key A blaze that led to a heavy rock classic.

Opposite Ian Gillan of Deep Purple

Key People
Paul Revere And The Raiders

Many would assume from their mop-topped singer Mark Lindsay and their name that this band were nothing more than a gimmicky answer to the U.S. success of The Beatles and their compatriots. But though Paul Revere is an iconic figure in the Americans' war against the British, it wasn't quite as simple as that: those two names were in fact the genuine first names of band founder, keyboardist Paul Revere Dick. Additionally, as far back as 1961, they had released a single presciently titled "Like Long Hair".

Not that they didn't trade on patriotism when – after a hiatus following that first bout of activity when Dick became a conscientious objector after being drafted – they re-formed when the British Invasion was in full swing. Their image was based around revolutionary war costumes. However, the music with which they implied they were repelling the invaders was no gimmick: hits like "Kicks," "(I'm Not Your) Stepping Stone," "Good Thing," and "Him Or Me –

What's It Gonna Be?" packed a real garagey crunch, as did their lyrics' (now dated but then sort-of daring) inclination to snarl at ladies.

Despite evolving as artists, their lightweight image worked against them as the '60s progressed and they shortened their name to The Raiders in 1970. On July 24, 1971 they secured their last brush with glory when their Native American-sympathetic single "Indian Reservation" made U.S. No. 1.

Sean Egan

Role Recording Artists

Date 1971

Nationality USA

Why It's Key An American band who made capital out of an image that implied they were repelling the British Invasion.

Key Person
Melanie

It's appropriate that quintessential hippie chick Melanie Safka, born in 1947, found a route to a wide general public by her appearance at the ultimate hippie festival, Woodstock. Carole King might have been the most commercially successful female singer-songwriter of the era but having a background in early '60s Brill Building pop she was really too old to fit the bill. Gentle, fey, anti-establishment, pro-ecology Joni Mitchell most certainly did fit the bill, but Melanie – who was all those things too – seemed to take it one step further. Perhaps significantly, Mitchell wrote festival anthem "Woodstock" although she had not appeared at Woodstock. Melanie's "Lay Down (Candles In The Rain)" was a far more personal document based on her experience of playing there during a thunderstorm.

A graduate of the Greenwich Village folk scene, Melanie was a natural representative of the liberated, beads-and-bangles image associated with hippiedom, but her compositions had a broad mainstream appeal.

Her 1971 hit "What Have They Done To My Song Ma?" was a knife in the ribs of music biz manipulators who she felt had wronged her but that didn't stop it becoming a variety show favorite. Meanwhile, her irresistibly infectious, innuendo-laden "Brand New Key" – which made U.S. No. 1 on December 25, 1971 – revealed that, for all her seeming innocence, she could be as predatory as any man.

Johnny Black

Role Recording Artist

Date 1971

Nationality USA

Why It's Key There had been hippie chicks before and there would be hippie chicks after, but Melanie Safka was the first to take that image to the bank.

Opposite Melanie

Key People
The Osmond family

When The Osmonds made U.S. No. 1 on February 13, 1971, with "One Bad Apple," it started the biggest family-oriented phenomenon popular music has seen. For the next two years, this Mormon clan from Utah – in various configurations – dominated the charts worldwide. So successful were they that they had their own animated television series. Yet they became – beyond their fanatical fanbase of teenage girls and pre-teens – a byword for the anodyne and artistically worthless.

Such a judgment wasn't quite fair or accurate. The Osmonds first appeared on the public radar in 1962, when as a pre-pubescent barbershop singing outfit they were regulars on *The Andy Williams Show*. It was Williams who suggested to the kids that they should learn musical instruments. This they proceeded to do, including new arrival Donny, who became a proficient pianist. The Osmonds were also capable of generating their own material; Alan, Merrill, and Wayne usually collaborating in composition, including on the fine, thumping 1972 hit "Crazy Horses." Yet the family's genuine abilities were undermined by the dual solo careers of some of its members. 13-year-old Donny was so cute that it seemed logical to give him records to release, but numbers such as his corny cover of Paul Anka's "Puppy Love" hardly gave the family street cred. When chubby youngest member Jimmy scored a novelty 1972 UK No. 1 with "Long Haired Lover From Liverpool," it cemented the family's placing in pop history among the feather-light.

Sean Egan

Role Recording Artists

Date 1971

Nationality USA

Why It's Key A musical family hoist by their own populist petard.

411

Opposite Alan, Wayne, Merrill, Jay, and Donny Osmond

Key Album *The Concert for Bangla Desh*
George Harrison And Friends

It's a fair guess that most rock fans in 1971 knew little or nothing about the troubles in Bangladesh, the densely populated, mostly Muslim country north of India. Perhaps George Harrison didn't either. But when Bengali sitar maestro Ravi Shankar called upon his friend the ex-Beatle to help displaced refugees of his war-torn homeland, Harrison embraced the cause. In the process he created the modern large-scale benefit concert, later expanded upon by Live Aid, Farm Aid, and many others.

Other artists had, of course, given charity performances before, but none had ever created such a wide-scale stir. Harrison, despite having scored with a massively popular solo album in *All Things Must Pass* in 1970, had not performed publicly since The Beatles' final show in 1966. Anticipation was high for the two concerts he booked into New York's Madison Square Garden on August 1, 1971, but fans got more than they bargained for when Harrison recruited such heavyweight pals as Bob Dylan (then semi-reclusive), Leon Russell, Eric Clapton, Billy Preston, Badfinger, fellow ex-Fab Ringo Starr and, of course, Shankar to join him at the unique event.

The two shows – one in the afternoon, one in the evening – were recorded and filmed for posterity, and the resultant album *The Concert For Bangla Desh* (using an alternative spelling), when released the following December, was a huge success, not only perching at No. 2 on the charts but raising nearly U.S. $250,000 for the cause.

Jeff Tamarkin

Release Date December 1971

Nationality USA

Tracklisting Introduction, Bangla Dhun, Wah-Wah, My Sweet Lord, Awaiting On You All, That's The Way God Planned It, It Don't Come Easy, Beware Of Darkness, Band Introduction, While My Guitar Gently Weeps, Medley: Jumpin' Jack Flash/ Youngblood, Here Comes The Sun, A Hard Rain's Gonna Fall, It Takes A Lot To Laugh It Takes a Train To Cry, Blowin' In the Wind, Mr. Tambourine Man, Just Like A Woman, Something, Bangla Desh

Why It's Key When rock shoed it could save lives.

Key Album *Who's Next*
The Who

Who's Next should have been a disaster, for that's what it felt like it was to the people behind it as it was being created.

Originally, the follow-up studio album to The Who's epoch-marking rock opera *Tommy* was envisaged as a movie called *Lifehouse* with an attendant soundtrack album. The ideas behind Who leader Pete Townshend's film story were ambitious and complicated, as well as - as far as Townshend's bandmates and Who co-manager Kit Lambert were concerned - confused. Lambert all but sabotaged the project. The movie foundered when the promised production money failed to materialize. Sessions at a New York studio to complete the music were a failure due to Lambert being an erratic heroin addict.

A shaken Townshend asked producer Glyn Johns to mix the New York tapes. But when a Johns session resulted in the magnificent "Won't Get Fooled Again", they went with Johns' suggestion to start from scratch.

When *Who's Next* materialized on July 31 1971, it was a shattered and scattered *Lifehouse*: half the songs were cut and the tracks were sequenced for aesthetic, not narrative, reasons. It didn't matter, simply because of the brilliance of the music: thunderous, majestic rock like "Baba O'Riley" and "Bargain" alternating with beautiful, elegant balladry like "Getting In Tune" and "Love Ain't For Keeping", performed by band members each hitting their respective technical peak, making for what is by consensus one of the dozen greatest albums ever released.

Sean Egan

Release Date August 27, 1971 (UK); August 14, 1971 (USA)

Nationality UK

Tracklisting Baba O'Riley/Bargain/Love Ain't for Keeping/My Wife/Song Is Over/Getting in Tune/Going Mobile/Behind Blue Eyes/Won't Get Fooled again

Producer The Who/Glyn Johns

Original Label Decca (USA)/Track (UK)

Why It's Key The classic Who album with an utterly tortured genesis.

Key Album *Blue*
Joni Mitchell

By the time of the release of *Blue*, her fourth album, in June 1971, the 27-year-old Canuck Joni Mitchell had already made her mark as both a writer and performer, providing Judy Collins with the U.S. Top 10 hit "Both Sides Now" and Crosby, Stills, Nash And Young with the U.S. Top 20 "Woodstock," while winning the 1969 Best Folk Performance Grammy Award for her second album, *Clouds*.

Her writing had always had a personal, introspective, seemingly autobiographical tone, but the songs on *Blue* took those tendencies to an extreme. Employing a spare backup (her own dulcimer strumming accompanied here and there by bass, guitar, pedal steel, and drums), Mitchell set the theme for the disc immediately on the lead-off track, "All I Want," noting that she was traveling on a lonely road. Thereafter, she traced the ups and downs of her romantic encounters in various locales, describing them in specific, ingenuous terms. It all ended up with

the harrowing "The Last Time I Saw Richard," in which the singer bravely declared that she would come out of her troubles like a butterfly escaping a cocoon.

Blue went on to become Mitchell's most critically acclaimed and honored album. Perhaps just as big an accolade for her as it being ranked 30th among the best albums of all time by *Rolling Stone* magazine in 2003 is the fact that Bob Dylan stated that his song "Tangled Up In Blue" was partly inspired by the Mitchell album.

William Ruhlmann

Release Date June 1971

Nationality Canada

Tracklisting All I Want, My Old Man, Little Green, Carey, Blue, California, This Flight Tonight, River, A Case Of You, The Last Time I Saw Richard

Why It's Key Raised the bar for confessional singer/songwriters.

Opposite Joni Mitchell

Key Performance **Marc Bolan invents glam rock on *Top Of The Pops***

By March 1971, Marc Bolan was on the top of the world, and at the top of the charts. Just three months after his band T Rex's "Ride A White Swan" frustratingly stalled at No. 2, their latest single, "Hot Love," had risen to No. 1 and the band were back at *Top Of The Pops*, to perform the hit for the nation.

Marc was looking cool that afternoon. He'd just picked up a new silver lamé jacket and matched it with hip-hugging white trousers. But, as he picked up his guitar to head out onto the soundstage, he felt a hand on his arm. He looked around; it was Chelita Secunda, a publicist friend of Bolan's wife June. "One thing before you go…" Deftly, Chelita daubed some eye-shadow across his face, and then brought out some glitter, patting it across his cheekbones, tiny teardrops that shimmered in the light. Musicians had worn make-up onstage before, but this was something new, something bold. He now looked glamorous – but, shockingly, glamorous in the way that a woman would

– something accentuated by his corkscrew curls, which always looked suspiciously like a lady's permanent. It didn't matter that the cameras didn't close in on Bolan's face until the final chorus of the performance, the "La la la" that chased "Hot Love" to its fade. One glimpse of it – a blinding sparkle beneath the studio lamps – was all it took to ignite glam rock, the dominant sartorial style of the UK charts over the following years.

Dave Thompson

Date March 24, 1971

Country UK

Why It's Key A spontaneous act ignites a whole new movement.

Opposite **Marc Bolan**

Key Event **Grand Funk Railroad sell out Shea Stadium**

Grand Funk Railroad, formed in the car fields outside Flint, Michigan, owed their success largely to the efforts of their manager, Terry Knight.

It wasn't hip or cool to like the power trio but their music, with its roots in the sound of acts like Cream and Link Wray, and their blue collar and patriotic image, struck a chord with the working class. However, none of that could quite explain why for a 12-month period, they were the biggest thing going. Knight, through media manipulation and clever promotional tactics – such as a giant billboard in the middle of Times Square – made a virtue of Grand Funk's no-frills approach to hard rock. The self-proclaimed "loudest band in the world" hit a commercial peak in 1970, when four of their albums were certified gold. Their subsequent tour broke several records. The most iconic of those broken records came in June 1971. Playing Shea Stadium was a move that inevitably invited comparisons to The Beatles because of the historic nature of the Fab Four's

first appearance there. Inviting comparisons to the biggest phenomenon in music history is usually a very unwise move, yet it's somehow in the nature of the way that Grand Funk Railroad seemed ever able to punch above their weight that they emerged from this situation triumphant – infuriatingly so, for their detractors. Their July 9, 1971, concert sold out in 71 hours, topping The Beatles' record. The record still stands.

Sara Farr

Date June 1971

Country USA

Why It's Key Showed that chutzpah can sometimes win out.

Key Album *Brian Jones Presents The Pipes Of Pan At Joujouka*

Rolling Stone Brian Jones was already dead by the time one of his most significant contributions made its appearance. A year before his July 1969 death in his own swimming pool, The Rolling Stones' co-founder had recorded a consortium of traditional trance musicians in the remote village of Joujouka, in Morocco's southern Rif Mountains. Jones had visited Morocco previously and had been introduced to the musicians via the Canadian writer and painter Brion Gysin and the Moroccan painter Mohamed Hamri. Entranced by the hypnotic, exotic music unknown to the outside world, Jones vowed to capture their spiritual, healing sounds and present them to the West. He set up a portable recorder and came away with several hours of tape: torrents of chanted vocals, unearthly pipes, and frenzied, nonstop percussion.

In 1971, excerpts of the obscure field recordings he'd made – even the musicians themselves had never before heard their music played back through an electronic machine – were released on The Rolling Stones' new self-named record label. It was, to be certain, utterly unlike anything they had recorded, yet it resonated with a segment of the Stones' audience open to experimenting with something so ancient it seemed brand new.

The Joujouka album marked the birth of World Music. While the concept of World Music is fatuous – a rather presumptuous umbrella title for music that originates from beyond the West – it undeniably helped spark curiosity about other ethnic music, opening the door a little bit wider for a deluge that continues.
Jeff Tamarkin

Release Date
October 1971

Nationality UK/Morocco

Tracklisting 55, War Song, Standing + One Half, Take Me With You Darling Take Me With You, Your Eyes Are Like A Cup Of Tea, I Am Calling Out, Your Eyes Are Like A Cup Of Tea (Reprise)

Why It's Key World music – whatever that is – starts here.

Key Song **"Stairway To Heaven"** Led Zeppelin

If American FM radio play, sheet music sales, and magazine polls are any guide, "Stairway To Heaven" is the most popular rock song ever recorded. Never having been released as a single and so unsullied by mainstream exposure makes it doubly treasured by fans.

By late 1970, their first two bluesy hard-rock albums and folk-tempered third had won Led Zeppelin a huge audience. What became the flagship track of their fourth album – whose title is comprised of four symbols not to be found on a keyboard and which was released on November 8, 1971 – encapsulated the contrasts of light and shade, wood and electricity, gentle folk and mega-decibel gut brutality that were the band's founding raison d'etre. Written round the log fire of a Welsh cottage under the inspiration of Lewis Spence's book *Magic Arts In Celtic Britain*, Robert Plant's ruminative lyric flowed in and around Jimmy Page's A minor tune whose introduction resembles the 1968 instrumental "Taurus" by the Los Angeles group Spirit, with whom Zeppelin had toured. The band developed the song until it grew into a dramatic eight minutes, a masterpiece of musical and atmospheric variety, and slow-burning tension-and-release.

A song so specific to a band's presentational style might have remained uncovered by other artists, but Tiny Tim, Frank Zappa, The Red Army Choir, Dolly Parton, Pat Boone, and Rolf Harris are among those who have downscaled this rock colossus for camp and catchpenny reasons.
Mat Snow

Release Date
November 1971

Nationality UK

Composers Jimmy Page, Robert Plant

Why It's Key The mystical epic that became the rock fan's favorite-ever song.

Key Event
Yes record *Fragile*

The Beatles started it, sequestering themselves in the studio for months on end while they perfected the final twiddle of their latest opus. By the end of the '60s, any band with a shred of self-respect had similar perfectionist bents, none more so than the members of the progressive rock movement.

Yes, across the course of their first three LPs, had certainly gained a reputation for faultless finesse, and the arrival of keyboard virtuoso Rick Wakeman in their ranks, in late summer 1971, could only embed those predilections even deeper. So what a shock it was when the band's next album, *Fragile*, shot out of the traps on November 26, 1971.

Subsequently Yes admitted they did it for the money – the equipment Wakeman needed didn't come cheaply, so, absurdly, they banged out a new album to finance his arsenal. Written on the spot, and recorded live in the studio, *Fragile*, said Wakeman, was "a giant jigsaw, with everybody linking up ideas." Amazingly, the album was very good. Not only did it not sound rushed but some of Yes' proudest achievements, including "Roundabout," "Long Distance Runaround," and "Heart Of The Sunrise," emerged from the sessions. The only lasting tragedy was that they never recorded under such pressure again. Had they done so, their career might have turned out to be even more brilliant than it did.

Dave Thompson

Release Date Late Summer 1971

Country UK

Why It's Key The haste in which an album is recorded brings origins of rock success to new levels of farce, whatever the record's merits.

Key Event Rod Stewart tops both the U.S. and UK albums and singles charts

In the '60s, The Beatles had topped UK and U.S. single and album charts all at the same time but never technically with the same product. It took Rod Stewart to achieve what even the mighty Fabs hadn't.

Still the frontman of The Faces but increasingly becoming better known for his solo albums, in 1971 Stewart recorded his LP masterpiece, *Every Picture Tells A Story*. As usual, it was made up of a highly unusual mixture of folk, soul, and rock, an epic version of "(I Know) I'm Losing You" rubbing shoulders with Stewart's beautiful rustic evocation of frontier life, "Mandolin Wind." It also featured a collaboration between Stewart and classical guitarist Martin Quittenton about the artist's first sexual conquest.

Despite a raunchy theme and a catchy, jangling melody set off by an arresting mandolin solo, all ddriven home by Stewart's unique emotional rasp, Mercury Records didn't think that the song was hit material, relegating it to a B-side. Instead, "Reason To Believe" was chosen as the album's single. But fate in the form of DJ opinion intervened, and "Maggie May" was given the radio play she deserved; on October 9, 1971, the song topped the singles charts in the UK. It had made the top spot in the United States on October 2, the same day as the album had topped the U.S. album charts. With the album also lodged at No. 1 in Britain, it made for an unprecedented double-double whammy.

Melissa Blease

Date October 9, 1971

Country UK

Why It's Key Set a new standard for transatlantic commercial success.

Key Performance *Jesus Christ Superstar* and *Godspell* stage musicals

Godspell and *Jesus Christ Superstar* both started life in 1970, as a master's thesis project and a commercially released album respectively. Both post-modern depictions of the life of Christ eventually made it to Broadway in 1971, though tackled the same source material with profound differences in treatment.

Jesus Christ Superstar by Andrew Lloyd Webber (music) and Tim Rice (lyrics), is an extravagant rock opera about the last weeks of Christ's life. Its score ranges from Mary Magdeleine's plaintive "I Don't Know How To Love Him" to "King Herod's Song," a music hall strut, to the anthemic title track. As the latter's (then rather shocking) lyric might suggest, the language is highly colloquial. Contrastingly, *Godspell*, by Stephen Schwartz (music and lyrics) and John Michael Tebelak (book), is notable for its economy of presentation. Based specifically on the gospel of Saint Matthew, its narrative is mostly implicit in a progression of lessons and parables told by Jesus to his apostles, the

company a troupe of clowns in a playground who assume Biblical personae. Though pop-rock, the songs are hymn-flavored, including the rousing "Prepare Ye The Way Of The Lord," the vampish "Turn Back, O Man," and the show's hit, the gently gospel "Day By Day."

Ultimately, though, the two creations probably have more in common than differences. Whatever the street language and pop culture trappings, both are almost surprisingly non-sacrilegious, treating respectfully an icon it was fashionable for the prevailing hippie culture to dismiss.

David Spencer

Date 1971

Country UK/USA

Godspell
Director John-Michael Tebelak

Cast Stephen Nathan, Peggy Gordon

Composer Stephen Schwartz

Jesus Christ Superstar (opposite) **Director** Jim Sharman

Cast Paul Nicholas, Stephen Tate

Composers Andrew-Lloyd-Webber, Tim Rice

Why It's Key The New Testament married with song and dance. Twice.

Key Event
The London Rock 'n' Roll Show

On August 5, 1972, London's Wembley Stadium was filled with people clamoring to see artists 15 years past their peak. Starring Chuck Berry, Little Richard, Jerry Lee Lewis, Bo Diddley, Bill Haley And His Comets, and newer acts who supposedly shared the '50s esthetic (The MC5, Alice Cooper, and Roy Wood), The London Rock 'n' Roll Show was an all-day greatest hits affair attracting unreformed teddy boys and curious longhairs alike.

Its subtitle – Legends Of The '50s – made it one of the very first rock shows to explicitly trade on nostalgia. Previously it had been thought that rock 'n' roll stars' careers died as their audiences grew up. While their fame and past achievements could always guarantee them a crowd somewhere, the original rockers' chart activity was non-existent and they were essentially has-beens living in reduced circumstances.

Then something unexpected happened. The original rock fans, now adults with disposable incomes,

showed themselves to be nostalgic for the idols of their youth, the rebelliousness of whose music had not previously been thought to chime with such sentimentality. In 1969, doo-wop revivalists Sha Na Na were a hit at Woodstock. Also, in 1969, John Lennon appeared on the same bill as Little Richard, Jerry Lee Lewis, Bo Diddley, and Chuck Berry at a rock 'n' revival concert in Toronto.

Within three months of the Wembley show, Chuck Berry would, in "My Ding-A-Ling," have his biggest ever hit. The notion of sell-by dates for rock stars was soon obsolete.

Mat Snow

Date August 5, 1972

Country UK

Why It's Key The start of the revival industry.

Key Person
Alice Cooper

As Vincent Furnier of Detroit, Michigan, he might never have had a single hit but, as Alice Cooper, the gender-bending queen of grand guignol, he parlayed shock-rock into a lifelong multi-platinum career.

Cooper's hard rock band – which was actually collectively called Alice Cooper in the beginning – were relatively restrained until the Toronto Rock 'n' Roll Festival of September 1969. A fan threw a live chicken onto the stage and, playing along, Alice threw it back. The following day the media was reporting a Cooper-directed mass gore-fest. Too smart to deny a story which had given him the biggest boost of his career, Furnier, born in 1948, began wearing make-up that made his eyes seem to be bleeding black blood and incorporating guillotines, electric chairs, and live snakes into his stage act. Gig attendances rocketed and on August 12, 1972, he reaped the rewards in record sales when the relentlessly surging teen riot incitement "School's Out" hit No. 1 in the UK, even though the pun

"We got no principals" meant nothing in "headmaster"-led British schools.

Other anthems like "Eighteen" were also successes but by 1974, Furnier had claimed the Alice Cooper name as his own. His quasi-feminist anthem "Only Women Bleed," however, didn't inaugurate a sensitive new direction and subsequent years have seen a corporatization by him of the Alice Cooper shock-rock imprimatur. It's an imprimatur subsequently adopted by Twisted Sister, Ozzy Osbourne, and – in the most blatant example – Marilyn Manson.
Johnny Black

Role Recording Artist

Date 1972

Nationality USA

Why It's Key New levels of outrageousness in rock.

Opposite **Alice Cooper**

Key Person
Al Green

Al Green, born in 1946, found a new way to sell soul to a mass audience, employing a Sam Cooke falsetto with a hint of Otis Redding's wounded, low-key posthumous hit "(Sittin' On) The Dock Of The Bay."

In 1967, Green met Willie Mitchell, producer at Memphis' Hi Records while drifting on the club circuit. Mitchell raised U.S. $1,500 to pay off Green's debts at home in Flint, Michigan and the singer moved to Memphis in 1968. He found his falsetto with a cover of The Temptations' "I Can't Get Next To You" in 1970, then sold a million with self penned "Tired Of Being Alone," a seductive musical sigh for the single man. "Let's Stay Together" became his first *Billboard* No. 1 on February 12, 1972, but Green had at first refused to record his own cowrite, thinking it too wimpy for a man's voice. But the sound came to define him and he sold like no other soul artist in the early '70s.

Green indulged heavily in women and drugs. When former girlfriend Mary Woodson forced her way into his Memphis house in October 1974 and scalded him with boiling grits before shooting herself, it set him on a spiritual path. By 1980, he had abandoned soul for the ministry, presiding over his own Memphis Church of the Full Gospel Tabernacle to this day. Gospel albums have replaced the soul that he did so much to imbue with a silky, soft touch.
Chris Goodman

Role Recording Artist

Date 1972

Nationality USA

Why It's Key Defined a new kind of soul star.

Key Song **"Without You"**
Harry Nilsson

Badfinger were blessed with a gifted songwriting partnership in Pete Ham and Tom Evans. Yet Badfinger's own version of "Without You" didn't quite hit the mark: "I couldn't get myself to sing it with real conviction," confessed Evans later. "It seemed like such a schmaltzy tune."

U.S. singer-songwriter Harry Nilsson disagreed. Haunted by the track, he teamed up with ace pop producer Richard Perry to turn it into a plaintive epic, its key line "I can't live if living is without you" sung with utter and moving sincerity. "Nilsson's version really showed what you can do with a song, production-wise, and with a good singer," Evans admitted. "It blew me away." "Without You" made U.S. No. 1 on February 19, 1972 and also reached the top in the UK. It landed Nilsson a Grammy for Best Male Pop Vocal, and gave the songwriters two Ivor Novello Awards, for Best Song and International Hit of the Year.

In 1994, pop diva Mariah Carey's cover of the song outsold Nilsson's, on which it was based (ironically, Nilsson died the day it was released: January 24), and saw "Without You" nominated for the Ivor Novello Award for Best Song again. By that time, the legal wrangling that had contributed to Badfinger's demise (and the suicides of both Ham and Evans) saw the song cocredited to five writers. Today, it's Ham/Evans again. And Nilsson's is still the definitive version.

Robert Dimery

U.S. No. 1 Date
February 19, 1972

Nationality UK/USA

Composers Pete Ham, Tom Evans

Why It's Key A little touch of Nilsson turns a good song into a classic pop weepie.

Key Song **"Give Ireland Back To The Irish"**
Wings

1972 was the year when both John Lennon and Paul McCartney went political.

Lennon's album in June that year, *Some Time In New York City*, saw him recast himself as a protest singer by any other name. Two of the tracks on it – "Sunday Bloody Sunday" and "The Luck Of The Irish" – were inspired by the Bloody Sunday massacre in Belfast on January 30, 1972 in which 13 apparently unarmed Catholics were killed by British troops. For once, though, Lennon's statement-making thunder had been stolen by his normally more politically cautious ex-Beatles colleague. McCartney was so appalled by Bloody Sunday that he dashed off an anthemic response pleading with Britain to leave the province, released on February 25, 1972.

That McCartney was not speaking from a viewpoint of a radical was made clear by the opening verse line, "Great Britain you are tremendous," but it is that very lack of dogma that made the song so powerful. It certainly seemed to scare the powers that be: not only was it banned from the airwaves in the UK but enunciation of even its title was forbidden on them. In an age of national broadcasting monopolies and lack of alternative means of exposure like the internet, it essentially meant the public could not hear it – which makes it even more remarkable that the record still managed a UK Top 20 placing. In the Republic of Ireland it soared to the top.

Sean Egan

Release Date February 25, 1972

Nationality UK

Composer Paul McCartney, Linda McCartney

Why It's Key McCartney improbably out-radicalizes Lennon.

Key Song **"American Pie"**
Don McLean

On January 15, 1972, the epic lament "American Pie" – spread over both sides of a single – made U.S. No. 1 and catapulted the hitherto-obscure folkie Don McLean to international stardom. The song's elaborate, clearly allegorical lyrics immediately sparked intense debate and McLean was besieged with enquiries as to what it all meant. "It means I don't ever have to work again," he ultimately took to replying.

Although its writer has never offered a line-by-line analysis, the central themes of "American Pie" are beyond reasonable dispute. With veiled references to, amongst others, The Beatles ("the sergeants"), The Rolling Stones ("Jack Flash"), Bob Dylan ("the jester"), and the Byrds, McLean traced popular music's evolution and cultural impact on America from "the day the music died" (February 3, 1959, when Buddy Holly, Ritchie Valens, and the Big Bopper perished in an airplane crash) to Woodstock and the horrors of Altamont. But while the song brilliantly charted a generation's loss of innocence, it also reflected McLean's personal '60s odyssey, as he undertook the same journey from carefree adolescence (he was 13 when Holly died) to the cynicism and alienation of what he'd describe as "the darker realities of adulthood." All of this would of course not mean much were the lyric not borne, as it was, on superb music with an exhilarating chorus.

McLean also sang the hell out of it, something that made Madonna's passionless, truncated dance-floor remake (2000) sound even more execrable.
David Wells

U.S. No. 1 Date
January 15, 1972

Nationality USA

Composer Don McLean

Why It's Key The history of rock 'n' roll in eight-and-a-half spellbinding minutes.

1970-1979

423

Key People
Uriah Heep

Few groups have minted as much critical derision as Uriah Heep. This veteran British band's style includes elements of progressive rock, jazz, and even country but their essential nature was perfectly summed up by the UK title of their debut album: *Very 'Eavy, Very 'Umble* (1970). The album was eponymous in the United States, where it led *Rolling Stone*'s Melissa Mills to famous pronounce, "If this group makes it I'll have to commit suicide." Other writers have derided Uriah Heep as "The worst music I've ever heard in my life" and likened them to a foul odor.

Nonetheless, Heep – named after a character in Charles Dickens' *David Copperfield* – did indeed make it, particularly with album *Demons And Wizards*, released in May 1972 and considered their masterpiece by those whose nostrils aren't so sensitive. *Innocent Victim* came out in 1977, a period that saw the band temper their indulgences and even nod toward pop – which didn't stop another journo opining, "I've always loathed them and thought… *Innocent Victim*… was the nadir of a worthless career."

Since relegated to cult status in America and Britain, the band remain popular in Europe, Japan, and even Russia, where stadium shows are a regular proposition. All the discouraging words and innumerable line-up changes – guitarist Mick Box has been the only ever-present – haven't hobbled a band whose continued existence perhaps owes a debt to that shopworn saying, "Bad publicity beats none at all."
Ralph Heibutzki

Role Recording Artists

Date 1972

Nationality UK

Why It's Key Possibly the most hated rock group ever to achieve success.

Key People
Hawkwind

Much as legitimate literature had long regarded science fiction as its idiot bastard offspring, so rock 'n' roll had always tended to treat anything remotely off-world as a joke. Hits like "Martian Hop" by The Ran-Dells or "Mr Spaceman" by The Byrds were little more than novelty discs, and it wasn't until the end of the '60s that material like Pink Floyd's "Interstellar Overdrive," The Grateful Dead's "Dark Star," and Jefferson Starship's *Blows Against The Empire* began to treat science fiction seriously as a source for rock music. Early in 1972, Elton John's "Rocket Man" and David Bowie's … *Ziggy Stardust*… album suggested that singer-songwriters too were looking beyond the earth for inspiration, but no rock band did more to further the connection than Hawkwind.

Originally perceived as a "people's band," regularly playing free concerts and festivals, Hawkwind were the first outfit to commit themselves completely and permanently to science-fiction subject matter, with music swamped in spacey synthesizer sounds and albums bearing such titles as *In Search Of Space* and *Space Ritual*. Hawkwind's lyrics were liberally sprinkled with androids, time machines, and aliens, so it was perhaps no surprise that they forged a lengthy professional association with science fiction/fantasy author Michael Moorcock. While many might find such fare forbidding, they had one moment of complete accessibility, when their spaceship anthem "Silver Machine" – which entered the UK chart on July 1, 1972 – soared to No. 3.

Gavin Michie

Role Recording Artists

Date 1972

Nationality UK

Why It's Key Established science fiction as a legitimate means of expression for serious rock artists.

Key Event
David Bowie declares "I'm gay"

By early 1972, David Bowie was at his wits' end. More than two years had elapsed since "Space Oddity" had given him his sole hit single and he could feel the breath of One Hit Wonderdom on his cheek.

The media adored Bowie's records and they received wide airplay. But the public ignored them and Bowie knew if he was ever going to make it big, first he needed to make a splash.

A year before, he piqued some interest by wearing a dress on the sleeve of his album *The Man Who Sold The World*, such androgyny being a rarity back then. So when the man from *Melody Maker*, Michael Watts, dropped by for an interview, the conversation inevitably wound its way towards sex… and Bowie dropped the bombshell. "I'm gay and always have been," he declared, not letting the fact that he was married with a child get in the way of the story.

Days before the story was printed on January 22, 1972, Bowie predicted "all fucking hell is going to be let loose." He was right. But while a curious press beat a path to his door, a fascinated public trampled a wider one to the stores. In an age when kids thought rock could no longer shock, they had found a star who repulsed their parents – and exulted in it by buying his records. Three months later, Bowie grabbed that much-needed second hit, "Starman," and this time there was no trouble following up.

Dave Thompson

Date January 22, 1972

Country UK

Why it's Key An artist exploits the publicity machine to his own advantage.

Opposite **David Bowie**

Key People
Roger Cook and Roger Greenaway

Members of obscure close harmony group The Kestrels, Roger Cook and Roger Greenaway began writing together in 1965, when they penned "You've Got Your Troubles," a UK No. 2 hit for The Fortunes. After an almost equally successful follow-up, "Here It Comes Again," the duo recorded as David And Jonathan: ironically, their first hit was a cover version (the Lennon/McCartney song "Michelle") but the highly infectious "Lovers Of The World Unite" was an original composition.

In 1968 they abandoned David And Jonathan to concentrate on writing, although they continued to record with others: Cook as lead singer of Blue Mink, while Greenaway and another ex-Kestrel, Tony Burrows, had a novelty hit as The Pipkins with "Gimme Dat Ding." But the Cook-Greenaway writing team continued unabated: they teamed up with Tony Macaulay to pen the ballad "Home Lovin' Man" for Andy Williams, and quickly reworked a jingle they'd

written for Coca-Cola as "I'd Like To Teach The World To Sing," a massive worldwide success for the New Seekers. They also worked extensively in the early '70s with The Hollies, writing "Gasoline Alley Bred" and, with the band's lead singer Allan Clarke, "Long Cool Woman (In A Black Dress)," a magnificent, Creedence Clearwater Revival-style retro-rocker that entered the *Billboard* Top 40 on July 8, 1972, peaking at No. 2. The Cook-Greenaway partnership collapsed in 1975 when a disillusioned Cook moved to Nashville, where he became a successful country music songwriter.
David Wells

Role Songwriters

Date 1972

Nationality UK

Why It's Key Unsuccessful harmony pop singers reinvent themselves as bespoke songwriters.

Key Person
Neil Young

Born in 1945, Canadian musician Neil Young left Buffalo Springfield in 1968 and proceeded to forge a career almost acclaimed as that of Bob Dylan. A perennial influence on singer/songwriters, he is also – unlike Dylan – cited by punk, grunge, shoegazers, alt. rock, and alt. country artists as a major influence.

Young released two solo albums before adding to an already famous trio to make up Crosby, Stills, Nash, And Young. His solo projects veered between country-tinged folk rock and electric squall. 1971's *After The Gold Rush* showcased both but it was *Harvest* (1972) that established his stardom. An accessible album, it featured the love-lorn, Dylanesque "Heart Of Gold," which proved that his unstinting high-pitched, nasal vocals could sound beautiful as it made U.S. No. 1 on March 18 1972.

Ever contrary, Young followed up with albums dubbed the "Doom Trilogy" by critics, as he fled from "middle of the road" stardom, one of which, 1975's

Tonight's The Night, a visceral expression of grief after heroin overdoses by two friends (Crazy Horse guitarist Danny Whitten and roadie Bruce Berry), is recognized as proto-punk rock. Young continued to veer from light to dark, roots rock to synth-pop, to the point of being sued by his company boss David Geffen in the '80s for releasing music "unrepresentative" of himself. His capacity to surprise is endless. After a brief flirtation with hard right Eighties politics, he released the anti-corporate "This Note's For You" and the coruscating protest song "Rockin' In The Free World."
Chris Goodman

Role Recording Artist

Date 1972

Nationality USA

Why It's Key Possibly the most contrary son-of-a-gun ever to become a major star.

Opposite **Neil Young**

Key Event
Mott The Hoople split up

On March 26, 1972, Ian Hunter, lead singer and rhythm guitarist with English rock band Mott The Hoople, sat down to write a lyric expressing his anguish at the fact that the Hoople had just decided to split up. Despite a fanatical live following and four well-regarded, if inconsistent, albums, a commercial breakthrough for the ensemble had never materialized. "Rock 'n' roll's a loser's game" ran the mordant refrain of the composition in question, "The Ballad Of Mott The Hoople."

Then a miracle occurred. A fan heard of the split and decided to try to help them. That fan happened to be David Bowie, just about to become one of the biggest stars in the world via his … *Ziggy Stardust*… album. He gave them a song to record – "All The Young Dudes" – that finally gained them a genuine hit.

It also seemed to focus their minds. Many of their own songs now followed the template of "… Dudes," mythologizing rock in the way that Bowie's song did –

although not glamorizing it. Their classic 1973 album *Mott* was a set almost exclusively dedicated to the subject of the trials and tribulations of being in a struggling rock band. The centerpiece of it was that cry of despair "The Ballad Of Mott The Hoople."

Hunter had a knack for the valediction. The next time the Hoople split – for good this time in 1974 – he penned the moving farewell and thank-you to Hoople fans "Saturday Gigs."
Sean Egan

Date March 26, 1972

Country UK

Why It's Key A band saved by a fairy godmother.

Key Album *The Rise And Fall Of Ziggy Stardust And The Spiders From Mars* David Bowie

The release of David Bowie's fifth album was always going to be a big deal, ever since he told *Melody Maker* he was gay at the start of the year. A series of flamboyant radio and television appearances raised the fever, particularly a landmark spot on *Top Of The Pops*, performing "Starman." *Ziggy…* , that single's parent album, released in June 1972, did the rest.

It was a superb record of mostly skeletal rock 'n' roll, many of whose tracks involved an androgynous alien who came to a dying earth and became a rock star before being destroyed by his band, The Spiders From Mars. That Bowie's band had the same name, that he himself seemed half-man, half-woman, that he dressed on stage as Ziggy, all served to create the first "role" in rock, one that blurred the distinctions between performer and performance. It was the blueprint for fame that the chameleon-like Bowie would follow for several years afterwards.

Maybe the world did not, as the opening song insisted, have just "five years left to cry in." But Bowie was already aware, as the song "Ziggy Stardust" stated, that the kids would kill the man, and that he'd have to break up the band. Almost everything Bowie was to achieve over the next 12 months was laid out in the career of Ziggy Stardust – the fictional person – as related on this album. Once that song cycle was over, David Bowie – the real person – simply created another character to replace him.
Dave Thompson

Release Date June 1972

Nationality UK

Tracklisting Five Years, Soul Love, Moonage Daydream, Starman, It Ain't Easy, Lady Stardust, Star, Ziggy Stardust, Suffragette City, Rock 'n' Roll Suicide

Producers David Bowie, Ken Scott

Original Label RCA

Why It's Key The album that pioneered the idea of artists as canvas.

Key Performance *Cabaret*
the movie

With director Harold Prince came the era of "concept musicals": productions revolving around an issue. His first was *Cabaret* (1966), based on Christopher Isherwood's *Berlin Stories* (1946) and John van Druten's play adaptation *I Am A Camera* (1955), about the star-crossed relationship between a young writer and an expatriate British nightclub singer in Germany as the Nazis are rising to power. Its bracing score by *Chicago*'s redoubtable John Kander (music) and Fred Ebb (lyrics) was subdivided between "book" numbers, furthering the action; and Brecht/Weill influenced commentary, sung in the Kit Kat Klub by a decadent emcee.

While daringly dark, the writer was portrayed as strictly heterosexual and some anti-Semitic references were softened. The movie, however, tackled those issues unflinchingly. Directed and choreographed by Bob Fosse and released in October 1972, it stunningly dispensed with the book numbers, and indeed, most of Joseph Stein's libretto in favor of a new treatment by screenwriter Jay Presson Allen. The score became a showcase for Joel Grey (the emcee) and Liza Minelli (the singer, now American). More Kit Kat numbers joined the deceptively inviting "Wilkommen" and the celebratory title song, including the rapacious "Money, Money" (usually referred to as "Money Makes The World Go Around") and the torchy "Maybe This Time."

The multi-Oscared movie made such an impact that, for the first time ever, a film musical had a retroactive influence on its stage forebear. Subsequent revivals worldwide absorbed some of the film's renovations in tone and score.
David Spencer

Movie Release Date October 1972

Country USA

Director Bob Fosse

Cast Joel Grey, Liza Minelli, Michael York

Composer John Kander, Fred Ebb

Why It's Key The movie musical that made its stage source more daring.

Key Song **"Nights In White Satin"**
The Moody Blues

Originally issued in late 1967 as The Moody Blues attempted a symphonic pop relaunch of their ailing career, the majestic "Nights In White Satin" not only installed the band as market leaders of a new sub-genre that merged rock with the classics; it would also endure as a timeless love song. Initially, though, it was merely a track on their latest album, *Days Of Future Passed* (1967), recorded with the aid of conductor Peter Knight.

An ethereal, lovelorn ballad that, like Procul Harum's "A Whiter Shade Of Pale," fused a contemporary psychedelic pop sense of dislocation with a neo-classical feel, "Nights In White Satin" had chiefly been inspired by Justin Hayward's emotional distress at being caught between two love affairs. Nevertheless, the song's title was prosaically literal, he admitted: "Somebody had actually given me some white satin sheets! They were totally useless…"

"Nights In White Satin" topped the French charts for several weeks when issued as a single. In March 1968 it became The Moody Blues' first UK Top 20 hit since "Go Now" (1964), although, curiously, it wasn't issued in 45 rpm format in the United States, where another *Days Of Future Passed* track, "Tuesday Afternoon," instead became a minor success. By 1972, though, the band's U.S. following had reached almost messianic proportions, and "Nights In White Satin" (simultaneously reissued in Britain, where it peaked at the No. 9 spot) was belatedly released as a single in the United States, entering the *Billboard* Top 40 on September 2, 1972 and eventually making No. 2.
David Wells

U.S. Chart Entry Date September 2, 1972

Nationality UK

Composer Justin Hayward

Why It's Key A pacesetter for orchestral rock.

Key Album *Fog On The Tyne*
Lindisfarne

Asked what was the biggest selling album in the UK in 1972, most will assume works by names like David Bowie, Don McLean, or the Stones would be in the frame. Few would guess the correct answer: *Fog On The Tyne* by the decidedly less famous quartet Lindisfarne.

Released in October 1971, it was the second album of the band based in the North-East England city of Newcastle-upon-Tyne. Named after a mordantly witty song which referenced the city's river penned by frontman Alan Hull, *Fog On The Tyne* brilliantly merged plangent melodies, ragged harmonies, and a lyrical vision that, on songs like the title track, "City Song," and the Rab Noakes-donated "Together Forever," updated the oldest folk tradition of all: the life and times of the young, unemployed, provincial male. All of this was rendered in the local "Geordie" dialect.

In recession-hit early '70s Britain, the album's localized themes were magnified into national concerns. With the help of the UK Top Five 5 success of "Meet Me On The Corner," *Fog On The Tyne* spent a year in the album charts, including four weeks at No. 1. Its sales belatedly brought debut album *Nicely Out Of Tune* and its own single "Lady Eleanor" into view.

Yet removed from his working-class roots and unable to write on the road, Hull suffered a major writing block. The band would come again, but *Fog On The Tyne* remains their commercial and cultural apex.
David Wells

Date 1972

Nationality UK

Tracklisting Meet Me On The Corner, Alright On The Night, Uncle Sam, Together Forever, January Song, Peter Brophy Don't Care, City Song, Passing Ghosts, Train In G Major, Fog On The Tyne

Why It's Key British rock embraces the provincial and yields improbable dividends.

Key Song "I Am Woman"
Helen Reddy

"I Am Woman" was first released in 1971 as a track on Helen Reddy's debut album, *I Don't Know How To Love Him*. Though Reddy, who cowrote the number with Ray Burton, regarded it as "my statement as a feminist," she didn't think of the self-empowering song as an anthem – or a hit. But when the number was featured in the soundtrack of the feminist documentary *Stand Up And Be Counted* the following year, Reddy wrote another verse, rerecorded the song, and released it as a single in May 1972.

Though opening with the forceful line "I am woman, hear me roar," the music was light, melodic pop, which helped the message go down easily. But the song initially received little airplay, due to the resistance of radio programers who didn't want to be seen supporting "women's libbers." Some critics were also derisive, finding the song "not effective either as propaganda or as schlock." In response, Reddy appeared on as many television variety shows as she could, and listener requests, primarily from women, helped push the song up the charts. On December 9, 1972, the record became Reddy's first U.S. No. 1 single.

The song later won the Grammy for Best Contemporary Female Pop Vocal Performance, and there was some further controversy when Reddy, accepting the award, thanked God "because She makes everything possible."
Gillian G. Gaar

Release Date May 1972

Nationality USA

Composers Helen Reddy, Ray Burton

Why It's Key The first feminist song to crack the mainstream.

Opposite **Helen Reddy**

Key Performance *The Harder They Come*
the movie

Though there had been quite a few reggae hits in Britain by the early '70s, and even a few in the United States, this lilting, bobbing, and often hypnotic form of music for the most part remained a specialized minority taste. The 1972 film *The Harder They Come* was crucial in changing that, and not only by featuring a wealth of classic reggae music in its soundtrack. It also gave dimension to the Jamaican culture that had fostered the style, both via its gritty portrayal of street life in Kingston and the charismatic performance of lead actor (and reggae star) Jimmy Cliff.

Cliff and other reggae musicians are also seen performing in the movie itself, which, in its combining of thriller outlaw drama and great music, remarkably does not shy away from portraying the seediness of the Jamaican music industry, and the desperate poverty that drives many to be a part of it, no matter how much exploitation is involved. Though only a modest seller upon initial release, the soundtrack LP (featuring

songs by Cliff and other top reggae acts such as Desmond Dekker and The Maytals) in essence became reggae's chief ambassador to the world. Like the film, it was instantly embraced by non-Jamaican critics, selling steadily over a period of decades, just as the movie continued to play art houses indefinitely. With Bob Marley's international breakthrough on its heels, reggae would never be a minority taste again.
Richie Unterberger

Movie Release Date 1972

Nationality Jamaica

Director Perry Henzell

Cast Jimmy Cliff, Janet Barkley, Basil Keane

Composer Jimmy Cliff

Why It's Key The chief agent of spreading the popularity of reggae on an international level.

Key Song "Tie A Yellow Ribbon Round The Old Oak Tree" Dawn

Songs have always given heart to soldiers risking life and limb for their country in far-off lands, from Vera Lynn's "We'll Meet Again" (World War II) to The Shirelles' "Dedicated To The One I Love" (Vietnam). Curiously though, Dawn's infectious "Tie A Yellow Ribbon… " – which nowhere mentions war in its lyric – has probably touched more war-torn hearts more directly than any song before or since.

Tony Orlando didn't think the song was a hit when the group Dawn – which was effectively him – recorded it, but on April 21, 1973, this tale of a man returning home after a spell in jail sat astride both U.S. and UK singes charts. The protagonist tells his former sweetheart that he'll stay on his bus unless she indicates she still wants him with the signal of a yellow ribbon. Before long, a tradition of tying ribbons around trees to welcome loved ones home sprang up in real life. In 1981, when 52 U.S. hostages returned safely from Iran after 444 days as political prisoners, they

found America festooned with yellow ribbons. The track became a hit all over again and the symbol has been used ever since to signify support for troops in conflicts including the Gulf War and the invasion of Iraq. "Tie A Yellow Ribbon… " is now estimated to be the second most-covered song of all time, with over 1,000 versions on record.
Gavin Michie

Release Date
February 1973

Nationality USA

Composer Larry Brown, Irwine Levine

Why It's Key A seemingly facile pop smash inspires an international emblem of hope.

Opposite Tony Orlando and Dawn

Key People
Slade

In this day and age of boyband syrup, it is astonishing to realize that numbered amongst the hits of Slade – also teen idols in their day – are some of the most raucous singles ever released: anthemic melodies, stomping rhythm effects, and vocalist Noddy Holder's booming voice all combined to exquisitely deafening effect, exemplified by "Cum On Feel The Noize," which became their fourth of six UK No. 1s on February 23, 1973.

Slade's 17 Top 20 hits in their home country between 1971 and 1976 were almost all written by Holder and bassist Jim Lea. Their image, though, was a complete contrast to their sonic crunch, particularly the ever-more garish get-ups of lead guitarist Dave Hill, who clearly didn't think that his high fringe and buck teeth were absurdity enough. The apotheosis of their success was their 1973 chart-topper "Merry Xmas Everybody," whose moving vignettes of Yuletide family life displayed their common touch.

Their fortunes started to dwindle with the soundtrack to their movie *Flame* (1974), which saw them dispense with their formula as they added brass, glossy production, and a reflective tone. Though a fine album, it seemed to bewilder the kids. Meanwhile, their frequent absences from the country as they vainly attempted to break the United States led to their 1977 album being sardonically titled after a refrain often to be heard in Britain at the time: *Whatever Happened To Slade?*

Hill and drummer Don Powell still tour as Slade.
Sean Egan

Role Recording Artists

Date 1973

Nationality UK

Why It's Key The chart sensations with an edge.

Opposite Dave Hill of Slade

Key Song "Send In The Clowns"
A Little Night Music

What is both the blessing and curse of Stephen Sondheim's work is that it is so specifically tailored for its dramatic context that only rarely does a crossover hit song emerge. Moreover, his recent inclination to spurn the populist approach hardly makes him Hit-Parade friendly. But the affecting, melancholic "Send In The Clowns" from *A Little Night Music* – has become one of those songs known even to those who don't watch musicals.

Typically for Sondheim, the song's creation was an accident of necessity, without any populist goal in mind. Late in the show (set in Sweden at the turn of the twentieth century), the lead romantic couple, actress Desiree and lawyer Frederick, hit an impasse, leading to a moment of loss and regret. Sondheim agreed to director Harold Prince's diktat that it was a moment for Desiree to sing. Unfortunately, he now had to write the "eleven o'clock number" for a star – Glynnis Johns – with limited vocal range and breath support. He opted to keep its range within an octave and employ short, simple phrases with sufficient spaces between. Thus as Sondheim put it in a television interview, the song (written overnight) was contrived to go: "Isn't it rich? – breathe, breathe – Isn't it queer? – breathe, breathe - Losing my timing this late in my career – breathe, breathe – Send in the clowns… " The pulsing consequence was all the more poignant.
David Spencer

Opening Night February 25, 1973

Nationality USA

Composer Stephen Sondheim

Why It's Key Rare latter-day standard from notoriously "difficult" composer.

Key Person
Eric Clapton

Organized by Pete Townshend, Eric Clapton's "comeback" concert at London's Rainbow Theatre on January 13, 1973, saw a return to the limelight for British rock's leading guitar hero.

Having acquired the nickname "God" for his fretboard skills with The Yardbirds, blues purist Clapton quit rather than play pop such as "For Your Love." After a brief but significant stint with John Mayall's Bluesbreakers, in 1966 he formed the legendary, highly influential psychedelic blues power trio Cream. When they disbanded in late 1968, Clapton assembled the supergroup Blind Faith, who released one album before falling apart. He also regularly undertook session work for friends, most famously playing on Beatles track "While My Guitar Gently Weeps."

Clapton's next major work was the December 1970 double LP *Layla And Other Assorted Love Songs* (issued as Derek And The Dominos), a tour de force whose title track is now firmly established as a classic.

After a lengthy struggle with heroin addiction, he returned in 1974 with the lovely *461 Ocean Boulevard*, which downplayed the guitar heroics in favor of a mellow and more song-oriented approach. Though remaining a haphazardly creative force, his career would continue to be interrupted by inner demons and personal tragedy. "Tears In Heaven," his grief-stricken response to the death of his four-year-old son, Conor, gave Clapton his biggest hit for a decade in early 1992: the song also featured on *Unplugged*, a graceful collection that topped the U.S. album charts later that year.

David Wells

Role Recording Artist

Date January 13, 1973

Nationality UK

Why It's Key The ultimate British guitar hero.

Opposite Eric Clapton

Key Song "Hocus Pocus"
Focus

Nobody really paid much attention when producer Mike Vernon signed Dutch act, Focus, in late 1970. Europeans couldn't rock. Or so insisted popular wisdom. In fact, it turned out that Focus could rock harder than almost anyone in sight.

"Hocus Pocus" was the record that proved it. A breakneck duet for mad axe and yodel, it was immediately obvious it was amongst the most distinctive records ever made, tracing the connection that nobody knew existed between uncompromising prog rock and novelty pop.

Guitarist Jan Akkerman's initial vision for "Hocus Pocus" called for bagpipes to duel with his stampeding guitar, before it was decided that yodeling – provided superbly by keyboardist Thijs van Leer – would be even stranger. But it was also effective. The single entered the *Billboard* Top 40 on April 21, 1973, and would go Top 10. The back catalog slammed into overdrive. In the UK, two Focus albums hit the Top 10

immediately and two 45s simultaneously stormed the singles chart.

Of all the ironies, the track that proved Holland was capable of rockin' was intended as a parody of rock, as later admitted by van Leer. "We did the song because we didn't have any outright rock songs on the album," he said. "There's yodeling and laughing in it, and even some crowd cheers. We wanted it humorous because of the great lack of humor in rock music. We enjoy the humor in classical and jazz."

Dave Thompson

Release Date January 1973

Nationality Holland

Composers Jan Akkerman, Thijs Van Leer

Why It's Key Low country rockers hit an artistic and commercial high.

Key People
Nicky Chinn and Mike Chapman

"If you're going to be in the music business, you gotta make hit records," Mike Chapman (born 1947 in Queensland) once pithily observed. A simple philosophy, it guided he and Nicky Chinn (a Londoner born in 1945) throughout the '70s, when the prodigious songwriting/production partnership ruled the British pop roost.

The duo's inaugural success came with the typically alliterative "Funny Funny," a January 1971 single for the previously unsuccessful Sweet. Sweet became their prime outlet. Chinnichap (as they were quickly dubbed) oversaw a run of hits for them that incrementally traded Archies-style bubblegum for hard rock ("Blockbuster" became the first No. 1 for both parties on January 27, 1973) before indulging the band's desire to be taken "seriously" with the epic "The Six Teens." Though glam was essentially a look, Chinnichap's association with Sweet ensured that their stomping, anthemic imprimatur in this period became defined as the glam rock sound, one they also conferred on tomboy rocker Suzi Quatro and quartet Mud. The latter's riproaring 1974 UK No. 1 "Tiger Feet" may well be the pair's most famous track. Chinnichap, though, were not one-trick ponies. They provided campfire sing-a-longs for New World, sultry ballads for Exile, and mature, reflective soft-rock like "If You Think You Know How To Love Me" for Smokie.

Slide-rule pop professionals, Chinnichap wrote some thirty UK Top Ten singles, including five chart-toppers. By the end of the '70s, however, Chapman was gradually moving away from his partner, independently producing such albums as Blondie's *Parallel Lines* (1978) and The Knack's *Get The Knack* (1979).
David Wells

Role Songwriters

Date 1973

Nationality UK/Australia

Why It's Key The writing team who were the kings of Glam rock.

Key Album *The Dark Side Of The Moon*
Pink Floyd

Pink Floyd were already established as a significant band in the realm of spacey progressive rock when they released their sixth album (not counting soundtracks and compilations), *The Dark Side Of The Moon* in their native Britain. After the departure of their early leader, Syd Barrett, who wrote much of their early material in a psychedelic pop style, the group became even more experimental, turning out lengthy instrumental compositions while maintaining a loyal following through touring.

Atom Heart Mother, their fourth album, topped the UK charts, and *Meddle*, their fifth, went top three but *The Dark Side Of The Moon* dwarfed those discs. At home, it charted for 367 weeks, and in the United States it went to No. 1, remained in the charts a record-breaking 741 weeks (it might still be in the regular album chart if *Billboard* hadn't changed the rules for older releases), and sold 15 million copies.

Why did it do so well? Pink Floyd managed to incorporate what they had learned from their experimentations into pop structures, relatively short, catchy songs that retained imaginative sonic ideas such as the chiming clocks in "Time" and the clinking coins in "Money." And lyricist Roger Waters wrote words reflecting on modern life that resonated with his listeners. The result was a leap into the mainstream for what had been a marginal music genre and worldwide acclaim for one of rock's more esoteric bands.
William Ruhlmann

Release Date
March 24, 1973

Nationality UK

Tracklisting Speak To Me, Breathe, On The Run, Time, The Great Gig In The Sky, Money, Us And Them, Any Colour You Like, Brain Damage, Eclipse

Why It's Key Massively popular album established progressive rock as a major musical genre.

Opposite Pink Floyd

Key Event **The Everly Brothers split up in public**

Beginning with "Bye Bye Love" in 1957, Don and Phil Everly had enjoyed seven years of huge record sales before losing their audience in the mid-'60s. However, even when their hitmaking days were behind them, they refused to become a nostalgia act like contemporaries Fats Domino and Chuck Berry and made even better and bolder music, especially on albums like the British beat-influenced *Two Yanks In England* (1966), the countrified *Roots* (1968), and the modern rock-oriented *Stories We Could Tell* (1972). The general public, however, were oblivious to the duo's new work – they wanted "Bye Bye Love," "Wake Up Little Susie," "All I Have To Do Is Dream," "Bird Dog," "(Till) I Kissed You," and the rest of their creamily sung classic run of hits.

The Everly Brothers, as far as the public were concerned, were frozen in time, the way they were when their audience was young. Frustration set in. By 1973, the Brothers felt they'd put in all the time that the duo was worth. Each had his own musical pursuits in mind. A catastrophic show at Knott's Berry Farm in California on July 14 brought the final, ignominious blow. The venue's director was so disgusted by what he felt to be the poor performance by Don that he stopped the show. Phil smashed his guitar and stalked off the stage. It would be 18 years before they worked together again.

Bruce Eder

Date July 14, 1973

Country USA

Why It's Key A classic rock act undone by their artistic ambition.

440

Key People
Sweet

Having scored early successes with shamelessly teenybop-oriented singles like "Funny Funny" and "Co-Co" (penned by the prolific hit-making duo Nicky Chinn and Mike Chapman), Sweet turned a corner with the heavy-riffing "Wig-Wam Bam," which entered the UK Top 75 on September 9, 1972. Their following series of Top 10 entries, although still master-minded by the Chinnichap duo, saw them shift effortlessly into relentlessly pounding heavy rock, albeit shot through with a frivolity that was essentially pop ("Blockbuster," "Hellraiser," "Ballroom Blitz," "Teenage Rampage"). Simultaneously, Sweet's classic line-up of Brian Connolly (vocals), Andy Scott (guitar), Steve Priest (bass), and Mick Tucker (drums) left no stone unturned in their relentless search for new eye-catching costumes, exploring every possibility inherent in outrageous coiffeur, glitter, sequins, face paint, loin cloths, and feathers, not to mention a penchant for shiny metallic thigh-length boots. This quest to go further out than T. Rex, Slade, and the rest won them recognition as the band who had taken the glam look to the outer limits.

This accolade proved a two-edged sword, with many critics writing them off as little more than low-grade teen fodder. In retrospect, however, it's hard to deny that Connolly's expressive vocalizing, Tucker's imaginative powerhouse percussion, and Scott's all-round musicianship set them apart from most of the competition. Indeed, when Scott replaced Chinnichap as Sweet's songwriter, he delivered gems like "Fox On The Run" and the Ivor Novello Award-winning "Love Is Like Oxygen."

Gavin Michie

Role Recording Artists

Date 1973

Nationality UK

Why It's Key The apex – or nadir? – of glam.

Key Event **Dr. Hook make the cover of *Rolling Stone***

Quasi comedy country-rock act Dr. Hook And The Medicine Show were a former New Jersey bar band consisting of lead singer/bassist Dennis Loccorriere, guitarist Ray Sawyer (the eye-patched Dr. Hook), steel guitarist George Cummings, keyboardist Bill Francis, and drummer Jay David. They had scored a transatlantic hit in 1972 with Shel Shelverstein's mawkish teen weeper parody "Sylvia's Mother" whose joke most purchasers seemed not to get.

Silverstein's "The Cover Of Rolling Stone" (1972) was of a different stripe. A racy, rollicking send-up of rock-star excess, it served up every cliché in the book by celebrating pill-popping, teenage blue-eyed groupies, limos, and an Indian guru but had one lament: despite increasingly success, the group depicted in the song couldn't get their smiling faces on the cover of *Rolling Stone*, with all the kudos and extra sales attached to the feat. Silverstein was a songwriter/humorist/*Playboy* cartoonist who also

penned Johnny Cash's "A Boy Named Sue." Delivered with typical twinkled-eyed panache by the band, the song was a Top 10 U.S. hit. It gave the then five-year-old magazine plenty of free publicity. Perhaps it is this that led the periodical to return the compliment on March 29, 1973, when they put Dr. Hook on the cover, albeit in caricature form courtesy of Gerry Gersten – although, frankly, it may have been just as much motivated by the kudos gained by the still "alternative" *Rolling Stone* being seen in the company of a band with such a stoned, ramshackle image.

Tierney Smith

Date March 29, 1973

Country USA

Why It's Key One good turn…

Key Album *Paris 1919*
John Cale

An album named after a famous peace conference and on which there are references to Shakespeare, Graham Greene, and Dylan Thomas hardly sounds like anything other than a forbidding affair, especially when its author is ex-Velvet Underground viola player John Cale. However, Cale's March 1973 album *Paris 1919* proved there was more to Cale than previously realized.

Paris 1919 was an album of defined beauty. It was also his most considered. "Everything else I've done has been off the cuff, but on *Paris 1919* I went into the studio with complete pieces," said Cale. The extra preparation reaped great rewards on a record that really did have something for everyone, from the Spanish influences of "Andalucia," the near-glam of "Macbeth," the Beatles-esque strings and horns of "Paris 1919," and the reggae flavors of "Graham Greene." Cale proved that he had come a long way from the screeching viola playing of the '60s and he

had a soft side that had previously only been shown via production work he'd undertaken for the likes of Nico. He used bluesy-country rockers Little Feat as his backing band and brought in the UCLA Symphony Orchestra for the string sections which softened the feel of the album.

John Cale proved to be one of the most versatile and surprising artists of the late twentieth century. With *Paris 1919* he added mainstream appeal to his already impressive avant garde and classical repertoire.

Rob Jovanovic

Release Date March 1973

Nationality UK

Tracklisting Child's Christmas In Wales, Hanky Panky Nohow, The Endless Plain Of Fortune, Andalucia, Macbeth, Paris 1919, Graham Greene, Half Past France, Antarctica Starts Here

Why It's Key A remarkable artist successfully fuses his rock 'n' roll, avant garde classical and literary leanings.

Key Album *Tubular Bells*
Mike Oldfield

"I was always listening to symphonies and piano concertos," remembered Mike Oldfield, "and I wondered if I could make my own kind of symphony using instruments that I could play... ". The more technically accomplished exponents of any thrusting young musical form invariably seek to push their music beyond its perceived boundaries. Ragtime composer Scott Joplin composed a ragtime opera, *Treemonisha*, in 1911, and jazz great Duke Ellington produced several ambitious orchestral suites in his later years. Rock audiences had to wait until 1973 for *Tubular Bells*, even if the Grateful Dead's side-length improvisation "Dark Star" (1969) and avant-garde composer Terry Riley's 18-minute-long keyboard suite "A Rainbow In Curved Air" (also 1969) were imaginative works that had found significant popularity among rock fans.

Teenage guitar prodigy Oldfield's guitar-based *Tubular Bells*, took the final step, starting with a single theme and then developing it in a series of multi-tracked variations to compose what was, effectively, rock's first symphony. The voice of comedic musician Vivian Stanshall hailing each instrument undermined suspicions of pomposity. Meanwhile, the opening theme's use on the soundtrack to film-of-the-moment *The Exorcist* gave the album some street cred.

Virgin Records owner Richard Branson was reluctant to release it and it took over a year to reach No. 1 in the UK chart but, ultimately, *Tubular Bells* made Branson and Virgin. It also arguably invented the New Age genre.

Johnny Black

Release Date
May 1973

Nationality UK

Tracklisting Tubular Bells (Part 1), Tubular Bells (Part 2)

Why It's Key Embraced the compositional techniques of classical music to create rock's first commercially successful full-length instrumental suite.

Key Performance **New York Dolls on** *The Old Grey Whistle Test*

As the New York Dolls finished their performance, the program cut to seated host Bob Harris, who literally laughed and said dismissively, "Mock rock." Such a reaction hardly indicated that what had just taken place was a stunning, epoch-marking television rock performance.

The date was November 27, 1973. The program was the BBC's *The Old Grey Whistle Test*, which when it began in 1971 was actually quite cutting-edge in its adult treatment of rock. However, without knowing it, the program began to epitomize what was wrong with the stultifying early '70s music scene – pandering to increasingly dull and self-indulgent artists.

The Dolls – a sort of younger, more streetwise, and more outrageous Rolling Stones – were on the program to lip-sync to two of the highlights of their eponymous debut album, the wailing "Jet Boy" and the sullen "Looking For A Kiss." They preened and pouted exhilaratingly, particularly androgynous singer/lyricist David Johansen and his rooster-headed musical foil Johnny Thunders. The contrast between their energy and color and the grayness of Harris and the era's music was stark. Future Smiths star Morrissey was among those bowled over by the performance. So was Steve Jones, soon to become known as a member of an even more outrageous ensemble, The Sex Pistols, who later opined, "I was fucking really knocked out by them."

The Dolls imploded after two albums but with this one performance provided ground rules for at least two musical generations.

Sean Egan

Date November 27, 1973

Country UK

Why It's Key The moment that, in retrospect, showed why punk had to happen.

Opposite New York Dolls

Key Album *Goodbye Yellow Brick Road*
Elton John

Goodbye Yellow Brick Road, the eighth studio album of keyboard wizard and treacle voiced singer Elton John was described by the artist himself as his White Album. Though not quite up to the standards of that Beatles work, it was a sprawling, picturesque double album where camp met pop, and a blockbuster that topped the U.S. charts for eight weeks.

John's partnership with lyricist Bernie Taupin had matured through albums as moodily cohesive as *Tumbleweed Connection* (1970) and as wisely crafted as *Honky Chateau* (1972). Now it was time to build a grand jukebox for the masses. Recorded almost under siege in Jamaica in a three-day stretch, *Goodbye Yellow Brick Road* boasted sumptuous ballads such as the haunting title track and the Marilyn Monroe tribute "Candle In The Wind," powerful rock (the Stonesesque "Saturday Night's Alright For Fighting"), glam parodies ("Bennie And The Jets"), bombastic epics served with a moog-rock dressing (11-minute opener "Funeral For A Friend [Love Lies Bleeding]"), and celluloid-tinged country ("Roy Rogers"). There's also downright filler, but "Jamaica Jerk Off" is excusable as novelty and "I've Seen That Movie Too" just because we love Elton. The whole thing was encased in a dazzling wraparound sleeve by Ian Beck. The songs, the band's solid musicianship, and Gus Dudgeon's sparkling production, makes this collection the crowning moment of even a career as long as John's.

Ignacio Julià

Release Date
October 5, 1973
Nationality UK

Tracklisting Funeral For A Friend (Love Lies Bleeding), Candle In The Wind, Bennie And The Jets, Goodbye Yellow Brick Road, This Song Has No Title, Grey Seal, Jamaica Jerk Off, I've Seen That Movie Too, Sweet Painted Lady, The Ballad Of Danny Bailey, Dirty Little Girl, All The Girls Love Alice, Your Sister Can't Twist (But She Can Rock 'n' Roll), Saturday Night's Alright For Fighting, Roy Rogers, Social Disease, Harmony

Why It's Key Elton John addresses his success with megalomania.

Opposite Elton John

Key Event Chilean singer Victor Jara is murdered by agents of the state

The popular Chilean folk singer-songwriter, poet, and political activist Victor Jara had been a supporter of Salvador Allende, Chile's elected socialist president, in the early '70s. After Allende was killed in a U.S.-backed military coup led by General Augusto Pinochet on September 11, 1973, Jara was among thousands of dissidents taken to Chile Stadium. There he was brutalized – his hands and ribs were broken – but he defied his captors by continuing to sing, until a machine gun ended his life.

Jara, born in 1932, had been active in the theater before turning to folk music in the '60s. His first recording was released in 1966 and by the early '70s he was well established, considered a founder of Chile's "New Song" movement. Many of Jara's songs fell under the banner of protest music, thus he became a prime target for the right-wing coup leaders. His body – containing 34 bullet wounds – was dumped by the side of a road.

Following his death, Jara's legend only grew. His songs have been covered by artists such as Arlo Guthrie and he has been mentioned in songs by Pete Seeger and The Clash. Although many of Jara's master recordings were burned after his demise, his wife Joan managed to smuggle some out of the country and they have since been released.

The Chile Stadium was renamed for Jara in 2003.

Jeff Tamarkin

Date September 15, 1973

Country Chile

Why It's Key Some of our more dramatic artists like to say they would die for their art. Victor Jara actually did.

Key Event
Death of Gram Parsons

With his work with The Byrds and The Flying Burrito Brothers and his two classic solo releases, *GP* (1972) and (posthumously) *Grievous Angel* (1973), Gram Parsons brought a hip rock sensibility to country music. His pioneering efforts inspired The Eagles, Wilco, and many others. Had Parsons lived out his life – rather than meeting his death at the Joshua Tree Inn in Southern California on September 19, 1973 where he overdosed at the age of 26 – he would have in all likelihood still have been acknowledged as a music trailblazer but not necessarily become a legend.

That side of things was helped by the fact that he sang with heartbreaking pathos, possessed rock star good looks, sported flashy Nudie tailored suits and got wasted with Rolling Stone Keith Richards. However, his iconic status was absolutely guaranteed by the bizarre circumstances surrounding the aftermath of his passing. It all started with an expressed desire on Parsons' part to one day be cremated in the Joshua

Tree Desert. Determined to honor his wishes, Parsons' manager Phil Kaufman and friend Michael Martin borrowed a hearse and headed to Los Angeles International Airport where they hijacked his body. They then drove to the desert, where they set Parsons and his coffin ablaze. The romantic gesture was ultimately futile – Parsons' wealthy Southern family got the body retrieved and buried in New Orleans – but would no doubt have been appreciated by Parsons, a man who had spent his life in an act of rebellion by marrying two forms of music considered inimical.

Tierney Smith

Date September 19, 1973

Nationality USA

Why It's Key The macabre pact that turned an artist from a mere talent into a myth.

Key Album *Jonathan Livingston Seagull*
Neil Diamond

Richard Bach's novel *Jonathan Livingston Seagull* was an archetypal hippy-drippy, counterculture bible, a tome that had pride of place on early '70s student bookshelves beside *The Tibetan Book Of The Dead* and *Zen And The Art Of Motorcycle Maintenance*. A novella about a seagull with an allegory about life experience it was a huge bestseller and resulted almost inevitably in a movie.

However, a full-length fictional movie about a bird was always going to be technically problematic and the reviews were rotten and box-office receipts mediocre. The soundtrack by Neil Diamond, though, miraculously sidestepped the stigma attached to the project, winning a Golden Globe and selling hugely. The track "Be" was pulled from it to become a minor U.S. hit single.

Though no doubt loyal Diamond fans made their purchases, it's difficult to imagine that this largely vocal-less, impressionistic music was bought by the

normal audience for Diamond's usually more pop-smart material. Diamond had spent much of his career in a quest to be perceived as a heavyweight rock artist, but no matter how long he grew his hair and how artistically ambitious his albums, somehow his attempts to be "credible" never really took. He was too clean-cut to seem alternative and his music, finely crafted though it was, never possessed grit, or even truly fast tempos. It's possible that this soundtrack is what finally, and fleetingly, got him the campus demographic he sought.

Sean Egan

Release Date 1973

Nationality USA

Tracklisting Prologue, Be, Flight Of The Gull, Dear Father, Skybird, Lonely Looking Sky, The Odyssey: Be/Lonely Looking Sky/Dear Father, Anthem, Be, Skybird, Dear Father, Be

Why It's Key Showed that the fortunes of a movie and a soundtrack were not necessarily intertwined.

Key Performance *The Rocky Horror Show* stage musical

The abolition of theatrical censorship in the UK in the late '60s was bound to bring some changes. Who knew that those changes would come in the form of a "sweet transvestite from transsexual Transylvania"? Tim Curry's portrayal as the corset-bound, sexually omnivorous Frank 'N' Furter being visited by an unsuspecting innocent young couple created a most unlikely London sensation.

Rock musicals *Hair* (1967) and *Godspell* (1971) may have showed Broadway that guitars had a place on the Great White Way but those seemed harmless when it came to Richard O'Brien's *The Rocky Horror Show*. After opening at London's Royal Court Theatre Upstairs on June 19, 1973, it went on to play for 2,358 nights before moving to Chelsea and then to the West End's Comedy Theatre for 600 more shows. O'Brien – the show's creator and composer – thought the show would only run for the original five weeks, saying by then they would have "exhausted our potential

audience." Perhaps he didn't count on the old-fashioned attraction of a good tune, camp anthems like "Time Warp" and "Damn It Janet" setting toes a-tapping despite the outrageous setting.

The U.S. production was a flop as was the 1975 film, *The Rocky Horror Picture Show*. It wasn't until small theaters across the United States – the first, reportedly being Waverly Theater in New York – started holding midnight screenings, complete with audience participation, that the film became the cult phenomenon that it is today.

Leila Regan-Porter

Opening Night June 19, 1973

Nationality UK

Director Jim Sharman

Cast Christopher Malcolm, Julie Covington, Tim Curry

Composer Richard O'Brien

Why It's Key Pushed the envelope for musicals – and set the standard for many an androgynous character.

1970-1979

Key Person
Ry Cooder

Having proved himself a peerless sideman with Captain Beefheart, Taj Mahal and The Rolling Stones, roots guitarist Ry Cooder released an eponymous debut solo album in 1971 wherein he revolutionized bottleneck guitar technique, making it obvious that a major new rock virtuoso had arrived.

Subsequent releases found him re-interpreting the music of his American folk heritage until, by his album *Paradise And Lunch*, he was the undisputed master of blue-eyed folk-blues. Contemporaries including Taj Mahal and Leon Redbone were also exploring and revitalizing acoustic blues and ragtime, but Cooder made it accessible to millions. Combined with his peerless virtuosity, Cooder's seemingly insatiable desire to learn about exotic musics subsequently led him into dalliances with Tex-Mex, Hawaiian, rock, acoustic blues and many other styles.

His evocative and understated scores added an air of intrigue and authenticity to movies *Paris, Texas*

(1984), *The Long Riders* (1980) and *Geronimo* (1993), making him the natural choice to play the slide guitar accompaniments to *Crossroads* (1986) the movie biography of blues legend Robert Johnson. It was a fascination for Cuban music, however, which brought him his greatest acclaim when he acted as producer of the Academy Award-nominated documentary *The Buena Vista Social Club* (1997). Since the millennium, perhaps seeking bigger challenges, Cooder has released two fascinating concept pieces, *Chavez Ravine* (2005) and *My Name Is Buddy* (2006), musically eclectic song cycles with linking storylines.

Johnny Black

Role Recording Artist

Date 1974

Nationality USA

Why It's Key Seamlessly blended Americana roots music with mainstream rock to achieve a new, enduringly popular hybrid.

Key Song "Waterloo"
ABBA

In the early '70s, rock and pop music was strictly an Anglo-American artform. The rest of Europe was resigned to entering traditional national folk songs in the Eurovision Song Contest. In 1973 though, Swedish songwriters Benny Andersson and Björn Ulvaeus, along with their manager Stig Anderson, tried their hand at Eurovision with a Phil Spector-ish pop tune. "Ring Ring." Though a hit single across Europe, it failed to represent Sweden in the contest.

Andersson, Anderson, and Ulvaeus made a second attempt at Eurovision with a revised sound and a new handle: an acronym of the Christian names of performers Björn Ulvaeus, Benny Andersson, Agnetha Faltskog, and Anni-Frid Lyngstad: "ABBA." "Waterloo" was a song that, almost absurdly, likened a man's surrender to his lover's charms with Napoleon's 1815 downfall but an exhilarating melody and a rhythm section like a herd of stampeding elephants quelled any doubts in the listener – and the judges.

In contrast to the derision generally poured on Eurovision entrants, "Waterloo" was a success even with serious American critics. The *Washington Post* heard "a playful spirit cutting loose... a work overloaded with enchantments of childhood – hula hoops, a candy store, King Kong, smooching during recess, every carefree delight wrapped into one fun-filled package."

The Eurovision-winning single hit No. 1 in the UK and No. 6 in the United States, forever sealing the ABBA trademark in pop's consciousness. More glory, though, was to come.

David McNamee

Release Date March 1974

Nationality Sweden

Composer Benny Andersson, Stig Anderson, Björn Ulvaeus

Why It's Key The song that achieved the feat of both winning Eurovision and being perceived as artistically heavyweight.

Opposite **ABBA**

Key Person
Paul Anka

Unlike many teen idols, Paul Anka was no manufactured talent. Anka was only fifteen – a similar age to his target audience – when his self-written "Diana" appeared in 1957. Its success on both sides of the Atlantic (No. 1 in the UK, No. 2 in the United States) led to a string of angst-filled, self-penned hits – "Lonely Boy," "Put Your Head On My Shoulder," "Puppy Love" – while he gave "It Doesn't Matter Anymore" to Buddy Holly, with whom he'd recently toured.

The hits dried up in the early '60s, but, away from the spotlight, Anka continued to prosper. In addition to writing the theme tune to Johnny Carson's *Tonight Show*, he supplied Tom Jones with "She's A Lady" and came up with English language lyrics to an obscure French song. Recorded by everyone from Elvis Presley to Sex Pistol Sid Vicious, the valedictory "My Way" was adopted by Frank Sinatra as his signature tune, although the song's triumphant, stridently self-congratulatory tone was a bit questionable.

In 1974 he wrote and sang "(You're) Having My Baby," which became his first U.S. chart-topper since "Lonely Boy" 15 years earlier. Both that song and its Top Ten follow-up, the adultery-themed "One Man Woman, One Woman Man," acknowledged that, like Anka himself, the singer's original audience had grown up and were attempting to navigate the myriad complexities of adulthood. That songs could help them do it showed that chart pop had come a long way since "Diana" – which had been about Anka's babysitter.

David Wells

Role Songwriter/Recording Artist

Date 1974

Nationality USA

Why It's Key The songwriter who grew up in public – and reflected it in his work.

Key People
Emerson, Lake, And Palmer

The Ontario Speedway California Jam that took place on April 6, 1974, is a legend: a spellbinding location, a fascinating opening bill, and a trio of headliners, each of whom was capable of filling the place in their own right.

Everybody pulled out all the stops. Black Sabbath turned in a stunning performance and Deep Purple erupted through an impetuous one. Meanwhile, keyboardist Keith Emerson, bassist Greg Lake, and drummer Carl Palmer – known as Emerson, Lake, And Palmer to their millions upon millions of fans – put on what Palmer still insists was the best show of their lives.

As was their wont, this trio of technoflash virtuosos blended rock and classical music. Organ duelling with percussion, guitars, and vocals ethereal on the battlefield, ELP were at their peak. If musical perfection was the sum of their performance, that alone would ensure the evening's immortality. But visually too, ELP were breathtaking, for how could anyone hope to upstage the sight of Keith Emerson, strapped onto a grand piano, levitating off the ground and then, still playing, executing a succession of somersaults?

In later years, it became fashionable to dismiss ELP as pretentious, an algebraic concoction of masturbatory noodles and Hobbit-humping lyrics. But they defined prog-rock, the musical genre that dominated the first half of the '70s and albums like *Tarkus* (1971) and *Brain Salad Surgery* (1973) not only graced the homes of umpteen people in those days considered to be hip but endure as monuments to their refusal to accept the concept of musical boundaries.
Dave Thompson

Role Recording Artists

Date 1974

Nationality UK

Why It's Key The undisputed potentates of progressive rock.

Opposite **Carl Palmer**

Key Event
A Chorus Line workshop

Director and choreographer Michael Bennett wanted to create some sort of stage show about the dancers who were usually anonymous and unacknowledged by the theater that depended on them.

At first, though, the ideas of he and his original collaborators Michon Peacock and Tony Stevens were vague. Feeling his way, Bennett made his first step a giant rap session in mid-January 1974 at an exercise center in Manhattan. The eighteen dancers who attended were simply asked why they started dancing, with some of the responses taped. Stories of dysfunctional childhoods, aching ambition, and sexual confusion poured out. A second tape-recorded rap session took place in February. Bennett got New York's Shakespeare Festival interested in the project enough to grant a paltry U.S. $100 per week for the dancers and rehearsal space and a skeleton crew at the city's Public Theater. There were no particular deadlines and no pressure. Some might have thought that this unprecedentedly relaxed way of working was simply asking for trouble, or at least self-indulgence. In fact, it resulted in a show – A Chorus Line – that would become the most successful musical of all time. Show dancer Baayork Lee recalled, "When you're a pilgrim and pioneer, you're just putting one foot in front of the other. We didn't know what we were doing… We didn't have any title for it." A new word would be added to the theater lexicon as a consequence of this pioneering: the "workshop" was born.
Sean Egan

Date January 1974

Country USA

Why It's Key A new creative way for the musical.

Key Song "Seasons In The Sun"
Terry Jacks

On March 2, 1974, this record topped the U.S. charts on its way to selling six million copies worldwide. However, that was the culmination of a long and somewhat unlikely journey for Jacques Brel's 1961 original "Le Moribond" ("The Dying Man"). Translated into English by author Rod McKuen, it had already been the subject of covers by The Kingston Trio and Nana Mouskouri. Jacks himself produced a demo version of the song for The Beach Boys, but was only persuaded to release the song on his own label after a newspaper delivery boy overheard the master tape.

In keeping with the lighter tone of Jacks' version, his own amended lyric makes the narrator's apparent suicide, suggested but not explicit in Brel's version, more opaque, while references to his wife's infidelity are absent altogether. Musically, the original's fatalistic charm had subsided to something almost carefree. McKuen was nonplussed by events, but contented himself with buying a new roof for his house with the royalty stream. Jacks himself subsequently found himself confined to "one hit wonder" status.

Critics often point to "Seasons In The Sun"'s maudlin key changes as the reason it is regularly adapted to soccer terrace chants. Maybe so, but it's emotional appeal is widespread: it has been covered by artists as disparate as boy band Westlife (who topped the UK charts with it) and Nirvana. Indeed, it was the first record that Kurt Cobain ever purchased.
Alex Ogg

Release Date
February 1974

Nationality France/USA

Composers Jacques Brel, Rod McKuen

Why It's Key Reestablished saccharine pop after years of increasing earnestness in music.

Key Event
Television play CBGBs

At the tail end of 1973, former opera singer Hilly Kristal opened his music venue CBGBs in New York's The Bowery – an area that is a byword for scuzziness - intending it to be a platform for local country, bluegrass, and blues artists, hence the venue's acronymous title.

However, in early 1974 Kristal was approached by "three scruffy dudes in torn jeans and T shirts" looking for a place for their band to play. The group was Television. On March 31, 1974, the band – Tom Verlaine (vocals and lead guitar), Richard Hell (bass), Billy Ficca (drums), and Richard Lloyd (guitar) – made their first appearance at CBGBs. Although Kristal later recalled the debut to be "terrible" and "non-sensical," Television began a long residency.

By April, Television's audience boasted such admiring luminaries as Lenny Kaye and "punk poetess" Patti Smith while, aside from gigs with Patti Smith, Television's subsequent CBGBs opening bands included Blondie forerunners Angel And The Snake, The Modern Lovers, Talking Heads, and The Ramones. The Dead Boys, The Dictators, and The Voidoids also became synonymous with the venue.

These bands' style ranged from pop to abrasive rock to avant garde but all had in common an "edge." Though steeped in the lore of rock, they also seemed aware of its current somnambulance and to feel a duty to instill a fresh energy to the form. This spirit can – and would – be summed up in a word: punk.
Kevin Maidment

Date March 31, 1974

Country USA

Why It's Key The birth of a legendary venue – and of a movement.

Key Album *Pretzel Logic*
Steely Dan

Few mainstream rock bands managed to sustain a reputation for being as cunningly subversive as Steely Dan. And it's not just because they appropriated their name from a dildo in William Burroughs' novel *Naked Lunch*.

After the expansively jazzy sophomore jam slump of *Countdown To Ecstasy* (1973), both fans and critics expected the band to return to the guitar-centered boogie of their debut, *Can't Buy A Thrill* (1972). Not Steely Dan. On *Pretzel Logic*, released March 1974, core members Walter Becker (bass) and Donald Fagen (keyboards, vocals) instead set about crafting impeccably smooth pop songs crammed incongruously with capricious musical marriages and cryptic wordplay.

Take U.S. Top 5 single "Rikki Don't Lose That Number" and its easy listening cocktail of syncopated samba and a bop motif borrowed from Horace Silver's "Song For My Father." Witness the sarcasm telegraphed in the title of "Any Major Dude Will Tell You," a ballad whose cynically offhanded lyric about life is framed by tender minor-key electric piano and layered acoustic guitar. Or the equally unfussy piano-pop of "Barrytown" which actually camouflages a contemptuous critique of small town life in Fagen's deceptively genial bleat and a vocal melody that openly echoes The Beatles' "Tell Me What You See."

It was this genre-referential pop sedition that secured *Pretzel Logic* a cult fan base, prompting high profile critics like Robert Christgau to rhapsodize over an "album [that] sums up their chewy perversity as aptly as its title."
Miles Keylock

Release Date March 1974

Nationality USA

Tracklisting Rikki Don't Lose That Number, Night By Night, Any Major Dude Will Tell You, Barrytown, East St. Louis Toodle-Oo, Parker's Band, Through With Buzz, Pretzel Logic, With A Gun, Charlie Freak, Monkey In Your Soul

Why It's Key The album stuffed full of knowing winks – and great tunes.

Key Song "This Town Ain't Big Enough For Both Of Us" Sparks

Joint Sparks frontmen the Mael brothers make unlikely bandmates, let alone siblings, but the partnership of deadpan, mustachioed keyboard player Ron and waiflike, frenetic, tousle-headed singer Russell makes for one of pop's most enduring images. Born and raised in southern California, a fascination with the original Britpop sound led to the Maels relocating to England in the early '70s, where they abandoned the conventional rock line-up to become one of the first electronic pop duos.

Sparks' first single "This Town Ain't Big Enough For Both Of Us" – originally intended to be a wry, ironic comment on film script clichés – entered the UK Top 75 on May 4, 1974. The opening track on the album *Kimono My House* (1974), the song combines Russell's powerful, quasi-hysterical falsetto vocals with frantic, almost double-time electronic beats, gunshot effects and glam rock overtures to create a multilayered three-minute melodrama. The whole thing almost sounds ridiculous, but is also undeniably infectious. Of the falsetto, Ron Mael later explained, "'This Town Ain't Big Enough For Both Of Us' was written in A, and by God it'll be sung in A… If you're coming up with most of the music, then you have an idea where it's going to go. And no singer is gonna get in my way."

"This Town… " peaked at UK No. 2, paving the way for similarly styled chart successes "Amateur Hour" and "Something For The Girl With Everything."
Melissa Blease

Release Date March 1974

Nationality USA

Composer Ron Mael

Why It's Key Eccentric L.A. electro-pop pioneers redefine glam rock – and possibly pop per se.

Key Album *Journey To The Centre Of The Earth* Rick Wakeman

An in-demand session musician, the classically trained pianist Rick Wakeman had been a member of folk ensemble The Strawbs before joining prog rock juggernauts Yes in 1971. The album *The Six Wives Of Henry VIII* established him as a solo performer in early 1973 but it was Wakeman's first post-Yes release, *Journey To The Centre Of The Earth*, that gave him his biggest commercial success and became a cornerstone creation of the symphonic rock genre.

Wakeman's plans for a musical interpretation of Jules Verne's celebrated science-fiction novel involved a cast of thousands, including the London Symphony Orchestra and *Blow-Up* star David Hemmings as narrator. However, the British arm of Wakeman's record company, A&M, weren't convinced by the idea, and gave him such a meager budget that he was unable to meet studio costs. Determined to pursue the project, the musician remortgaged his house, raising sufficient funds to instead record the work live at the London Royal Festival Hall on January 18, 1974 – the same day that he received a writ from his local dairy for non-payment of his milk bill.

The huge financial gamble paid off. Though UK A&M were reluctant to release the work, *Journey To The Centre Of The Earth* – a suitably epic combination of prog rock pomp and classical arrangements, with Wakeman's virtuoso synthesizer work always at the heart of the matter – topped the British charts on May 25 and made No. 3 in America, where it was quickly certified gold.

David Wells

Release Date May 1974

Nationality UK

Tracklisting The Journey-Recollection, The Battle-The Forest

Why It's Key Artist 1 Record Company 0.

Opposite **Rick Wakeman**

1970-1979

455

Key Person
Nick Drake

Though a 2004 BBC radio documentary on him was narrated by Hollywood star Brad Pitt, Nick Drake's death 30 years earlier from an overdose of antidepressants went largely unnoticed. After all, it had been nearly three years since the last of his three albums, none of which had sold more than a few thousand copies, while his aversion to interviews and live performances had exacerbated his obscurity.

Former University of Cambridge student Drake had signed to Island in 1969. Made with arranger Robert Kirby and producer/mentor Joe Boyd, *Five Leaves Left* (1969) and *Bryter Layter* (1970) were stunning showcases for his intimate, wistful songs but received only tepid reviews. When Boyd returned to America, Drake retreated further into himself before recording a third album in October 1971. An impossibly stark, bleak work, *Pink Moon* sold even fewer copies than its predecessors. When he eventually returned to the studio in July 1974, his physical appearance and declining musicianship shocked the returning Boyd. Though disputed by some family members, 26-year-old Drake's death on November 25, 1974, was officially recorded as suicide.

Drake remained the lost boy of the British folk/singer-songwriter scene for many years. A 1979 box set, *Fruit Tree*, sold poorly, but introduced him to a new generation of musicians. By the time the title track of *Pink Moon* appeared in a television commercial in 2000, the monthly retro-rock magazines and Sunday supplements had ensured that the posthumous cult of Nick Drake was in full flow.

David Wells

Role Recording Artist

Date 1974

Nationality UK

Why It's Key Hitherto-ignored singer-songwriter posthumously becomes a legend.

Key Song "Autobahn"
Kraftwerk

Perhaps it was the fact that it was an anthem to the open road that made "Autobahn" (German for "freeway") appeal to a nation weaned on Chuck Berry and Beach Boys car anthems. Nevertheless, it was still completely astonishing that a record by an act almost completely unknown outside European avant garde circles, intoned in German, neither rocking, funky, nor country, and trimmed down from 22 minutes to 4, could, following its entrance on the then very conservative *Billboard* singles chart on April 12, 1975, eventually reach U.S. No. 25. (It also made UK No. 11).

The fifth album by Florian Schneider and Ralf Hütter and the third under the band name Kraftwerk ("power station"), *Autobahn* was the last to be produced in his Cologne studio by producer/engineer Konrad "Conny" Plank, a key figure in the so-called Krautrock movement. Synthesizers and electronic treatments had, by *Autobahn*'s recording in the summer of 1974 fixed Kraftwerk's signature sound.

To be heard on the title track hit are electronic percussion pads played by Wolfgang Flür, a MiniMoog playing the bass line with added analog echo, phasing on synths for the chords and vocals treated by a vocoder.

Like all Kraftwerk's subsequent songs addressing the texture of modern life, the song displays an ambiguity, celebrating the power and leisure that technology affords while expressing faint unease at the attendant sense of repetition and loss of control, the latter underlined by inhumanly monotone singing.

Mat Snow

Release Date
September 1974

Nationality Germany

Composers Florian Schneider, Ralf Hütter, Emil Schult

Why It's Key U.S. drive-time hit that announced the arrival of German avant garde rock to the international stage.

Opposite **Kraftwerk**

Key Album *The Snow Goose*
Camel

Concept albums had come a long way since *SF Sorrow* (arguably) first ushered in the genre in 1968, and the journey had not been scenic. Vast, sprawling conceits with grandiose titles were now the norm, epic prognostications that sacrificed every virtue one normally expected to find on a record – catchy tunes, singable lyrics, hummable hooks – in favor of impenetrable concepts, multitudinous chord changes, and lyric sheets cribbed from a Sanskrit Thesaurus.

But, within the sordid realms that swirled around the conceit of the concept, there was always room for invention and maneuver. Ray Davies and The Kinks pulled it off once or twice, and The Who's *Quadrophenia* (1973) was a simply stunning achievement. It was Camel, however, who truly realigned the beast, by shrugging off every one of the genre's most ingrained habits and rendering their tale a wholly lyric-less one.

Formed by former Shotgun Express keyboardist Pete Bardens, Camel occupied the musical middle ground between Emerson, Lake, And Palmer and The Moody Blues, eminently capable of the vast symphonic statement but with a sharp eye for invention and delivery, too. Realigning novelist Paul Gallico's *Snow Goose* was their most demanding statement, but – released in April 1975 – it was their most successful, too, a series of wordless movements and textures that, whether you'd read the book or not, translated its themes into beautiful melody that still sounds fulfilling today.

Dave Thompson

Release Date April 1975

Nationality UK

Tracklisting The Great Marsh, Rhayader, Rhayader Goes To Town, Sanctuary, Fritha, The Snow Goose, Friendship, Migration, Rhayader Alone, Flight Of The Snow Goose, Preparation, Dunkirk, Epitaph, Fritha Alone, La Princesse Perdue, The Great Marsh

Why It's Key Maybe not the first rock concept album based on fiction but surely the first instrumental one.